OFFICIAL TOURIST BOARD GUIDE

New 41st Edition

B&Bs and Hotels

England's star-rated guest accommodation

2016

Penelope, Viscountess Cobham
Chairman of VisitEngland

Stunning countryside, vibrant cities, open coastlines, history and heritage, accommodation to meet your every need...but let me give you even more great reasons to stay in England in 2016!

Thought by many to be England's greatest landscape-gardener, 2016 sees the 300th anniversary of the birth of Lancelot "Capability" Brown. Brown was born in beautiful Northumberland, in England's north-east, but his legacy includes more than 200 sites across England which claim association with him. Bowood House in Wiltshire, Blenheim Palace in Oxfordshire and Burghley House in Lincolnshire, will all be joined by many other grand houses this summer in celebrating the achievements of this great man with exhibitions and special events throughout the year.

In honour of Brown VisitEngland has designated 2016, "Year of the Garden", and in England they come in all guises. Wonderful Westonbirt Arboretum in Gloucestershire will be offering visitors a "never seen before" perspective when it opens its Treetop Walkway 13 metres up in the canopy; Hampton Court Palace has teamed up with a Chelsea-winning gardener to plan the new "Magic Garden" – an adventure playground with history at its heart featuring a jousting area, five tiltyard towers and a breathing dragon! Magic of another sort will be experienced by visitors to the Derren Brown Psychological Theme Park, the first in the world, when it opens in March at Thorpe Park in Surrey; whilst London's Royal Academy of Arts will be showing a major exhibition: Painting the Modern Garden: Monet to Matisse.

"Exhibitionism" of another sort is on view at the Saatchi Gallery in London where the Rolling Stones will host a comprehensive and immersive insight into the group. National treasures of a different kind will be on view at Durham Cathedral when it opens previously hidden spaces within the Cathedral Cloister and a major restoration project at Rievaulx Abbey in the North Yorks Moors National Park ensures you're guaranteed a fascinating insight into the lives of the people who founded these wonderful sites.

The moors are synonymous with the Bronte sisters and visitors to the Bronte Parsonage Museum in picturesque Haworth can celebrate the 200th anniversary of the birth of Charlotte, best known for her novel, Jane Eyre. Stratford-on-Avon, meanwhile, will mark 400 years of Shakespeare's timeless legacy with many exciting new projects coming to fruition including at his family home, New Place, where the story of Shakespeare's mature years as a successful writer and citizen of his home town will be told.

England's city destinations continue to offer great opportunities to explore and experience new activities. In Bristol, gardens will form the backdrop of a new inland surfing lake, The Wave: Bristol, currently in development and set to bring together people of all ages and abilities. For those seeking coastal waves, Hastings Pier will reopen this summer promising to offer an eclectic range of activities from farmers markets to circus and sport. Brighton sea-front will bring the countryside in range when the British Airways i360 opens. This 162-metre high observation tower is designed, engineered and manufactured by the team responsible for the London Eye and will offer stunning views of the South Downs national park.

As Chairman of VisitEngland I am extremely proud of the constant investment in and development of the tourism experiences in England. I do hope you will enjoy discovering England in 2016 and come to share my passion for it as a destination to holiday and work in.

Contents

Further Information

Useful Indexes

How to use this guide

This official VisitEngland guide is packed with information from where to stay, to how to get there and what to see on arrival. In fact, this guide captures everything you need to know when exploring England.

Choose from a wide range of quality-assessed accommodation to suit all budgets and tastes. This guide contains a comprehensive listing of bed and breakfast properties participating in the VisitEngland Quality Assessment Scheme, as well as hotels, guesthouses, farmhouses, inns, hostels and campus accommodation.

Each property has been visited annually by professional assessors, who apply nationally agreed standards, so that you can book with confidence knowing your accommodation has been checked and rated for quality.

Check out the places to visit in each region, from towns and cities to spectacular coast and countryside, plus historic homes, castles and great family attractions! Maps show accommodation locations, selected destinations and some of the National Cycle Networks.

For even more ideas go online at www.visitengland.com.

Regional tourism contacts and tourist information centres are listed – contact them for further information. You'll also find events, travel information, maps and useful indexes.

Accommodation entries explained

Each accommodation entry contains detailed information to help you decide if it is right for you. This has been provided by proprietors and our aim is to ensure that it is as objective and factual as possible.

ASHBOURNE, Derbyshire   Map ref 4B2   SatNav DE6 1QU B

visitEngland ★★★★ GUEST ACCOMMODATION

visitEngland Silver AWARD

B&B PER ROOM PER NIGHT
S: £61.00 - £83.00
D: £66.00 - £88.00

Peak District Spa
Buxton Road, Nr Alsop en le Dale, Ashbourne, Derbyshire DE6 1QU T: (01335) 310100
F: 01335 310100 E: PeakDistrictSpa@rivendalecaravanpark.co.uk
W: www.peakdistrictspa.co.uk £ BOOK ONLINE

Occupying a secluded location on part of Rivendale's 37 acre site with its own parking, terrace and garden with superb views over Eaton Dale. Ideal for cycling, walking & outdoor pursuits (fly fishing lake on site). Convenient Chatsworth, Alton Towers, Carsington Water. All rooms with en suites, oak or travertine floors, under floor heating. Ground floor rooms accessible for wheelchairs,

Directions: Travelling north from Ashbourne towards Buxton on the A515, find Rivendale on the RHS.

Bedrooms: 2 double, 2 twin. Ground floor rooms with wheelchair access & shower room wet rooms en suite. 1st floor rooms with over bath showers en suite
Open: All year except closes 2nd Jan - 31st Jan

Site: ❀ P Payment: 💳 Leisure: ⚓ ♪ ▶ ∪ Property: 🛏 🗄 🖊 Children: 🚼 🛏 🍼 Catering: 🍴 🍽
Room: 🔌 🚿 📶 📺 🛁 🍵

1. Listing under town or village with map reference
2. Rating (and/or) Award where applicable
3. Prices per room per night for bed and breakfast (B&B)
4. Establishment name, address, telephone and email
5. Website information
6. Satellite navigation
7. Indicates whether a property is a Hotel (H) or Guest Accommodation (B)
8. Accessible rating where applicable
9. Walkers, cyclists, pets and families welcome where applicable
10. Travel directions
11. Indicates when the establishment is open
12. At-a-glance facility symbols

5

Key to symbols

Information about many of the accommodation services and facilities is given in the form of symbols.

Site Features

- **P** Private parking
- ✳ Garden
- € Euros accepted
- 💳 Visa/Mastercard/Switch accepted

Leisure Facilities

- ⚲ Tennis court(s)
- 🏊 Swimming pool – outdoor
- 🏊 Swimming pool – indoor
- 🧖 Sauna on site
- 💆 Health/beauty facilities on site
- 🏋 Gym on site
- ♣ Games room
- ∪ Riding/pony-trekking nearby
- ▶ Golf available (on site or nearby)
- 🎣 Fishing nearby
- 🚴 Cycles for hire nearby

Property Facilities

- 🔥 Real log/coal fires
- 🛗 Passenger lift
- 🌙 Night porter
- 🛋 Lounge for residents' use
- 🧺 Laundry facilities
- 💻 WiFi or internet access
- 🐕 Dogs/pets accepted by arrangement
- 🎀 Conference facilities
- ❄ Air conditioning

Children

- 🪑 High chairs available
- 🛏 Cots available
- 👶 Children welcome

Catering

- 🍽 Special diets available
- 🍷 Licenced (table or bar)
- 🍴 Evening meals

Room Facilities

- 📀 DVD player
- 📺 Television
- 📡 Satellite/cable/freeview TV
- ☎ Telephone
- ☕ Tea/coffee making in bedrooms
- 💇 Hairdryer
- 🛌 Bedrooms on ground floor
- 🛏 Four-poster bed(s)
- 🚬 Smoking rooms available

Campus/Hostels

- ▦ Cooking facilities available

Visitor Attraction Quality Scheme

 Participating attractions are visited by a professional assessor. High standards in welcome, hospitality, services, presentation; standards of the toilets, shop and café (where provided) must be achieved to receive this VisitEngland award.

Visitor Attraction Quality Scheme Accolades

For top-scoring attractions where visitors can expect a really memorable visit.

For 'going the extra mile', ensuring that visitors are really well looked after.

For small, well-run attractions that deserve a special mention.

For particularly innovative and effective interpretation or tour, telling the story to capture visitors' imaginations.

For attractions with cafes and restaurants that consistently exceed expectations.

Pets Come Too - accommodation displaying this symbol offer a special welcome to pets. Please check for any restrictions before booking.

Businesses displaying this logo have undergone a rigorous verification process to ensure that they are sustainable (green). See page 23 for further information.

VisitEngland's Breakfast Award recognises hotels and B&Bs that offer a high quality choice of breakfast, service and hospitality that exceeds what would be expected at their star rating. Look out for the following symbol in the entry 🍴

National Accessible Scheme

The National Accessible Scheme includes standards for hearing and visual impairment as well as mobility impairment – see pages 10-11 for further information.

Welcome Schemes

Walkers, cyclists, families and pet owners are warmly welcomed where you see these signs – see page 9 for further information.

Motorway Service Area Assessment Scheme
The star ratings cover a wide range of aspects of each operation including cleanliness, the quality and range of catering and also the quality of the physical aspects, as well as the service provided. – See page 276 for further information.

A special welcome

To help make booking your accommodation easier, VisitEngland has four special Welcome schemes which accommodation in England can be assessed against. Owners participating in these schemes go the extra mile to welcome walkers, cyclists, families or pet owners to their accommodation and provide additional facilities and services to make your stay even more comfortable.

For further information go online at www.qualityintourism.com/quality-schemes/welcome-schemes

Families Welcome

If you are searching for the perfect family holiday, look out for the Families Welcome sign. The sign indicates that the proprietor offers additional facilities and services catering for a range of ages and family units. For families with young children, the accommodation will have special facilities such as cots and highchairs, storage for push-chairs and somewhere to heat baby food or milk. Where meals are provided, children's choices will be clearly indicated, with healthy options also available. They'll have information on local walks, attractions, activities or events suitable for children, as well as local child-friendly pubs and restaurants. However, not all accommodation is able to cater for all ages or combinations of family units, so do remember to check for any restrictions before confirming your booking.

Welcome Pets!

Do you want to travel with your faithful companion? To do so with ease make sure you look out for accommodation displaying the Welcome Pets! sign. Participants in this scheme go out of their way to meet the needs of guests bringing dogs, cats and/or small birds. In addition to providing water and food bowls, torches or nightlights, spare leads and pet washing facilities, they'll buy in pet food on request and offer toys, treats and bedding. They'll also have information on pet-friendly attractions, pubs, restaurants and recreation. Of course, not everyone is able to offer suitable facilities for every pet, so do check if there are any restrictions on the type, size and number of animals before you confirm your booking.

Walkers Welcome

If walking is your passion, seek out accommodation participating in the Walkers Welcome scheme. Facilities include a place for drying clothes and boots, maps and books for reference and a first-aid kit. Packed breakfasts and lunches are available on request in hotels and guesthouses, and you have the option to pre-order basic groceries in self-catering accommodation. On top of this, proprietors provide a wide range of information including public transport, weather forecasts, details of the nearest bank, all night chemists and local restaurants and nearby attractions.

Cyclists Welcome

Are you an explorer on two wheels? If so, seek out accommodation displaying the Cyclists Welcome symbol. Facilities at these properties include a lockable undercover area, a place to dry outdoor clothing and footwear, an evening meal if there are no eating facilities available within one mile and a packed breakfast or lunch on request. Information is also available on cycle hire, cycle repair shops, maps and books for reference, weather forecasts, details of the nearest bank, all night chemists and much much more.

National Accessible Scheme

Finding suitable accommodation is not always easy, especially if you have to seek out rooms with level entry or large print menus. Use the National Accessible Scheme to help you make your choice.

Additional help and guidance on accessible tourism can be obtained from the national charity Tourism for All:

Tourism for All

Tourism for All UK
7A Pixel Mill
44 Appleby Road
Kendal, Cumbria LA9 6ES

Information helpline
0845 124 9971
(lines open 9-5 Mon-Fri)
E info@tourismforall.org.uk
W www.tourismforall.org.uk
www.openbritain.net

Proprietors of accommodation taking part in the National Accessible Scheme have gone out of their way to ensure a comfortable stay for guests with hearing, visual or mobility needs. These exceptional places are full of extra touches to make everyone's visit trouble-free, from handrails, ramps and step-free entrances (ideal for buggies too) to level-access showers and colour contrast in the bathrooms. Members of staff may have attended a disability awareness course and will know what assistance will really be appreciated.

Appropriate National Accessible Scheme symbols are included in the guide entries (shown opposite). If you have additional needs or specific requirements, we strongly recommend that you make sure these can be met by your chosen establishment before you confirm your reservation. The index at the back of the guide gives a list of accommodation that has received a National Accessible Scheme rating.

For more information on the NAS and tips and ideas on holiday travel in England go to: **www.visitengland.com/accessforall**

The criteria VisitEngland has adopted does not necessarily conform to British Standards or to Building Regulations. They reflect what the organisation understands to be acceptable to meet the practical needs of guests with mobility or sensory impairments and encourage the industry to increase access to all.

England

Mobility Impairment Symbols

 Older and less mobile guests
Typically suitable for a person with sufficient mobility to climb a flight of steps but who would benefit from fixtures and fittings to aid balance.

 Part-time wheelchair users
Typically suitable for a person with restricted walking ability and for those who may need to use a wheelchair some of the time and can negotiate a maximum of three steps.

 Independent wheelchair users
Typically suitable for a person who depends on the use of a wheelchair and transfers unaided to and from the wheelchair in a seated position. This person may be an independent traveller.

 Assisted wheelchair users
Typically suitable for a person who depends on the use of a wheelchair and needs assistance when transferring to and from the wheelchair in a seated position.

  Access Exceptional is awarded to establishments that meet the requirements of independent wheelchair users or assisted wheelchair users shown above and also fulfil more demanding requirements with reference to the British Standards BS8300.

Visual Impairment Symbols

 Typically provides key additional services and facilities to meet the needs of visually impaired guests.

Typically provides a higher level of additional services and facilities to meet the needs of visually impaired guests.

Hearing Loss Symbols

 Typically provides key additional services and facilities to meet the needs of guests with hearing loss.

 Typically provides a higher level of additional services and facilities to meet the needs of guests with hearing loss.

11

Peace of Mind with Star Ratings

Many hotels and bed and breakfast properties in England are star rated by VisitEngland. We annually check that our standards are comparable with other British tourist boards to ensure that wherever you visit you receive the same facilities and services at any star rated accommodation.

All the accommodation in this guide is annually checked by VisitEngland assessors and an on site assessment is made every year. This means that when you see the Quality Rose marque promoting the star rating of the property, you can be confident that we've checked it out.

The national standards used to assess accommodation are based on VisitEngland research of consumer expectations. The independent assessors decide the type (classification) of accommodation, for example if it's a 'small hotel', 'country house hotel', 'bed and breakfast', 'guest accommodation' etc. and award star ratings based on the quality of the service and accommodation offered, as well as, where appropriate, a further special quality award.

Our assessors consider every aspect of your stay, such as the warmth of welcome, comfort of furnishings, including beds, food quality (breakfast and dinner for hotels, breakfast for guest accommodation), cleanliness and the level of care offered.

The Quality Rose marque helps you decide where to stay, giving you peace of mind that the

accommodation has been thoroughly checked out before you check in.

Accommodation Types

Always look at or ask for the classification of accommodation, each offers a very distinct experience.

The hotel designators you'll find in this guide are:

Hotel – minimum of 5 bedrooms, but more likely to have over 20.

Small Hotel – maximum of 20 bedrooms, usually more personally run.

Country House Hotel – set in ample grounds or gardens, in a rural or semi-rural location and an emphasis on peace and quiet.

Town House Hotel – maximum of 50 rooms in a city or town-centre location, high quality with distinctive and individual style, high ratio of staff to guests. Dinner may not be served but room service available. Might not have a dining room so breakfast may be served in bedroom.

Metro Hotel – can be any size and in a city or town centre location - offering full hotel services, but not dinner (although will be within easy walking distance of a range of places to eat).

Budget Hotel – part of a large, 'branded' hotel group offering clean and comfortable en suite facilities, many with 24-hour reservations. Budget hotels are not awarded individual star ratings.

Accredited Hotel – accredited hotels have been visited by VisitEngland assessors to check the standards of cleanliness and maintenance meet or exceed guests' expectations. This annual assessment does not include an overnight stay and no star ratings are awarded.

Looking for something a little different?

Within this guide you'll find some interesting alternatives to hotels. **Restaurants with Rooms** are just that – the restaurant is the main business and they will be licensed. **Hotel Boats** are generally narrow boats and are worked by a crew. They can be booked by individuals or groups and provide all the services of a hotel, including meals and refreshments.

Star ratings you can trust

Hotels are awarded a rating from 1 to 5 stars. All star ratings assure you of certain services which are:

- All rooms have an en suite or private bathroom
- Designated reception and staff available during day and evening (24 hrs in case of emergency)
- Licence to serve alcohol
- Access to hotel at all times for registered guests
- Dinner available at least five days a week (except Town House or Metro Hotels)

- All statutory obligations will be met, including Fire Safety

The bed and breakfast designators you'll find in this guide are:

Guest Accommodation – wide range of establishments from one-room bed and breakfast to larger properties, which may offer dinner and hold an alcohol licence.

Bed and Breakfast – accommodating generally for no more than six people, the owners of these establishments welcome you into their home as a special guest.

Guest House – generally comprising more than three rooms. Dinner may be available (if it is, it will need to be booked in advance). May possibly be licensed.

Farmhouse – bed and breakfast, and sometimes dinner, but always on a farm.

Inn – pubs with rooms, and many with restaurants as well.

Room Only – accommodation that either does not offer breakfast or, if it does, it will not be served (ie self-service or breakfast pack)

Hostel – safe, budget-priced, short-term accommodation for individuals and groups. The Hostel classification includes Group Hostel, Backpacker and Activity Accommodation (all of which are awarded star ratings).

Campus – accommodation provided by educational establishments, including university halls of residence and student village complexes. May be offered on a bed and breakfast or sometimes on a self-catering basis.

OFFICIAL TOURIST BOARD GUIDES

New 41st Edition

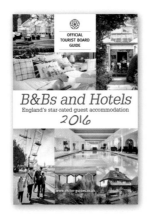
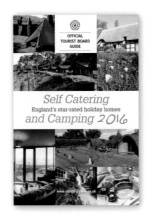

There are many guides to guest accommodation, but there's only ONE VisitEngland guide THE Official Tourist Board Guide to star-rated guest accommodation in England.

Book your accommodation online

Visit our websites for detailed information, up-to-date availability and to book your accommodation online. Includes over 20,000 places to stay, all of them star rated.

www.visitor-guides.co.uk

www.visitor-guides.co.uk

Star ratings you can trust

All bed and breakfast accommodation that is awarded a star rating (from 1 to 5 stars) will assure you of minimum standards, so you can be confident that you will find the basic services that you would expect, such as:

- A clear explanation of booking charges, services offered and cancellation terms.
- A full cooked breakfast or substantial continental breakfast.
- May offer ensuite facilities, but also shared bathroom facilities.
- For a stay of more than one night, rooms cleaned and beds made daily.
- Printed advice on how to summon emergency assistance at night.
- All statutory obligations will be met, including Fire Safety.

To achieve higher star ratings, an increasing level of facilities and services are offered. For example, at 3-star, bed and breakfast must offer a guest bathroom which cannot be shared with the owners and bedrooms must have a washbasin if not en suite. At 4-star, 50% of bedrooms will be en suite or with private bathroom. At 5-star, all rooms must be en suite or with a private bathroom.

Star ratings are based on a combination of the range of facilities, the level of service offered and quality - if an establishment offers facilities required to achieve a certain star rating but does not achieve the quality score required for that rating, a lower star rating is awarded. Accommodation with limited facilities but high quality standards may be capped at a lower star rating, but may achieve a Silver or Gold Award.

Gold and Silver Awards

How can you find those special places to stay – those that, regardless of the range of facilities and services, achieve top scores for quality (for hospitality and service, bedrooms and bathrooms, food and cleanliness)? Look for VisitEngland's Gold and Silver Awards. These awards are given to establishments offering the highest level of quality within their particular star rating.

High star ratings mean top quality in all areas and all the services expected of that classification. Lower star ratings with a Silver or Gold Award indicate more limited facilities or services but top quality. You may therefore find that a 2-star Gold Award hotel offering superior levels of quality may be more suited to your needs if, for example, enhanced services such as a concierge or 24-hour room service are not essential for your stay.

Sometimes a bed and breakfast establishment has exceptional bedrooms and bathrooms and offers guests a very special welcome, but cannot achieve a higher star rating because, for example, there are no en suite bedrooms. This is sometimes the case with period properties. Look out for accommodation with Gold or Silver Awards which recognise quality rather than specific facilities.

VisitEngland's unique Gold and Silver Awards are given in recognition of exceptional quality. A list of all Gold and Silver Award winning accommodation with a detailed entry in this guide is given on page 296.

The more stars, the higher the quality and the greater the range of facilities and level of service. The following refers to the Hotel scheme:

★★ Two-Star must provide
Dinner five nights a week (unless Metro hotel)

★★★ Three-Star must provide
All en suite bedrooms (i.e. no private bathrooms)
Telephones in all rooms
Room service during core hours
A permanently staffed reception

★★★★ Four-Star must provide
Enhanced guest services e.g. 24 hour room service, porterage, afternoon tea etc.
Superior bedrooms and bathrooms

★★★★★ Five-Star must provide
Some permanent suites
Enhanced services, such as concierge, valet parking etc.

Gold and Silver Awards

VisitEngland's unique Gold and Silver Awards are given in recognition of exceptional quality in hotel and bed and breakfast accommodation.

VisitEngland professional assessors make recommendations for Gold and Silver Awards during assessments. They look for aspects of exceptional quality in all areas, in particular, housekeeping, hospitality, bedrooms and bathrooms.

While star ratings are based on a combination of quality, the range of facilities and the level of service offered, Gold and Silver Awards are based solely on quality. Therefore a 2 star property with limited facilities but exceptional quality could still achieve the Gold Award status.
Hotels and Bed & Breakfast establishments with a Gold or Silver Award are featured below. Detailed entries for these properties are also included in the regional pages and can be found using the property index on page 307.

An index of Gold and Silver Award-winning properties with a detailed entry in this guide can be found at the back of the book.

Gold Award Hotels with entries in the regional pages

Coworth Park
Ascot, Berkshire

Barnsley House
Barnsley,
Gloucestershire

**Stanley House
Hotel & Spa**
Blackburn, Lancashire

Clare House
Grange-over-Sands,
Cumbria

Langley Castle Hotel
Hexham,
Northumberland

Chewton Glen
New Milton, Hampshire

Scafell Hotel
Rosthwaite, Cumbria

Rye Lodge Hotel
Rye, Sussex

Hotel Riviera
Sidmouth, Devon

**Calcot Manor
Hotel & Spa**
Tetbury,
Gloucestershire

**Lindeth Howe
Country House Hotel**
Windermere, Cumbria

Silver Award Hotels with entries in the regional pages

Hell Bay Hotel
Bryher, Isles of Scilly

The Pier House Hotel
Charlestown, Cornwall

**Stoke by Nayland
Hotel, Golf & Spa**
Colchester, Essex

Treglos Hotel
Constantine Bay,
Cornwall

Cavendish Hotel
Eastbourne, Sussex

Budock Vean Hotel
Falmouth, Cornwall

The Grange Hotel
Newark,
Nottinghamshire

**Barnsdale Lodge
Hotel**
Oakham, Rutland

**The Coniston Hotel,
Country Estate & Spa**
Skipton, North Yorkshire

**St Michael's
Manor Hotel**
St. Albans, Hertfordshire

Gold Award Guest Accommodation
with entries in the regional pages

Abbey Guest House
Abingdon-on-Thames,
Oxfordshire

The Old Pump House
Aylsham, Norfolk

Marlborough House
Guest House
Bath, Somerset

**Fenham Farm
Coastal Bed
& Breakfast**
Berwick-upon-Tweed,
Northumberland

**Pendragon
Country House**
Camelford, Cornwall

**Mitchell's of Chester
Guest House**
Chester, Cheshire

**Cladda House B&B
and Self Catering
Apartments.**
Dartmouth, Devon

**Hever Castle Luxury
Bed & Breakfast**
Edenbridge, Kent

Glebe House Muston
Grantham,
Lincolnshire

Decoy Barn
Great Yarmouth,
Norfolk

Colton House
Rugeley,
Staffordshire

**The Barn &
Pinn Cottage
Guest House**
Sidmouth, Devon

The Close B&B
Stroud, Gloucestershire

**The Downs,
Babbacombe**
Torquay, Devon

Bradle Farmhouse
Wareham, Dorset

Beryl
Wells, Somerset

**Meadow View Guest
House**
Wighton, Norfolk

Silver Award Guest Accommodation
with entries in the regional pages

Peak District Spa
Ashbourne, Derbyshire

Yorkshire Bridge Inn
Bamford, Derbyshire

Pulteney House
Bath, Somerset

Alannah House
Berwick-upon-Tweed,
Northumberland

**4 Star Phildene
Blackpool**
Blackpool, Lancashire

**Willow Tree
Cottage B&B**
Bognor Regis, Sussex

Gurney Manor Mill
Bridgwater, Somerset

Broseley House
Broseley, Shropshire

Causeway House B&B
Castleton, Derbyshire

George Bell House
Chichester, Sussex

1 Maytham Cottages
Cranbrook, Kent

Castle View
Durham, Co Durham

**Kiln Farm
Guest House**
Elmswell, Suffolk

**Yewfield Vegetarian
Guest House**
Hawkshead Hill,
Cumbria

**St Anne's
Guest House**
Heacham, Norfolk

The Baskerville
Henley-on-Thames,
Oxfordshire

Church Oast
Hernhill, Kent

Burleigh Mead
Keswick, Cumbria

Cowscot House
Kirkby Malzeard,
North Yorkshire

Bosavern House
Lands End, Cornwall

**Redhouse Farm
Bed & Breakfast &
Self-Catering**
Lincoln, Lincolnshire

Beach House
Lymington, Hampshire

The Limes
Maidstone, Kent

Old Lodge Malton
Malton, North
Yorkshire

Hillborough House
Milton-under-
Wychwood,
Oxfordshire

**Treetops Guest
House**
Moreton-In-Marsh,
Gloucestershire

Overcliff Lodge
Mundesley, Norfolk

Bryn Clai
Ringmer, Sussex

**Killerby Cottage
Farm**
Scarborough, North
Yorkshire

Tredower Barton
St. Minver, Cornwall

Great Field Farm B&B
Stelling Minnis, Kent

Adelphi Guest House
Stratford-upon-Avon,
Warwickshire

Glenlee Guest House
Swanage, Dorset

**The Mill
at Gordleton**
Sway, Hampshire

Ness House
Teignmouth, Devon

**The Gallery
Bed & Breakfast**
Thirsk,
North Yorkshire

The Westgate
Torquay, Devon

Newhouse Farm
Trowbridge, Wiltshire

**Spring Cottage
Bed & Breakfast**
Truro, Cornwall

Lulworth Cove Inn
Wareham, Dorset

**Village Limits
Country Pub,
Restaurant & Motel**
Woodhall Spa,
Lincolnshire

**Avondale
Guest House**
York, North Yorkshire

VisitEngland Awards for Excellence

A warm welcome and a great night out was anticipated when it was announced that NewcastleGateshead were set to host VisitEngland's 2015 Awards for Excellence and guests at this prestigious annual celebration were not disappointed.

The coming together of a signature destination, the Sage Gateshead, and the best that tourism in England can offer was a heady mix. With fifteen categories featuring amazing experiences and top quality establishments the winners epitomised the care, attention and customer-centric approach that England's tourism businesses deliver in droves.

The Awards are open to all businesses that meet the category criteria and operators from across the country compete for a place on a roll of honour which spans 26 years of excellence in tourism. This year a panel of expert judges considered 345 entries and you can find a full list of the winners at www.visitenglandawards.org

The prestigious Large Hotel of the Year, Gold Award, was claimed by north-east favourite, Matfen Hall Hotel, Golf & Spa. The lovingly restored ancestral home of Sir Hugh and Lady Blackett and now the leading independently owned hotel in the region, Matfen is a 19th century country house set in the heart of some of Northumberland's most beautiful countryside. Built in the 15th century Silver Award

winner, Ellenborough Park Hotel & Spa, can claim to be the grand dame of English country houses. Located adjacent to Cheltenham's Racecourse in the heart of the Cotswolds, this secluded historic hideaway offers a luxurious break from the everyday. If you'd prefer to have access to the sea then Chewton Glen Hotel & Spa, this year's Bronze Award winner, can offer you the best of every world! A few minutes walk from the sea and set in 130 acres of Hampshire countryside on the edge of the New Forest National Park this is a very special place. If a castle is more to your liking then Peckforton Castle, in Cheshire, guarantees a fairytale stay. With an enchanting medieval exterior, bedrooms are individually designed to ensure contemporary comfort. Dating from the 16th century, the Manor House in Moreton-in-the-March promises a relaxed, friendly, unpretentious and quintessentially English experience in a charming Cotswold setting.

The Small Hotel of the Year Award provided a tantalising glimpse of the breadth of beautiful venues on offer in England. Gold winner Brockencote Hall Hotel in Worcestershire recently underwent a £6million refurbishment to ensure this classic Victorian

mansion offers an experience worthy of the 70 acres of beautiful parkland in which it sits. An excellent touring base on the Devon-Cornwall border, Tavistock's The Horn of Plenty offers stunning views, guaranteed comfort and a menu which showcases a passion for British food – 90% of produce served is sourced from the south-west. Old and new sit comfortably together in the magnificent manor house which is Mallory Court Hotel in Royal Leamington Spa. Handsome bedrooms, unobtrusive service and breath-taking grounds provided a winning combination and our Bronze Award. If the Lake District is your destination of choice then don't miss the Cedar Manor Hotel and Restaurant set in Windermere and with a fantastic reputation for fine dining and sesonal modern British menus. Meanwhile the Talbot Hotel, in Malton in stunning North Yorkshire, provides traditional elegance and warm hospitality for a stay of complete relaxation in a fully-restored lovely gade II* listed building. Guests looking to get far away from their day to day will not be disappointed with a stay at the Hell Bay Hotel on the Isles of Scilly, set in a picturesque cove facing the Atlantic Ocean and offering a friendly and private oasis of calm.

Colton House in Staffordshire, took the Gold Award in the B&B of the year category by offering a high quality, friendly but luxurious home from home experience in a Grade II* listed property on the edge of Cannock Chase. The experience at Swan House, our Silver Award winner, offers a complete contrast in a five-star gold boutique, 15th century B&B in historic Hastings Old Town. At the Bronze Award winning Old Rectory of St James Guest House in Telford a quintessentially English experience is offered with afternoon tea on

arrival and charming experiences and service at every turn. Exceeding expectations is the mantra of the team at Mere Brook House on the Wirral, Merseyside where homemade cakes are freely available as part of a generous and enchanting experience. Nestled in large gardens and close to the sea Lower Barns Boutique B&B provides a magical getaway beloved by guests looking to spend precious time together. This is a hiding place, to rest, relax and discover what really matters.

Large Hotel of the Year 2015

GOLD WINNER
Matfen Hall Hotel, Golf & Spa, Tyne & Wear

SILVER WINNER
Ellenborough Park Hotel & Spa, Gloucestershire

BRONZE WINNER
Chewton Glen Hotel & Spa, Hampshire ★ ★ ★ ★ ★

HIGHLY COMMENDED
Peckforton Castle, Cheshire

The Manor House Hotel, Gloucestershire ★ ★ ★ ★

Small Hotel of the Year 2014

GOLD WINNER
Brockencote Hall Hotel, Worcestershire

SILVER WINNER
The Horn of Plenty, Devon

BRONZE WINNERS
Mallory Court Hotel, Warwickshire

HIGHLY COMMENDED
Cedar Manor Hotel & Restaurant, Cumbria

Hell Bay Hotel, Isles of Scilly ★ ★ ★ ★

The Talbot Hotel, North Yorkshire

Bed & Breakfast / Guest Accommodation of the Year 2015

GOLD WINNER
Colton House, Staffordshire ★ ★ ★ ★ ★

SILVER WINNER
Swan House, East Sussex ★ ★ ★ ★ ★

BRONZE WINNERS
The Old Rectory of St James Guest House, Shropshire ★ ★ ★ ★

HIGHLY COMMENDED
Lower Barns Boutique B&B, Cornwall

Mere Brook House, Merseyside ★ ★ ★ ★ ★

Guest Accommodation of the Year

Colton House

Lying in the heart of rural Staffordshire, the magnificent Georgian Grade II listed Colton House is a luxury guesthouse like no other. Believed to date back to 1730, the building itself has a rich history, having played host to royalty and heads of state in the past, while the accommodation oozes five-star quality.

The current custodians of this fine building, Ron and Gay Lawrence, fell in love with the house and its magnificent sweeping staircase in 1977, believing it would make the perfect home for their three children and Afghan dog. In fact, it exceeded their expectations but once the children had flown the nest and they'd both taken early retirement things became a little too quiet for this energetic couple. So they decided to convert the family home on the edge of Cannock Chase into a five-star B&B.

They started out with just two rooms before renovating the whole house to create 11 luxury en-suite rooms. It has been a long and challenging journey but has paid off in a big way with a thriving business that now boasts the VisitEngland accolade of being the best B&B in the country in 2015.

Ron and Gay didn't have any experience in the hospitality industry before embarking on their ambitious plan 11 years ago. Ron had been a civil engineer in the water industry while Gay had undertaken a total of 49 jobs, ranging from working for J Lyons Corner Shops making birthday cakes to being a Civil Servant.

"It was after the children had left that we got bored and missed the buzz of having people about and so decided to start a B&B," says Gay. "We really had no idea what to expect when we first started, but it's been a hugely rewarding venture."

The couple, who employ four part-time housekeepers, a part-time handyman and gardener, are the only ones working full-time and it means long days, getting up at 5am and not retiring to bed before midnight.

"We really had no idea what to expect when we first started, but it's been a hugely rewarding venture."
Gay

"We put a lot of time and effort into the business," adds Gay, "but we enjoy what we do. We love meeting new people and learning about their interests."

The interior of the building has been lovingly restored to retain the original elegance of the house. There are magnificent fireplaces, one of which displays the coat of arms of the family, original oak panelling and a wide, sweeping staircase. This was specially designed to accommodate the caged crinolines worn by early residents.

Set across 1.5 acres, the grounds are completely available to all guests and feature a large lawn, flower borders, secret gazebo and kitchen garden. Strategically placed seating offers beautiful views.

"We take delight in our guests having a memorable stay at Colton House," says Gay. "It's a wonderful building which we love to share with other people.

"Winning the VE Excellence Award created a great deal of excitement for both Ron and myself, and provided lots of press coverage for the business."

For guests staying at Colton House there are lots of things to see and do in the area. Walkers have the chance to experience the delights of the Peak District and Cannock Chase, while water enthusiasts can try their hand at narrow boating on the many canals. There are lots of heritage properties within easy driving distance, along with the National Memorial Arboretum, the Potteries, and the breweries of Burton on Trent.

Over the past few years Colton House has set some very high standards for guest accommodation but the Lawrences are not resting on their laurels. "We are consistently striving for improvements in quality," says Gay. "That's what sets us apart from the rest."

As well as winning gold in the Bed & Breakfast/Guest Accommodation of the Year category at the VisitEngland Excellence Awards, Colton House were also Highly Commended for Sustainable Tourism.

**Contact details: Colton House, tel 01889 578580
email mail@coltonhouse.com, website www.coltonhouse.com**

There are hundreds of "Green" places to stay and visit in England from small bed and breakfasts to large visitor attractions and activity holiday providers. Businesses displaying this logo have undergone a rigorous verification process to ensure that they are sustainable (green) and that a qualified assessor has visited the premises.

We have indicated the accommodation which has achieved a Green award... look out for the ⚘ symbol in the entry.

Sustainable Tourism in England

More and more operators of accommodation, attractions and events in England are becoming aware of sustainable or "green" issues and are acting more responsibly in their businesses. But how can you be sure that businesses that 'say' they're green, really are?

Who certifies green businesses?

There are a number of green certification schemes that assess businesses for their green credentials. VisitEngland only promotes those that have been checked out to ensure they reach the high standards expected. The members of those schemes we have validated are truly sustainable (green) businesses and appear amongst the pages of this guide with our heart-flower logo on their entry.

 Businesses displaying this logo have undergone a rigorous verification process to ensure that they are sustainable (green) and that a qualified assessor has visited the premises.

At the moment we promote the largest green scheme in the world - Green Tourism Business Scheme (GTBS) - and the Peak District Environmental Quality Mark.

Peak District Environmental Quality Mark

This certification mark can only be achieved by businesses that actively support good environmental practices in the Peak District National Park. When you buy a product or service that has been awarded the Environmental Quality Mark, you can be confident that your purchase directly supports the high-quality management of the special environment of the Peak District National Park.

Green Tourism Business Scheme

 Green Tourism is the market leading sustainable certification programme for the tourism sector in the UK and Internationally. From small bed and breakfasts to large visitor attractions and activity holiday providers. A Green Tourism Award means that a business works responsibly, ethically and sustainably, contributes to their community, is reducing their impact on the environment and aims to be accessible and inclusive to all visitors and staff.

With over 2,100 Green Tourism businesses all independently inspected graded Bronze, Silver or Gold they identify businesses that are really making a difference, so you can choose the greenest option with confidence.

How are these businesses being green?

Any business that has been certified 'green' will have implemented initiatives that contribute to reducing their negative environmental and social impacts whilst trying to enhance the economic and community benefits to their local area.

Many of these things may be behind the scenes such as energy efficient boilers, insulated lofts or grey water recycling, but there are many fun activities that you can expect to find too. For example, your green business should be able to advise you about traditional activities nearby, the best places to sample local food and buy craft products, or even help you to enjoy a 'car-free' day out.

Large Hotel of the Year

Chewton Glen Hotel & Spa

Celebrating its 50th anniversary in 2016, Chewton Glen in Hampshire provides a quintessentially English hotel experience that offers guests modern-day luxury in an 18th Century building.

From modest beginnings it has expanded into an iconic hotel, containing 70 luxurious bedrooms and suites, an outstanding spa, plus fabulous leisure and sporting facilities.

A member of the prestigious Relais & Chateaux group, Chewton Glen is set amidst sweeping lawns, woods and parkland on the southern edge of the 900,000-acre New Forest, and only a 10-minute walk from the sea.

Although its origins as a country house date back to the 1700s, Chewton Glen's journey to success as a five-star hotel began in 1966 when the property was bought by Martin Skan and his brother Trevor.

Over the past five decades constant transformation and improvements have created a world-class property that has set the standard for hospitality and service. The hotel continues to develop and innovate and the addition of the distinctive Treehouse Suites has drawn acclaim from across the globe.

"The success of Chewton Glen has been built on passion," says Andrew Stembridge, Managing Director of Chewton Glen. "The passion of our founders, the Skans, was so infectious that staff could not help but share it.

"Much has changed over the last half-century – new management, new ownership – but that spirit still lives on. It is passion that sets Chewton Glen apart from the rest, and passion will no doubt keep it at the top for the next 50 years."

The interior design of the hotel is stunning, combining a sophisticated mix of modern fabrics with traditional country house furniture and antiques. Each of the spacious bedrooms and suites is individually styled to provide the ultimate in luxury and comfort.

"The little touches are what people remember," adds Andrew. "Attention to detail is hugely important and a meticulous eye for detail helps in the hotel's search for perfection. We constantly try to see how we can do things better."

"At the heart of everything we have done for the past 50 years is the belief that the guest comes first. This forms our desire to please, to go that extra mile. It is inherent in everything the team at Chewton Glen does."

"One of our greatest strengths is the equal respect we have for every guest. For example, we have had a multitude of celebrities staying with us. We never talk about them and we never make a particular fuss of them, which is why they are able to remain under the radar and actually relax. We feel it is our job to ensure that whenever anyone is with us, they have a proper break."

The award-winning Dining Room offers the flexibility of formal dining, al fresco lunches, family celebrations and corporate entertaining. Heading up the culinary team is Luke Matthews, whose passion is the preparation of fish dishes and providing a healthier style of cooking. He uses fresh ingredients grown in the hotel's own Kitchen Garden and Nursery, alongside locally sourced products.

The leisure and sporting facilities include an impressive 17 metre ozone-treated indoor swimming pool, state of the art gymnasium, a purpose-built tennis centre with two indoor and two outdoor courts, a par-3 golf course and driving range, clay pigeon shooting, and croquet lawn.

Although it is probably the wonderful setting and the award-winning facilities that prompt discerning travellers to stay at Chewton Glen initially, it is without question the hotel's team who make guests come back time and time again.

"If you were to ask someone to name 10 world-class hotels, they might talk about the Peninsula in Hong Kong, the Dorchester in London, the Bel-Air in Los Angeles," says Andrew. 'But I still find it quite bizarre sometimes when Chewton Glen is included with them.

"It is not the biggest building or even the most impressive location. But it does deserve its place in that list. What makes Chewton Glen so successful is the overall package. I genuinely do not think there is anywhere else quite like it."

Contact details:
tel 01425 275 341
email reservations@chewtonglen.com
website www.chewtonglen.com

"Attention to detail is hugely important and a meticulous eye for detail helps in the hotel's search for perfection. We constantly try to see how we can do things better."
Andrew

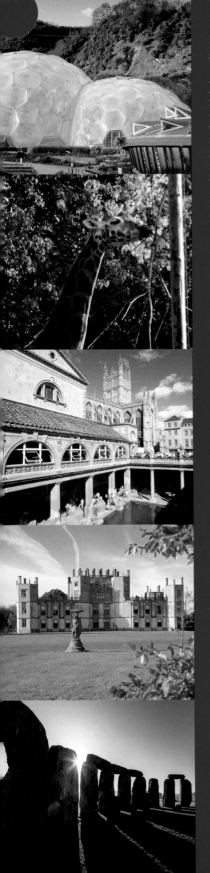

Don't Miss...

Eden Project
St. Austell, Cornwall PL24 2SG
(01726) 811911
www.edenproject.com
Explore your relationship with nature at the world famous Eden Project,
packed with projects and exhibits about climate and the environment,
regeneration, conservation and sustainable living. Be inspired by
cutting-edge buildings, stunning year round garden displays, world-
class sculpture and art, as well as fabulous music and arts events. See
all the sights and immerse yourself in nature with a walk among the the
treetops on the Rainforest Canopy Walk or a ride on the land train.

Paignton Zoo
Paignton, Devon TQ4 7EU
(0844) 474 2222
www.paigntonzoo.org.uk
One of Britain's top wildilfe attractions, Paignton Zoo has all the usual
suspects with an impressive collection of lions, tigers, gorillas, orangutans,
rhinos and giraffes. It is also home to some of the planet's rarest creatures
and plants too. For a day jam-packed with family fun and adventure
there's Monkey Heights, the crocodile swamp, an amphibian ark and a
miniature train, as well as the hands-on interactve Discovery Centre.

Roman Bath
Bath, Somerset BA1 1LZ
(01225) 477785
www.romanbaths.co.uk
Bathe in the naturally hot spa water at the magnificent baths
built by the romans, indulge in a gourmet getaway, or enjoy a romantic
weekend exploring the wealth of historic architecture. You can find all of
this in the beautiful city of Bath and attractions such as Longleat Safari
Park and Stonehenge are all within easy reach too.

Sherborne Castle & Gardens
Sherborne, Dorset DT9 5NR
(01935) 812072
www.sherbornecastle.com
Built by Sir Walter Raleigh in c1594, the castle reflects various styles from
the Elizabethan hall to the Victorian solarium, with splendid collections
of art, furniture and porcelain. The grounds around the 50-acre lake were
landscaped by 'Capability' Brown and the 30 acres of tranquil lakeside
gardens are the perfect place to escape.

Stonehenge
Amesbury, Wiltshire SP4 7DE
(0870) 333 1181
www.english-heritage.org.uk/stonehenge
The Neolithic site of Stonehenge in Wiltshire is one of the most famous
megalithic monuments in the world, the purpose of which is still largely
only guessed at. This imposing archaeological site is often ascribed
mystical or spiritual associations and receives thousands of visitors from
all over the world each year.

South West

Cornwall & Isles of Scilly, Devon, Dorset,
Gloucestershire, Somerset, Wiltshire

A spectacular combination of ancient countryside and glorious coastline, Britain's South West is its most popular holiday area. It stretches from the soft stone and undulating hills of the Cotswolds in the north, through Wiltshire with its historic monuments, to the wild moors, turquoise waters, golden sands and pretty harbours of Dorset, Devon and Cornwall. The beauty of this region and all it has to offer never fails to delight.

Gloucestershire

Wiltshire

Somerset

Devon   Dorset

Cornwall

Explore – South West

Cornwall

Spectacular turquoise seas and white sands dotted with fishing harbours, beautiful gardens and the remnants of Cornwall's fascinating industrial heritage draw visitors from far and wide. The pounding waves to be found along the coastline attract surfers from all over to the world famous beaches around Newquay and make Cornwall a mecca for watersports enthusiasts of all kinds.

The majestic and largely untouched wilderness of Bodmin Moor is only one example of the rich natural environment that can be found here, with miles of walking paths criss-crossing the impressive landscape. This walkers paradise has something for everyone, with The Cornish Way - over 200 miles of inter-linking trails connecting Bude to Land's End – and the spectacular 300 mile long South West Coast Path National Trail with its beautiful views of secluded coves, sandy beaches and jaw-dropping cliffs.

West Cornwall's captivating light and landscape has intrigued and inspired artists since the early 19th century. St Ives is at the heart of today's vibrant art scene, with local arts and crafts galleries rubbing shoulders with international stars such as the Tate St Ives and the Barbara Hepworth Museum and Sculpture Garden.

Cornwall also has a diverse history reaching back to prehistoric, Celtic and medieval roots and there are a huge number of heritage attractions in this corner of the country. St Michael's Mount is an ancient island of myth and legend, Tintagel Castle overlooks the dramatic windswept Atlantic coast, while Grade I listed Port Eliot House & Gardens is a hidden gem nestling beside a secret estuary near Saltash.

Devon

Take a hike or a mountain bike and discover the rugged beauty of Exmoor, explore the drama of the craggy coastline, or catch a wave on some of the region's best surf beaches. North Devon is also rich in heritage with many stately homes and historic attractions including Hartland Abbey and the picturesque Clovelly village, where the steep pedestrianised cobbled main street, takes you to a beautiful deep-blue harbour.

Stunningly beautiful, Dartmoor is perhaps the most famous of Devon's National Parks and offers miles of purple, heather-clad moorland, rushing rivers and stone tors. Walk the length and breadth of the moor or cycle the Drake's Trail, where you'll come across wild ponies and plenty of moorland pubs, perfect for a well earned rest. Head east and discover the imposing Blackdown Hills Area of Outstanding Natural Beauty, stopping off in one of the area's picture-postcard villages for a delicious Devon Cream Tea.

Plymouth is famous for its seafaring heritage, with Plymouth Hoe as the backdrop for Sir Francis Drake's legendary game of bowls, as well as being one of the most beautiful natural harbours in the world. Climb Smeaton's Tower for the incredible views if you're feeling energetic, visit the world-famous Plymouth Gin Distillery at Sutton Harbour, or take the kids to the National Marine Aquarium for an afternoon of fishy fun.

Torquay, gateway to the English Riviera, boasts elegant Victorian villas, iconic palm trees, a sweeping sandy beach and a rich maritime history. Paignton offers great days out including its famous zoo, and the traditional fishing harbour of Brixham is awash with seafood restaurants, waterside pubs and cafés. This whole area is also home to a huge selection of beaches from small, romantic coves to larger, award-winning stretches. The Jurassic Coast is a UNESCO World Heritage Site which stretches for 95 miles along the Devon/Dorset coast, revealing 185 million years of geology and is a must for visitors to the South West.

Dorset

Stretching from historic Lyme Regis in the west to Christchurch in the east, and including a number of designated heritage areas, the whole Dorset coastline is a treasure trove of geology. Interesting landforms are plentiful - Durdle Door, Lulworth Cove, the Isle of Portland with the famous Portland Bill lighthouse and the shingle bank of Chesil Beach to name but a few. Weymouth and Portland are two of the best sailing locations in Europe and offer water sports galore, as well as pretty harbours. For traditional English seaside resorts visit Victorian Swanage, or Bournemouth with its fine sandy beach, perfect for families.

Inland, enchanting market towns, quaint villages and rolling countryside play host to delightful shops, museums, family attractions, historic houses and beautiful gardens such as the Sub-Tropical Gardens at Abbotsbury. Explore Dorset's natural beauty on foot or by bicycle at Stoborough Heath and Hartland Moor nature reserves.

Gloucestershire

A perfect base for for touring the Cotswolds, Cheltenham is an elegant spa town of Regency town houses and leafy squares, award winning gardens and an array of impressive sporting and cultural events such as The Cheltenham Gold Cup or The Cheltenham Festival of music.

Tewkesbury, famous for its fine half-timbered buildings, alleyways and 12th Century Norman Abbey, is one of the best medieval townscapes in England. Enjoy a riverside stroll along the River Severn or a boat trip along the Avon. Grade I listed Sudeley Castle & Gardens, set against the dramatic backdrop of the Cotswolds, is well worth a visit and at the centre of the Severn Vale, Gloucester is a vibrant and multicultural city with an impressive cathedral. It combines historic architecture with numerous visitor attractions, quirky shops and mouth-watering tearooms, restaurants and pubs, and is only a stone's throw from the ancient woodlands of Forest of Dean.

Somerset & Bristol

The maritime city of Bristol is packed with historic attractions, exciting events and fabulous festivals. Cabot Circus offers first class shopping, while stylish restaurants and cafés on the Harbourside serve up locally produced food to tempt and delight. Out and about, Isambard Kingdom Brunel's Clifton Suspension Bridge and the Bristol Zoo Gardens are firm favourites.

Topped by the tower of the ruined 15th Century church, Glastonbury Tor is the stuff of myth and legend, rising high above the Somerset Levels near the delightful town of Glastonbury. Believed to be the site of a Saxon fortress, it has breathtaking views reaching to Wells, the Mendips and the Bristol Channel in the North, Shepton Mallet and Wiltshire in the East, South to the Polden Hills and to the Quantocks and Exmoor in the West.

Wiltshire

Surrounded by stunning scenery and home to a magnificent Cathedral, a wealth of heritage and cultural, dining and shopping venues, the medieval city of Salisbury is the jewel in the crown of South West England's rural heartland.

Further afield you can find an abundance of quintessential English market towns and villages. Marlborough, famed for its charming high street and independent shops, is stylish and sophisticated with a cosmopolitan café culture, while Wilton, the ancient capital of Wessex, is home to Wilton House and a beautiful Italianate Church.

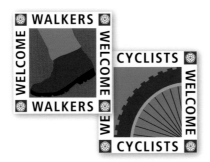

Visit – South West

 Attractions with this sign participate in the Visitor Attraction Quality Assurance Scheme.

Cornwall

Blue Reef Aquarium
Newquay, Cornwall TR7 1DU
(01637) 878134
www.bluereefaquarium.co.uk
Over 40 naturally themed habitats take you on a fantastic journey from Cornish waters to exotic seas.

Boardmasters
Trebelsue Farm, Watergate Bay, Cornwall TR8 4AN
www.boardmasters.co.uk
Europe's largest surf and music festival, takes place at Fistral Beach and Watergate Bay in early August.

Cornwall Film Festival
November, Cornwall
www.cornwallfilmfestival.com
A month long festival of fabulous films.

Cornwall's Crealy Great Adventure Park
Wadebridge, Cornwall PL27 7RA
(01841) 540276
www.crealy.co.uk/cornwall
Enter the magical land of Cornwall's Crealy and hold on tight for a thrilling ride.

Crantock Bale Push
September, Crantock, nr Newquay
www.balepush.co.uk
Teams pushing giant hay bales around the village.

Lost Gardens of Heligan
St. Austell, Cornwall PL26 6EN
(01726) 845100
www.heligan.com
An exploration through Victorian Productive Gardens & Pleasure Grounds, a sub-tropical Jungle and more.

Minack Theatre
Porthcurno, Cornwall TR19 6JU
(01736) 810181
www.minack.com
Cornwall's world famous Minack open-air theatre.

National Maritime Museum Cornwall
Falmouth, Cornwall TR11 3QY
(01326) 313388
www.nmmc.co.uk
Award-winning museum with something for everyone.

National Seal Sanctuary
Helston, Cornwall TR12 6UG
(01326) 221361
www.sealsanctuary.co.uk
The National Seal Sanctuary rescues, rehabilitates and releases over 40 seal pups a year.

Newquay Fish Festival
September, Newquay, Cornwall
www.newquayfishfestival.co.uk
Three days celebrating Newquay harbour and delightful fresh local produce.

Newquay Zoo
Newquay, Cornwall TR7 2LZ
(01637) 873342
www.newquayzoo.org.uk
Multi-award winning Zoo set in sub-tropical lakeside gardens and home to over 130 species of animals.

Royal Cornwall Show
June, Wadebridge, Cornwall, PL27 7JE
www.royalcornwallshow.org
A fascinating glimpse into rural life, enjoy 3 days of Cornish heritage, entertainment, displays and fairs.

St Michaels Mount
Marazion, Cornwall TR17 0HS
(01736) 710265
www.stmichaelsmount.co.uk
Explore the amazing island world and discover legend, myth and over a thousand years of incredible history.

Tate St Ives
St. Ives, Cornwall TR26 1TG
(01736) 796226
www.tate.org.uk
An introduction to modern and contemporary art, including works from the Tate Collection.

Devon

The Agatha Christie Festival
September, Torquay, Devon
www.agathachristiefestival.co.uk
Celebrate the world's most famous crime writer, Dame Agatha Christie. A literary festival with a murder mystery twist!

Bicton Park Botanical Gardens
Budleigh Salterton, EX9 7BJ
(01395) 568465
www.bictongardens.co.uk
Magnificent gardens, streams, woodlands and features. Take a walk through the arboretum before a relaxing meal at the Orangery Restaurant.

Bournemouth Air Festival
August, Bournemouth, Devon
www.bournemouthair.co.uk
Free four-day seafront air show.

Brixham Pirate Festival
May, Brixham, Devon
www.brixhampirates.com
Brixham turns pirate with live music, games, re-enactments, skirmishes on the Golden Hind.

Clovelly Village
(01237) 431781
www.clovelly.co.uk
Most visitors consider Clovelly to be unique. Whatever your view, it is a world of difference not to be missed.

Custom House Visitor Centre
Exeter, Devon EX2 4AN
(01392) 271611
www.exeter.gov.uk/customhouse
Discover the history of Exeter in 15 minutes at the Quay House Visitor Centre on Exeter's Historic Quayside.

Dartmouth Castle
Dartmouth, Devon TQ6 0JN
(01803) 833588
www.english-heritage.org.uk/dartmouthcastle
For over six hundred years Dartmouth Castle has guarded the narrow entrance to the Dart Estuary and the busy, vibrant port of Dartmouth.

Dartmouth Steam Railway
Queens Park Station, Torbay Road, Paignton TQ4 6A
(01803) 555872
www.dartmouthrailriver.co.uk
Running Paignton along the spectacular Torbay coast and through the wooded slopes bordering the Dart estuary, with stunning scenery and seascapes.

Escot Gardens, Maze & Forest Adventure
Ottery St. Mary, Devon EX11 1LU
(01404) 822188
www.escot-devon.co.uk
Historical gardens and fantasy woodland surrounding the ancestral home of the Kennaway family.

Fishstock
September, Brixham, Devon
www.fishstockbrixham.co.uk
A one-day festival of seafood and entertainment held in Brixham.

Hartland Abbey & Gardens
(01237) 441496/234
www.hartlandabbey.com
Hartland Abbey is a family home full of history in a beautiful valley leading to a wild Atlantic cove.

Ilfracombe Aquarium
Ilfracombe, Devon EX34 9EQ
(01271) 864533
www.ilfracombeaquarium.co.uk
A fascinating journey of discovery into the aquatic life of North Devon.

Kents Cavern
Torquay TQ1 2JF
01803 215136
www.kents-cavern.co.uk
Kents Cavern is one of Europe's top prehistory Stone Age caves with an extensive labyrinth of spectacular and easily accessible caverns open daily all year.

Plymouth City Museum and Art Gallery
Devon PL4 8AJ
(01752) 304774
www.plymouth.gov.uk/museumpcmag.htm
The museum presents a diverse range of contemporary exhibitions, from photography to textiles, modern art to natural history.

Dorset

Athelhampton House and Gardens
Athelhampton, Dorchester, Dorset DT2 7LG
(01305) 848363
www.athelhampton.co.uk
*One of the finest 15th century Houses in England
nestled in the heart of the picturesque Piddle Valley.*

Christchurch Food and Wine Festival
May, Christchurch, Dorset BH23 1AS
www.christchurchfoodfest.co.uk
*Celebrity chefs, over 100 trade stands, culinary treats,
cookery theatres and some eminent food critics.*

Corfe Castle Model Village and Gardens
Corfe Castle, Dorset BH20 5EZ
(01929) 481234
www.corfecastlemodelvillage.co.uk
*Detailed 1/20th scale model of Corfe Castle and
village before its destruction by Cromwell.*

Dorset County Museum
Dorchester, Dorset, DT1 1XA
(01305) 257180
www.dorsetcountymuseum.org
*Follow Dorset through time; visit the nostalgic
Victorian Gallery, walk on real Roman mosaic floors
and discover the dinosaurs that roamed the lands
and seas.*

Dorset Knob Throwing Festival
May, Cattistock, nr Dorchester, Dorset
www.dorsetknobthrowing.com
World famous quirky festival.

Forde Abbey & Gardens
Chard, Dorset TA20 4LU
(01460) 220231
www.fordeabbey.co.uk
*Founded 850 years ago, Forde Abbey was converted
into a private house in c.1649.*

Larmer Tree Festival
July, Cranborne Chase, North Dorset
(01725) 552300
www.larmertreefestival.co.uk
*Boutique festival featuring over 70 diverse artists,
a comedy club, street theatre, carnival procession.*

Lulworth Castle & Park
Wareham, Dorset BH20 5QS
0845 450 1054
www.lulworth.com
Enjoy historic buildings & stunning landscapes.

Lyme Regis Fossil Festival
May, Lyme Regis, Dorset
www.fossilfestival.co.uk
*A natural science and arts cultural extravaganza on
the UNESCO World Heritage Jurassic Coast.*

Portland Castle
Portland, Dorset DT5 1AZ
(01305) 820539
www.english-heritage.org.uk/portland
Coastal fort built by Henry VIII to defend Weymouth.

Sherborne Abbey Music Festival
April - May, Sherborne, Dorset
www.sherborneabbeyfestival.org
*Five days of music performed by both nationally
acclaimed artists and gifted young musicians.*

Sturminster Newton Cheese Festival
September, Sturminster, Dorset
www.cheesefestival.co.uk
A celebration of the region's dairy heritage.

Swanage Regatta
July - August, Swanage, Dorset
www.swanagecarnival.com
The South's premier carnival.

Bristol

At-Bristol
Bristol BS1 5DB
(0845) 345 1235
www.at-bristol.org.uk
*21st century science and technology centre, with
hands-on activities, interactive exhibits.*

Avon Valley Railway
Bristol BS30 6HD
(0117) 932 5538
www.avonvalleyrailway.org
*Much more than your average steam train ride.
A whole new experience or a nostalgic memory.*

The Bristol Hippodrome
Bristol, BS1 4UZ
(01173) 023310
www.atgtickets.com/venues/bristol-hippodrome
One of the country's top provincial theatres, staging major West End and Broadway productions.

Bristol Zoo Gardens
Bristol BS8 3HA
(0117) 974 7300
www.bristolzoo.org.uk
Your passport for a day trip into an amazing world of animals, exhibits and other attractions.

Brunel's SS Great Britain
Bristol BS1 6TY
(0117) 926 0680
www.ssgreatbritain.org
Award-winning attraction showing the world's first great ocean liner and National Brunel Archive.

City Sightseeing The Bristol Tour
Central Bristol BS1 4AH
(03333) 210101
www.citysightseeingbristol.co.uk
Open-top bus tours, with guides and headphones, around the city of Bristol. Runs daily through summer.

Gloucestershire

Chavenage
Chavenage, Tetbury, Gloucestershire GL8 8XP
(01666) 502329
Elizabethan Manor Chavenage House, a TV/ Film location is still a family home, offers unique experiences, with history, ghosts and more.

Corinium Museum
Cirencester, Gloucestershire GL7 2BX
(01285) 655611
www.coriniummuseum.org
Discover the treasures of the Cotswolds as you explore its history at this award winning museum.

Forest Food Showcase
October, Forest of Dean, Gloucestershire
www.forestshowcase.org
A celebration of the foods and fruits of the forest. Held at Speech House on the first Sunday in October.

Gloucester Cathedral
Gloucestershire GL1 2LX
(01452) 528095
www.gloucestercathedral.org.uk
A place of worship and an architectural gem.

Gloucester Waterways Museum
Gloucester GL1 2EH
(01452) 318200
Closed for refurbishment, opens summer 2016. A Victorian warehouse, interactive displays and galleries.

Hidcote Manor Garden
Chipping Campden, Gloucestershire GL55 6LR
(01386) 438333
www.nationaltrust.org.uk/hidcote
Rare trees and shrubs, outstanding herbaceous borders and unusual plants from all over the world.

Painswick Rococo Garden
Painswick, Gloucestershire GL6 6TH
(01452) 813204
www.rococogarden.org.uk
A fascinating step back to a flamboyant and sensual period of English Garden Design

Sudeley Castle Gardens and Exhibition
Winchcombe, Gloucestershire GL54 5JD
(01242) 602308
www.sudeleycastle.co.uk
Award-winning gardens surrounding Castle and medieval ruins.

Westonbirt, The National Arboretum
Tetbury, Gloucestershire GL8 8QS
(01666) 880220
www.forestry.gov.uk/westonbirt
600 acres with one of the finest collections of trees.

Somerset

Bridgwater Arts Centre
Bridgwater, Somerset, TA6 3DD
(01278) 422700
www.bridgwaterartscentre.co.uk
A beautiful Georgian building; be entertained by one of the evening shows, relax in the cosy bar, or stroll through the local gallery.

Glastonbury Abbey

Somerset BA6 9EL
(01458) 832267
www.glastonburyabbey.com
Somewhere for all seasons! From snowdrops and daffodils in the Spring, to family trails and quizzes and Autumn colour on hundreds of trees.

Glastonbury Festival

June, Pilton, Somerset
www.glastonburyfestivals.co.uk
Known for its contemporary music, but also features dance, comedy, theatre, circus, cabaret and other arts.

Haynes International Motor Museum

Yeovil, Somerset BA22 7LH
(01963) 440804
www.haynesmotormuseum.co.uk
More than 400 vehicles displayed in stunning style, dating from 1886 to the present day.

The Jane Austen Centre

Bath, Somerset BA1 2NT
(01225) 443000
www.janeausten.co.uk
Celebrating Bath's most famous resident.

Number One Royal Crescent

Bath, Somerset BA1 2LR
(01225) 428126
www.bath-preservation-trust.org.uk
Restored and authentically furnished town house shows fashionable life in 18th century Bath.

West Somerset Railway

Minehead, Somerset TA24 5BG
(01643) 704996
www.west-somerset-railway.co.uk
Longest independent steam railway in Britain.

Wiltshire

Bowood House and Gardens

Bowood, Calne, Wiltshire, SN11 0LZ
(01249) 812102
www.bowood.org
Stately home with formal grounds and woodlands created by master landscaper Capability Brown.

Longleat

Warminster, Wiltshire BA12 7NW
(01985) 844400
www.longleat.co.uk
A wealth of exciting attractions including Longleat House along with lots of special events to keep you and your family entertained.

Old Sarum

Salisbury, Wiltshire SP1 3SD
(01722) 335398
www.english-heritage.org.uk/oldsarum
Discover the story of the original Salisbury. The mighty Iron Age hill fort where the first cathedral stood and where our ancestors left their mark.

Salisbury Cathedral

Salisbury, Wiltshire SP1 2EJ
(01722) 555120
www.salisburycathedral.org.uk
Britain's finest 13th century cathedral with the tallest spire in Britain. Discover nearly 800 years of history, the world's best preserved Magna Carta (AD 1215).

Stourhead House and Garden

Warminster, Wiltshire BA12 6QD
(01747) 841152
www.nationaltrust.org.uk/stourhead
A breathtaking 18th century landscape garden with lakeside walks, grottoes and classical temples.

Wilton House

Wilton House, Wilton, Wiltshire SP2 0BJ
(01722) 746714
www.wiltonhouse.com
Wilton House has one of the finest art collections in Europe and is set in magnificent landscaped parkland featuring the Palladian Bridge.

Tourist Information Centres

When you arrive at your destination, visit the Tourist Information Centre for quality assured help with accommodation and information about local attractions and events, or email your request before you go.

Axminster	The Old Courthouse	01297 34386	touristinfo@axminsteronline.com
Barnstaple	Museum of North Devon	01271 375000 / 346747	info@staynorthdevon.co.uk
Bath	Abbey Chambers	0906 711 2000	tourism@bathtourism.co.uk
Bideford	Burton Art Gallery	01237 477676	bidefordtic@torridge.gov.uk
Blandford Forum	Riverside House	01258 454770	blandfordtic@btconnect.com
Bodmin	Shire Hall	01208 76616	bodmintic@visit.org.uk
Bourton-on-the-Water	Victoria Street	01451 820211	bourtonvic@btconnect.com
Bradford on Avon	The Greenhouse	01225 865797	tic@bradfordonavon.co.uk
Braunton	The Bakehouse Centre	01271 816688	brauntonmuseum@yahoo.co.uk
Bridport	Bridport Town Hall, Bucky Doo Square	01308 424901	bridport.tic@westdorset-weymouth.gov.uk
Bristol : Harbourside	E Shed	0906 711 2191	ticharbourside@destinationbristol.co.uk
Brixham	Hobb Nobs Gift Shop	01803 211 211	holiday@englishriviera.co.uk
Bude	Bude Visitor Centre	01288 354240	budetic@visitbude.info
Budleigh Salterton	Fore Street	01395 445275	info@visitbudleigh.com
Cartgate	South Somerset TIC	01935 829333	cartgate.tic@southsomerset.gov.uk
Chard	The Guildhall	01460 260051	chard.tic@chard.gov.uk
Cheltenham	Municipal Offices	01242 522878	info@cheltenham.gov.uk
Chippenham	Hight Street	01249 665970	info@chippenham.gov.uk
Chipping Campden	The Old Police Station	01386 841206	info@campdenonline.org
Christchurch	49 High Street	01202 471780	enquiries@christchurchtourism.info
Cirencester	Corinium Museum	01285 654180	cirencestervic@cotswold.gov.uk
Combe Martin	Seacot	01271 883319	mail@visitcombemartin.co.uk
Dartmouth	The Engine House	01803 834224	holidays@discoverdartmouth.com
Dawlish	The Lawn	01626 215665	dawtic@teignbridge.gov.uk
Dorchester	11 Antelope Walk	01305 267992	dorchester.tic@westdorset-weymouth.gov.uk
Exeter	Visitor Information Centre	01392 665700	tic@exeter.gov.uk

Exmouth	Travelworld	01395 222299	tic@travelworldexmouth.co.uk
Falriver	11 Market Strand	0905 325 4534	vic@falriver.co.uk
Fowey	5 South Street	01726 833616	info@fowey.co.uk
Frome	The Library	01373 465757	touristinfo@frome-tc.gov.uk
Glastonbury	The Tribunal	01458 832954	info@glastonburytic.co.uk
Gloucester	28 Southgate Street	01452 396572	tourism@gloucester.gov.uk
Honiton	Lace Walk Car Park	01404 43716	honitontic@btconnect.com
Ilfracombe	The Landmark	01271 863001	marie@visitilfracombe.co.uk
Ivybridge	The Watermark	01752 897035 / 892220	info@ivybridgewatermark.co.uk
Launceston	The White Hart Arcade	01566 772321	info@launcestontic.co.uk
Looe	The Guildhall	01503 262072	looetic@btconnect.com
Lyme Regis	Guildhall Cottage	01297 442138	lymeregis.tic@westdorset-weymouth.gov.uk
Lynton and Lynmouth	Town Hall	01598 752225	info@lyntourism.co.uk
Malmesbury	Town Hall	01666 823748	tic@malmesbury.gov.uk
Melksham	32 Church Street	01225 707424	info@visit-melksham.com
Mere	The Library, Barton Lane	01747 860546	
Minehead	19 The Avenue	01643 702624	minehead.visitor@hotmail.com
Modbury	5 Modbury Court	01548 830159	modburytic@lineone.net
Moreton-in-Marsh	High Street	01608 650881	moreton@cotswold.gov.uk
Newquay	Municipal Offices	01637 854020	newquay.tic@cornwall.gov.uk
Newton Abbot	6 Bridge House	01626 215667	natic@teignbridge.gov.uk
Ottery St Mary	10a Broad Street	01404 813964	info@otterytourism.org.uk
Padstow	Red Brick Building	01841 533449	padstowtic@btconnect.com
Penzance	Station Approach	01736 335530	beth.rose@nationaltrust.org.uk
Plymouth	Plymouth Mayflower Centre	01752 306330	barbicantic@plymouth.gov.uk
Poole	Enefco House	0845 2345560	info@pooletourism.com
Salcombe	Market Street	01548 843927	info@salcombeinformation.co.uk
Salisbury	Fish Row	01722 342860	visitorinfo@salisburycitycouncil.gov.uk
Scilly, Isles Of	Hugh Street, Hugh Town	01720 424031	tic@scilly.gov.uk
Seaton	The Underfleet	01297 21660	visit@seaton.gov.uk
Shaftesbury	8a Bell Street	01747 853514	tourism@shaftesburydorset.com
Shepton Mallet	70 High Street	01749 345258	enquiries@visitsheptonmallet.co.uk
Sherborne	3 Tilton Court	01935 815341	sherborne.tic@westdorset-weymouth.gov.uk
Sidmouth	Ham Lane	01395 516441	ticinfo@sidmouth.gov.uk
Somerset	Sedgemoor Services	01934 750833	somersetvisitorcentre@somerset.gov.uk
South Molton	1 East Street	01769 574122	visitsouthmolton@btconnect.com
St Austell	Southbourne Road	01726 879 500	staustelltic@gmail.com
St Ives	The Guildhall	01736 796297	info@stivestic.co.uk
Street	Clarks Village	01458 447384	info@streettic.co.uk
Stroud	Subscription Rooms	01453 760960	tic@stroud.gov.uk
Swanage	The White House	01929 422885	mail@swanage.gov.uk
Swindon	Central Library	01793 466454	infocentre@swindon.gov.uk
Taunton	Market House	01823 340470	tauntontic@tauntondeane.gov.uk
Tavistock	The Den	01626 215666	teigntic@teignbridge.gov.uk
Tetbury	33 Church Street	01666 503552	tourism@tetbury.org
Tewkesbury	100 Church Street	01684 855040	tewkesburytic@tewkesbury.gov.uk
Tiverton	Tiverton Museum	01884 256295	tivertontic@tivertonmuseum.org.uk
Torquay	The Tourist Centre	01803 211 211	holiday@englishriviera.co.uk
Torrington	Castle Hill	01805 626140	info@great-torrington.com
Totnes	The Town Mill	01803 863168	enquire@totnesinformation.co.uk
Trowbridge	Civic Centre	01225 765072	tic@trowbridge.gov.uk
Truro	Municipal Building	01872 274555	tic@truro.gov.uk
Wareham	Discover Purbeck	01929 552740	tic@purbeck-dc.gov.uk
Warminster	Central Car Park	01985 218548	visitwarminster@btconnect.com
Wellington	30 Fore Street	01823 663379	wellingtontic@tauntondeane.gov.uk
Wells	Wells Museum	01749 671770	visitwellsinfo@gmail.com
Weston-Super-Mare	The Winter Gardens	01934 417117	westontic@parkwood-leisure.co.uk
Wimborne Minster	29 High Street	01202 886116	wimbornetic@eastdorset.gov.uk
Winchcombe	Town Hall	01242 602925	winchcombetic@tewkesbury.gov.uk
Woolacombe	The Esplanade	01271 870553	info@woolacombetourism.co.uk
Yeovil	Petters House	01935 462781	yeoviltic@southsomerset.gov.uk

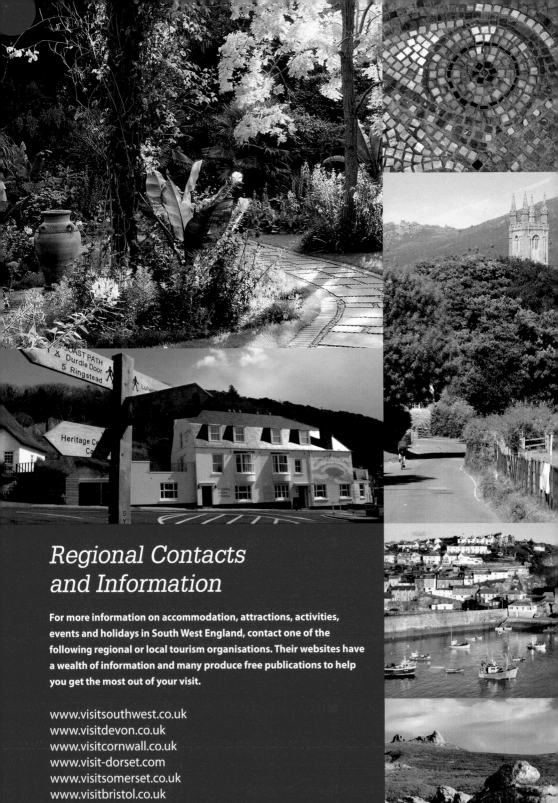

Regional Contacts and Information

For more information on accommodation, attractions, activities, events and holidays in South West England, contact one of the following regional or local tourism organisations. Their websites have a wealth of information and many produce free publications to help you get the most out of your visit.

www.visitsouthwest.co.uk
www.visitdevon.co.uk
www.visitcornwall.co.uk
www.visit-dorset.com
www.visitsomerset.co.uk
www.visitbristol.co.uk
www.visitbath.co.uk
www.southwestcoastpath.org.uk

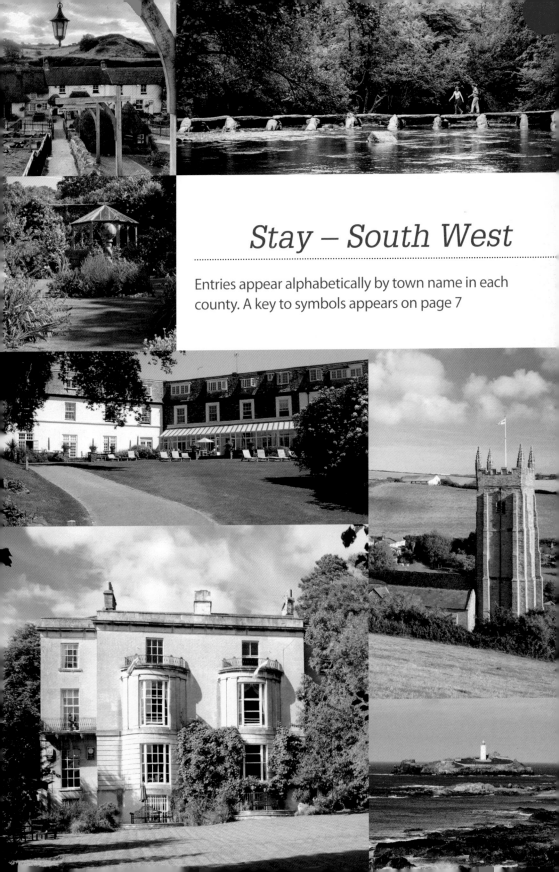

Stay – South West

Entries appear alphabetically by town name in each county. A key to symbols appears on page 7

CAMELFORD, Cornwall   Map ref 1B2

Pendragon Country House

Old Vicarage Hill, Davidstow, Camelford, Cornwall PL32 9XR **T:** (01840) 261131
E: enquiries@pendragoncountryhouse.com
W: www.pendragoncountryhouse.com **£ BOOK ONLINE**

Beautifully presented, family-run luxury country guest house set in mature grounds offering bed & breakfast at its best. 7 en suite rooms offer a wide range of accommodation, from a spacious single to a grand superior king with a four-poster bed. **Directions:** From the East, entering Davidstow continue past church. Signposted Pendragon Country House will be on the right hand side 1/4 mile from A39. **Bedrooms:** All en suite, TV/DVD, tea tray and luxury furnishings **Open:** All Year except 24th-27th Dec

B&B PER ROOM PER NIGHT
S: £60.00 - £65.00
D: £95.00 - £140.00
EVENING MEAL PER PERSON
£27.00 - £50.00

Site: ❀ **P** Payment: ⊞ € Leisure: ⚓ ► ∪ ✦ Property: ♈ ➳ 🐾 🎎 ⌚ 🐾 ∅
Children: ⛷ ☷ 🅰 Catering: (✗ ♈ 🍽 Room: ♋ 🍴 📺 📀 🎐 🛏

CHARLESTOWN, Cornwall   Map ref 1B3

The Pier House Hotel

Harbour Front, Charlestown Road, St Austell, Cornwall PL25 3NJ **T:** (01726) 67955
F: 01726 69246 **E:** pierhouse@btconnect.com
W: www.pierhousehotel.com

B&B PER ROOM PER NIGHT
S: £70.00 - £97.00
D: £118.00 - £148.00

The Pier House Hotel is situated on the picturesque harbour of Charlestown with stunning views of the port and coastline of St Austell bay. Experience the ultimate luxury that you would expect from one of the premier hotels in Cornwall. **Directions:** Please see our website for full directions. **Bedrooms:** 7 single, 17 double, 3 twin, 3 family **Open:** All year except Christmas day

Site: ❀ Payment: ⊞ Leisure: ♪ ► ∪ Property: ☷ 🎎 ● Children: ⛷ ☷ 🅰 Catering: (✗ ♈ 🍽
Room: ♋ 🍴 📞 📀 📺 🎐

Looking for something else?

The official and most comprehensive guide to independently inspected, quality-assessed accommodation.

B&Bs and Hotels
B&Bs, Hotels, farmhouses, inns, campus and hostel accommodation in England.

Self Catering and Camping
Self-catering holiday homes, approved caravan holiday homes, serviced apartments, boat accommodation, holiday cottage agencies, Touring parks, camping holidays and holiday parks and villages in England.

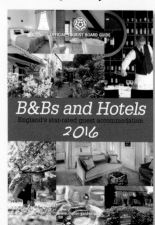

B&Bs and Hotels
England's star-rated guest accommodation
2016

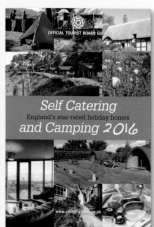

Self Catering
England's star-rated holiday homes
and Camping 2016

Now available in all good bookshops and online at:
www.visitor-guides.co.uk

CONSTANTINE BAY, Cornwall Map ref 1B2 SatNav PL28 8JH [H]

Treglos Hotel

Constantine Bay, Padstow PL28 8JH **T:** (01841) 520727 **F:** 01841 521163
E: stay@tregloshotel.com
W: www.tregloshotel.com **£ BOOK ONLINE**

B&B PER ROOM PER NIGHT
S: £73.50 - £115.00
D: £141.00 - £230.00
HB PER PERSON PER NIGHT
£98.00 - £139.50

SPECIAL PROMOTIONS
Prices vary throughout the seasons - please contact or visit website for further details.

This luxurious hotel on the North Cornish coast has 42 rooms and suites, many with dramatic views over Constantine Bay. Facilities include indoor pool, whirlpool, treatment rooms and award-winning restaurant. Treglos has its own golf course and self-catering apartments. Beaches and coastal paths are within a short stroll. Please contact for evening meal prices.

Directions: Please contact us for directions.

Bedrooms: 3 single, 23 double/twin, 10 family, 6 suite.
Open: February - November.

Site: ❀ P **Payment:** ⊞ **Leisure:** 🏊 ♪ ▶ ∪ ◕ ✕ ☂ **Property:** 🐾 🐴 🖼 🛏 ☾ ◐ ∅ **Children:** 🧸 🛏 🚶 **Catering:** (✕ 🍷 🍴 **Room:** 🍷 ♨ 📞 📺 DVD 🍴

FALMOUTH, Cornwall Map ref 1B3 SatNav TR11 5LG [H]

Budock Vean Hotel

Nr Helford Passage, Mawnan Smith, Falmouth, Cornwall TR11 5LG **T:** (01326) 250288
F: 01326 250892 **E:** relax@budockvean.co.uk
W: www.budockvean.co.uk **£ BOOK ONLINE**

B&B PER ROOM PER NIGHT
S: £73.00 - £141.00
D: £73.00 - £282.00
EVENING MEAL PER PERSON
£41.00

SPECIAL PROMOTIONS
See website for details
-
www.budockvean.co.uk/offers

On a quiet bend of the tranquil Helford River nestles the award-winning 4 star Budock Vean Hotel. Set in 65 acres of glorious gardens, woodlands and its own golf course – The Budock Vean is a sanctuary for rest and relaxation. With an AA Rosette restaurant renowned for amazing food, relaxing treatments in the Natural Health Spa, luxury self catering holiday homes, tennis courts, kayaking and boat trips along the river, you can be as active or as relaxed as you wish.

Directions: Please contact us for directions.

Bedrooms: 7 single, 24 double, 23 twin, 2 family, 1 suite
Open: All year except January 2 - 20 2016.

Site: ❀ P **Payment:** ⊞ **Leisure:** 🏊 ♪ ▶ ∪ ✕ 🚴 ☂ **Property:** 🍷 🐴 🖼 🛏 ☾ ◐ ∅ **Children:** 🧸 🛏 🚶 **Catering:** (✕ 🍷 **Room:** 🍷 ♨ 📞 📺 📠

LANDS END, Cornwall Map ref 1A3
SatNav TR19 7RD **B**

B&B PER ROOM PER NIGHT
S: £40.00 - £50.00
D: £80.00 - £98.00

Bosavern House
Bosavern, St. Just, Lands End TR19 7RD **T:** (01736) 788301 **E:** info@bosavern.com
W: www.bosavern.com

C17th country house in attractive grounds. Centrally heated, comfortable accommodation. Most rooms have sea or moorland views. Home cooking using local produce. Ideally situated for exploring West Cornwall. Ample parking. **Directions:** Take A3071 from Penzance towards St Just, turn left onto B3306 signed Lands End. Bosavern House is 0.5 mile on left. **Bedrooms:** 1 single, 3 double, 2 twin, 2 family **Open:** All year except Christmas

 Site: ✿ P Payment: 💷 € Leisure: ♿ 🏌 ⚲ Property: 🖥 ☎ Children: ⏰ 🏥 ⚥ Catering: 🍴 🍲
Room: 🖐 🛀 📺 ♨ 🚪

LOOE, Cornwall Map ref 1C2
SatNav PL13 2DG **H**

B&B PER ROOM PER NIGHT
S: £50.00 - £72.00
D: £100.00 - £154.00
HB PER PERSON PER NIGHT
£52.00 - £92.00

SPECIAL PROMOTIONS
Special-event packages. Extensive range of conference and business facilities. Weddings and special occasions. Christmas and New Year celebrations.

Hannafore Point Hotel and Spa
Marine Drive, West Looe, Looe PL13 2DG **T:** (01503) 263273
E: stay@hannaforepointhotel.com
W: www.hannaforepointhotel.com

A warm welcome awaits you. Set in picturesque Cornish village with spectacular, panoramic sea views. Indulge in superb home-cooked food. Dining options include quality local produce and fresh fish. The terrace is a popular rendezvous for cream teas or cocktails. Spa pool, gym, sauna, steam and beauty therapies.

Directions: A38 from Plymouth, then A387 to Looe. Cross over stone bridge, turn 1st left (sign 'Hannafore') and uphill until overlooking bay.

Bedrooms: 4 single, 33 dble
Open: All year

Site: ✿ Payment: 💷 Leisure: ♿ 🏌 ⏱ ∪ 🎾 ⚲ Property: 🏌 🐕 🖥 ☎ ◐ Children: ⏰ 🏥 ⚥
Catering: 🍴 🍲 Room: 🖐 🛀 ✆ 📻 📺 ♨ 🚪 🛏

The Official Tourist Board Guide to **B&Bs and Hotels 2016**

NEWQUAY, Cornwall   Map ref 1B2   SatNav TR7 2NQ B

Harrington Guest House
25 Tolcarne Road, Newquay TR7 2NQ **T:** (01637) 873581
E: harringtonguesthouse@yahoo.com
W: www.harringtonguesthouse.com **£ BOOK ONLINE**

B&B PER ROOM PER NIGHT
S: £25.00 - £34.00
D: £46.00 - £58.00

The Harrington is a Bed & Breakfast with a central location situated within a short walk of all that Newquay resort has to offer. 5 mins walk from train station and local buses. Excellent value rooms with free Wi-Fi and free parking. **Bedrooms:** En suite, flatscreen TV, tea and coffee facilities **Open:** All year except Christmas

Site: P Payment: Leisure: Property: Children: Catering: Room:

PENZANCE, Cornwall   Map ref 1A3   SatNav TR18 3AE H

Hotel Penzance
Britons Hill, Penzance TR18 3AE **T:** (01736) 363117 **F:** 01736 361127
E: reception@hotelpenzance.com
W: www.hotelpenzance.com **£ BOOK ONLINE**

B&B PER ROOM PER NIGHT
S: £85.00 - £95.00
D: £145.00 - £210.00
EVENING MEAL PER PERSON
£25.50

Enjoy high levels of comfort and friendly service at this award winning hotel. The Bay restaurant presents fine food served all day with evening a la carte and tasting menus. Traditional or contemporary-style rooms with sea views across Penzance Harbour. **Directions:** Enter Penzance on A30. At roundabout keep left towards Town Centre. Third turn right onto Britons Hill. Hotel 70m on right. **Bedrooms:** 4 single, 12 doubles, 9 twin. All Superior and most Classic rooms have sea views **Open:** All year

Site: Payment: Leisure: Property: Children: Catering: Room:

PENZANCE, Cornwall   Map ref 1A3   SatNav TR18 4HG H

Queens Hotel
The Promenade, Penzance, Cornwall TR18 4HG **T:** (01736) 362371 **F:** 01736 350033
E: enquiries@queens-hotel.com
W: www.queens-hotel.com **£ BOOK ONLINE**

SPECIAL PROMOTIONS
We have regular promotions, please check our offers webpage at www.queens-hotel.com/category/offers/

The Queens Hotel is the gateway to West Cornwall offering comfort and style, as well as great service and food. Enjoy a striking destination inspired by an extraordinary landscape, and a resilient culture rich in heritage. As a true family hotel, guests are welcome to bring their pets.

Directions: The Queens Hotel is located in the middle the promenade of Penzance, on one of the longest promenades in the UK. Just head to the seafront and you'll find us.

Bedrooms: All rooms en suite, with TV, Wi-Fi, tea and coffee and room service
Open: All year

Site: P Payment: Leisure: Property: Children: Catering: Room:

ST. AGNES, Cornwall Map ref 1B3

SatNav TR5 0XX **B**

★★★
FARMHOUSE

B&B PER ROOM PER NIGHT
S: £27.50 - £30.00
D: £50.00 - £60.00

Little Trevellas Farm

Trevellas, St Agnes TR5 0XX **T:** (01872) 552945 **F:** 01872 552945
E: velvet-crystal@xlninternet.co.uk
W: www.stagnesbandb.co.uk **£ BOOK ONLINE**

A 250-year-old house on a working farm on the B3285 provides a peaceful, comfortable base for a holiday that will appeal to lovers of both coast and countryside. Wi-fi now available. In the case of one night stays, a £5 surcharge will be added to room rates.
Directions: Please contact us for directions. **Bedrooms:** 1 single, 1 double, 1 twin **Open:** All year

Site: P Property: 🐾 🖼 **Catering:** 🍴 **Room:** ✻ 📺

ST. AGNES, Cornwall Map ref 1B3

SatNav TR5 0PA **B**

★★
GUEST HOUSE

B&B PER ROOM PER NIGHT
S: £25.00 - £50.00
D: £50.00 - £60.00

Penkerris

Penwinnick Road (B3277), St. Agnes TR5 0PA **T:** (01872) 552262 **E:** penkerris@gmail.com
W: www.penkerris.co.uk

Edwardian house with parking, lawned garden for relaxation and games, cosy lounge and delightful dining room serving real food. Close to dramatic cliff walks and iconic surfing beaches (nearest 1km). Beach hut available. Ideal location, central for all of Cornwall.
Directions: From A30, big roundabout at Chiverton, 3 miles to village on B3277. Penkerris is just inside St Agnes village and 30mph sign and before the Museum. **Bedrooms:** 2 double, 2 twin, 2 family, 2 singles. **Open:** All year

Site: ✿ **P Payment:** 💷 € **Leisure:** 🚴 ⛳ **Property:** 🐾 🖼 📖 **Children:** 🚲 🍴 🏊 **Catering:** 🍴 **Room:** ✻ 📺

ST. MINVER, Cornwall   Map ref 1B2   SatNav PL27 6RG B

★★★ FARMHOUSE
Silver AWARD

B&B PER ROOM PER NIGHT
D: £64.00 - £80.00

Tredower Barton
St Minver, Wadebridge, Cornwall PL27 6RG **T:** (01208) 813501
E: dally.123@btinternet.com

Tredower Barton is a farm bed and breakfast set in beautiful countryside near the North Cornish coast. New for 2014, a lovely garden/sun room with beautiful panoramic views available for guests' use. Delicious breakfast and relaxing stay guaranteed. Near to local attractions, Padstow, Port Isaac, Eden Project & Heligan Gardens only 45 mins. Wi-Fi available. **Directions:** 3 miles from Wadebridge on road B3314 to Port Issac. **Bedrooms:** 1 twin, 1 family (can be used as family or double).
Open: Easter to October.

Site: ✿ P Leisure: 🦽 ▶ ✈ ✎ Property: 📺 ♨ Children: 🛏 🎠 ♣ Room: 📶 ☕ 📺 🎽 🖨

TRURO, Cornwall   Map ref 1B3   SatNav TR2 4JA B

★★★★ BED & BREAKFAST
Silver AWARD

B&B PER ROOM PER NIGHT
S: £57.00 - £65.00
D: £70.00 - £75.00

Spring Cottage B&B
Probus, Truro, Cornwall TR2 4JA **T:** (01872) 520307 **E:** info@springcottage.co.uk
W: www.springcottage.co.uk **£ BOOK ONLINE**

Chris and David warmly welcome you to Spring Cottage, a quality B&B in a listed 17th century Cornish cottage, lovingly restored to provide stylish en suite accommodation. Truro five miles, Eden Project and Heligan within easy reach.

Bedrooms: En suite rooms with showers, TV, free Wi-Fi. **Open:** All year except Christmas and New Year.

Site: ✿ P Payment: 💳 Property: 📺 Room: 📶 📺 📀

BRYHER, Isles of Scilly   Map ref 1A3   SatNav TR23 0PR H

★★★★ HOTEL
Silver AWARD

B&B PER ROOM PER NIGHT
S: £115.00 - £365.00
D: £170.00 - £570.00

EVENING MEAL PER PERSON
£36.50 - £42.50

SPECIAL PROMOTIONS
Please see our website for all special rates and breaks.

Hell Bay Hotel
Bryher, Isles of Scilly TR23 0PR **T:** (01720) 422947 **F:** 01720 423004
E: contactus@hellbay.co.uk
W: www.hellbay.co.uk **£ BOOK ONLINE**

Bryher's only hotel and England's last boasts a spectacular, natural location that blends with the contemporary style of the hotel to produce a unique venue. All accommodation is beautifully appointed, and most bedrooms have direct sea views. The award-winning food and informal service combine to complete the experience.

Directions: Flights from Exeter, Newquay or Land's End or ferry from Penzance all to the neighbouring island of St Mary's. A local boat transfer will take you to Bryher, a 15 minute journey.

Bedrooms: 4 family, 21 suite
Open: March to October

Site: ✿ Payment: 💳 Leisure: 🎵 ▶ ♨ ⚓ 🎿 ⛹ ☂ ✈ ✎ Property: 🐾 📺 🖥 ♨ ∅ Children: 🛏 🎠 ♣
Catering: ❌ 🍽 🍴 Room: 📶 ☕ 🕭 📺 📀 🎽 🖨

BRIXHAM, Devon   Map ref 1D2

SatNav TQ5 9AJ **H**

VisitEngland
★★★
HOTEL

Berry Head Hotel

Berry Head Road, Brixham TQ5 9AJ **T:** (01803) 853225 **F:** 01803 882084
E: stay@berryheadhotel.com
W: www.berryheadhotel.com

B&B PER ROOM PER NIGHT
S: £55.00 - £78.00
D: £96.00 - £168.00
HB PER PERSON PER NIGHT
£58.00 - £94.00

SPECIAL PROMOTIONS
Special-event packages. Extensive range of conference and business facilities. Weddings and special occasions. Christmas and New Year celebrations.

Steeped in history, nestling on the water's edge in acres of outstanding natural beauty. Traditional hospitality, excellent, friendly and personal service with attention to detail. Comfortable accommodation, thoughtfully equipped. Imaginative menus, varied dining options, featuring quality local produce and fresh fish. Lounge, bars and terrace, popular with locals and residents.

Directions: Enter Brixham, continue to harbour and around, up King Street for 1 mile to Berry Head.

Bedrooms: 3 single, 12 dble, 10 twin, 7 family
Open: All year

Site: ✿ **Payment:** 💷 € **Leisure:** ♿ ♪ ▶ ☾ ☂ **Property:** ⚑ 🖥 🔒 ◗ **Children:** ⛵ 🛏 🚶 **Catering:** ♟ 🍴
Room: ♜ ☕ ☎ 📻 📺 🎧 🎿 🛗

DARTMOUTH, Devon   Map ref 1D3

SatNav TQ6 9EF **B**

VisitEngland
★★★★
BED & BREAKFAST

VisitEngland
Gold
AWARD

Cladda House B&B and Self Catering Apartments

88-90 Victoria Road, Dartmouth, Devon TQ6 9EF **T:** (01803) 835957 / 07967060003
E: BandB@cladda-dartmouth.co.uk
W: www.cladda-dartmouth.co.uk

B&B PER ROOM PER NIGHT
S: £75.00 - £85.00
D: £85.00 - £98.00

SPECIAL PROMOTIONS
Please call for Reductions on Weekly Lets and Details of Dartmouth Festivals - Music Festival - Regatta Week - Food Festival - Galleries Weeks, Candelit Christmas, Christmas and New Year.

Family run B & B in Dartmouth Town with 4 Quality En suite Super King Double, Twin & Standard Double Rooms & 2 Self Contained 1 Bedroom (S/K orTwin) + Living Room (Sofa Bed) Suites. Spacious for 2 or Small Families, Walkers, Golfers, etc. Our own FREE GUARANTEED on-site parking. A Stroll to Dartmouth's Waterfront, Restaurants, Pubs, Varied indivdual Shops and Galleries. Debit/ Credit Cards accepted.

Directions: Description of getting to Dartmouth and detailed where to find us Map of Dartmouth showing our On-site Parking at back of Cladda House in Ford Valley sent with all of our Booking Confirmations.

Bedrooms: All Rooms En-suite, Free WiFi, Flat Screen Colour TV/DVD, Hair Dryer, Alarm Clock/ Radio, Quiet Fridge & Full Hospitality Tray.
Open: All Year

Site: ✿ **P** **Payment:** 💷 € **Leisure:** ♪ ▶ **Property:** 🐾 🖥 **Children:** ⛵ 🛏 🚶 **Catering:** 🍴
Room: ♜ ☕ 📺 📀 🛗

Langstone Cliff Hotel

Mount Pleasant Road, Dawlish Warren, Dawlish, Devon EX7 0NA **T:** (01626) 868000
F: 01626 868006 **E:** info@langstone-hotel.co.uk
W: www.langstone-hotel.co.uk **£ BOOK ONLINE**

B&B PER ROOM PER NIGHT
S: £69.00 - £150.00
D: £69.00 - £150.00
EVENING MEAL PER PERSON
£8.50 - £35.00

SPECIAL PROMOTIONS
Children under 10 free
when sharing with 2
adults. Special cabaret
weekend breaks
throughout the year.

Set in 19 acres of Devon woodland overlooking the sea close to Exeter and Torquay. Extensive leisure facilities include 2 swimming pools, snooker, tennis, table tennis, fitness room and hairdressing Salon. Regular entertainment, children welcome, dinner dance and cabaret weekends, Dance Holidays, extensive Christmas and New Year Programme.

Directions: From M5 jct 31 follow A379 for Dawlish. Turn left at harbour after Starcross. Follow road approx 1.5 miles, hotel is on left.

Bedrooms: 1 single, 19 dble, 8 twin, 30 family, 6 suite
Open: All year

Site: ❋ P Payment: 🆔 Leisure: ♪ ♪ ♻ ✗ ♨ ⚡ ✈ Property: ♟ 🐈 📧 🅱 🎯 ⊙ Children: 🍼 🛏 ♿ Catering: (✗ ♙ 🍴 Room: 🍵 ♨ ☎ 🖥 🔌

Globe Inn

Frogmore, Nr Kingsbridge TQ7 2NR **T:** (01548) 531351 **E:** info@theglobeinn.co.uk
W: www.theglobeinn.co.uk

B&B PER ROOM PER NIGHT
S: £60.00 - £70.00
D: £85.00
EVENING MEAL PER PERSON
£10.00 - £20.00

The inn is situated in the pretty village of Frogmore, between Kingsbridge and Dartmouth, in glorious unspoilt South Hams countryside. The pub has undergone tasteful renovation and now boasts 8 well appointed en suite bedrooms. Downstairs the pub has a cosy bar restaurant frequented be friendly locals.
Directions: Via Kingsbridge take the A379 to Dartmouth and Torcross. After 2 miles, look out for the Inn on the left as you enter Frogmore. **Bedrooms:** 5 double, 2 twin, 1 family. All rooms en suite
Open: All year

Site: ❋ P Payment: 🆔 Leisure: ♪ ♪ Property: 🐈 📧 ♻ Children: 🍼 ♿ Catering: (✗ ♙ 🍴 Room: 🍵 ♨ 🖥

Blue Waters Lodge

4 Leighon Road, Paignton TQ3 2BQ **T:** (01803) 557749 **E:** info@bluewaterslodge.co.uk
W: www.bluewaterslodge.co.uk

B&B PER ROOM PER NIGHT
D: £55.00 - £65.00

Blue Waters Lodge offers a warm friendly greeting and is conveniently situated within easy strolling distance of the seafront, shops and entertainments, yet still in a quiet location for a peaceful holiday. **Directions:** Please see website for details. **Bedrooms:** Free Wi-Fi, Freeview flatscreen TV, clock radio alarm, complimentary beverages and snacks, hairdryer and complimentary toiletries. Unlimited street parking. **Open:** All year

Site: ❋ P Payment: 🆔 Property: 📧 ♻ Children: 🍼 🛏 Catering: ♙ 🍴 Room: 🍵 ♨ 🖥

VisitEngland
★★
HOTEL

Redcliffe Lodge Hotel
1 Marine Drive, Paignton TQ3 2NJ **T:** (01803) 551394 **F:** 01803 551394
E: redcliffelodge@gmail.com
W: www.redcliffelodge.co.uk **£ BOOK ONLINE**

B&B PER ROOM PER NIGHT
S: £20.00 - £35.00
D: £40.00 - £70.00
HB PER PERSON PER NIGHT
£35.00 - £50.00

SPECIAL PROMOTIONS
2-4 year olds half-price
when sharing with
adults. Winter 2 night
breaks, B&B and 3
course evening meal
from £30pppn.

Redcliffe Lodge occupies one of Paignton's finest seafront positions, in its own grounds with a large, free car park. All rooms are en suite and comfortably furnished with modern facilities. Licensed bar. Panoramic views from both our sun lounge and dining room, where you will enjoy our high standard of cuisine.

Directions: Follow A3022 to Paignton seafront. The hotel is situated at the end of Marine Drive, on the right adjacent to Paignton Green.

Bedrooms: 2 single, 10 dble, 3 twin, 2 family
Open: All year

Site: ✿ P Payment: 🔲 Leisure: ♿ ♪ ▶ ☺ Property: ⌦ ⌦ ▣ ▣ ◐ Children: ☺ ⊞ ⚲
Catering: (✗ ⍑ ⌦ Room: ⌦ ♨ ▣ 📺 ⌦

PLYMOUTH, *Devon*   Map ref 1C2 — SatNav PL1 2RQ **B**

B&B PER ROOM PER NIGHT
S: £32.00 - £50.00
D: £54.00 - £64.00

Athenaeum Lodge

4 Athenaeum Street, The Hoe, Plymouth PL1 2RQ **T:** (01752) 665005 **F:** 01752 395222
E: athenaeumlodge@gmail.com
W: www.athenaeumlodge.com £ **BOOK ONLINE**

Elegant, Grade II Listed guesthouse, ideally situated on The Hoe. Centrally located for the Barbican, Theatre Royal, Plymouth Pavilions, Ferry Port and the National Marine Aquarium. City centre and university are a few minutes walk. Wi-Fi. **Directions:** Please see website for comprehensive directions. **Bedrooms:** 3 double, 2 twin, 3 family **Open:** All year except Christmas and New Year

Site: **P** Payment: ⊞ Leisure: ♪ ▶ Property: ▦ Children: ⚑ Catering: ⅏ Room: ⚑ ♨ ⓐ ⓣⓥ ☕

PLYMOUTH, *Devon*   Map ref 1C2 — SatNav PL1 3BS **B**

B&B PER ROOM PER NIGHT
S: £35.00 - £40.00
D: £55.00 - £60.00

Caraneal

12-14 Pier Street, West Hoe, Plymouth PL1 3BS **T:** (01752) 663589 **F:** 01752 663589
E: caranealhotel@hotmail.com
W: www.caranealplymouth.co.uk £ **BOOK ONLINE**

Caraneal is a cosy family-run establishment near the famous Hoe and seafront and within easy walking distance of the city centre and the historic Barbican. Free Wi-Fi Available. **Directions:** From A38 follow signs for City Centre, then the Hoe and Seafront. On seafront pass Plymouth Dome and turn right at the next mini-roundabout. **Bedrooms:** 5 double, 2 twin **Open:** All year except Christmas and New Year

Site: **P** Payment: ⊞ Leisure: ♿ ♪ Property: ▦ Children: ⚑ ⊞ ⅊ Catering: ⅏ Room: ⚑ ♨ ⓐ ⓣⓥ ☕ 🚗

SIDMOUTH, *Devon*   Map ref 1D2 — SatNav EX10 0ND **B**

B&B PER ROOM PER NIGHT
S: £43.00 - £50.00
D: £79.00 - £119.00
EVENING MEAL PER PERSON
£19.50 - £23.50

SPECIAL PROMOTIONS
3+ nights 1 for free, 2+ Nights & 7+ Nights Special Rates please see our website for details.

Open over Christmas & New Year.

Special occasions & functions by arrangement.

Please enquire for details.

The Barn & Pinn Cottage Guest House

Bowd, Sidmouth, Devon EX10 0ND **T:** (01395) 513613
E: barnpinncottage@btinternet.com
W: www.thebarnandpinncottage.co.uk

This beautiful 15th Century thatched cottage nestles within two acres of award-winning gardens, 5 minutes drive from Sidmouth. All en suite rooms have full central heating, Digital TV, and tea/coffee making facilities. Dinner available Thur-Sun. Good home cooking, varied menu, well stocked bar. Comfortable guest lounge, large private car park.

Directions: Located on A3052 12 miles from Exeter, 15 miles from Lyme Regis. Between Newton Poppleford and Sidford. 5 mins from beach at Sidmouth using B3176.

Bedrooms: 1 single, 3 double, 1 kingsize, 2 luxury four posters with private garden, 2 twin. 1 holiday let as B&B or self catering. Family rooms possible.
Open: All year

Site: ❋ **P** Payment: ⊞ Leisure: ♿ ♪ ▶ ∪ Property: ⋔ Children: ⚑ Catering: ⅏ ⅏ Room: ⚑ ♨ ⓐ ⓣⓥ ☕ 🚗

South West - Devon

★★★★ HOTEL | **Gold AWARD**

B&B PER ROOM PER NIGHT
S: £109.00 - £188.00
D: £218.00 - £356.00
HB PER PERSON PER NIGHT
£129.00 - £232.00

SPECIAL PROMOTIONS
Seasonal breaks available throughout the year. Christmas and New Year programme also available.

Hotel Riviera

The Esplanade, Sidmouth, Devon EX10 8AY **T:** (01395) 515201 **F:** 01395 577775
E: enquiries@hotelriviera.co.uk
W: www.hotelriviera.co.uk **£ BOOK ONLINE**

The Hotel Riviera is splendidly positioned at the centre of Sidmouth's esplanade, overlooking Lyme Bay. With its mild climate and the beach just on the doorstep, the setting echoes the South of France and is the choice of the discerning visitor in search of relaxation and quieter pleasures. Glorious sea views can be enjoyed from the recently re-designed en suite bedrooms, all of which are fully appointed and have many thoughtful extras. In the elegant bay-view dining room guests are offered a fine choice of dishes from extensive menus, prepared by English trained chefs with local seafood being a particular speciality. The hotel has a long tradition of hospitality and is perfect for unforgettable holidays, long weekends, unwinding breaks and all the spirit of the glorious Festive Season… you will be treated to the kind of friendly personal attention that can only be found in a private hotel of this quality.

Directions: Sidmouth is 165 miles from London and 13 miles from M5 exit 30 then follow A3052.

Bedrooms: 7 single, 10 doubles, 7 twin, 2 suite
Open: All year

Site: P Payment: ▦ **Leisure:** ♠ **Property:** ♠ ♞ ▦ ◧ ♨ ● **Children:** ❧ ▦ ♣ **Catering:** ♅ ♟ ▥ **Room:** ☎ ♨ ♣ ◧ TV DVD

★★★★ INN | **Silver AWARD**

B&B PER ROOM PER NIGHT
D: £100.00 - £140.00
EVENING MEAL PER PERSON
£15.00 - £25.00

Ness House

Ness Drive, Shaldon, Nr Teignmouth, Devon TQ14 0HP **T:** (01626) 873480
E: nesshouse.shaldon@hall-woodhouse.co.uk
W: www.theness.co.uk **£ BOOK ONLINE**

The Ness House is a Georgian property, built in 1810, on the outskirts of Shaldon village overlooking the Teign Estuary and only a stones throw from the beach. The Smugglers Tunnel can be found 20 yards away, leading you down to the secluded Ness Beach, sheltered by the Ness Cliff. The ferry which runs between Teignmouth and Shaldon is also a 'must', when visiting the area.

Directions: If you follow the road next to the Ness a little further up, you will find a pay and display car park with plenty of spaces.

Bedrooms: Recently refurbished to a luxurious and comfortable standard, including flatscreen TV and Bluetooth radio. Unbeatable sea views available on request.
Open: We are open year-round

Site: ☼ **Property:** ♞ ▦ ∅ **Children:** ❧ ▦ ♣ **Catering:** ♅ ♟ **Room:** ☎ ♨ TV

TORQUAY, Devon Map ref 1D2 SatNav TQ2 6RQ

VisitEngland
★★★ HOTEL

Best Western Livermead Cliff Hotel

Sea Front, Torquay TQ2 6RQ **T:** (01803) 299666 **F:** (01803) 294496
E: info@livermeadcliff.co.uk
W: www.livermeadcliff.co.uk **£ BOOK ONLINE**

B&B PER ROOM PER NIGHT
S: £35.00 - £110.00
D: £60.00 - £230.00
HB PER PERSON PER NIGHT
£40.00 - £140.00

Best Western

Privately owned, 3 star Best Western hotel on the water's edge with direct access to the beach. Panoramic views, sea view lounge and en suite rooms, licensed bar and stunning new Riviera Terrace. Free parking. Free Wi-Fi. Ideally located for touring the SW of England. **Directions:** Please contact us for directions. **Bedrooms:** 13 single, 29 double, 14 twin, 8 family, 1 suite **Open:** All year

Site: ✿ **Payment:** ⊞ **Leisure:** ⚓ ♪ ▶ ♒ **Property:** ⚷ ⚘ 🚗 🚲 ◐ **Children:** 🍼 🛏 🏃 **Catering:** ♟ 🍴 Room: ☎ ♨ ☏ 📺 ♨ 📠

TORQUAY, Devon Map ref 1D2 SatNav TQ2 6RH

VisitEngland
★★★ HOTEL

Corbyn Head Hotel

Sea Front, Torquay, Devon TQ2 6RH **T:** (01803) 213611 **F:** 01803 296152
E: info@corbynhead.com
W: www.corbynhead.com **£ BOOK ONLINE**

B&B PER ROOM PER NIGHT
S: £39.00 - £121.00
D: £69.00 - £250.00
EVENING MEAL PER PERSON
£23.50 - £29.50

The Corbyn Head Hotel is one of Torquay's leading hotels with its seafront location. Most bedrooms enjoy stunning sea views, many have private balconies. Outdoor Swimming Pool. Free Wi-Fi. Free on-site parking. **Directions:** Torquay Seafront, turn right and follow signs for Cockington Village. Hotel on right. **Bedrooms:** 3 single, 29 double, 10 twin, 3 family **Open:** All year

Site: ✿ **P Payment:** ⊞ **Leisure:** ⚓ ☀ ⚡ ↗ **Property:** ⚷ ⚘ 🚗 🚲 ♨ ◐ **Children:** 🍼 🛏 🏃 **Catering:** (✗ 🍴 🍴 Room: ☎ ♨ ☏ 📺 📠

TORQUAY, Devon Map ref 1D2 SatNav TQ1 3LN

VisitEngland
★★★★ GUEST ACCOMMODATION

VisitEngland
Gold AWARD

The Downs, Babbacombe

Seafront, 41-43 Babbacombe Downs Road, Babbacombe, Torquay TQ1 3LN
T: (01803) 328543 **F:** 01803 670557 **E:** enquiries@downshotel.co.uk
W: www.downshotel.co.uk **£ BOOK ONLINE**

B&B PER ROOM PER NIGHT
S: £63.00 - £78.00
D: £78.00 - £93.00
EVENING MEAL PER PERSON
£18.95

SPECIAL PROMOTIONS
Stay 3 or more nights & get 1 extra night free, available Jan & Feb. In Oct & Nov stay 3 nights or more, midweek, and get dinner on us one night for free! Stay 7 nights to get a long stay discount.

The Downs, Babbacombe in Torquay is family run with 12 ensuite rooms, 8 with balconies & uninterrupted sea views over Lyme Bay. We have a Lounge Bar and Restaurant serving optional evening meals and are fully licensed. We have an elegant feel whilst maintaining a comfortable, relaxed atmosphere. Dogs & Children welcome.

WINNERS OF SOUTH DEVON TOURISM & HOSPITALITY AWARDS 2013 - B&B, GUEST HOUSE.

Directions: M5 South to Torquay A380, at Torquay Harbour take left at r/a to Babbacombe. On entering Babbacombe take right turn into Princes Street, left onto Babbacombe Downs Rd, we are on the left.

Bedrooms: All bedrooms are fully en suite with simple yet stylish oak furniture and pocket sprung beds, luxurious toiletries & towels, in keeping with a 4*hotel.
Open: All year, Christmas breaks available.

Site: **P Payment:** ⊞ **Leisure:** ▶ **Property:** ⚘ 🚗 ♨ **Children:** 🍼 🛏 🏃 **Catering:** (✗ 🍴 🍴 Room: ☎ ♨ ☏ 📺

VisitEngland
★★★
HOTEL

B&B PER ROOM PER NIGHT
S: £35.00 - £110.00
D: £60.00 - £230.00
HB PER PERSON PER NIGHT
£40.00 - £140.00

Livermead House Hotel

Torbay Road, Seafront, Torquay TQ2 6QJ **T:** (01803) 294361 **F:** 01803 200758
E: info@livermead.com
W: www.livermead.com £ BOOK ONLINE

The Livermead House Hotel in Torquay, situated on the edge of the Cockington Valley was built in 1820 and is positioned on Torquay's sea front. The hotel offers breathtaking sea views, beautifully manicured lawns and exceptionally high standards of service and cuisine from award winning Chef, Tony Hetherington.
Directions: Full directions and map available on our website.
Bedrooms: 7 single, 34 double, 25 twin, 1 family, all en suite
Open: All year

Site: ✿ Payment: 💳 Leisure: ♨ 🎵 🏃 ♿ 🎯 🏹 Property: ☂ 🐕 🚭 🅿 🌙 Children: 🐴 🏢 ⚲ Catering: 🍷 🍴 Room: 📶 ☕ 📞 📺 🎦

VisitEngland
★★★★
HOTEL

B&B PER ROOM PER NIGHT
S: £75.00 - £105.00
D: £99.00 - £180.00
EVENING MEAL PER PERSON
£15.00 - £40.00

SPECIAL PROMOTIONS
Year round offers available, see website for details, or ring our friendly reception team.

The Osborne Hotel

Hesketh Crescent, Meadfoot Beach, Torquay TQ1 2LL **T:** (01803) 213311 **F:** 01803 296788
E: enq@osborne-torquay.co.uk
W: www.osborne-torquay.co.uk £ BOOK ONLINE

The Osborne Hotel, known by the discerning as 'The Country House Hotel by the Sea', is the centrepiece of an elegant Regency crescent. Most Rooms provide panoramic views of the broad sweep of Torbay. There are 2 hotel restaurants, the gourmet Langtry's offering regional specialities, and the more informal Brasserie.

Directions: From Torquay harbour, turn left at clocktower signposted Meadfoot Beach, turn right at traffic lights. Follow road straight ahead to the bottom of the hill.

Bedrooms: 1 single, 16 dble, 5 twin, 2 family, 8 suite
Open: All year

Site: ✿ P Payment: 💳 Leisure: 🎵 🏃 🎯 ⚲ ♨ 🏹 Property: ☂ 🚭 🅿 🌙 Children: 🐴 🏢 ⚲ Catering: 🍷 🍴 Room: 📶 ☕ 📞 📺 🎦

VisitEngland
★★★★
GUEST
ACCOMMODATION

VisitEngland
Silver
AWARD

B&B PER ROOM PER NIGHT
S: £39.00 - £44.00
D: £67.00 - £92.00

The Westgate

Falkland Road, Torquay, Devon TQ2 5JP **T:** (01803) 295350 **E:** stay@westgatehotel.co.uk
W: www.westgatehotel.co.uk £ BOOK ONLINE

An elegant Victorian villa retaining its period charms offering quality bed and breakfast. Ideal location near Torre Abbey & conference centre. Walking distance to beach, town, harbour & station . Free on-site parking & WiFi. Bar & lounge. **Directions:** Follow signs to Torre Abbey and confence centre, turn sharp left at traffic lights outside Torre Abbey - see The Westgate 400m on left. **Bedrooms:** En-suite rooms, flat screen TV, beverage trays. **Open:** Spring, Summer, Autumn.

Site: P Payment: 💳 Property: 🚭 🅿 Children: 🐴5 Catering: 🍷 Room: 📶 ☕ 📺 🎦

TORQUAY, Devon   *Map ref 1D2*   SatNav TQ2 5PD **B**

VisitEngland
★★★
GUEST HOUSE

B&B PER ROOM PER NIGHT
S: £50.00 - £75.00
D: £60.00 - £80.00

Whitburn Guest House

Saint Lukes Road North, Torquay, Devon TQ2 5PD **T:** (01803) 296719
E: lazenby1210@btinternet.com
W: www.whitburnguesthouse.co.uk **£ BOOK ONLINE**

Anne and Joe warmly welcome you to our clean comfortable guest house, 5 mins walk or local bus to harbour, beach, seafront, town centre shops, clubs, restaurants. Lovely residential area and parking. Full cooked breakfast included in price. **Directions:** At Seafront go up Shedden Hill, take 2nd right into St Lukes Road, then 1st left into St Lukes Road North. Whitburn Guest House 150 metres on left. **Bedrooms:** En suite or private rooms, Freeview TV, tea, coffee. **Open:** All year

Site: P Payment: 💶 Leisure: 🐾 ♪ ► Property: 🖥 🏠 Children: 👶 🛏 ♿ Room: ♨ 🕐 📺 📀 ♿

BLANDFORD FORUM, Dorset   *Map ref 2B3*   SatNav DT11 7AJ **B**

VisitEngland
★★★★
INN

B&B PER ROOM PER NIGHT
D: £100.00 - £170.00

The Crown Hotel

West Street, Blandford Forum, Dorset DT11 7AJ **T:** (01258) 456 626
E: crownhotel.blandford@hall-woodhouse.co.uk
W: www.crownhotelblandford.co.uk **£ BOOK ONLINE**

One of the oldest inns in Dorset, the Crown Hotel is set in the picturesque Georgian town of Blandford; a perfect example of traditional British hospitality. The beautifully panelled walls and carefully restored Oak floors make this the perfect place to explore the wonderful Georgian town of Blandford and the wider beauty of the Blackmore Vale.

Directions: Located on the edge of Blandford Forum opposite Morrisons on West Street.

Bedrooms: Please refer to website for latest information on our bedrooms.
Open: We are open year round.

Site: ❀ P Payment: 💶 Property: 🐾 🐴 🖥 ◗ ⌀ Children: 👶 🛏 ♿ Catering: 🍴 ♟ Room: 🍵 ♨ 📞 📺

Sign up for our newsletter

Visit our website to sign up for our e-newsletter and receive regular information on events, articles, exclusive competitions and new publications.

www.visitor-guides.co.uk

BOURNEMOUTH, Dorset   Map ref 2B3 — SatNav BH1 3PF [B]

B&B PER ROOM PER NIGHT
S: £65.00 – £120.00
D: £85.00 – £130.00
EVENING MEAL PER PERSON
£23.00

Balincourt

58 Christchurch Road, Bournemouth BH1 3PF **T:** (01202) 552962 **F:** 01202 552962
E: reservations@balincourt.co.uk
W: www.balincourt.co.uk **£ BOOK ONLINE**

Elegant family-run Victorian guest accommodation. Prime location for attractions, seafront and town centre. Tastefully decorated en suite rooms. Warm and friendly service. Children minimum age 14 years. Evening meals by prior arrangement. **Directions:** Please contact for directions. **Bedrooms:** Special occasion flowers, chocolates, champagne available on request **Open:** All Year

Site: ✿ P **Payment:** 💳 **Leisure:** ♪ ▶ ⚲ **Property:** 🖥 ♨ ⌖ **Catering:** 🍴✗ 🍷 🍽 **Room:** 🍵 ☕ 📺

BRIDPORT, Dorset   Map ref 2A3 — SatNav DT6 3LB [H]

B&B PER ROOM PER NIGHT
S: £84.00 - £122.00
D: £130.00 - £155.00

SPECIAL PROMOTIONS
Please check our website or call for our current offers.

Bridge House Hotel

115 East Street, Bridport, Dorset DT6 3LB **T:** (01308) 423371 **F:** 01308 459573
E: info@bridgehousebridport.co.uk
W: www.bridgehousebridport.co.uk **£ BOOK ONLINE**

18th Century Georgian character town house, next to the river and its gardens. Offers quiet elegance, traditional ambience and friendly service. Elegant lounge, ten en suite bedrooms and a fully licensed wine bar, offering the ideal venue for functions, from parties to funerals, buffets to full bespoke menus, using fresh local quality produce. Free parking, near the town centre.

Directions: Located at the eastern end of Bridport's main street; 400m from the town centre and 200m before the roundabout on the right-hand side.

Bedrooms: 3 single, 3 double, 1 twin, 3 family
Open: All year

Site: ✿ P **Payment:** 💳 € **Leisure:** ♿ ♪ ▶ ♻ **Property:** ⚲ 🐾 🖥 🛏 ♨ **Children:** 🍼 🛏 🪑
Catering: 🍷 🍽 **Room:** 🍵 ☕ 📞 📻 📺

BRIDPORT, Dorset   Map ref 2A3 — SatNav DT6 3LY [B]

B&B PER ROOM PER NIGHT
D: £70.00 – £140.00

The Tiger Inn

14-16 Barrack Street, Bridport DT6 3LY **T:** (01308) 427543
E: jacquie@tigerinnbridport.co.uk
W: www.tigerinnbridport.co.uk

Award winning 'CAMRA - West Dorset town Pub of the Year 2012'. Free house. Excellent town centre location. Boutique style bedrooms, all en suite, flatscreen TV and free Wi-Fi. **Directions:** Please contact us for directions. **Bedrooms:** 5 double, 2 family. **Open:** All year

Site: ✿ **Payment:** 💳 **Leisure:** ♿ ♪ ▶ ♻ **Property:** 🖥 **Children:** 🍼 🪑 **Catering:** 🍷 🍽 **Room:** 🍵 ☕ 📻 📺

DORCHESTER, Dorset Map ref 2B3 — SatNav DT1 1UP H

Wessex Royale Hotel

32 High West Street, Dorchester DT1 1UP **T:** (01305) 262660 **F:** 01305 251941
E: info@wessexroyalehotel.co.uk
W: www.wessexroyalehotel.co.uk **£ BOOK ONLINE**

A delightful Georgian building with 27 comfortable en suite rooms. Guests can relax in the cosy lounge area and our a la carte restaurant is open from 6pm each evening. **Directions:** Please see our website for map and full directions. **Bedrooms:** 2 single, 15 double, 5 twin, 2 family, 3 suite. **Open:** All year except Christmas and New Year.

B&B PER ROOM PER NIGHT
S: £85.00 - £109.00
D: £99.00 - £185.00
HB PER PERSON PER NIGHT
£74.50 - £104.50

Site: ✿ **Payment:** 💳 **Leisure:** ♿ ♪ ▶ ∪ **Property:** 🍴 ▤ ◐ **Children:** 🚼 ▦ ☆ **Catering:** 🍽 🍴
Room: 🍵 📶 ☎ 📺 🛁

EYPE, Dorset Map ref 1D2 — SatNav DT6 6AL H

Eype's Mouth Country Hotel

Eype, Bridport, Dorset DT6 6AL **T:** (01308) 423300 **F:** 01308 420033
E: info@eypesmouthhotel.co.uk
W: www.eypesmouthhotel.co.uk **£ BOOK ONLINE**

Picturesque village of Eype, Bridport amidst downland and cliff tops of Heritage Coastline. Stunning sea views, lovely walking nearby, excellent hospitality, food and drink, in peaceful surroundings of family-run hotel. Perfect for relaxing. **Directions:** A35, Bridport bypass, take turning to Eype, also signed to service area, then 3rd right to beach. Hotel 0.5 miles down lane. **Bedrooms:** 1 single, 12 dble, 3 twin, 1 family **Open:** All year

B&B PER ROOM PER NIGHT
S: £82.50 - £107.50
D: £112.50 - £132.50
EVENING MEAL PER PERSON
£26.00 - £28.00

Site: ✿ P **Payment:** 💳 € **Leisure:** ♿ ♪ ▶ ∪ **Property:** 🍴 🐾 ▤ ♨ **Children:** 🚼 ▦ ☆
Catering: (✗ 🍽 🍴 **Room:** 🍵 📶 📺 🛁

SWANAGE, Dorset Map ref 2B3 — SatNav BH19 1PQ B

Glenlee Guest House

6 Cauldon Avenue, Swanage, Dorset BH19 1PQ **T:** (01929) 425794
E: info@glenleeswanage.co.uk
W: www.glenleeswanage.co.uk **£ BOOK ONLINE**

B&B PER ROOM PER NIGHT
S: £78.00 - £88.00
D: £88.00 - £98.00
EVENING MEAL PER PERSON
£22.00

SPECIAL PROMOTIONS
Spring offer: £13 off per room per night if you stay three nights or more in March/ April/May. Autumn offer: £8 off per room per night if you stay two nights or more in September or October.

Expect a warm welcome and a friendly atmosphere at the Glenlee, in a delightful position overlooking Beach Gardens, with its putting greens, bowling green and tennis courts. It's just a short walk to the award-winning sandy beach and a level stroll along the seafront to the town centre. Evening meals offered on selected weeks (please check). Private car park with a space for each room. Free Wi-Fi.

Directions: Entering Swanage from Wareham & Corfe Castle on A351 (Victoria Ave), follow signs for Main Beach Car Park. Take next left after car park into Northbrook Rd, then fourth right turning into Cauldon Ave.

Bedrooms: All bedrooms en suite with either walk-in shower or bath with shower over. Flat-screen TV, fast free Wi-Fi, tea & coffee, DAB clock radio, hairdryer.
Open: Open March to November.

Site: ✿ P **Payment:** 💳 **Property:** ▤ ♨ **Children:** 🚼³ **Catering:** (✗ 🍽 🍴 **Room:** 🍵 📶 📺 🛁

SWANAGE, Dorset   Map ref 2B3

SatNav BH19 1LT

The Pines Hotel

Burlington Road, Swanage BH19 1LT **T:** (01929) 425211 **F:** 01929 422075
E: reservations@pineshotel.co.uk
W: www.pineshotel.co.uk **£ BOOK ONLINE**

B&B PER ROOM PER NIGHT
S: £74.00
D: £148.00 - £198.00
EVENING MEAL PER PERSON
£6.75 - £33.50

Family-run hotel in Purbeck countryside at quiet end of Swanage Bay. Access to beach for walks encompassing coastal views. Friendly staff, refurbished sea-facing lounges and highly acclaimed seaview restaurant. **Directions:** A351 to seafront. Turn left then 2nd or 3rd turn on your right (either Victoria road or Burlington road). We are at the end of these roads. **Bedrooms:** 2 single, 15 double, 8 twin, 8 family, 8 suite. **Open:** All year

WAREHAM, Dorset   Map ref 2B3

SatNav BH20 5NU

Bradle Farmhouse

Bradle Farm, Church Knowle, Wareham, Dorset BH20 5NU **T:** (01929) 480712
F: 01929 481144 **E:** info@bradlefarmhouse.co.uk
W: www.bradlefarmhouse.co.uk **£ BOOK ONLINE**

B&B PER ROOM PER NIGHT
S: £75.00 - £85.00
D: £85.00 - £90.00

Picturesque farmhouse set in the heart of Purbeck. Fine views of Corfe Castle and surrounding countryside, with many spectacular walks. Large spacious rooms, delicious breakfast with home produce and a warm welcome assured. Local pub 1 mile. **Directions:** A351 from Wareham to Corfe Castle. At Corfe take a right turn at the foot of the castle signed Church Knowle. After Church Knowle turn left 1 mile. **Bedrooms:** Spacious rooms all en suite, TVs and Tea/coffee facilities **Open:** All Year except Christmas

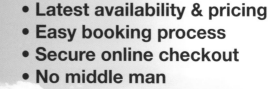

- **Latest availability & pricing**
- **Easy booking process**
- **Secure online checkout**
- **No middle man**
- **Real customer reviews**

BOOK WITH CONFIDENCE

GUESTLINK | ONLINE TOURISM SOLUTIONS

www.visitor-guides.co.uk • www.roomcheck.co.uk
www.ukgreatbreaks.com • and many more!

Kingston Country Courtyard

Kingston, Nr Corfe Castle, Wareham, Dorset BH20 5LR   **T:** (01929) 481066   **F:** 01929 481256
E: relax@kingstoncountrycourtyard.com
W: www.kingstoncountrycourtyard.com

B&B PER ROOM PER NIGHT
S: £40.00 - £60.00
D: £120.00 - £170.00
HB PER PERSON PER NIGHT
£60.00 - £70.00

Kingston Country Courtyard gives you a taste of authentic farmstead life in an Area of Outstanding Natural Beauty. Tastefully converted outbuildings, high beamed ceilings, thick Purbeck stone walls. Bed and Breakfast or Self Catering apartments available. Some dog friendly rooms by arrangement. Views of the Castle from the garden. Limited Wi-Fi...enjoy an escape from the city!

Directions: From Wareham, take the A351 towards Swanage. On leaving the village of Corfe Castle, turn right on to the B3069 - signposted to Kingston, up the hill, round a sharp left bend, we are on the left.

Bedrooms: En suite, TVs, tea and coffee, kettles in rooms
Open: All year round except Xmas & New Year

Site: ❀ **P** **Leisure:** ఉ ♪ ▶ ♆ **Property:** ☍ 🐾 ⛴ ▣ ♨ **Children:** ⛺ ᕟ ‡ **Catering:** ♟ 🍴
Room: 📶 ☕ 📺 📀 🛁 🎴

Lulworth Cove Inn

Main Road, West Lulworth, Dorset BH20 5RQ   **T:** (01929) 400333
   E: lulworthcoveinn@hall-woodhouse.co.uk
W: www.lulworth-coveinn.co.uk   **£ BOOK ONLINE**

B&B PER ROOM PER NIGHT
D: £85.00 - £160.00
EVENING MEAL PER PERSON
£15.00 - £25.00

Situated on the doorstep of Lulworth Cove, the Lulworth Cove Inn boasts stunning coastal views and scenic Jurassic footpaths. Only a few of minutes' drive from Durdle Door the Lulworth Cove Inn is an idyllic location for paradise seekers.

Directions: End of B3070, down Main Road, Lulworth Cove on the left at the end opposite Heritage Centre Carpark.

Bedrooms: Each unique bedroom is finished to a luxurious, comfortable standard with flatscreen TV, bluetooth radio and tea & coffee making facilities
Open: We are open year-round

Site: ❀ **Payment:** 💷 **Property:** ⛴ ⌀ **Children:** ⛺ ‡ **Catering:** (✗ ♟ **Room:** 📶 ☕ 📺

For **key to symbols** see page 7

VisitEngland
★★★
GUEST HOUSE

AcQua Beach Weymouth

131 The Esplanade, Weymouth, Dorset DT4 7EY **T:** (01305) 776900 **F:** 01305 791099
E: info@acquabeachhotel.co.uk
W: www.acquabeachhotel.co.uk **£ BOOK ONLINE**

B&B PER ROOM PER NIGHT
S: £40.00 - £55.00
D: £60.00 - £140.00

If you're looking for a funky B&B overlooking Weymouth's beautiful seafront then you've come to the right place. Relax in our rooms; have a coffee overlooking the sea, or when the sun goes down enjoy a cocktail in the gorgeous Bar AcQuA. **Directions:** Located opposite the beach on Weymouth's Esplanade; a mere 5 minute walk from the railway station and the Jubilee Clock. **Bedrooms:** All en suite with flatscreen TV and hospitality tray **Open:** All year

Site: **P** Payment: 💷 Leisure: 🚲 ⚓ ♻ Property: 📺 🏥 Children: 🛏 🛌 ♿ Catering: 🍷 🍽 Room: 🌐 🚰 📺

VisitEngland
★★★★
INN

Smugglers Inn

Osmington Mills, Weymouth, Dorset DT3 6HF **T:** (01305) 833125
E: smugglersinn.weymouth@hall-woodhouse.co.uk
W: www.smugglersinnosmingtonmills.co.uk **£ BOOK ONLINE**

B&B PER ROOM PER NIGHT
D: £100.00 - £120.00
EVENING MEAL PER PERSON
£15.00 - £25.00

Nestled on the edge of the Jurassic coast, boasting stunning views and scenic footpaths, the Smugglers Inn is an idyllic location for those wishing to escape the hustle of everyday. Dating back to the 13th century, the Inn is known to have been the home of some of the most notorious smugglers of the age. In its present day, the Inn offers award-winning Badger cask ales and fresh dishes.

Directions: Located in Osmington Mills from A353 take Mills Road, follow to the end, carpark on the right, Smugglers Inn on the left.

Bedrooms: Smuggler's Inn offers 4 En-Suite rooms with WiFi access. All rates are per room, per night inc. breakfast and free car park pass. **Open:** We are open year-round

Site: ❀ Payment: 💷 Property: 🐾 📺 ♻ Children: 🛏 ♿ Catering: (✕ 🍷 Room: 🌐 🚰 📺

Need more information?

Visit our websites for detailed information, up-to-date availability and to book your accommodation online. Includes over 20,000 places to stay, all of them star rated.
www.visitor-guides.co.uk

BARNSLEY, Gloucestershire   Map ref 2B1   SatNav GL7 5EE H

Barnsley House

Barnsley, Cirencester GL7 5EE **T:** (01285) 740000 **E:** reception@barnsleyhouse.com
W: www.barnsleyhouse.com

B&B PER ROOM PER NIGHT
S: £182.00 - £582.00
D: £200.00 - £600.00

Luxury 18 bedroom hotel, once the home of the late famous garden designer Rosemary Verey. Beautiful Cotswold house built in 1697 set in stunning gardens, with contemporary bedrooms. We now have a hydrotherapy pool. Weekend prices vary.
Directions: Centre of Barnsley, on the B4425 (Cirencester to Bibury and Burford road), 4 miles NE of Cirencester.
Open: All year

Site: ✿ P **Payment:** 💳 **Leisure:** ♿ ♪ ▶ ♂ ⚷ **Property:** 🏆 🐕 📺 🏠 ♨ 🌓 ◐ ⌀ **Children:** ♿14 🛏 🎎
Catering: (✕ 🍽 🍴 **Room:** 📞 ♨ 🕯 📻 📺 🎮 🍴 🚪

BOURTON-ON-THE-WATER, Gloucestershire Map ref 2B1   SatNav GL54 2AR B

The Lansdowne

Lansdowne, Bourton on the Water, Gloucestershire GL54 2AR **T:** (01451) 820673
E: info@thelansdownecotswolds.co.uk
W: www.lansdownevilla.co.uk £ BOOK ONLINE

B&B PER ROOM PER NIGHT
S: £55.00
D: £75.00

The Lansdowne (formerly Lansdowne villa) is a 12 bedroomed guest house just a 2 minute walk from the centre of Bourton on the Water. All rooms are en suite, there is free Wi Fi throughout as well as ample private parking.
Bedrooms: King-size, double, twin and single beds.
Open: All year

Site: P **Leisure:** ♿ ▶ ♂ **Property:** 📺 🏠 **Room:** 📞 ♨ 📺 🚪

CIRENCESTER, Gloucestershire   Map ref 2B1   SatNav GL7 1LF B

Riverside House

Watermoor, Cirencester GL7 1LF **T:** (01285) 647642 **F:** 01285 647615
E: riversidehouse@mitsubishi-cars.co.uk
W: www.riversidehouse.org.uk £ BOOK ONLINE

B&B PER ROOM PER NIGHT
S: £55.50 - £65.50
D: £71.00 - £81.00
EVENING MEAL PER PERSON
£10.00 - £18.00

SPECIAL PROMOTIONS
Special group discounts are available at weekends. Ideal for clubs and societies.

Recently refurbished bed and breakfast accommodation within walking distance of the historic market town of Cirencester. Riverside House makes an ideal base for exploring the Cotswolds with easy access to the M4/M5. Fully licensed restaurant open for evening meals Monday to Thursday. Built in the grounds of The Colt Car Company.

Directions: Located just off A419 opposite the Tesco superstore.

Bedrooms: 15 double, 9 twin
Open: All year

Site: ✿ P **Payment:** 💳 **Leisure:** ♿ ♪ ▶ ♂ **Property:** 📺 **Children:** 🛏 **Catering:** 🍽 🍴
Room: 📞 ♨ 🕯 📻 📺

GLOUCESTER, Gloucestershire Map ref 2B1   SatNav GL12LG H

English Holiday Cruises

The Edward Elgar, Alexandra Quay, The Docks, Gloucester GL1 2LG **T:** (01452) 410411
F: 01452 357959 **E:** sales@englishholidaycruises.co.uk
W: www.englishholidaycruises.co.uk **£ BOOK ONLINE**

HB PER PERSON PER NIGHT
£110.00 - £165.00

SPECIAL PROMOTIONS
Includes 3 Meals/day free tea/coffee, welcome drink, wine at dinner, outside tours & WiFi. Live entertainment on one night. Special low prices & singles rates in April and October.

For an unusual holiday in England, book a cruise with English Holiday Cruises in the Cotswolds Severn vale. Board their Hotel Boat Edward Elgar in Gloucester, unpack, relax and sail through glorious countryside to fascinating destinations steeped in history.

The meals are delicious and the crew really care! Why travel to the Rhine when 97% of guests recommend us? From only £220 all-inclusive.

Directions: Gloucester is easy to reach by car, train or coach. Passengers board MV Edward Elgar in the Historic Docks of Gloucester and secure parking is available nearby.

Bedrooms: 4-Star Hotel Boat standard. All cabins are twin-bedded, with a window, heating/air conditioning, ample storage and en suite shower, basin and WC.
Open: 40 Cruise dates available from April to October.

Payment: ⊞ **Property:** ⊛ ⚊ 🖥 🗄 ♨ ◐ **Catering:** ⟨✗ ⚊ 🍴 **Room:** ⌇ ☎

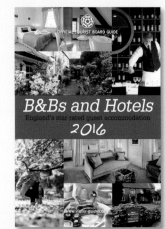
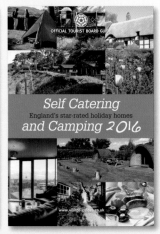

MORETON-IN-MARSH, Gloucestershire Map ref 2B1 — SatNav GL56 0HE B

Treetops Guest House

London Road, Moreton in Marsh, Gloucestershire GL56 0HE **T:** (01608) 651036
F: 01608 651036 **E:** treetops1@talk21.com

B&B PER ROOM PER NIGHT
S: £55.00
D: £80.00 - £85.00

Family guesthouse on A44, set in 0.5 acres of secluded gardens, yet only 5 minutes' walk to the village centre. **Directions:** Please contact for directions. **Bedrooms:** 2 double, 2 superior double, 2 twin all ensuite. **Open:** All year except Christmas.

Site: ❄ **P Payment:** 🖃 **Property:** 🖥 ♨ **Children:** 🐾 🛏 ♿ **Catering:** 🍴 **Room:** 🖥 ♨ 📺 🔌

STOW-ON-THE-WOLD, Gloucestershire Map ref 2B1 — SatNav GL54 1JH B

Corsham Field Farmhouse

Bledington Road, Stow on the Wold, Gloucestershire GL54 1JH **T:** (01451) 831750
E: farmhouse@corshamfield.co.uk
W: www.corshamfield.co.uk

B&B PER ROOM PER NIGHT
S: £45.00 - £60.00
D: £55.00 - £80.00

Charming farmhouse with warm welcome and spectacular views. Peaceful location one mile from Stow. Garden. Car park. Relaxing lounge. Free Wi-Fi. Ideal for Cotswold villages, Stratford, Blenheim and Warwick. Excellent pub food 5 minutes walk **Directions:** A436 from Stow on the Wold for 1 mile, fork right onto B4450 Bledington Road. We are 1st farm on right opposite the Oddington turn. **Bedrooms:** 2 double, 2 twin, 3 family **Open:** All year except Christmas

Site: ❄ **P Payment:** € **Leisure:** ♫ ▶ **Property:** 🖥 ♨ **Children:** 🐾 **Room:** 🖥 ♨ 📺 🔌

STROUD, Gloucestershire Map ref 2B1 — SatNav GL6 9JE B

The Close B&B

The Close, Well Hill, Minchinhampton, Stroud, Gloucestershire GL6 9JE **T:** (01453) 883338
E: theclosebnb@gmail.com
W: www.theclosebnb.co.uk **£ BOOK ONLINE**

B&B PER ROOM PER NIGHT
S: £65.00 - £75.00
D: £85.00 - £95.00

Historic Town House offering stylish and comfortable accommodation, the perfect place for a short break in the Cotswolds. Set in a charming small market town with shops and cafes nearby. Wonderful walking country with beautiful views. **Directions:** 2nd house on the left, from the top of Well Hill. **Bedrooms:** Spacious rooms with en suites, TVs and tea/coffee making facilities. **Open:** Open February - December (closed Jan).

Site: ❄ **P Payment:** 🖃 **Leisure:** ▶ ○ **Property:** 🐴 🖥 ♨ 🐾 **Catering:** 🍴 **Room:** 🖥 ♨ 📺

TETBURY, Gloucestershire Map ref 2B2 — SatNav GL8 8YJ H

Calcot Manor Hotel & Spa

Tetbury, Gloucestershire GL8 8YJ **T:** (01666) 890391 **F:** 01666 890394
E: reception@calcotmanor.co.uk
W: www.calcotmanor.co.uk **£ BOOK ONLINE**

B&B PER ROOM PER NIGHT
S: £174.00 - £504.00
D: £199.00 - £529.00

A charming Country House Hotel, set in peaceful gardens, renowned for the excellence of its restaurant and the informality of its Gumstool Inn. Calcot has excellent facilities for children including family suites with bunk beds, baby listening facilities and an Ofsted-registered crèche. For adults there's the luxury of Calcot Spa, boasting seven treatment rooms, indoor pool and an outdoor hot tub by a blazing fire. **Directions:** 3 m West of Tetbury on A4135. **Bedrooms:** 7 dbl, 15 twin, 12 family, 1 suite **Open:** All year

Site: ❄ **Payment:** 🖃 **Leisure:** ♿ ♫ ▶ ○ 🎯 ♨ 🎣 ♿ **Property:** 🐴 🖥 🅿 ○ **Children:** 🐾 🛏 ♿ **Catering:** 🍷 🍴 **Room:** 🖥 ♨ 🔌 📺 🔌

AA
★★★★
Guest House

B&B PER ROOM PER NIGHT
S: £69.00
D: £95.00 - £150.00

SPECIAL PROMOTIONS
Please see website for
the current special
promotions.

The Bailbrook Lodge

35/37 London Road West BA1 7HZ **T:** (01225) 859090 **F:** 01225 852299
E: bookings.bailbrook0411@siteminder.co.uk
W: www.bailbrooklodge.co.uk **£ BOOK ONLINE**

A Grade II Listed country house with 14 rooms, excellently situated a mile and a half from the city centre, in a delightful, relaxing location with lovely lawns and gardens. We have 15 individually decorated and furnished bedrooms providing the utmost in comfort and charm to make your stay truly enjoyable. 5 of our 15 rooms include four-poster beds, the only boutique B&B or hotel in Bath offering this number of four-poster beds.
Car parking is free.

Directions: From the M4: come off at junction 18 and take A46, come off at Bath exit and at the roundabout turn left to Batheaston, hotel is immediately on the left.

Bedrooms: En suite, flat screen tv, quality teas and fresh ground coffee, biscuits, mineral water, cotton slippers.
Open: All year

Site: ✿ P Payment: 💳 Leisure: ▶ Property: ♟ 🖥 🏛 Children: 👶 🎠 🛝 Catering: ♟ 🍴
Room: 📺 🛁 TV 📀 🔌

VisitEngland
★★★
HOSTEL

B&B PER ROOM PER NIGHT
S: £32.00 - £36.00
D: £58.00 - £65.00

f 🐦

Bath YMCA

International House, Broad Street Place, Bath BA1 5LH **T:** (01225) 325900 **F:** 01225 462065
E: stay@bathymca.co.uk
W: www.bathymca.co.uk

The YMCA is centrally located, just a minute away from all the major tourist attractions, we have over 200 beds in the form of dormitories, singles, twins, triples and quad rooms. Dorms from £21 per person per night. **Directions:** From the bus or train station walk north up Manvers Street. Go past Bath Abbey on your left and, keeping the river Avon on you right, continue via Orange Grove (on left) and High Street to Walcot Street or Broad Street. **Open:** All year

Site: ✿ Payment: 💳 Leisure: ♿ ▶ 🔍 ✗ 🏊 Property: ⊛ ♟ 🖥 TV 🔔 Children: 👶 🎠 🛝 Catering: 🍴
Bedroom: 📺 🔌

VisitEngland
★★★★
GUEST
ACCOMMODATION

VisitEngland
Gold
AWARD

B&B PER ROOM PER NIGHT
S: £95.00 - £145.00
D: £95.00 - £155.00

f

Marlborough House Guest House

1 Marlborough Lane, Bath BA1 2NQ **T:** (01225) 318175 **F:** 01225 466127
E: mars@manque.dircon.co.uk
W: www.marlborough-house.net **£ BOOK ONLINE**

Enchanting vegetarian townhouse in Bath's city centre, featuring elegant rooms, unique breakfast menu, and relaxing atmosphere. Close to theatre and excellent restaurants. **Directions:** M4 junct 18 to Bath. A4 into city centre via Queen Square, take Charlotte Street exit, continue for 1 minute Marlborough La will be on your right. **Bedrooms:** 2 double, 2 twin, 2 family **Open:** All year except Christmas

🏆 Site: ✿ P Payment: 💳 € Leisure: ♿ Property: ⊛ 🖥 Children: 👶 🎠 🛝 Catering: ♟ 🍴 Room: 📺
🛁 📞 📀 TV 🔌

South West - **Somerset**

Pulteney House

14 Pulteney Road, Bath BA2 4HA **T:** (01225) 460991 **F:** 01225 460991
E: pulteney@tinyworld.co.uk
W: www.pulteneyhotel.co.uk **£ BOOK ONLINE**

B&B PER ROOM PER NIGHT
S: £60.00 - £90.00
D: £85.00 - £160.00

SPECIAL PROMOTIONS
Reduced rates for stays of 3 nights or more - each booking assessed individually.

Large, elegant, Victorian house in picturesque gardens. Large, private car park with CCTV. 5-10 minutes walk from city centre. An ideal base for exploring Bath and surrounding areas. All rooms (except one) are en suite. All have hairdryer, TV with Freeview/Sat, hospitality tray and radio/alarm clocks. Free Wi-Fi in all rooms.

Directions: Pulteney House is situated on A36, which runs through Bath. For more detailed directions please refer to our website.

Bedrooms: 2 singles, 8 doubles, 4 twins, 3 family. Twin rates inc. in double rates. Family rates £125 - £160.
Open: All year except Christmas

Site: ❂ P **Payment:** ⊞ **Property:** ▭ **Children:** ⚲ ⊞ ⚶ **Catering:** ⚱ **Room:** ⚲ ⚶ ⊚ ⊺ ⚶ ⚶

The Royal Hotel

Manvers Street BA1 1JP **T:** (01225) 463134 **F:** 01225 442931 **E:** info@royalhotelbath.co.uk
W: www.royalhotelbath.co.uk **£ BOOK ONLINE**

B&B PER ROOM PER NIGHT
S: £70.00 - £89.00
D: £120.00 - £150.00
EVENING MEAL PER PERSON
£12.95 - £22.00

SPECIAL PROMOTIONS
Always available - see our website for details.

The Royal is Grade II listed, designed by Brunel and opened as a hotel in 1846. The present owners (since 1995) have ensured that this lovely property is maintained to a high standard and retains its character.

Our stylish restaurant "Brasserie Brunel" offers French specialities with grills including steaks. We have an excellent reputation for food and a friendly, relaxing atmosphere.

Directions: By car: A46 off M4 (Jct 18) to City Centre. By train: directly opposite Bath Spa railway station.

Bedrooms: En suite, digital TVs and DVD players, modem points, hair dryer, trouser press, tea and cafetiere ground coffee, biscuits and mineral water.
Open: All year

Site: P **Payment:** ⊞ **Property:** ⚲ ▭ ⚶ ◐ **Children:** ⚲ ⊞ ⚶ **Catering:** (✕ ⚱ **Room:** ⚲ ⚶ ⚶ ⊺ ⚶ ⚶

South West - Somerset

BRIDGWATER, Somerset Map ref 1D1 · SatNav TA5 2HW B

VisitEngland ★★★★ GUEST ACCOMMODATION
VisitEngland Silver AWARD

B&B PER ROOM PER NIGHT
S: £40.00 - £50.00
D: £70.00 - £80.00

Gurney Manor Mill
Gurney Street, Cannington, Bridgwater TA5 2HW **T:** (01278) 653582
E: gurneymill@yahoo.co.uk
W: www.gurneymill.co.uk

Old watermill and barn conversion, alongside a stream with waterfall, pond and wildlife. Situated in picturesque village at gateway to Quantock Hills. Ideal location for touring the beautiful Historical West Country and South West. **Directions:** Cannington (Bridgwater). Turn right into East St, turn right into Gurney St. Gurney Manor Mill is after Gurney Manor. **Bedrooms:** 2 double, 1 twin, 1 family **Open:** All year

Site: ✿ **P Payment:** 💷 **Leisure:** ♪ ▶ **Property:** 🐾 🖥 🖵 **Children:** 🧸 🎮 🍼 **Catering:** 🍴 **Room:** 🔌 🖥 📺 🛋 🚿

BRISTOL, Somerset Map ref 2A2 · SatNav BS13 8AG B

VisitEngland ★★★ GUEST ACCOMMODATION

B&B PER ROOM PER NIGHT
S: £55.00
D: £65.00

EVENING MEAL PER PERSON
£9.50 - £19.50

SPECIAL PROMOTIONS
Stay Fri and Sat night and get Sunday night free (incl Bank Holiday weekends).

The Town & Country Lodge
A38 Bridgwater Road, Bristol BS13 8AG **T:** (01275) 392441 **F:** 01275 393362
E: reservations@tclodge.co.uk
W: www.tclodge.co.uk

Highly comfortable lodge offering genuine value for money. Splendid, rural location on the A38 only three miles from central Bristol and handy for airport, Bath, Weston and all major local attractions. Excellent restaurant offering bar menus. Ideal for functions, wedding receptions and conferences.

Directions: Situated on A38 halfway between Airport and city centre. From North M5 exit J18 Avonmouth. A4 Bristol Airport. From South exit M5 J22. A38 Bristol.

Bedrooms: 4 single, 11 double, 14 twin, 7 family. **Open:** All year except Christmas.

Site: ✿ **P Payment:** 💷 **Leisure:** ♪ ▶ **Property:** 🖥 **Children:** 🧸 **Catering:** 🍷 🍴 **Room:** 🔌 🖥 📞 🛋 📺 🚿

CHEDDAR, Somerset *Map ref 1D1* SatNav BS28 4SN **B**

BED & BREAKFAST

B&B PER ROOM PER NIGHT
S: £50.00
D: £72.00

EVENING MEAL PER PERSON
£8.95 - £18.95

Yew Tree Farm

Wells Road, Theale, Nr Wedmore, Somerset BS28 4SN **T:** (01934) 712475 **F:** 01934 712475
E: yewtreefarm@yewtreefarmbandb.co.uk
W: www.yewtreefarmbandb.co.uk

17th century farmhouse nr Cheddar, Wells and Wookey. Idyllic walks fishing/golf/cycling. 1, 2, 3 course home cooked and freshly prepared evening meals available, as well as snacks and cream teas. Large secure off street parking area available and free Wi-Fi. Additional £10 surcharge for pets per night. **Directions:** From Wells, take B3139 towards Burnham-on-Sea. Drive through Wookey, Henton, Panborough. **Bedrooms:** 1 double, 1 twin, 1 family. **Open:** All year

Site: ❁ **P Payment:** € **Leisure:** ♪ ▶ ∪ **Property:** ⊫ ⛳ ▣ **Children:** ⌕ ⏢ ⏀ **Catering:** ✗ ⊞
Room: ⊠ ⬤ ⓪ ⏢ ⏢

DUNSTER, Somerset *Map ref 1D1* SatNav TA24 6SF **H**

HOTEL

B&B PER ROOM PER NIGHT
S: £65.00 - £90.00
D: £90.00 - £140.00

EVENING MEAL PER PERSON
£17.00 - £27.00

SPECIAL PROMOTIONS
Discounted rates for longer stays and midweek bookings. Ring for newsletter for information on special events. Group bookings welcome.

Yarn Market Hotel

25-33 High Street, Dunster TA24 6SF **T:** (01643) 821425 **F:** 01643 821475
E: hotel@yarnmarkethotel.co.uk
W: www.yarnmarkethotel.co.uk **£ BOOK ONLINE**

Within Exmoor National Park, our hotel is ideal for walking, riding, fishing. Family-run with a friendly, relaxed atmosphere. All rooms en suite with colour TV. Four-poster and superior rooms available. Non-smoking. Home-cooked dishes to cater for all tastes. Group bookings welcomed. Conference facilities. Special Christmas and New Year breaks.

Directions: From M5 jct 25 follow signs for Exmoor/Minehead A358/A39. Dunster signed approx 0.5 miles from A39 on left. Hotel in village centre beside Yarn Market.

Bedrooms: 2 single, 12 dbl, 7 twin, 2 family.
Open: All year

Site: ❁ **Payment:** ▣ € **Leisure:** ♨ ♪ ▶ ∪ **Property:** ♟ ⛳ ⊟ ▣ ♘ **Children:** ⌕ ⏢ ⏢
Catering: ✗ ▼ ⊞ **Room:** ⊠ ⬤ ⏢ ⊞

WELLS, Somerset *Map ref 2A2* SatNav BA5 3JP **B**

GUEST ACCOMMODATION Gold AWARD

B&B PER ROOM PER NIGHT
S: £80.00 - £100.00
D: £100.00 - £160.00

Beryl

Off Hawkers Lane, Wells, Somerset BA5 3JP **T:** (01749) 678738 **F:** 01749 670508
E: stay@beryl-wells.co.uk
W: www.beryl-wells.co.uk

A small Victorian Gothic mansion in a beautiful part of Somerset, Beryl is just 1 mile from Wells Cathedral. A warm and friendly welcome awaits every guest in this family-run home. Experience a stay for luxury bed and breakfast at 'Beryl'. Byworth and Nowell fine jewellery in the coach house. **Directions:** In Wells, follow signs to the Horringtons until you reach a Budgens BP Garage. Then turn left into Hawkers Lane. We are right at the top of the hill. **Open:** All year except Christmas

Site: ❁ **P Payment:** ▣ **Leisure:** ↯ **Property:** ⊟ ▣ ♘ ⌀ **Children:** ⌕ ⏢ ⏢ **Catering:** ▼ ⊞ **Room:** ⊠ ⬤
⦾ ⏢ ⏢ ⊞

CRICKLADE, Wiltshire   Map ref 2B2

SatNav SN6 6DD **B**

VisitEngland
★★★★
GUEST ACCOMMODATION

B&B PER ROOM PER NIGHT
D: £85.00

The Red Lion
74 High Street, Cricklade SN6 6DD **T:** (01793) 750776 **E:** info@theredlioncricklade.co.uk
W: www.theredlioncricklade.co.uk **£ BOOK ONLINE**

Situated on the Thames path, The Red Lion Inn dates back to the 1600s. Roaring log fires, 10 traditional ales including 5 brewed in our own on site micro brewery (Hop Kettle Brewery). A contemporary restaurant serving homemade and seasonal food, a traditional bar area serving pub classics, a garden and 5 recently built en suite bedrooms.

Directions: Located just off the A419 between Swindon and Cirencester, which is minutes from junction 15 of the M4.

Bedrooms: 3 double, 2 twin.
Open: All year

Site: ✿ Payment: 🖃 Leisure: ✿ ♪ ▶ ♒ Property: ♟ 🐾 🖼 ∅ Children: 🚼 ✦ Catering: (✗ ♟ 🍴
Room: ✎ ♨ 🅐 📺 🎦 ♨

MANNINGFORD ABBOTS, Wiltshire   Map ref 2B2

SatNav SN9 6HZ **B**

VisitEngland
★★★★
BED & BREAKFAST

B&B PER ROOM PER NIGHT
S: £40.00
D: £60.00 - £85.00
EVENING MEAL PER PERSON
£15.00 - £17.00

Huntly's Farmhouse
Manningford Abbots, Pewsey SN9 6HZ **T:** (01672) 563663 / 07900 211789
E: gimspike@esend.co.uk
W: www.huntlys.co.uk

Peaceful, thatched 17th century farmhouse including horse-stabling/grazing. Good walking country. Heated outdoor swimming pool. Free range and organic food. Family room comprises 1 twin adjoining separate single room. **Directions:** Turn off A345 SW of Pewsey signed Manningford Abbotts. Huntlys is 0.5 mile on RHS just past turn to Sharcott. Opposite post box in wall.
Bedrooms: 1 double, 1 family **Open:** All year

Site: ✿ P Leisure: ✿ ♪ ▶ ♒ ⚘ Property: 🐾 🖼 🎞 Children: 🚼5 Catering: (✗ 🍴 Room: ✎ ♨ 🅐 📺

MARLBOROUGH, Wiltshire Map ref 2B2
SatNav SN8 3DP **B**

VisitEngland
★★★
FARMHOUSE

B&B PER ROOM PER NIGHT
D: £70.00

Suddene Park Farm
Burbage, Marlborough, Wiltshire SN8 3DP **T:** (01672) 810296
E: peter.devenish@btconnect.com
W: www.suddeneparkfarm.co.uk

Situated in a beautiful secluded Wiltshire farm house, 6 miles South of Marlborough, with spacious room, lovely outlook and easy access to local attractions. Adjacent to the Savernake Forest, The Vale of Pewsey and The Kennet & Avon Canal. **Directions:** From Burbage High Street turn into Taskers Lane, take 3rd left onto Wolf Hall Road, after 1/2 mile follow road through "S" bend. Our drive is on the right. **Bedrooms:** En suite, TV, Wi-Fi, tea and coffee, microwave and fridge. **Open:** All year except Christmas and New Year.

Site: ✿ P Property: 🐕 🖥 Children: 🛏 🚼 ⚡ Room: 🔌 💧 📺 ⬜ ♨

MELKSHAM, Wiltshire Map ref 2B2
SatNav SN12 8EF **H**

VisitEngland
★★
SMALL HOTEL

B&B PER ROOM PER NIGHT
S: £65.00 - £90.00
D: £90.00 - £110.00
HB PER PERSON PER NIGHT
£85.00 - £110.00

Shaw Country Hotel
Bath Road, Shaw, Nr Melksham, Wiltshire SN12 8EF **T:** (01225) 702836 **F:** 01225 790275
E: shawcountryhotel@hotmail.co.uk
W: www.shawcountryhotel.com **£ BOOK ONLINE**

Four hundred year old farmhouse in own grounds, nine miles from Bath. Licensed bar and restaurant, with table d'hote and a la carte menus. All rooms en suite. **Bedrooms:** 3 single, 7 double, 3 twin **Open:** All year

Site: ✿ Payment: 💳 Property: 🍴 🐕 🖥 📶 Children: 🛏 🚼 ⚡ Catering: 🍴 🍳 Room: 🔌 💧 📻 📺 ♨

SALISBURY, Wiltshire Map ref 2B3
SatNav SP5 4LH **B**

B&B PER ROOM PER NIGHT
S: £38.00 - £42.00
D: £50.00 - £55.00

Evening Hill
Blandford Road, Coombe Bissett, Salisbury, Wiltshire SP5 4LH **T:** (01722) 718561
E: info@eveninghill.com
W: www.eveninghill.com

A quiet village location 10 mins from the city of Salisbury. Ideal for visiting Salisbury city and Cathedral, Stonehenge, New Forest, Bath, Southampton, Portsmouth, Winchester. **Directions:** 2 miles South of Salisbury on the A354. Drive through the village of Coombe Bissett 500 meters past the church on right hand side. **Bedrooms:** 1 double, 1 family **Open:** All year

Site: ✿ P Payment: 💳 Property: 🐕 🖥 📶 Children: 🛏 🚼 ⚡ Catering: 🍳 Room: 🔌 💧 📻 📺 ♨

TROWBRIDGE, Wiltshire Map ref 2B2
SatNav BA14 6LF **B**

VisitEngland
★★★★
BED & BREAKFAST

VisitEngland
Silver
AWARD

B&B PER ROOM PER NIGHT
S: £44.00 - £60.00
D: £75.00 - £90.00

Newhouse Farm
Littleton, Semington, Trowbridge, Wiltshire BA14 6LF **T:** (01380) 870349
E: stay@newhousefarmwilts.co.uk
W: www.newhousefarmwilts.co.uk

Former Victorian farmhouse, lovely gardens and grounds with wildflower meadow. Warm welcome, comfortable spacious rooms. Ideal touring centre for Longleat, Bowood, Lacock and Bath. Perfect for walking and cycling along the Kennet and Avon Canal. Great pubs nearby. **Directions:** On A361 between Trowbridge and Devizes. No.49 bus stops outside. **Bedrooms:** 2 double and 1 twin room, all en suite **Open:** All year

Site: ✿ P Property: 🖥 📶 📻 Children: 🛏 🚼 ⚡ Catering: 🍳 Room: 🔌 💧 📺 ♨

For **key to symbols** see page 7

Don't Miss...

Beaulieu National Motor Museum, House and Garden ⊕

Beaulieu, Hampshire SO42 7ZN
(01590) 612345
www.beaulieu.co.uk
In the New Forest, Beaulieu is one of England's top family days out.
There's lots to enjoy including the world famous National Motor
Museum, home to a stunning and historic collection of automobiles;
Palace House, home of the Montagu family; historic Beaulieu Abbey
founded in 1204 by Cistercian Monks, and World of Top Gear features
vehicles from some of the most ambitious challenges.

Portsmouth Historic Dockyard ⊕

Portsmouth, Hampshire PO1 3LJ
(023) 9283 9766
www.historicdockyard.co.uk
Portsmouth Historic Dockyard offers a great day out for all the family
and spans over 800 years of British Naval history. The state-of-the-art
Mary Rose Museum is home to the remains of Henry VIII's flagship and an
astounding collection of 400 year old artefacts recovered from the sea.

The Royal Pavilion Brighton ⊕

Brighton, East Sussex BN1 1EE
03000 290900
www.brighton-hove-rpml.org.uk/RoyalPavilion
This spectacularly extravagant seaside palace was built for the
Prince Regent, later King George IV, between 1787 and 1823. Housing
furniture, works of art and a splendid balconied tearoom overlooking
the gardens, it is one the most extraordinary and exotic oriental
buildings in the country.

Turner Contemporary Art Gallery

Margate, Kent, CT19 1HG
(01843) 233000
www.turnercontemporary.org
Situated on Margate's seafront, Turner Contemporary is a welcoming
space that offers world-class exhibitions of contemporary and historical
art, events and activities. Taking inspiration from Britain's best-known
painter JMW Turner and designed by internationally acclaimed David
Chipperfield Architects, this gleaming structure hovering over the town
is the largest exhibtiion space in the South East outside of London and
admission to the gallery is free.

Windsor Castle

Windsor, Berkshire SL4 1NJ
(020) 7766 7304
www.royalcollection.org.uk
Built by Edward III in the 14th century and restored by later monarchs,
Windsor Castle is the largest and oldest occupied castle in the world
and has been the family home of British kings and queens for almost
1,000 years. It is an official residence of Her Majesty the Queen and
encapsulates more than 900 years of English history. St George's Chapel
within the Castle Precincts is the spiritual home of the Order of the
Garter, the oldest order of chivalry in the world.

South East

Berkshire, Buckinghamshire, Hampshire, Isle of Wight, Kent, Oxfordshire, Surrey, Sussex

The Thames sweeps eastwards in broad graceful curves, cutting through the beeches of the Chiltern Hills. Miles of glorious countryside and historic cities offer heritage sites, gardens, parks and impressive architecture for you to visit. In the far south, fun-filled resorts and interesting harbours are dotted along 257 miles of delightful coastline and the Isle of Wight is a only a short ferry ride away. The South East of England is an area of great beauty that will entice you to return again and again.

Oxfordshire
Buckinghamshire
Berkshire
Surrey   Kent
Hampshire
Sussex
Isle of Wight

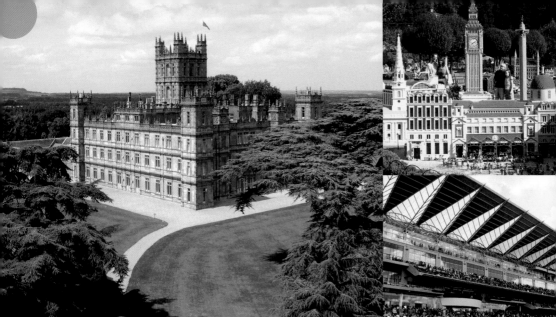

Explore – South East

Berkshire

Renowned for its royal connections, the romantic county of Berkshire counts Windsor Castle as its most famous building. Cliveden House, former seat of the Astor family and now a famous hotel, is nearby. Highclere Castle, the setting for Downton Abbey, as well as Eton College and Ascot Racecourse can be found here too.

For fun-filled days out, explore the models and exciting events at fabulous Legoland in Windsor, or take budding scientists in the family to The Lookout Discovery Centre at Bracknell and The Living Rainforest at Thatcham for plenty of interactive hands-on activities.

Buckinghamshire

Buckinghamshire, to the north east of the region, is home to the most National Trust properties in the country including the magnificent french chateau-style Waddesdon Manor near Aylesbury, idyllic Claydon House near Buckingham and Hughendon in High Wycombe, the former home of Benjamin Disraeli. And don't forget to get some fresh air in the magnificent 'Capability' Brown landscape at Stowe, now a famous public school.

The city of Milton Keynes has its infamous concrete cows and the delights of its vast shopping centre but there's plenty more to see and do in the county. Experience a hands-on history lesson at the fascinating Chiltern Open Air Museum or get your adrenalin pumping and test your head for heights with a zip wire adventure at Go Ape Wendover Woods. For a gentler pace, enjoy a tranquil bike ride through beautiful countryside along the meandering Thames.

Hampshire & Isle Of Wight

Historic Winchester is a must-visit for its charming medieval streets, imposing Cathedral, vibrant galleries and stylish, independent shops. The ancient heaths and woodlands of the New Forest National Park were once a royal hunting ground for William the Conqueror and deer, ponies and cattle continue to roam free. Cycle, walk or go horseriding in this tranquil, car-free environment or visit attractions such as the National Motor Museum at Beaulieu and Exbury Gardens & Steam Railway for a great day out.

Coastal Hampshire, with the Solent, Southampton Water and the Isle of Wight, is one of the sailing playgrounds of England. Nearby Portsmouth Harbour has Nelson's Victory, the Mary Rose and the ironclad HMS Warrior. Stroll gently around the picturesque village of Lymington or explore the cliffs along the coast. The Isle of Wight can be reached by ferry and has amazing beaches, exciting events such as Bestival, or a step back in time, counting Osborne House and Carisbrooke Castle among its historic gems.

Kent

The Garden of England is a diverse county full of romantic villages and unmissable heritage. The opulent Leeds Castle, surrounded by its shimmering lake and set in 500 acres of spectacular parkland and gardens, has attractions and events aplenty. Take a tour of Kent's rural past with a scenic cruise along the River Medway to Kent Life, a museum and working farm with animals galore and a real sense of nostalgia for bygone days.

At the northeast tip of the county, where stunning sea- and sky-scapes famously inspired JMW Turner, Margate is home to the brilliant Turner Contemporary art gallery and the Shell Grotto, a subterranean wonder lined with 4.6 million shells. Broadstairs hosts an acclaimed annual folk festival taking place all over the town, there's hardly a venue that isn't bursting with song, music and dance. Ramsgate is also a firm favourite, with its sophisticated café culture, marina and award-winning sandy beach.

Oxfordshire

Oxford's dreaming spires, echoing quads and cloistered college lawns have a timeless beauty. The Ashmolean Museum, Britain's oldest public museum, opened in 1683 and contains gold and jewellery believed to have belonged to King Alfred, the lantern carried by Guy Fawkes and riches from ancient Egypt and Greece. The Bodleian Library, founded in 1596, contains over one million volumes, including a copy of every book published in the UK since 1900. Just north of Oxford at Woodstock sits magnificent Blenheim Palace, the birthplace of Sir Winston Churchill. Oxfordshire's quiet paths and roads are perfect for cycling, and charming picture postcard villages like Great Tew make excellent rest points.

Surrey

Ashdown Forest, now more of a heath, covers 6400 acres of upland, with a large deer, badger and rare bird population. The heights of Box Hill and Leith Hill rise above the North Downs to overlook large tracts of richly wooded countryside, containing a string of well protected villages. The Devil's Punchbowl, near Hindhead, is a two mile long sandstone valley, overlooked by the 900-ft Gibbet Hill. Farnham, in the west of the country, has Tudor and Georgian houses flanking the 12th century castle. Nearby Aldershot is the home of the British Army and county town Guildford is a contemporary business and shopping centre with a modern cathedral and university. The north of the county borders Greater London and includes the 2400 acre Richmond Park, Hampton Court Palace and Kew Gardens.

Sussex

Sussex is a popular county for those wanting a short break from the hustle and bustle of London. Cosmopolitan Brighton, surely the capital of East Sussex, oozes culture, boutique hotels, marina, shops and 'buzz'. The eccentric Royal Pavilion testifies to its history as the Regency summer capital of Britain.

To the west is the impressive Arundel Castle, with its famous drama festival, nearby popular marinas and Wittering sands. Bognor Regis is a traditional seaside resort with a blue flag beach and the usual attractions. Littlehampton, with its award-winning beaches and architecture including the East Beach Cafe and the Stage by the Sea, is a popular destination and a great base for exploring the beautiful Sussex Coast.

To the east the impressive Beachy Head and Seven Sisters cliffs provide a dramatic backdrop for Eastbourne. The Sussex section of the South Downs National Park stretches from Beachy Head to Harting Down with miles of open chalk grassland, lush river valleys and ancient forests to explore.

If heritage is your thing then Sussex has a plethora of historic houses and gardens and three of the historic cinque ports. Rye in particular, with its cobbled streets, transports the visitor back three centuries. The 1066 Story is told at Battle, near Hastings and Groombridge Place, Great Dixter and Borde Hill all feature stunningly beautiful heritage gardens.

Visit – South East

 Attractions with this sign participate in the Visitor Attraction Quality Assurance Scheme.

Berkshire

Ascot CAMRA Beer Festival
Ascot Racecourse, October
An action packed day of flat racing and an array of over 280 real ales, ciders and perries to sample at the Ascot CAMRA Beer Festival as well as traditional pub games, a quiz and live music.

French Brothers Ltd
Windsor, Berkshire SL4 5JH
(01753) 851900
www.boat-trips.co.uk
Large range of public trips on weather-proof vessels departing from Windsor, Runnymede and Maidenhead.

Go Ape! Bracknell, Swinley Forest
Berkshire RG12 7QW
(0845) 643 9215
www.goape.co.uk
Go Ape! and tackle a high-wire forest adventure course of rope bridges, Tarzan swings and zip slides up to 35 feet above the forest floor.

Highclere Castle and Gardens
Newbury, Berkshire RG20 9RN
(01635) 253210
www.highclerecastle.co.uk
Visit the spectacular Victorian Castle which is currently the setting for Downton Abbey. Splendid State Rooms, Library and Egyptian Exhibition in the Castle Cellars, plus gardens inspired by Capability Brown.

LEGOLAND® Windsor
Berkshire SL4 4AY
(0871) 222 2001
www.legoland.co.uk
A theme park and Lego-themed hotel, with over 55 interactive rides and attractions, there's just too much to experience in one day!

The Look Out Discovery Centre
Bracknell, Berkshire RG12 7QW
(01344) 354400
www.bracknell-forest.gov.uk
A hands-on, interactive science exhibition with over 80 exhibits, set in 1,000 hectares of Crown woodland.

Reading Festival
August, Reading, Berkshire
www.readingfestival.com
The Reading and Leeds Festivals are a pair of annual music festivals that take place simultaneously.

REME Museum of Technology
Reading, Berkshire RG2 9NJ
(0118) 976 3375
www.rememuseum.org.uk
The museum shows the developing technology used by the Royal Electrical and Mechanical Engineers in maintaining and repairing the army's equipment since 1942.

Royal Ascot Races
June, Ascot, Berkshire SL5 7JX
(0844) 346 3000
www.ascot.co.uk
Britain's most valuable race meeting, attracting many of the world's finest racehorses to compete for more than £5.5milllion in prize money.

Buckinghamshire

Aerial Extreme Milton Keynes
Milton Keynes, Buckinghamshire MK15 0DS
0845 652 1736
www.aerialextreme.co.uk/courses/willen-lake
Amaze yourself as you take each of the challenges head on.

Bekonscot Model Village and Railway
Beaconsfield, Buckinghamshire HP9 2PL
(01494) 672919
www.bekonscot.co.uk
Use your imagination in this unique world of make-believe that has delighted generations of visitors.

Gulliver's Land
Milton Keynes, Buckinghamshire MK15 0DT
(01908) 609001
www.gulliversfun.co.uk
Family theme park with 40 rides aimed at children between 2 and 12 years.

Kop Hill Climb
September, Princes Risborough, Buckinghamshire
www.kophillclimb.org.uk
In the 1900s Kop Hill Climb was one of the most popular hill climbs in the country for cars and motorcycles. Now the spirit of the climb is revived.

Marlow Regatta
June, Eton Dorney, Buckinghamshire
www.themarlowregatta.com
Marlow Regatta is one of the multi-lane regattas in the British Rowing calendar.

Milton Keynes Theatre
Milton Keynes, Bucks MK9 3NZ
www.atgtickets.com/venues/milton-keynes-theatre
Managed by the Ambassador Theatre Group, this modern 1400 seater theatre and entertainment centre offers West End and world class production and events, making every visit memorable.

National Trust Stowe
Buckinghamshire MK18 5DQ
(01280) 817156
www.nationaltrust.org.uk/stowe
Over 40 temples and monuments, laid out against an inspiring backdrop of lakes and valleys.

Reading Real Ale and Jazz Festival
June, Reading, Buckinghamshire
www.readingrealalejazzfest.co.uk
This year's festival is going to be the biggest and best yet, featuring some of the best jazz acts on the circuit.

Roald Dahl Festival
July, Aylesbury Town Centre, Buckinghamshire
www.aylesburyvaledc.gov.uk/dahl
An annual celebration of the famous author, including a 500-strong parade of pupils, teachers and musicians with puppets and artwork based on the Roald Dahl stories.

Roald Dahl Museum and Story Centre
Great Missenden, Buckinghamshire HP16 0AL
(01494) 892192
www.roalddahl.com/museum
Where Roald Dahl (1916-1990) lived and wrote many of his well-loved books.

Waddesdon Manor
Aylesbury, Buckinghamshire HP18 0JH
(01296) 653226
www.waddesdon.org.uk
This National Trust property houses the Rothschild Collection of art treasures and wine cellars. It also features spectacular grounds with an aviary, parterre and woodland playground, licensed restaurants, gift and wine shops.

Xscape
Milton Keynes, Buckinghamshire MK9 3XS
01908 397007
www.xscape.co.uk
Xscape, Milton Keynes offers a unique combination of extreme sports and leisure activities for all ages.

Hampshire & Isle Of Wight

Alton Summer Beer Festival
May, Alton, Hampshire
www.altonbeerfestival.co.uk
Celebrating the cultural heritage of Alton as a traditional area for brewing, based on the clear waters rising from the source of the River Wey, and locally grown hops.

Blackgang Chine
Chale, Isle of Wight PO38 2HN
(01983) 730330
www.blackgangchine.com
The UK's oldest amusement park overlooking the stunning South coast of the Isle of Wight. Great family fun in over 40 acres of spectacular cliff-top gardens.

Cowes Week
August, Cowes, Isle of Wight
www.aamcowesweek.co.uk
Cowes Week is one of the longest-running regular regattas in the world with up to 40 daily races for around 1,000 boats.

Dinosaur Isle
Sandown, Isle of Wight PO36 8QA
(01983) 404344
www.dinosaurisle.com
Britain's first purpose built dinosaur museum and visitor attraction, in a spectacular pterosaur shaped building, on Sandown's blue flag beach. Walk back through fossilised time and meet life sized replica dinosaurs.

Exbury Gardens and Steam Railway
Beaulieu, Hampshire SO45 1AZ
(023) 8089 1203
www.exbury.co.uk
World famous woodland garden, home to the Rothschild Collection of rhododendrons, azaleas, camellias, rare trees and shrubs, with its own steam railway.

Isle of Wight Festival
June, Newport, Isle of Wight
www.isleofwightfestival.com
Annual music festival featuring some of the UK's top acts and bands.

Isle of Wight Walking Festival
May, Isle of Wight
www.isleofwightwalkingfestival.co.uk
The festival boasts 16 days of unbeatable, informative and healthy walks.

Marwell Zoo
Winchester, Hampshire SO21 1JH
(01962) 777407
www.marwell.org.uk
A chance to get close to the wonders of the natural world – and play a big part in helping to save them.

New Forest and Hampshire Show
July, New Park, Brockenhurst, Hampshire
www.newforestshow.co.uk
The show attracts, on average, 95,000 visitors every year and brings together a celebration of traditional country pursuits, crafts, produce and entertainment.

Osborne House
East Cowes, Isle of Wight PO32 6JX
(01983) 200022
www.english-heritage.org.uk/daysout/properties/osborne-house
Step into Queen Victoria's favourite country home and experience a world unchanged since the country's longest reigning monarch died here just over 100 years ago.

Paultons Family Theme Park
Romsey, Hampshire SO51 6AL
(023) 8081 4442
www.paultonspark.co.uk
A great family day out with over 60 different attractions and rides included in the price!

Shanklin Chine
Shanklin, Isle of Wight PO37 6BW
(01983) 866432
www.shanklinchine.co.uk
Historic gorge with dramatic waterfalls and nature trail. The Isle of Wight's oldest tourist attraction, which first opened in 1817.

Southampton Boat Show
September, Southampton, Hampshire
www.southamptonboatshow.com
See the best boats and marine brands gathered together in one fantastic water-based show.

Ventnor Botanic Gardens
St. Lawrence, Isle of Wight PO38 1UL
(01983) 855397
www.botanic.co.uk
Basking in the microclimate of The Undercliff, Ventnor Botanic Garden on the Isle of Wight is one of the great gardens of Britain . A place where the pleasure of plants can be enjoyed to the fullest.

Winchester Hat Fair
July, Winchester, Hampshire
www.hatfair.co.uk
Named after the tradition of throwing donations into performer's hats, it's Britain's longest running festival of street theatre and outdoor arts.

Kent

Bedgebury National Pinetum & Forest
Cranbrook, Kent TN17 2SL
(01580) 879820
www.forestry.gov.uk/bedgebury
Ideal for cycling, walking, running and riding and adventure play. Visit the National Pinetum, one of the world's finest conifer collections, perfect for picnics.

Canterbury Cathedral
Canterbury, Kent
(01227) 762862
www.canterbury-cathedral.org/
One of the oldest and most famous Christian structures in England, stunning Canetrbury Cathedral is a holy place and part of a World Heritage Site.

Deal Castle
Deal, Kent CT14 7BA
(01304) 372762
www.english-heritage.org.uk
One of the finest Tudor artillery castles built by the order of King Henry VIII. Explore the castle's interior and outside, admire the squat, rounded bastions and canons of its defences.

Deal Festival of Music and the Arts
June/July, Deal, Kent
(01304) 370220
www.dealfestival.co.uk
Experience great classical and contemporary music from some of the world's finest music-makers, as well as theatre, opera, cinema and dance .

Dickens Festival
June, Rochester, Kent
www.visitmedway.org/events/festivals
A weekend of colourful celebration honouring one of England's greatest writers with costumed parades, street acts, competitions, readings and fair.

Hever Castle & Gardens
Hever, Edenbridge Kent TN8 7NG
(01732) 865224
www.hevercastle.co.uk
A romantic 13th century moated castle with magnificently furnished interiors, award winning gardens, miniature Model House Exhibition, Yew Maze and a unique Splashing Water Maze.

The Historic Dockyard Chatham
Kent ME4 4TZ
(01634) 823807
www.thedockyard.co.uk
A unique, award-winning maritime heritage destination with a fantastic range of attractions, iconic buildings and historic ships to explore, plus a fabulous programme of touring exhibitions, events and activities.

Kent & East Sussex Railway
Tenterden, Kent TN30 6HE
(01580) 765155
www.kesr.org.uk
Rural light railway enables visitors to experience travel and service from a bygone age aboard restored Victorian coaches and locomotives.

Leeds Castle
Maidstone, Kent ME17 1PL
(01622) 765400
www.leeds-castle.com
With 500 acres of beautiful parkland and gardens, daily activities, flying falconry displays, special events and attractions including a hot air balloon festival and a triathlon, Leeds Castle is one of the best days out in Kent,

Quex Park & Powell-Cotton Museum
Birchington, Kent CT7 0BH
(01843) 842168
www.quexpark.co.uk
Quex Park is home to the Powell-Cotton Museum and the Powell-Cotton family's extraordinary collection of natural history, ethnography and fine and decorative arts.

Rochester Castle
Kent ME1 1SW
(01634) 335882
www.visitmedway.org/site/attractions/rochester-castle-p44583
One of the finest keeps in England. Also the tallest, measures 113 feet high, 70 feet square and has walls 12 feet thick in places, partly built on the Roman city wall. Good views from the battlements over the River Medway.

Oxfordshire

Blenheim Palace
Woodstock, Oxfordshire OX20 1PX
(0800) 849 6500
www.blenheimpalace.com
Birthplace of Sir Winston Churchill and home to the Duke of Marlborough, Blenheim Palace, one of the finest baroque houses in England, is set in over 2,000 acres of landscaped gardens.

Didcot Railway Centre
Oxfordshire OX11 7NJ
(01235) 817200
www.didcotrailwaycentre.org.uk
Living museum recreating the golden age of the Great Western Railway. Steam locomotives and trains, Brunel's broad gauge railway, engine shed and small relics museum.

Henley Royal Regatta
July, Henley, Oxfordshire
www.hrr.co.uk
Attracting thousands of visitors over a five-day period and spectators will be thrilled by over 200 races of international standard.

Oxford Official Guided Walking Tour
owtours@visitoxfordshire.org
A fascinating and entertaining way to explore and learn about this unique city, its history, University, famous people and odd traditions. Covering a wide range of topics from an introduction to the city and its University to Inspector Morse, Harry Potter, J.R.R. Tolkien and more.

Surrey

British Wildlife Centre
Lingfield, Surrey RH7 6LF
(01342) 834658
www.britishwildlifecentre.co.uk
The best place to see and learn about Britain's own wonderful wildlife, with over 40 different species including deer, foxes, otters, badgers, pine martens and red squirrels.

Guildford Cathedral
Surrey GU2 7UP
(01483) 547860
www.guildford-cathedral.org
New Anglican Cathedral, the foundation stone of which was laid in 1936. Notable sandstone interior and marble floors. Restaurant and shops.

Investec Derby
June, Epsom Racecourse, Surrey
www.epsomderby.co.uk
The biggest horse race in the flat-racing calendar.

Loseley Park
Guildford, Surrey GU3 1HS
(01483) 405120
www.loseleypark.co.uk
A beautiful Elizabethan mansion standing in ancient Surrey Parkland. Still the home of the More-Molyneux family, it is remarkably unchanged since 1562 when Sir William More laid the first stones .

RHS Garden Wisley
Woking, Surrey GU23 6QB
(0845) 260 9000
www.rhs.org.uk/wisley
Enjoy a day out at the world-class Wisley garden, stretching over 240 glorious acres. Join in the fun with all year round events.

RHS Hampton Court Palace Flower Show
July, Hampton Court, Surrey
www.rhs.org.uk
One of the biggest events in the horticulture calendar.

Thorpe Park
Chertsey, Surrey KT16 8PN
(0871) 663 1673
www.thorpepark.com
Thorpe Park Resort is an island like no other, with over 30 thrilling rides, attractions and live events.

Wings & Wheels
August, Dunsfold Aerodrome, Surrey
www.wingsandwheels.net
A popular family day out featuring an outstanding variety of dynamic aviation, motoring displays and iconic cars.

Sussex

1066 Battle Abbey and Battlefield
East Sussex TN33 0AD
(01424) 775705
www.english-heritage.org.uk
An abbey founded by William the Conqueror on the site of the Battle of Hastings.

Arundel Festival
August, Arundel, Sussex
www.arundelfestival.co.uk
Ten days of the best music, theatre, art and comedy.

Arundel Wetland Centre
West Sussex BN18 9PB
(01903) 883355
www.wwt.org.uk/visit/arundel
WWT Arundel Wetland Centre is a 65-acre reserve in an idyllic setting, nestled at the base of the South Downs National Park.

Brighton Festival
29 New Road, Brighton BN1 1UG
(01273) 709709
www.brightonfestival.org
A sensational programme of art, theatre, dance, music, literature and family shows starting with a Children's Parade winding its way through the city.

Brighton Lanes
Brighton, East Sussex
www.visitbrighton.com/shopping/the-lanes
From quirky stores, vintage antiques and boutiques to live music, funky restaurants and cutting edge art, Brighton Lanes is crammed with interesting independent shops and watering holes.

Brighton Fringe
May, Brighton, Sussex
www.brightonfestivalfringe.org.uk
One of the largest fringe festivals in the world, offering cabaret, comedy, classical concerts, club nights, theatre and exhibitions, as well as street performances.

British Airways i360
Brighton BN1 2LN
(03337) 720360
www.britishairwaysi360.com
Take a flight into the skies and see Sussex as you've never seen it before. The 450 feet high British Airways i360 will offer breath-taking 360 degree views of up to 26 miles from the world's first vertical cable car. Lift-off summer 2016!

Chichester Cathedral
West Sussex PO19 1RP
(01243) 782595
www.chichestercathedral.org.uk
A magnificent Cathedral with treasures ranging from medieval stone carvings to world famous 20th century artworks.

Denmans Garden
Fontwell, West Sussex BN18 0SU
(01243) 542808
www.denmans-garden.co.uk
Beautiful 4 acre garden designed for year round interest through use of form, colour and texture. Beautiful plant centre, award-winning and fully licensed Garden Café.

Eastbourne Beer Festival
October, Winter Gardens, Eastbourne, Sussex
www.visiteastbourne.com/beer-festival
*Eastbourne's annual beer festival features over 120
cask ales, plus wines, international bottled beers,
ciders and perries. Each session features live music.*

Eastbourne Festival
July, Eastbourne, Sussex
www.eastbournefestival.co.uk
*Eastbourne Festival is an Open Access Arts Festival
which takes place annually for three weeks. It has
become recognised as an annual showcase for local
professional and amateur talent.*

England's Medieval Festival
August, Herstmonceux Castle, Sussex
www.englandsmedievalfestival.com
A celebration of the Middle Ages.

Fishers Adventure Farm Park
Billingshurst, West Sussex RH14 0EG
(01403) 700063
www.fishersfarmpark.co.uk
*Award-winning Adventure Farm Park and open all
year. Ideally suited for ages 2-11 years. Huge variety
of animals, rides and attractions from the skating rink,
to pony rides, toboggan run, bumper boats, theatre
shows and more!*

Glorious Goodwood
July, Chichester, Sussex
www.goodwood.com
*Bursting with fabulous fashions, succulent
strawberries, chilled Champagne and top horse
racing stars, as well as music and dancing.*

Glyndebourne Festival
May - August, Lewes, Sussex
www.glyndebourne.com
*An English opera festival held at Glyndebourne, an
English country house near Lewes.*

Great Dixter House and Gardens
Rye, East Sussex TN31 6PH
(01797) 252878
www.greatdixter.co.uk
*An example of a 15th century manor house with
antique furniture and needlework. The house is
restored and the gardens were designed by Lutyens.*

London to Brighton Bike Ride
June, Ends on Madeira Drive, Brighton, Sussex
www.bhf.org.uk/london-brighton
*The annual bike ride from the capital to the coast in
aid of the British Heart Foundation. The UK's largest
charity bike ride with 27,000 riders.*

Pashley Manor Gardens
Wadhurst, East Sussex TN5 7HE
(01580) 200888
www.pashleymanorgardens.com
*Pashley Manor Gardens offer a blend of romantic
landscaping, imaginative plantings, fine old trees,
fountains, springs and large ponds plus exciting
special events.*

Petworth House and Park
West Sussex GU28 0AE
(01798) 342207
www.nationaltrust.org.uk/petworth
*Discover the National Trust's finest art collection
displayed in a magnificent 17th century mansion
within a beautiful 700-acre park. Petworth House
contains works by artists such as Van Dyck,
Reynolds and Turner.*

RSPB Pulborough Brooks
West Sussex RH20 2EL
(01798) 875851
www.rspb.org.uk
*Set in the scenic Arun Valley with views to the South
Downs, the two mile circular nature trail leads
around this beautiful reserve.*

Tourist Information Centres

When you arrive at your destination, visit the Tourist Information Centre for quality assured help with accommodation and information about local attractions and events, or email your request before you go.

Aldershot	Prince's Hall	01252 320968	aldershotvic@rushmoor.gov.uk
Ashford	Ashford Gateway Plus	01233 330316	tourism@ashford.gov.uk
Aylesbury	The Kings Head	01296 330559	tic@aylesburyvaledc.gov.uk
Banbury	Castle Quay Shopping Centre	01295 753752	banbury.tic@cherwell-dc.gov.uk
Battle	Yesterdays World	01797 229049	battletic@rother.gov.uk
Bexley (Hall Place)	Central Library	0208 3037777	touristinfo@bexleyheritagetrust.org.uk
Bicester	Unit 86a Bicester Village	01869 369055	bicestervisitorcentre@valueretail.com
Bracknell	The Look Out Discovery Centre	01344 354409	thelookout@bracknell-forest.gov.uk
Brighton	Brighton Centre Box Office	01273 290337	visitor.info@visitbrighton.com
Buckingham	The Old Gaol Museum	01280 823020	buckinghamtic@touismse.com
Burford	33a High Street	01993 823558	burford.vic@westoxon.gov.uk
Burgess Hill	Burgess Hill Town Council	01444 238202	touristinformation@burgesshill.gov.uk
Canterbury	Beaney House	01227 378100	canterburyinformation@canterbury.gov.uk
Chichester	The Novium	01243 775888	chitic@chichester.gov.uk
Deal	The Landmark Centre	01304 369576	info@deal.gov.uk
Dover	Dover Museum	01304 201066	tic@doveruk.com
Eastbourne	Cornfield Road	0871 663 0031	tic@eastbourne.gov.uk

Faringdon	The Corn Exchange	01367 242191	tic@faringdontowncouncil.gov.uk
Faversham	Fleur de Lis Heritage Centre	01795 534542	ticfaversham@btconnect.com
Folkestone	20 Bouverier Place	01303 258594	chris.kirkham@visitkent.co.uk
Fordingbridge	Kings Yard	01425 654560	fordingbridgetic@tourismse.com
Gosport	Gosport TIC, Bus Station Complex	023 9252 2944	tourism@gosport.gov.uk
Gravesend	Towncentric	01474 337600	info@towncentric.co.uk
Guildford	155 High Street	01483 444333	tic@guildford.gov.uk
Hastings	Queens Square	01424 451111	hic@hastings.gov.uk
Hayling Island	Central Beachlands	023 9246 7111	tourism@havant.gov.uk
Henley-on-Thames	Town Hall,	01491 578034	vic@henleytowncouncil.gov.uk
High Wycombe	High Wycombe Library	01494 421892	tourism_enquiries@wycombe.gov.uk
Horsham	9 The Causeway	01403 211661	visitor.information@horsham.gov.uk
Lewes	187 High Street	01273 483448	lewes.tic@lewes.gov.uk
Littlehampton	The Look & Sea Centre	01903 721866	jo-lhvic@hotmail.co.uk
Lymington	St Barbe Museum	01590 676969	office@stbarbe-museum.org.uk
Lyndhurst & New Forest	New Forest Museum	023 8028 2269 / 023 8028 5492	info@thenewforest.co.uk
Maidenhead	Maidenhead Library	01628 796502	maidenhead.tic@rbwm.gov.uk
Maidstone	Maidstone Museum	01622 602169	tourism@maidstone.gov.uk
Marlow	55a High Street	01628 483597	tourism_enquiries@wycombe.gov.uk
Midhurst	North Street	01730 812251	midtic@chichester.gov.uk
Newbury	The Wharf	01635 30267	tourism@westberks.gov.uk
Oxford	Visit Oxfordshire, Oxford Information Centre	01865 252200	info@visitoxfordshire.org
Petersfield	County Library	01730 268829	petersfieldinfo@btconnect.com
Portsmouth	D-Day Museum	023 9282 6722	vis@portsmouthcc.gov.uk
Princes Risborough	Tower Court	01844 274795	risborough_office@wycombe.gov.uk
Ringwood	Ringwood Gateway	01425 473883	town.council@ringwood.gov.uk
Rochester	95 High Street	01634 338141	visitor.centre@medway.gov.uk
Romsey	Museum & Tourist Information Centre	01794 512987	romseytic@testvalley.gov.uk
Royal Tunbridge Wells	Unit 2 The Corn Exchange	01892 515675	touristinformationcentre@tunbridgewells.gov.uk
Sandwich	The Guildhall	01304 613565 / 617197	tourism@sandwichtowncouncil.gov.uk
Seaford	37 Church Street	01323 897426	seaford.tic@lewes.gov.uk
Sevenoaks	Stag Community Arts Centre	01732 450305	tic@sevenoakstown.gov.uk
Swanley	Library & Information Centre	01322 614660	touristinfo@swanley.org.uk
Tenterden	Tenterden Gateway	08458 247 202	
Thame	Town Hall	01844 212833	oss@thametowncouncil.gov.uk
Thanet	The Droit House	01843 577577	visitorinformation@thanet.gov.uk
Tonbridge	Tonbridge Castle	01732 770929	tonbridge.castle@tmbc.gov.uk
Winchester	Guildhall	01962 840500	tourism@winchester.gov.uk
Windsor	Old Booking Hall	01753 743900	windsor.tic@rbwm.gov.uk
Witney	3 Welsh Way	01993 775802 / 861780	witney.vic@westoxon.gov.uk

Regional Contacts and Information

For more information on accommodation, attractions, activities, events and holidays in South East England, contact one of the following regional or local tourism organisations. Their websites have a wealth of information and many produce free publications to help you get the most out of your visit.

www.visitsoutheastengland.com
email enquiries@tourismse.com or
call (023) 8062 5400.

www.visitnewbury.org.uk
www.visitbuckinghamshire.org
www.visit-hampshire.co.uk
www.visitisleofwight.co.uk
www.visitkent.co.uk
www.visitoxfordandoxfordshire.com
www.visitsurrey.com
www.visitbrighton.com

Stay – South East

Entries appear alphabetically by town name in each county. A key to symbols appears on page 7

ASCOT, Berkshire   Map ref 2C2   SatNav SL5 7SE [H]

Coworth Park

Blacknest Road, Ascot, Berkshire SL5 7SE **T:** (01344) 876 600
E: reservations.CPA@dorchestercollection.com
W: www.dorchestercollection.com **£ BOOK ONLINE**

B&B PER ROOM PER NIGHT
D: £340.00

EVENING MEAL PER PERSON
£30.00

SPECIAL PROMOTIONS
Our Spa and Stay offer includes luxury accommodation for two with English breakfast, 50 minute luxury spa treatment for two, use of the relaxation room, followed by smoothies in the Spatisserie.

Coworth Park is Dorchester Collection's 70-room luxury country house hotel and spa set in 240 acres of picturesque Berkshire parkland. Seasonal ingredients and exceptional service feature across the three dining experiences - Restaurant Coworth Park, The Barn and The Spatisserie. Enjoy quintessential English activities from horse riding to polo, or relax in the award-winning luxury spa and pool.

Directions: Coworth Park is just 45 minutes from central London and 20 minutes from London Heathrow airport. Situated near to Ascot and bordering on Windsor Great Park.

Bedrooms: The 70 guestrooms, situated in the Mansion House and in cottages and stables, blend traditional and contemporary design with bespoke furnishings
Open: All year

Site: ✿ P **Payment:** 🖃 **Leisure:** 🏊 ▶ ᘁ ⚒ 🏹 ⚲ ✎ 🎾 🎣 **Property:** ⓫ 🍽 🖥 🖂 🏛 ◐ 🔌 **Children:** 🚼 🛏 🏃
Catering: (✕ 🍷 **Room:** 🍵 ♨ ☎ 🖥 📺 💿 🎧 🎮

WINDSOR, Berkshire   Map ref 2D2   SatNav RG42 6LD [H]

Stirrups Country House Hotel

Maidens Green, Bracknell RG42 6LD **T:** (01344) 882284 **F:** 01344 882300
E: reception@stirrupshotel.co.uk
W: www.stirrupshotel.co.uk **£ BOOK ONLINE**

Stirrups, with its Tudor origins, is located between Bracknell, Ascot and Windsor and is the perfect venue for visits to Legoland Windsor (three miles). Round off your day by relaxing in the oak-beamed bar, by the inglenook fire, prior to dinner. Please contact for prices.
Directions: Stirrups lies on the B3022, 200 metres south of the crossroads in Maidens Green Village. **Bedrooms:** 19 dbl, 4 twin, 7 family, 6 suite - all en suite. **Open:** All year

Site: ✿ P **Payment:** 🖃 **Property:** 🍽 🖥 🖂 🏛 ◐ **Children:** 🚼 🛏 🏃 **Catering:** (✕ 🍷 🍴 **Room:** 🍵 ♨ ☎ 🖥 📺 🎧 🎮

GREAT MISSENDEN, Buckinghamshire   Map ref 2C1   SatNav HP16 0AX [B]

Forge House

Forge House, 10 Church Street, Great Missenden, Buckinghamshire HP16 0AX
T: (01494) 867347 / 07717 949710

B&B PER ROOM PER NIGHT
D: £75.00 - £80.00

Set in the wooded Chiltern Hills, quiet village location - a charming 18th century beamed house traditionally refurbished with three en suite double bedrooms. Set in the home village of Roald Dahl, Forge House welcomes walkers and cyclists alike and is only a 35 minute trip from Marylebone London station. Please contact for prices for single occupancy. **Bedrooms:** 2 double rooms, 1 twin room, 1 single room, all en suite **Open:** All Year

Site: ✿ P **Payment:** € **Leisure:** 🏊 ▶ ᘁ **Property:** 🏛 ✎ **Children:** 🚼5 **Catering:** 🍴 **Room:** 🍵 ♨ 🖥 📺 💿

The Three Lions

Stuckton, Fordingbridge SP6 2HF T: (01425) 652489 F: 01425 656144
E: the3lions@btinternet.com
W: www.thethreelionsrestaurant.co.uk

B&B PER ROOM PER NIGHT
S: £79.00
D: £125.00
HB PER PERSON PER NIGHT
£70.00 - £85.00

SPECIAL PROMOTIONS
Weekend Two Day
Break £235 incl
continental breakfast
£360 with 3 course
dinners Mid Week
£215 to £340
respectively.

A restaurant with rooms in the New Forest. Come and stay, relax and enjoy English/French cuisine cooked by Mike a constantly hands on (former) Michelin starred chef. Cosy informal bar, log fire, conservatory and gardens with sauna and hot tub. Three times Hampshire Restaurant of the Year, Good Food Guide. National Newcomer of the Year, Good Hotel Guide. We are family, cyclist and walker friendly & accept pets.

Directions: 15 mins M27 jct 1. 15 mins Salisbury. Locate Total garage east of Fordingbridge, follow brown tourist signs to the Three Lions.

Bedrooms: 2 dble, 2 twin, 3 family
Open: All year

Site: Payment: Leisure: Property: Children: Catering: Room:

Wellington Arms

Stratfield Turgis, Hook, Hampshire RG27 0AS T: (01256) 882214
E: wellingtonarmsreception.basingstoke@hall-woodhouse.co.uk
W: www.wellingtonstratfieldturgis.co.uk £ BOOK ONLINE

B&B PER ROOM PER NIGHT
D: £90.00 - £120.00

Whether you are looking for a relaxing weekend getaway from it all or convenient business stopover, this original 17th century farmhouse and now grade II listed hotel located on the outskirts of the Duke of Wellington's estate is the perfect setting.

Directions: From M3/M4 take A33, Wellington Arms is halfway along.

Bedrooms: Our historic hotel and rooms are steeped in charm and character. Each of our bedrooms show off genuine period features and home comfort.
Open: We are open year-round.

Site: Payment: Leisure: Property: Children: Catering: Room:

★★★★
INN

Silver
AWARD

B&B PER ROOM PER NIGHT
D: £95.00 - £160.00

EVENING MEAL PER PERSON
£15.00 - £25.00

Beach House

Milford on Sea, Lymington, Hampshire SO41 0PT T: (01590) 643044
E: beachhouse.reception@hall-woodhouse.co.uk
W: www.beachhousemilfordonsea.co.uk £ BOOK ONLINE

Situated on the edge of the New Forest, 200 yards from the beach with breath-taking views of the Isle of Wight and the Needles, the Beach House is a Grade II listed Victorian mansion built in 1897. Originally built for the Siemens Family as their 'Beach House', it's a beautiful example of Arts and Crafts architecture with restored oak-panelled interior, stained glass windows and vintage furniture.

Directions: From M27: take jct 1 or 2, take A337 signposted to Lyndhurst. Drive through Lyndhurst and Brokenhust, through Lymington, take B3058, stay on, Beach House on left.

Bedrooms: Each room decorated in a unique style, tea & coffee tray, flat screen TV, bluetooth radio
Open: We are open year-round

Site: ✿ P Payment: 💷 Property: 🐕 🚗 ⌀ Children: ざ ⅄ Catering: (✗ ⅄ Room: 🖓 🖑 📺 🔌 📠

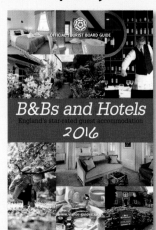
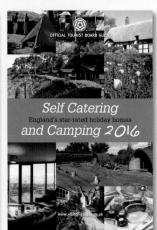

NEW MILTON, NEW FOREST, *Hampshire*   *Map ref 2B3*   *SatNav BH23 5QL* H

VisitEngland ★★★★★ HOTEL

VisitEngland *Gold* AWARD

B&B PER ROOM PER NIGHT
D: £377.00 –
£1652.00

SPECIAL PROMOTIONS
Two night minimum
stay at weekends.

Chewton Glen
New Milton, New Forest, Hampshire BH25 6QS   T: (01425) 282212
F: 01425 272310   E: reservations@chewtonglen.com
W: www.chewtonglen.com

VisitEngland Awards for Excellence 2015 BRONZE WINNER

An English Original. Chewton Glen is a luxury countryhouse hotel and spa set in 130 acres of Hampshire countryside on the edge of the New Forest National Park, and just a few minutes walk from the sea. A very special place, Chewton Glen is a proud member of Relais & Châteaux, is one of the finest luxury hotels in the UK and has been voted 'Best Hotel for Service in the UK' and listed as one of the 'World's Best Hotels' by Conde Nast Traveller readers. The unsurpassed heritage of effortlessly gracious English hospitality and the balance between heritage and evolution is what makes Chewton Glen a 5 star, luxury country house hotel and spa that constantly surprises.

Directions: Please contact us for directions.

Bedrooms: 35 Double, 23 Suites, 12 Treehouse Suites.
Open: All year

Site: ✿ Payment: ▦ € Leisure: ♿ ♪ ▶ ♒ ✗ ♨ ⚞ ⚲ ⚘ Property: ⊛ ♟ ▤ ▯ ◑ Children: ⚘ ⇙ ♨ ⚲ ⚲ ✗
Catering: ♟ ♨ Room: ♨ ☏ ▣ ▣ ◔

PORTSMOUTH, *Hampshire*   *Map ref 2C3*   *SatNav PO1 3HS* H

VisitEngland ★★ HOTEL

B&B PER ROOM PER NIGHT
S: £53.00 – £73.00
D: £92.00 – £145.00
EVENING MEAL PER PERSON
£15.75 – £18.50

SPECIAL PROMOTIONS
Minimum 3 night
breaks Sunday to
Thursday from £56.00
pp per night. Friday
and Saturday from £65
pp per night.

Royal Maritime Club
75-80 Queen Street, Portsmouth PO1 3HS   T: (023) 9282 4231   F: 023 9229 3496
E: info@royalmaritimeclub.co.uk
W: www.royalmaritimeclub.co.uk   **£ BOOK ONLINE**

Situated at the heart of Portsmouth's unique naval heritage area. Within walking distance of HMS Victory, HMS Warrior, the Mary Rose, Gunwharf Quays shopping complex. Rail, coach, ferry links nearby.

Directions: Take the M275 Portsmouth(W) and then follow signs to Historic Waterfront/Historic Dockyard.

Bedrooms: 20 single, 33 dble, 19 twin, 8 family, 20 superior
Open: All year except Christmas and New Year

Payment: ▦ Leisure: ⚲ Property: ♟ ▤ ▯ ◑ Children: ⚘ ♨ ⚲ Catering: ♟ ♨ Room: ♨ ⬩ ▣ ▣ ◔

SOUTHAMPTON, Hampshire   Map ref 2C3
SatNav SO31 5DQ [B]

B&B PER ROOM PER NIGHT
S: £52.50
D: £67.50

The Prince Consort
Victoria Road, Netley Abbey, Southampton, Hampshire SO31 5DQ   T: (02380) 452676
E: info@theprinceconsortpub.co.uk
W: www.theprinceconsortpub.co.uk

Grade 2 listed Victorian Pub with separate annexe B&B in the Heart of Netley Abbey. Close to Hamble, Southampton, Winchester and Portsmouth. Rates include breakfast. **Directions:** Situated near A27 & M27 and mainline train links to and from Southampton and Portsmouth. Within easy walking distance of Hamble. **Bedrooms:** 4 double, 3 twin. **Open:** All year

Site: ❀ **P** **Payment:** 💷 **Leisure:** 🎵 ⌶ ♻ **Property:** 🐾 🖥 **Children:** 🛏 🍴 ♿ **Catering:** 🍴 🍷 🍽
Room: 🛁 🍷 📶 📺 🍴

SWAY, Hampshire   Map ref 2C3
SatNav SO41 6DJ [B]

B&B PER ROOM PER NIGHT
S: £115.00 - £245.00
D: £150.00 - £295.00
EVENING MEAL PER PERSON
£23.95 - £47.00

The Mill At Gordleton
Silver Street, Hordle, Lymington SO41 6DJ   T: (01590) 682219
E: info@themillatgordleton.co.uk
W: www.themillatgordleton.co.uk

A beautiful individual privately owned small restaurant with rooms, wonderful river, gardens. Homemade, local and organic food. We care passionately about the environment which is reflected in everything we do. **Directions:** A337 Lyndhurst to Brockenhurst to Lymington. Over two mini roundabouts first right Sway Road. The Mill at Gordleton Hotel 2m. **Bedrooms:** 3 kings, 3 twins, 2 suite. **Open:** All year except Christmas day.

Site: ❀ **Payment:** 💷 **Leisure:** 🎵 ♻ **Property:** 🖥 **Children:** 🛏 🍴 ♿ **Catering:** 🍷
Room: 📶 🛁 📞 📶 📺

WINCHESTER, Hampshire   Map ref 2C3
SatNav SO23 9SR [B]

B&B PER ROOM PER NIGHT
S: £55.00 - £60.00
D: £65.00 - £70.00

12 Christchurch Road
12 Christchurch Road, Winchester SO23 9SR   T: (01962) 854272 / 07879 850076
E: pjspatton@yahoo.co.uk

Elegant Victorian house furnished with style. Easy, pleasant walk to city centre, cathedral, museums, shops and water meadows. Breakfast in conservatory, overlooking beautiful gardens (NGS), with home-made bread, preserves and local produce. **Directions:** Please contact us for directions. **Bedrooms:** 1 double, 1 twin. Comfortable and well furnished **Open:** All year except Christmas and New Year

Property: 🐾 🖥 **Children:** 🛏 🍴 ♿ **Catering:** 🍽 **Room:** 📶 🛁

SANDOWN, Isle of Wight   Map ref 2C3
SatNav PO36 8JR **B**

VisitEngland
★★★
GUEST ACCOMMODATION

B&B PER ROOM PER NIGHT
S: £29.00 - £35.00
D: £58.00 - £70.00

SPECIAL PROMOTIONS
Check our website for ferry inclusive specials.

The Montpelier
5 Pier Street, Sandown PO36 8JR   **T:** (01983) 403964 / 07771 936651
E: steve@themontpelier.co.uk
W: www.themontpelier.co.uk

The Montpelier is situated opposite the pier and beaches with the High St just around the corner. We offer B&B, room-only and ferry-inclusive from Southampton. Rooms are en suite, most with sea views and all have a fridge. Room only £4pn less.

Directions: Make your way to Sandown Pier and Esplanade and as you come into Pier Street we are the blue building 15 metres down on your left.

Bedrooms: 1 single, 3 double, 2 twin, 2 family.
Open: All year

Payment: 💷 € **Leisure:** 🎵 ▶ **Property:** 🖭 **Children:** 🐕 🎠 **Catering:** 🍴 **Room:** 🕿 🐾 📺

ASHFORD, Kent   Map ref 3B4
SatNav TN25 5NB **B**

VisitEngland
★★★★
GUEST ACCOMMODATION

B&B PER ROOM PER NIGHT
S: £50.00 - £60.00
D: £90.00

Bulltown Farmhouse Bed & Breakfast
Bulltown Lane, West Brabourne, Ashford, Kent TN25 5NB   **T:** (01233) 813505
E: lily.wilton@bulltown.co.uk
W: www.bulltown.co.uk

Stunning 15th Century timber framed farmhouse with wealth of beams surrounded by cottage garden in Area of Outstanding Natural Beauty. Rooms have unspoilt views. All en suite. Guest lounge with large inglenook fireplace. Local produce used. **Directions:** See website for directions but under 4 miles from Junction 10 M20. **Bedrooms:** 1 double, 1 twin, 1 family **Open:** All year

Site: ✿ P **Payment:** € **Leisure:** ♿ 🎵 ▶ ↺ **Property:** 🖭 🖥 **Children:** 🐕 🎠 🧗 **Catering:** 🍴 **Room:** 🕿 🐾

CANTERBURY, Kent   Map ref 3B3
SatNav CT1 3JT **B**

VisitEngland
★★★
BACKPACKERS

B&B PER ROOM PER NIGHT
S: £25.00 - £35.00
D: £20.00 - £30.00
BED ONLY PER NIGHT
£10.00 - £24.50

Kipps Independent Hostel
40 Nunnery Fields, Canterbury CT1 3JT   **T:** (01227) 786121   **E:** kippshostel@gmail.com
W: www.kipps-hostel.com   **£ BOOK ONLINE**

Self-catering backpackers hostel only a short walk from the Cathedral and City Centre. We offer accommodation for individuals and Groups . Excellent facilities including kitchen, garden, lounge free Wifi, and nightly events. **Directions:** Please go to our website www.kipps-hostel.com for directions. **Bedrooms:** Private/family and dormitory rooms **Open:** All year

Site: ✿ P **Payment:** 💷 € **Leisure:** 🎣 **Property:** 🖭 📶 📺 **Catering:** 🍴 **Bedroom:** 🐾 ☎

CRANBROOK, Kent   Map ref 3B4

1 Maytham Cottages

Frogs Lane, Rolvenden Layne, Cranbrook TN17 4NH   T: (01580) 241484
E: jobeddows@aol.com
W: rolvendenbedandbreakfast.co.uk

A pretty grade II Lutyens cottage situated in the peaceful hamlet of Rolvenden Layne. Ideal for numerous National Trust sites/gardens/coast. Just 200 yards from excellent pub. We are the proud owners of a five star food hygene certificate. Always a warm welcome.
Directions: A28 Tenterden to Rolvenden village, left into Maytham Road, 1 mile then right into Frogs Lane, 100yds on the left.
Bedrooms: 1 king size & single with en suite bathroom. 1 double fourposter & 1 double, both with shower en suite. **Open:** All year

B&B PER ROOM PER NIGHT
S: £55.00 - £65.00
D: £80.00 - £90.00

 Site: ❀ **P** Leisure: 🚴 ⚓ ▶ ∪ Property: 🐕 🖂 ⌂ Children: 🍼 🛏 ♿ Catering: 🍴 Room: ☎ ♨ 🔌 📺 📀 🍳 📠

DOVER, Kent   Map ref 3C4

Farthingales Bed and Breakfast

Old Court Hill, Nonington, Dover, Kent CT15 4LQ   T: 07599 303494
E: farthingalesbandb@yahoo.co.uk
W: www.farthingales.co.uk

B&B PER ROOM PER NIGHT
S: £65.00 - £95.00
D: £75.00 - £85.00

SPECIAL PROMOTIONS
Local pub 5 minutes walk away.

Truly a rural retreat. Farthingales offers a unique blend of history and the comforts of 21st Century living in a beautiful Victorian building which was once the village shop. For those who enjoy living through medieval times, we offer rooms in our 15th Century Kentish hall house. A secluded venue for those travelling alone, as couples, families or groups.

Directions: Via A2 towards Dover, turn off at Wingham/Aylesham exit and follow signs for Nonington. Left at The Royal Oak pub into Vicarage Lane under the tunnel of trees. We're opposite St Mary's Church.

Bedrooms: Twin and double in converted village shop. Lounge and en suites, plus a 15th Century suite with lounge, dining room and large en suite. £95 per night.
Open: All year

Site: ❀ **P** Payment: 💷 Leisure: 🚴 Property: 🖂 ⌂ ✎ Room: ♨ 🔌 📺 📀

Book your accommodation online

Visit our websites for detailed information, up-to-date availability and to book your accommodation online. Includes over 20,000 places to stay, all of them star rated.

www.visitor-guides.co.uk

EDENBRIDGE, Kent   Map ref 2D2   SatNav TN8 7NG B

Hever Castle Luxury Bed & Breakfast

Hever Castle, Hever, Edenbridge, Kent TN8 7NG T: (01732) 861800 F: 01732 867860
E: stay@hevercastle.co.uk
W: www.hevercastle.co.uk/stay/bed-breakfast £ BOOK ONLINE

B&B PER ROOM PER NIGHT
S: £105.00 - £255.00
D: £125.00 - £255.00

SPECIAL PROMOTIONS
Includes complimentary access to the castle and gardens.

Surrounded by glorious Kent countryside, Hever Castle in Kent offers luxury Bed and breakfast in the Astor Wing of Hever Castle, an Edwardian Wing created by William Waldorf Astor, designed in Tudor style. This period property boasts a fine collection of 28, stunning five-star Gold graded bedrooms. On offer you will find an abundance of rich fabrics, crisp linens, panelled walls, perhaps a golden chaise longue or a glimpse of the castle through leaded windows.

All bedrooms are en suite and individually styled, some offering four poster beds, some roll top baths and some walk in showers. All rooms blend modern day comforts with antique furnishings and original features. The fine collection of bedrooms offers a selection of double rooms, twin rooms, single rooms and some rooms that are suitable for families with young children.

Directions: Please see website.

Bedrooms: Luxurious toiletries, Wi-Fi, flat screen TV's and direct-dial telephones.
Open: All year

Site: P Payment: Leisure: Property: Children: Catering: Room:

GILLINGHAM, Kent   Map ref 3B3   SatNav ME7 5QT H

King Charles Hotel

Brompton Road, Gillingham ME7 5QT T: (01634) 830303 F: 01634 829430
E: reservations@kingcharleshotel.co.uk
W: www.kingcharleshotel.co.uk £ BOOK ONLINE

B&B PER ROOM PER NIGHT
S: £50.00
D: £60.00

SPECIAL PROMOTIONS
Special Sunday night rates. Please see website for details.

A privately owned, modern hotel, situated in the heart of Medway. All bedrooms have en suite bathroom, tea/coffee facilities, hairdryer, telephone, TV and wireless internet. We offer extremely competitive group rates.

Directions: M2 jct 4 to Gillingham/Medway Tunnel. Turn left to Brompton before tunnel. We are on left.

Bedrooms: 4 single, 33 dble, 33 twin, 26 family, 2 suite
Open: All year

Site: P Payment: Leisure: Property: Children: Catering: Room:

HERNHILL, Kent   Map ref 3B3
SatNav ME13 9JW B

Church Oast
Church Oast, Hernhill, Faversham ME13 9JW T: (01227) 750974 E: jill@geliot.plus.com
W: www.churchoast.co.uk

B&B PER ROOM PER NIGHT
S: £48.00 - £58.00
D: £80.00 - £90.00

A warm welcome and luxury accommodation in converted Oast House in quiet picturesque village. Well equipped bedrooms with en-suite or private facilities. Award winning breakfasts served in stunning conservatory with views over garden and orchards. Guest lounge. Meals available in nearby pub and plenty of other eating places nearby. Near to Canterbury, Whitstable and Faversham.

Directions: From London M2 then A299 Margate first exit and follow signs to Hernhill. From Dover A2 to M2 roundabout 4th exit A299 then as above.

Bedrooms: 2 double, 1 flexible/family
Open: All year

Site: ❀ P Payment: € Leisure: ♪ ▶ ∪ Property: 🖥 Children: 🛏 🍴 Catering: 🍽 Room: 🍵 ♨

MAIDSTONE, Kent   Map ref 3B3
SatNav ME17 1RQ B

Ash Cottage
Penfold Hill, Leeds Village, Nr Maidstone, Kent ME17 1RQ T: (01622) 863142
E: rayne@ashcottagekent.co.uk
W: www.ashcottagekent.co.uk

B&B PER ROOM PER NIGHT
S: £62.00 - £75.00
D: £82.00 - £98.00

SPECIAL PROMOTIONS
Seasonal special offers available, please see website.

Hot tea, fresh cake, a good nights sleep, hearty breakfast, candlelight and home made jam. Welcome to Ash Cottage, a Channel 4 Four in a Bed winner for 2014, adjacent to Leeds Castle. Enjoy a relaxed breakfast in front of the inglenook, explore all Kent has to offer, recharge your batteries in our cottage garden or snug, stroll to a country pub. Sleep in goose feather and duck down in crisp cotton sheets and enjoy.

Directions: At M20 Junction 8 follow sign for Leeds Castle. Pass castle entrance, Ash Cottage on right after bridge and 30 mph sign before bend.

Bedrooms: 2 king en suite, 1 twin with private bathroom
Open: All year

Site: ❀ P Leisure: ▶ Property: 🖥 Children: 🛏10 Catering: 🍽 Room: 🍵 ♨ 📷 📺

MAIDSTONE, Kent Map ref 3B3 — SatNav ME14 2BD B

The Limes
118 Boxley Road, Maidstone ME14 2BD T: (01622) 750629 / 07889 594700
E: info@thelimesmaidstone.co.uk
W: www.thelimesmaidstone.co.uk £ BOOK ONLINE

B&B PER ROOM PER NIGHT
S: £50.00
D: £90.00

Large Georgian house, 2 star guest accommodation. Close to town centre, motorways, railway stations and shopping centres. Good location for walkers and cyclists. Off-road parking. Silver award for breakfast and a 5 star hygiene rating. Directions: From M2 Junction 3 take A229 to Maidstone. From M20 Junction 6 A229 Signposted Penenden Heath. Turn right at roundabout for town centre. Bedrooms: 3 single, 1 twin. Open: All year except Christmas and New Year.

Site: ✿ P Leisure: ♪ ▶ ☋ Property: ☷ ☕ Children: ⚤12 Catering: ⛾ Room: ☏ ✦ ☕ 📺

MAIDSTONE, Kent Map ref 3B3 — SatNav ME14 1BH H

The Townhouse Hotel
74 King Street, Maidstone, Kent ME14 1BH T: (01622) 663266 E: reservations@tthh.co.uk
W: www.tthh.co.uk £ BOOK ONLINE

Located in the heart of Maidstone, the hotel was built as a vicarage in 1802, retaining may original features. On site restaurant and bar. All rooms en suite. Wireless internet connection. Please see website for current prices. Bedrooms: All rooms are en suite. Open: All year

Payment: 💷 Property: ☷ Children: ⚤ ☷ ♣ Catering: ⓧ ☕ ⛾ Room: ☏ ✦ ☕ 📺

RAMSGATE, Kent Map ref 3C3 — SatNav CT11 8DT H

Comfort Inn Ramsgate
Victoria Parade, Ramsgate, Kent CT11 8DT T: (01843) 592345 F: 01843 580157
E: reservations@comfortinnramsgate.co.uk
W: www.comfortinnramsgate.co.uk £ BOOK ONLINE

B&B PER ROOM PER NIGHT
S: £35.00 - £50.00
D: £40.00 - £120.00

SPECIAL PROMOTIONS
Promotional rate available mid week and weekends, ring 01843 592345 for details.

Victorian Grade 2 Listed building with modern facilities situated on the cliff top with panoramic views of English Channel. Free Wi-Fi, well stocked bar selling local ale, restaurant offering wide variety of dishes, Beauty Salon. Sea view rooms, some with enclosed balcony, Garden. Free parking. Live Entertainment fortnightly.

Directions: From M2 take the A299 then A253 to Ramsgate. Follow signs for East Cliff. From Victoria Road turn left, hotel is on the left.
Bedrooms: 7 single, 14 double, 9 twin, 7 family, 7 suite
Open: All year

Site: ✿ Payment: 💷 € Leisure: ♿ ♪ ☋ Property: ⊛ ☕ ☷ ☕ ◑ Children: ⚤ ☷ ♣ Catering: ☕ ⛾ Room: ☏ ✦ ☕ ☕ 📺 ♨ 🛏

ROCHESTER, Kent   Map ref 3B4
SatNav ME1 1TN B

Medway Little Townhouse

14 Love Lane, Rochester, Kent ME1 1TN T: (01634) 408034 / 07752 457286
E: medwaylittletownhouse@hotmail.co.uk
W: www.medwaylittletownhouse.co.uk

B&B PER ROOM PER NIGHT
S: £45.00 - £55.00
D: £65.00 - £85.00
EVENING MEAL PER PERSON
£12.50 - £15.00

Medway Little Townhouse is situated in a quiet lane in the centre of Rochester tucked away just behind the Castle and Cathedral. Enjoy a sublime morning view of the Rochester Cruising Club's Yacht moorings on the river Medway, whilst eating a Full English or Continental Breakfast served on our conservatory enclosed balcony. 10 min walk from train station. Directions: Please see website. Bedrooms: Individually themed with period furniture and art, spectacular views, 2 rooms ensuite, 1 with adjacent bathroom. Open: All year

Site: P Property: ♒ ⬛ Ⓑ Children: ⛎ Catering: (✗ ☕ Room: ☇ ⬥ ⓐ 📺

ROYAL TUNBRIDGE WELLS, Kent   Map ref 2D2
SatNav TN4 9SS B

Badgers End Bed & Breakfast

47 Thirlmere Road, Royal Tunbridge Wells, Kent TN4 9SS T: (01892) 533176

B&B PER ROOM PER NIGHT
S: £35.00
D: £60.00

Modern house in quiet cul-de-sac with large garden backing onto woodland. Close to A26. Full English breakfast. Freeview TV plus broadband. Tea and coffee making facilities. Non smoking establishment throughout. Directions: 1.5 miles from Tunbridge Wells station. 1 mile from shopping centre. Varying directions, given upon request. Bedrooms: 1 single, 1 double Open: All year except Christmas

Leisure: ▶ Property: ⬛ Catering: 🍴 Room: ☇ ⬥ ⓐ 📺

SHORNE, Kent *Map ref 3B3*

HOTEL

B&B PER ROOM PER NIGHT
S: £59.50 - £69.50
D: £69.50 - £79.50

The Inn on the Lake Hotel
Watling Street, Shorne, Gravesend DA12 3HB **T:** (01474) 823333 **F:** 01474 823175
E: reservations@innonlake.co.uk
W: www.innonlake.co.uk **£ BOOK ONLINE**

Set in 12 acres of woodland, the Inn on the Lake offers a friendly and comfortable stay in a modern, family run establishment. We have 80 bedrooms, many of them with direct access to the 2 beautiful lakes, offering en suite bathrooms, television, telephone, tea & coffee making facilities and hairdryer.

Directions: The hotel is situated on the A2 midway between Rochester and Dartford, just past Gravesend.

Bedrooms: 35 dbl, 35 twin, 8 family
Open: All year

Site: ❀ **Payment:** 🖃 € **Leisure:** ♪ ▶ **Property:** ♟ 🐾 ▦ ☽ **Children:** 🧸 🛏 ⚲ **Catering:** 🍽 🍴
Room: ☎ ♨ 📞 📺 🎧 ⟟

STELLING MINNIS, Kent *Map ref 3B4*

FARMHOUSE *Silver AWARD*

B&B PER ROOM PER NIGHT
S: £45.00 - £100.00
D: £80.00 - £120.00

Great Field Farm B&B
Misling Lane, Stelling Minnis, Canterbury CT4 6DE **T:** (01227) 709223 **F:** 01227 709223
E: greatfieldfarm@aol.com
W: www.great-field-farm.co.uk

Powered by solar, wind and ground source energy, we offer 3 spacious barn conversions with 2 en suite bedrooms each, sleeping 4-6, open plan kitchens/sitting rooms. Also Cottage suite, sleeps 2 plus sofa-bed. Beautiful views, hearty breakfasts with home grown produce. Free wi-fi. 10 minutes to Canterbury and Eurotunnel. 15 minutes to Folkestone and Ashford.

Directions: From M20 exit J11 onto B2068 to Canterbury. Look out for brown B & B signs after about 6 miles.

Bedrooms: 3 double, 4 twin, all en suite
Open: All year

Site: ❀ **P Payment:** 🖃 € **Leisure:** ⚲ ♪ ▶ ♻ **Property:** ▦ **Children:** 🧸 🛏 ⚲ **Room:** ☎ ♨ 📺 ⟟

ABINGDON, Oxfordshire   Map ref 2C1   SatNav OX14 3BT B

★★★
INN

B&B PER ROOM PER NIGHT
S: £60.00
D: £79.00
EVENING MEAL PER PERSON
£6.95 - £16.00

The Railway Inn

Station Road, Culham, Culham Station Nr Abingdon, Oxon OX14 3BT **T:** (01235) 528046
E: info@railwayinnculham.co.uk
W: www.railwayinnculham.co.uk

Bed and breakfast. Evening meals range from home made pies to steaks. Free house. Cask ales. Free parking. Friendly staff. No Sunday evening meals. No dogs policy. **Directions:** A415 2 miles East of Abingdon. Adjacent to main rail, London Paddington to Oxford. Close to A34, M40 and M4. 1 mile from Thames Path. **Bedrooms:** 4 double, 3 twin, 2 family and 1 Double de Luxe. **Open:** All year except Christmas.

Site: ✿ P Payment: 💳 Leisure: ♪ ▶ Property: 🚪 Children: 🛏 ⚡ Catering: 🍷 🍽 Room: 💧 ⚙ 📺

ABINGDON-ON-THAMES, Oxfordshire   Map ref 2C1   SatNav OX14 2BE B

VisitEngland
★★★★
GUEST HOUSE

VisitEngland
Gold
AWARD

B&B PER ROOM PER NIGHT
S: £60.00 - £85.00
D: £100.00 - £110.00

Abbey Guest House

136 Oxford Road, Abingdon-on-Thames, Oxford OX14 2AG
T: (01235) 537020 / 07976 627252 **E:** info@abbeyguest.uk
W: www.abbeyguest.uk **£ BOOK ONLINE**

We are a quiet, 'Home from Home', non smoking, multi-award winning, highly accessible B&B, in the historic town of Abingdon-on-Thames. Guests enjoy private parking, excellent bus services and local amenities, Fair Trade items + Free Wi-Fi. **Directions:** Oxford Road is the A4183. Detailed walking & driving directions, and information if travelling by bus, train or plane is available on the website. **Bedrooms:** Lift installed-ensures 7 en-suite rooms accessible **Open:** All Year - Add. Chge for Xmas & New Year

Site: ✿ P Payment: 💳 Property: 🚪 ♨ Children: 🛏 🚪
⚡ Catering: 🍽 Room: ⚙ 💧 📺 📀 ♪

BICESTER, Oxfordshire   Map ref 2C1   SatNav OX26 1TE H

VisitEngland
★★★★
HOTEL

B&B PER ROOM PER NIGHT
S: £85.00 - £170.00
D: £95.00 - £180.00

Bicester Hotel Golf and Spa

Bicester Hotel Golf and Spa, Green Lane, Chesterton, Bicester, Oxfordshire OX26 1TE
T: (01869) 241204 **E:** carol.barford@bicesterhgs.com
W: www.bicesterhotelgolfandspa.com **£ BOOK ONLINE**

A unique, independently run 52 bedroomed hotel with extensive leisure and spa facilities and an 18 hole golf course, set in 134 acres. Close to Bicester Village and other local attractions. **Directions:** Just minutes from J9 of M40 motorway. Direct rail links into London and Birmingham from Bicester North. **Bedrooms:** 19 Standard Double, 13 Standard Twin, 14 Superior Double, 4 Feature Rooms, 2 suite. **Open:** All year except Christmas day

Site: ✿ P Payment: 💳 Leisure: ♿ ♪ ▶ ∪ ✿ ♨ 🏊 ♨ ✎ Property: ⊛ 🍷 🖥 ◐ Children: 🛏 🚪 ⚡
Catering: (✗ 🍷 🍽 Room: ⚙ 💧 ☎ ⚙ 📺

Sign up for our newsletter

Visit our website to sign up for our e-newsletter and receive regular information on events, articles, exclusive competitions and new publications.
www.visitor-guides.co.uk

The Baskerville

Station Road, Lower Shiplake, Henley-on-Thames RG9 3NY T: (01189) 403332
E: enquiries@thebaskerville.com
W: www.thebaskerville.com £ BOOK ONLINE

B&B PER ROOM PER NIGHT
S: £100.00 - £200.00
D: £110.00 - £200.00
EVENING MEAL PER PERSON
£27.00 - £36.00

SPECIAL PROMOTIONS
Daily changing
specials.

Quality, award winning, traditional family run village inn situated on the Thames Path, a short walk from Shiplake station and just minutes from Henley-on-Thames. Outstanding food with menus that evolve with the seasons using fresh local produce. Excellent wine list, cosy, comfortable bar with a good choice of cask-conditioned ales. 50 cover restaurant and a garden with seating for 100.

Directions: From Henley-on-Thames, take Reading road for 2 miles, turn left down Station Road for 0.5 mile. Baskerville is on right after cross roads before station.

Bedrooms: 2 double, 1 twin, 1 family.
Open: All year

Site: ❋ P Payment: 💳 Leisure: ▶ Property: ♞ 🐾 ⚒ Ø Children: 🍼 ⌨ 🏃 Catering: (✕ ♟ ⅋
Room: 🌾 👄 ⌨ TV DVD

Hillborough House

The Green, Shipton Road, Milton-under-Wychwood, Near Burford OX7 6JH
T: (01993) 832352 F: 01993 832352 E: hillboroughhouse@btinternet.com
W: www.hillboroughhouse.co.uk £ BOOK ONLINE

B&B PER ROOM PER NIGHT
S: £60.00 - £80.00
D: £80.00 - £90.00

A Victorian village house with spacious en suite rooms overlooking the green with views to distant hills. You will be assured of a warm welcome and a great breakfast. **Directions:** Please contact us for directions. **Bedrooms:** 1 double, 1 twin, 1 family, all en suite
Open: All year except Christmas

Site: P Leisure: 🚴 ♪ ▶ ⛳ Property: 🐾 ⚒ 🔲 Children: 🍼 ⌨ 🏃 Catering: ⅋ Room: 🌾 👄 ⌨ TV DVD ♨

Abodes B&B

6 Blackman Close, Kennington, Oxford OX1 5NU T: (01865) 435229
E: info@abodesuk.com
W: www.abodesofoxford.com/bed-and-breakfast-oxford-6603 £ BOOK ONLINE

B&B PER ROOM PER NIGHT
S: £50.00 - £55.00
D: £75.00 - £85.00

We are a small but welcoming B&B. Luxury 4* double room & modern en-suite shower room & toiletries. Relaxing location to visit Oxford. Luxury linen & towels.TV Fridge. Continental breakfast. WIFI. Ample Free parking. Friendly Pet dog. **Directions:** From A34 in either direction take the Hinksey Interchange exit. Follow signs to Oxford then to Kennington. At roundabout turn up Upper Road. 4th left **Bedrooms:** Luxury Double En-suite **Open:** All year apart from Christmas & New Year

Site: P Payment: 💳 Leisure: ▶ Property: ⚒ Room: 🌾 👄 TV DVD

Arden Lodge

34 Sunderland Avenue, Oxford OX2 8DX **T:** (01865) 552076 **F:** 01865 512265
E: ardenlodge34@googlemail.com
W: www.ardenlodgeoxford.co.uk

B&B PER ROOM PER NIGHT
S: £40.00 - £50.00
D: £60.00 - £70.00

Arden Lodge is a modern, detached house set in a tree-lined avenue, in one of Oxford's most select areas. It offers 3 attractively furnished bedrooms, with private facilities, colour TV and beverage tray. An excellent base for touring: within easy reach of the Cotswolds, London, Stratford and Warwick. The position is convenient for Oxford City Centre, parks, river, meadows, golf course and country inns, including the world famous Trout Inn as featured in 'Inspector Morse'. Ample parking is available, and there is an excellent bus service, with Oxford City Centre about 10 minutes away.

Directions: Please contact us for directions.

Bedrooms: 1 single, 1 double, 1 twin
Open: All year except Christmas

Site: **P** Leisure: ▶ Property: ▦ Children: ⛏ 🛉 Catering: 🍴 Room: 🖲 🛠 📞 📺

The Buttery

11 Broad Street, Oxford OX1 3AP **T:** (01865) 811950 **F:** 01865 811951
E: enquiries@thebutteryhotel.co.uk
W: www.thebutteryhotel.co.uk **£ BOOK ONLINE**

B&B PER ROOM PER NIGHT
S: £75.00 - £139.00
D: £99.00 - £159.00

Set on Broad Street, surrounded by historic Oxford colleges and museums, The Buttery welcomes you to explore the wonders of Oxford from its central location. Spacious well-furnished en suite rooms. **Directions:** Please contact us for directions.
Bedrooms: 1 single, 9 double, 3 twin, 3 family. **Open:** All year

Payment: 💷 Property: ▦ ◑ Children: ⛏ 🛏 🛉 Catering: 🍴 Room: 🖲 🛠 📞 📱 📺

Cotswold House

363 Banbury Road, Oxford OX2 7PL **T:** (01865) 310558 **E:** d.r.walker@talk21.com
W: www.cotswoldhouse.co.uk **£ BOOK ONLINE**

B&B PER ROOM PER NIGHT
S: £69.00 - £85.00
D: £110.00 - £150.00

A well-situated and elegant property, offering excellent accommodation and service. Cotswold House is in a most desirable part of Oxford. Free parking and Wi-Fi. **Directions:** Exit Oxford ring road on North side, following sign to Summertown. We are half a mile on right as you head towards city centre. **Bedrooms:** 2 single, 2 double, 1 twin, 2 family, 1 deluxe suite **Open:** All year

Site: **P** Payment: 💷 Property: ▦ Children: ⛏³ Room: 🖲 🛠 📺 ♨

SatNav OX1 4PL B

Newton House Guest House B&B Oxford

82-84 Abingdon Road, Oxford OX1 4PL **T:** (01865) 240561 **F:** 01865 244647
E: stay@newtonhouseoxford.co.uk
W: www.newtonhouseoxford.co.uk **£ BOOK ONLINE**

B&B PER ROOM PER NIGHT
S: £66.00 - £99.00
D: £74.00 - £110.00

SPECIAL PROMOTIONS
Ask about special offers.

Close to Oxford's city centre, on foot, bus, coach, train or car. A perfect opportunity to visit Oxford's university central city attractions, research facilities, museums, hospitals. Family-run with a personal touch, free Wi-Fi, car park, English traditional breakfast, vegetarian and continental. Special diets catered for.

Directions: Situated on A4144 (OX1 4PL) Postal code 1/2 mile (800 mtrs) from the city centre 10 to 15 min walk see us on google maps.

Bedrooms: 8 double, 4 twin, 2 family, all en suite
Open: All year

Site: P Payment: £ € **Leisure:** 🚴 🏊 **Property:** 📺 🌙 **Children:** 👶 🛏 🏃 **Catering:** 🍴
Room: 🍵 🛁 📞 📠 📺

SatNav OX2 6EH B

Park House

7 St Bernards Road, Oxford OX2 6EH **T:** (01865) 310824 **E:** krynpark@hotmail.com

B&B PER ROOM PER NIGHT
S: £40.00 - £45.00
D: £60.00 - £70.00

Traditional Victorian terraced house in north Oxford, ten minutes walk from city centre and within easy reach of all amenities. Friendly and relaxed atmosphere. Single night bookings on Fridays and Saturdays carry £10 surcharge. **Directions:** Please contact us for directions. **Bedrooms:** 1 single, 2 double **Open:** All year except Christmas

Site: ⚘ **P Payment:** € **Leisure:** 🚴 **Property:** 🐕 📺 📶 **Children:** 👶 🛏 🏃 **Catering:** 🍴 **Room:** 🍵 🛁 📞 📺

For **key to symbols** see page 7

WOODSTOCK, Oxfordshire   Map ref 2C1   SatNav OX20 1HT B

The Duke of Marlborough

A44 Woodleys, Woodstock, Oxford OX20 1HT T: (01993) 811460 F: 01993 810165
E: sales@dukeofmarlborough.co.uk
W: www.dukeofmarlborough.co.uk

Family-run and friendly and well known locally for its good food. Situated close to Woodstock. Nearby Blenheim Palace and Oxford. Ideally situated for exploring the surrounding countryside.
Directions: We are positioned on the A44 Oxford to Stratford road just 2 mile north of Woodstock at the junction with the B4437.
Bedrooms: 4 double, 2 twin, 5 family, 2 suites. **Open:** All year

B&B PER ROOM PER NIGHT
S: £75.00 - £110.00
D: £90.00 - £140.00
EVENING MEAL PER PERSON
£9.95 - £30.00

Site: ✿ P Leisure: ♪ ▶ ♨ Property: 🖥 Children: 🏛 Catering: ❌ 🍴 🍽 Room: 🍵 🐾 📺

EAST MOLESEY, Surrey   Map ref 2D2   SatNav KT8 9DD

Kings Arms

2 Lion Gate, Hampton Court Road, East Molesey, Surrey KT8 9DD T: (02089) 771729
E: kingsarms.hamptoncourt@hall-woodhouse.co.uk
W: www.kingsarmshamptoncourt.co.uk **£ BOOK ONLINE**

B&B PER ROOM PER NIGHT
S: £70.00 - £160.00
D: £100.00 - £200.00
EVENING MEAL PER PERSON
£15.00 - £25.00

The Kings Arms is a 300 year old inn located on the Northern edge of Hampton Court Palace just outside the Lions Gate. The building is steeped in history and in parts of it date back to 1658. Originally built as a 'house of disrepute' for the soldiers garrisoned at Hampton Court Palace, today the inn offers guests characterful and unique rooms perfect for a relaxing stay.

Directions: Use of our four parking space is free to our Guests. Please ask at reception for a permit to display. On-street parking is limited to four hours. There's also long stay parking in Bushy Park.

Bedrooms: Our historic inn and rooms are steeped in charm and character. Each of our bedrooms show off genuine period features and home comforts.
Open: We are open year-round

Payment: 💷 Property: 🖥 ⌀ Children: 🐾 🧍 Catering: ❌ 🍴 Room: 🍵 🐾 📺

Need more information?

Visit our websites for detailed information, up-to-date availability and to book your accommodation online. Includes over 20,000 places to stay, all of them star rated.
www.visitor-guides.co.uk

BEXHILL-ON-SEA, Sussex   Map ref 3B4   SatNav TN40 2HH B

B&B PER ROOM PER NIGHT
S: £40.00 - £60.00
D: £70.00 - £90.00

Eve's Bed & Breakfast

20 Hastings Road, Bexhill-on-Sea, East Sussex TN40 2HH **T:** (01424) 733268
E: evesbandb@gmail.com
W: www.evesbandb.co.uk

Bexhill's Old Town is a gentle stroll from our friendly, family run Victorian 4 star B&B. We have 5 en suite bedrooms (2 double, 3 family, single occupancy available) that are spacious but cosy for you to relax in. Special offers available. **Bedrooms:** Ground floor room with wet room available. **Open:** All year

Site: ✿ P Payment: 💷 Property: 🐾 🚭 Children: 🚼 🛏 ☆ Catering: 🍴 Room: 📶 ☕ 📺 📀 ♿

BOGNOR REGIS, Sussex   Map ref 2C3   SatNav PO22 7AH B

B&B PER ROOM PER NIGHT
S: £60.00 - £90.00
D: £90.00 - £120.00

White Horses Bed & Breakfast

Clyde Road, Felpham, Bognor Regis, West Sussex PO22 7AH **T:** (01243) 824320
E: whitehorsesbandb@btinternet.com
W: www.whitehorsesfelpham.co.uk

White Horses is located in a quiet cul-de-sac overlooking the sea and Felpham beach. A modernised flint and brick house offering quality accommodation. A 3 mile promenade adjacent affords easy sea-side walking. Pubs and food outlets nearby. **Directions:** Please see website. **Bedrooms:** En suite, flat screen TV, hairdryer & tea/coffee tray. **Open:** All year

  Site: ✿ P Payment: 💷 € Leisure: ▶ Property: 🚭 Children: 🚼 🛏 ☆ Room: 📶 ☕ 📺

BOGNOR REGIS, Sussex   Map ref 2C3   SatNav PO22 9AG B

B&B PER ROOM PER NIGHT
S: £45.00
D: £70.00

Willow Rise

131 North Bersted Street, Bognor Regis, West Sussex PO22 9AG
T: (01243) 829544 / 07713 427224 **E:** gillboon@aol.com
W: www.willowrise.co.uk

Willow rise is a comfortable family B&B built in the 1930's with panoramic views of the south downs and Goodwood. Situated in a conservation area on the outskirts of the town, with execellent access to all amenities. **Directions:** Follow A259 from Chichester to Bognor Regis, left at Royal Oak Pub into North Bersted Street. Continue, B&B on left hand side. **Bedrooms:** En suite twin room £70, single room with ensuite, double room with private bathroom. **Open:** All Year excluding Christmas and New Year.

Site: ✿ P Payment: 💷 Leisure: 🎵 ▶ Property: 🐾 🚭 Children: 🚼 🛏 ☆ Catering: 🍴 Room: ☕ 📺 📀

BOGNOR REGIS, Sussex   Map ref 2C3   SatNav PO22 7EG B

B&B PER ROOM PER NIGHT
S: £60.00 - £75.00
D: £70.00 - £95.00

Willow Tree Cottage B&B

35 Bereweeke Road, Felpham, Bognor Regis, West Sussex PO22 7EG **T:** (01243) 828000
E: bookings@willowtreecottage.org.uk
W: www.willowtreecottage.org.uk

Minutes from the sea and the busy little village of Felpham, you'll find a warm welcome, a peaceful stay and sumptuous breakfasts. The homely accommodation ensures your stay is undisturbed by other guests.
Directions: From the centre of Felpham Village head towards the Fox Public House & go down Blakes Road, take the first turn left to the end of Bereweeke Rd.
Bedrooms: 1 king-sized double room and 1 twin bedded room.
Open: All year except Christmas and New Year.

Site: ✿ P Property: 🚭 Catering: 🍴 Room: 📶 ☕ 📺

BRIGHTON, Sussex   Map ref 2D3

SatNav BN2 9JA **B**

VisitEngland
★★★
HOSTEL

BED ONLY PER NIGHT
£15.00 - £80.00

Kipps Brighton

76 Grand Parade, Brighton BN2 9JA **T:** (01273) 604182 **E:** kippshostelbrighton@gmail.com
W: www.kipps-brighton.com **£ BOOK ONLINE**

Award winning hostel situated in the heart of Brighton.
We offer private rooms as well as dormitory rooms.
Excellent facilities, including a self catering kitchen, lounge &
outside patio. Views overlooking the historic Royal Pavillion.
Directions: We are situated in the centre of Brighton. Visit our
website to print off a map. **Bedrooms:** 1 single, 6 doubles, 4 twins,
& dormitory rooms **Open:** All year

Site: ✿ **Payment:** 💷 € **Leisure:** 🏊 ♪ ▶ ひ **Property:** 📺 🅰 📺 🔲 **Catering:** 🍴 🍷 **Room:** 🛋
Bedroom: ✋

CHICHESTER, Sussex   Map ref 2C3

SatNav PO19 7HW **B**

VisitEngland
★★★
BED & BREAKFAST

B&B PER ROOM PER NIGHT
S: £45.00
D: £65.00

The Cottage

22B Westhampnett Road, Chichester, W. Sussex PO19 7HW **T:** (01243) 774979
E: thecottagechichester@gmail.com
W: www.chichester-bedandbreakfast.co.uk

Just off the A27. A short walk from the town centre with its
Cathedral, cinema, bowling, shops, rail & bus stations, restaurants &
pubs. Goodwoods Festival of Speed & Revival, Airfield, golfing &
horse racing. The Tangmere Aviation Museum.
Directions: Westhampnett Road is located on the eastern side of
Chichester and is close to Portfield Retail park and Goodwood just
off the A27. **Bedrooms:** 1 double, 1 twin with complimentary tea
tray, TV. **Open:** All year except Christmas and New Year.

Site: P **Property:** 📺 **Children:** 👶 **Catering:** 🍴 **Room:** ✋ 📺 🛋

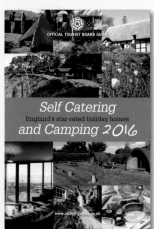

George Bell House

4 Canon Lane, Chichester, West Sussex PO19 1PX **T:** (01243) 813586
E: bookings@chichestercathedral.org.uk
W: www.chichestercathedral.org.uk / www.cathedralenterprises.co.uk

B&B PER ROOM PER NIGHT
S: £79.00
D: £117.00 - £138.00

SPECIAL PROMOTIONS
Seasonal Discounts -
30% discount on
bedroom rates from
2nd January - 10th
April 2016 (not
including breakfast)

George Bell House is a beautifully restored eight bedroom house situated in the historic precincts of Chichester Cathedral.

All bedrooms are en-suite, with tea & coffee facilities and offer stunning views of the Cathedral or gardens. Breakfast is available in the dining room of the house which looks out into the private garden.

Free Wi-Fi & parking available. Advance booking essential.

Directions: Turn though the archway into Canon Lane off South Street and George Bell House is the last house on the left before the next archway

Bedrooms: 4 x large double / twins, 3 x standard doubles & 1 x single room with disabled access
Open: All Year excluding Christmas and New Year

Site: ❀ P Payment: 💷 Property: 🍴 🖥 Children: 🚼 🍼 🎠 Catering: 🍽 Room: 📶 ♨ 📺 🍳

Millstream Hotel

Bosham Lane, Bosham Nr Chichester, West Sussex PO18 8HL **T:** (01243) 573234
F: 01243 573459 **E:** info@millstreamhotel.com
W: www.millstreamhotel.com **£ BOOK ONLINE**

B&B PER ROOM PER NIGHT
S: £79.00 - £149.00
D: £145.00 - £235.00

HB PER PERSON PER NIGHT
£92.00 - £125.00

SPECIAL PROMOTIONS
Please contact for à la
carte menu prices.

This charming English country hotel is situated in picturesque Bosham, just 4 miles west of Chichester. The bright and airy en suite bedrooms are all individually decorated. The Millstream Restaurant serves modern British cuisine and has 2 AA Rosettes. Alternatively, Marwick's Brasserie provides a contemporary and relaxed eating environment. Guests can enjoy afternoon tea in the gardens or lounge.

Bedrooms: Bedrooms are individually decorated, en suite, with fresh milk and water in the fridge, tea & coffee making facilities and dressing gowns
Open: All Year

Site: ❀ P Payment: 💷 Property: 🍴 🖥 🎯 ◐ Catering: 🍴 🍷 Room: 📶 ♨ ☎ 📺 🍳 🖥

EASTBOURNE, Sussex Map ref 3B4 SatNav BN21 4DH H

HOTEL ★★★★ **Silver AWARD**

B&B PER ROOM PER NIGHT
S: £65.00 - £117.00
D: £106.00 - £185.00
EVENING MEAL PER PERSON
£23.00 - £25.00

Cavendish Hotel

Grand Parade, Eastbourne, East Sussex BN21 4DH **T:** (01323) 410222 **F:** 01323 410941
E: reception756@britanniahotels.com
W: www.britanniahotels.com

A large 4* hotel on the English South Coast, stylish and unpretentious, elegant but relaxed. En suite bedrooms and fine dining complemented by the welcoming friendly and professional service. **Directions:** Located in Eastbourne on the South Coast, regular trains from London Victoria, Gatwick Airport is 43 miles away and good road links from M25. **Bedrooms:** 8 single, 42 dble, 64 twin, 5 suite **Open:** All year

Site: P Payment: Leisure: Property: Children: Catering: Room:

HENFIELD, Sussex Map ref 2D3 SatNav BN5 9RQ B

BED & BREAKFAST ★★★★

B&B PER ROOM PER NIGHT
S: £42.50 - £50.00
D: £75.00 - £90.00

No1 The Laurels B&B

1 The Laurels, Martyn Close, Henfield, West Sussex BN5 9RQ **T:** (01273) 493518
E: bookings@no1thelaurels.co.uk
W: www.no1thelaurels.co.uk **£ BOOK ONLINE**

A detached house faced with traditional knapped Sussex flint stones. Comfortable rooms, a warm welcome, easy access to Brighton. Many places of interest nearby. **Directions:** Please refer to website. **Bedrooms:** 1 single, 2 double and 1 twin **Open:** All year

Site: P Payment: Property: Children: Catering: Room:

RINGMER, Sussex   Map ref 2D3
SatNav BN8 5RU **B**

★★★★ GUEST ACCOMMODATION

Silver AWARD

Bryn Clai
Uckfield Road (A26), Ringmer, Lewes BN8 5RU   **T:** (01273) 814042
E: daphne@brynclai.co.uk
W: www.brynclai.co.uk   **£ BOOK ONLINE**

B&B PER ROOM PER NIGHT
S: £65.00 - £80.00
D: £80.00 - £90.00

Set in seven acres with beautiful garden. Parking. Comfortable interior. Large bedrooms (ground-floor rooms), views over farmland. Walking distance country pub with excellent food. Glyndebourne, South Downs and Brighton nearby.
Directions: From A26, 2 miles north of Lewes, 5 miles south of Uckfield. **Bedrooms:** 1 double, 1 twin, 2 family **Open:** All year

Site: ❀ P **Payment:** 🔲 **Leisure:** ♪ ▶ **Property:** 🛏 **Children:** ⛹ 🏠 ⚹ **Catering:** 🍽 **Room:** 🔲 🛁 📺 🔲 🔲

RYE, Sussex   Map ref 3B4
SatNav TN31 7EL **H**

★★★ HOTEL

The River Haven Hotel
Quayside, Winchelsea Road, Rye TN31 7EL   **T:** (01797) 227982   **F:** 01797 227983
E: info@riverhaven.co.uk
W: www.riverhaven.co.uk   **£ BOOK ONLINE**

B&B PER ROOM PER NIGHT
S: £60.00 - £85.00
D: £80.00 - £110.00
HB PER PERSON PER NIGHT
£58.50 - £73.50

Family-run hotel with restaurant. English breakfast, flat screen Freeview TVs, en suite bathrooms. Standard, superior & garden rooms with river views. Special breaks. Disability-friendly. Large car park free parking for guests. **Directions:** From Channel Ports & London M20 to exit 10 to Brenzett. Take A259 to Rye and follow ring road. Hotel is adjacent to the Quay. **Bedrooms:** 13 dble, 3 twin, 6 family. **Open:** All year except Christmas.

Site: ❀ **Payment:** 🔲 **Leisure:** ♿ ♪ ▶ **Property:** 🍴 🖥 ◑ **Children:** ⛹ 🏠 ⚹ **Catering:** 🍷 🍽 **Room:** 🔲 🛁 📞 📺 🔲

RYE, Sussex   Map ref 3B4
SatNav TN31 7LD **H**

★★★ TOWN HOUSE HOTEL

Gold AWARD

Rye Lodge Hotel
Hilders Cliff, Rye, East Sussex TN31 7LD   **T:** (01797) 223838   **F:** 01797 223585
E: info@ryelodge.co.uk
W: www.ryelodge.co.uk   **£ BOOK ONLINE**

B&B PER ROOM PER NIGHT
D: £130.00 - £250.00

SPECIAL PROMOTIONS
Champagne Celebreak! One night stay in the Champagne room with fruit, flowers, chocolates and Champagne in your room and enjoy dinner at the famous Mermaid Inn. The cost is £295.00.

Staying at Rye Lodge is always an enjoyable experience at any time of the year. The surroundings are elegant, the atmosphere relaxed - and the service second to none! Luxurious rooms and suites furnished to the highest standards with all the little extras that make such a difference. Room Service. Champagne Bar and Terrace, Leisure Centre with swimming pool and Sauna. Private car park.

Directions: http://ryelodge.co.uk/rye-lodge-maps/

Bedrooms: All rooms en suite with shower or bath
Open: All year

Site: P **Payment:** 🔲 **Leisure:** 🏊 ❄ **Property:** 🐾 🖥 **Children:** ⛹ 🏠 ⚹ **Catering:** 🍷 **Room:** 🔲 🛁 📞 📺 🔲

Don't Miss...

Buckingham Palace
London, SW1A 1AA
(020) 7766 7300
www.royalcollection.org.uk
Buckingham Palace is the office and London residence of Her Majesty
The Queen. It is one of the few working royal palaces remaining in the
world today. The State Rooms are used extensively by The Queen and
Members of the Royal Family and during August and September, when
The Queen makes her annual visit to Scotland, the Palace's nineteen
state rooms are open to visitors.

Houses of Parliament
Westminster, London SW1A 0AA
020 7219 4565
www.parliament.uk/visiting
Tours offer a unique combination of one thousand years of history,
modern day politics, and stunning art and architecture. Visit the Queen's
Robing Room, the Royal Gallery and the Commons Chamber, scene
of many lively debates. Stylish afternoon tea in the Terrace Pavillion
overlooking the River Thames can be added to many tours.

Madame Tussauds
Marylebone Road, London, NW1 5LR
(0871) 894 3000
www.madametussauds.com/London/
Experience the legendary history, glitz and glamour of Madame
Tussauds London. Visit the 14 exciting, interactive zones and come face-
to-face with some of the world's most famous stars. From Shakespeare to
David Beckham you'll meet leading figures from sport, showbiz, politics
and even royalty. Strike a pose with Usain Bolt, get up close and personal
with One Direction, receive a royal audience with Her Majesty the
Queen, or even plant a cheeky kiss on Prince Harry's cheek.

National Gallery
Westminster WC2N 5DN
(020) 7747 2888
www.nationalgallery.org.uk
Founded in 1824, housing one of the greatest collections of Western
European painting in the world, with over 2,300 paintings dating from
the mid-13th century to 1900. Discover inspiring art by world-class artists
including Botticelli, Caravaggio, Leonardo da Vinci, Monet, Raphael,
Rembrandt, Titian, Vermeer and Van Gogh. The Gallery aims to encourage
the widest possible access to the pictures as well as studying and caring
for the collection, which is on show 361 days a year, free of charge.

Natural History Museum
Kensington and Chelsea SW7 5BD
(020) 7942 5000
www.nhm.ac.uk
The world's most prestigious and pre-eminent museum of natural
history, exhibiting a vast range of specimens from various segments of
natural history. Revealing how the jigsaw of life fits together - animal,
vegetable or mineral, the best of our planet's most amazing treasures are
here for you to see - for free. Alongside the collection, a packed calendar
of year round activities, temporary exhibitions and special events as
diverse as David Attenborough's virtual reality Great Barrier Reef dive
and Crime Scene Live, an interactive night at the museum combining
real science and crime fiction, offers something for everyone.

London

London

Grand landmarks, gorgeous gardens, spectacular shopping, exciting attractions, museums, galleries, theatres, sporting venues and all the buzz and history of the capital - London's treasures are beyond measure. A single trip is never enough and you'll find yourself returning time and again to take in the many unforgettable sights and experiences on offer.

Explore – London

In the Central/West End area the most visited sights are the now public rooms of Buckingham Palace, the National Gallery in Trafalgar Square, Tate Britain on Millbank, Westminster Abbey, Houses of Parliament and Cabinet War Rooms.

Westminster Abbey, nearly a thousand years old, has tombs of many English kings, queens, statesmen and writers. The British Museum in Bloomsbury houses one of the world's largest selections of antiquities, including the Magna Carta, the Elgin Marbles and the first edition of Alice in Wonderland. This entire area can be well viewed from The London Eye on the South Bank.

No visit to London is complete without a spot of shopping. Head for bustling Oxford Street and the stylish shops on Regent Street and Bond Street, check out the trendy boutiques around Carnaby Street, or visit the iconic Liberty store.

For entertainment, enjoy a wide range of theatre, bars, restaurants and culture in Covent Garden and don't forget to take in a musical or an off-beat play and the amazing nightime atmosphere around Leicester Square. Madame Tussauds features all your favourite celebrities and super heroes, or if you fancy an historical fright, visit the London Dungeon near Tower Bridge or explore the streets of old London on a Jack the Ripper tour.

London's parks are its lungs. St James, the oldest, was founded by Henry VIII in 1532. Hyde Park, bordering Kensington, Mayfair and Marylebone, is the largest at 630 acres and one of the greatest city parks in the world. You can enjoy any number of outdoor activities, visit the Serpentine Galleries for contemporary art or Speakers' Corner, the most famous location for free speech in the world. Regents Park, with its zoo and outdoor theatre, lies north of Oxford Circus and was given to the nation by the Prince Regent.

In the North of the capital, trendy Camden is an eclectic mix of intriguing and unique experiences. Locals and visitors alike hunt for vintage treasures in the open air markets at Camden Lock and far-out attire in the alternative shops that line the high street, or spend time celebrity spotting or strolling along Regent's Canal. There's a different kind of food at every turn, from street vendors to swanky sushi restaurants, and Camden is also home to an extraordinary array of bars, live music and arts venues including the Roundhouse.

Heading East, St Pauls Cathedral in the city of London was redesigned by Sir Christopher Wren and the nearby the Tower of London, a medieval fortress dominated by the White Tower and dating from 1097, houses The Crown Jewels, guarded by the famous Beefeaters. Even further East, the Queen Elizabeth Olympic Park is the exciting legacy of the 2012 Olympic Games and is situated at the heart of a new, vibrant East London.

To the South East of the capital, Canary Wharf is one of Londons main financial centres and contains many of Europe's tallest buildings, including the second-tallest in Great Britain, One Canada Square. On the south bank, opposite Docklands, attractions include the National Maritime Museum incorporating the Royal Greenwich Observatory, the Cutty Sark and The O2, one of London's premier entertainment venues.

In November, the Lord Mayors Show will feature a parade of over 6,000 people, military marching bands, acrobats, a procession of decorated floats, a gilded State Coach that the Lord Mayor travels and starts with an RAF flypast. After the procession London's City Guides will be on hand to lead free guided tours of the City's more strange and wonderful corners, and in the evening fireworks will light up the sky over the river.
Visit their website for more information, www.lordmayorsshow.org.

Visit – London

 Attractions with this sign participate in the Visitor Attraction Quality Assurance Scheme.

Apsley House
Westminster W1J 7NT
(020) 7499 5676
www.english-heritage.org.uk
This great 18th century town house pays homage to the Duke's dazzling military career, which culminated in his victory at Waterloo in 1815.

Bank of England Museum
Bartholomew Lane, London EC2R 8AH
(020) 7601 5545
www.bankofengland.co.uk/museum
Housed within the impressive walls of the Bank of England, this fascinating museum takes you through the history of the bank since its foundation in 1694 to its role today as the nation's central bank.

Bateaux London Restaurant Cruisers
Westminster WC2N 6NU
(020) 7695 1800
www.bateauxlondon.com
Bateaux London offers lunch and dinner cruises, combining luxury dining, world-class live entertainment and five-star customer care.

The Boat Race
March, Putney Bridge
www.theboatrace.org
Boat crews from the universities of Oxford and Cambridge battle it out on the Thames.

British Museum
Camden WC1B 3DG
(020) 7323 8299
www.britishmuseum.org.uk
Collections that span over two million years of human history and culture, all under one roof.

Changing the Guard
Buckingham Palace, London SW1A 1AA
www.royalcollection.org.uk
Watch the Changing the Guard ceremony at Buckingham Palace for an impressive display of British pomp and ceremony at 11.30am every day.

Chinese New Year
February, Various venues
www.visitlondon.com
London's Chinese New Year celebrations are the largest outside Asia, with parades, performances and fireworks.

Chiswick House
Chiswick, London W4 2RP
(020) 8995 0508
www.english-heritage.org.uk/visit/places/chiswick-house/
Among the most glorious examples of 18th-century British architecture, the celebrated villa of Lord Burlington with impressive grounds, features Italianate garden with statues, temples, obelisks and urns. The gardens are the birthplace of the English Landscape Movement and have inspired countless gardens.

Churchill Museum and Cabinet War Rooms
Westminster SW1A 2AQ
(020) 7930 6961
www.iwm.org.uk
Learn more about the man who inspired Britain's finest hour at the highly interactive and innovative Churchill Museum, the world's first major museum dedicated to life of the 'greatest Briton'. Step back in time and discover the secret.

City of London Festival
June-July, Various venues
www.visitlondon.com
The City of London Festival is an annual extravaganza of music, dance, art, film, poetry, family and participation events that takes place in the city's Square Mile.

Cutty Sark King
William Walk, London SE10 9HT
www.rmg.co.uk/cutty-sark
Discover what life was like on board the legendary sailing ship Cutty Sark, the world's sole surviving tea clipper, and fastest ship of her time - now an award-winning visitor attraction.

Eltham Palace
Greenwich SE9 5QE
(020) 8294 2548
www.elthampalace.org.uk
A spectacular fusion of 1930s Art Deco villa and magnificent 15th century Great Hall. Surrounded by period gardens.

The Globe Theatre
Bankside, London SE1 9DT
(020) 7902 1400
www.shakespearesglobe.com
Globe Exhibition & Tour and Globe Education seek to further the experience and international understanding of Shakespeare in performance.

Goldsmiths Hall
Foster Lane, London EC2V 6BN
(020) 7606 7010
One of the Twelve Great Livery Companies of the City of London. The Goldsmiths' Company, based at the magnificent Goldsmiths' Hall in the City of London, regularly holds exhibitions and events to promote contemporary jewellers and silversmiths.

Greenwich Heritage Centre
Greenwich SE18 4DX
(020) 8854 2452
www.royalgreenwich.gov.uk
Local history museum with displays of archaeology, natural history and geology. Also temporary exhibitions, schools service, sales point and Saturday club.

Hampton Court Palace
Richmond upon Thames KT8 9AU
(0870) 752 7777
www.hrp.org.uk
This magnificent palace set in delightful gardens was famously one of Henry VIII's favourite palaces.

HMS Belfast
Southwark SE1 2JH
(020) 7940 6300
www.iwm.org.uk
HMS Belfast, launched 1938, served throughout WWII, playing a leading part in the destruction of the German battle cruiser Scharnhorst and in the Normandy Landings.

Hyde Park
London W2 2UH
(0300) 061 2000
www.royalparks.org.uk/parks/hyde-park
Explore one of the greatest city parks in the world, with outdoor sports, a spectacular children's playground, a packed calendar of open air events and a number of fascinating buildings and monuments, such as The Serpentine Bridge, the famous Archiles statue and the Diana Memorial Fountain.

Imperial War Museum
Southwark SE1 6HZ
(020) 7416 5000
www.iwm.org.uk
This award-winning museum tells the story of conflict involving Britain and the Commonwealth since 1914. See thousands of imaginatively displayed exhibits, from art to aircraft, utility clothes to U-boats.

Kensington Palace State Apartments
Kensington and Chelsea W8 4PX
(0844) 482 7777
www.hrp.org.uk
Home to the Royal Ceremonial Dress Collection, which includes some of Queen Elizabeth II's dresses worn throughout her reign, as well as 14 of Diana, Princess of Wales' evening dresses.

Kenwood House
Camden NW3 7JR
(020) 8348 1286
www.english-heritage.org.uk/visit/places/kenwood-house/
Beautiful 18th century villa with fine interiors, and a world class collection of paintings. Also fabulous landscaped gardens and an award-winning restaurant.

London Dungeon
County Hall, Riverside Building SE1 7PB
(020) 7403 7221
www.thedungeons.com/London
Exciting, scary and fun - the London Dungeon has a new home on the Southbank and lots of new scary stories about London's history for you to discover. Steel your nerves for some terrifying new experiences and hrilling new scary rides!

London Eye River Cruise Experience
Lambeth E1 7PB
(0871) 781 3000
www.londoneye.com
See London from a different perspective and enjoy a unique 40 minute circular sightseeing cruise on the river Thames.

London Fashion Weekend
www.londonfashionweekend.co.uk
London's largest and most exclusive designer shopping event. This four-day showcase brings you the ultimate fashion experience.

London Festival of Architecture
June
www.londonfestivalofarchitecture.org
A city-wide celebration of architectural experimentation, thinking and practice. See London's buildings in a new light during the Festival of Architecture.

London Film Festival
October, Various venues
www.bfi.org.uk/lff
A two-week showcase of the world's best new films, the BFI London Film Festival is one of the most anticipated events in London's cultural calendar, screening more than 300 features, documentaries and shorts from almost 50 countries.

London Transport Museum
Westminster WC2E 7BB
(020) 7379 6344
www.ltmuseum.co.uk
The history of transport for everyone, from spectacular vehicles, special exhibitions, actors and guided tours to film shows, gallery talks and children's craft workshops

London Wetland Centre
Richmond upon Thames SW13 9WT
(020) 8409 4400
www.wwt.org.uk
The London Wetland Centre is a unique wildlife visitor attraction just 25 minutes from central London. Run by the Wildfowl and Wetlands Trust (WWT), it is acclaimed as the best urban site in Europe to watch wildlife. Stroll among the lakes, ponds and gardens. The café is perfect for relaxing, and kids will love the play areas.

London Zoo
Regent's Park, London NW1 4RY
(020) 7722 3333
www.zsl.org/zsl-london-zoo
Come face to face with some of the hairiest, scariest, tallest and smallest animals on the planet - right in the heart of the capital.

Lord's Tour
Westminster NW8 8QN
(020) 7616 8595
www.lords.org/history/tours-of-lords/
Guided tour of Lord's Cricket Ground including the Long Room, MCC Museum, Real Tennis Court, Mound Stand and Indoor School.

Museums At Night
May, Various venues
www.visitlondon.com
Explore arts and heritage after dark at museums across London. Packed with special events, from treasure trails to pyjama parties, Museums at Night is a great opportunity to explore culture in a new light.

Museum of London
City of London EC2Y 5HN
(020) 7001 9844
www.museumoflondon.org.uk
Step inside Museum of London for an unforgettable journey through the capital's turbulent past.

National Maritime Museum
Greenwich SE10 9NF
(020) 8858 4422
www.nmm.ac.uk
Britain's seafaring history housed in an impressive modern museum. Themes include exploration, Nelson, trade and empire, passenger shipping, luxury liners, maritime London, costume, art and the sea, the future and environmental issues.

National Portrait Gallery
Westminster WC2H 0HE
(020) 7306 0055
www.npg.org.uk
The National Portrait Gallery houses the world's largest collection of portraits. Visitors come face to face with the people who have shaped British history from Elizabeth I to David Beckham. Entrance is free.

Notting Hill Carnival
August, Various venues
www.thenottinghillcarnival.com
2016 is the 50th anniversary of Europe's biggest street festival – where the streets of London come alive with colourful floats, street performers, music and tempting food stalls. A spectacular event!

RHS Chelsea Flower Show
May, Royal Hospital Chelsea
www.rhs.org.uk/Chelsea-Flower-Show
Experience the greatest flower show in the world at London's Royal Hospital Chelsea. The Chelsea Flower Show has been held in the grounds of the Royal Hospital Chelsea, London every year since 1913, apart from gaps during the two World Wars. Once Britain's largest flower show, it is still the most prestigious.

Ride London 2016
July, London
www.prudentialridelondon.co.uk
RideLondon is the world's greatest festival of cycling and takes place the weekend immediately after the Tour de France. With five events to enjoy on closed roads over a summer weekend in July there's really something for everyone.

Royal Academy of Arts
Piccadilly, London W1J 0BD
(020) 7300 8000
www.royalacademy.org.uk
A varied varied programme of exciting exhibitions and events at the Royal Academy of Arts in 2016. The landmark exhibition Painting the Modern Garden: Monet to Matisse (30 Jan-20 Apr 2016) uses the work of Monet as a starting point to examine the role gardens played in the evolution of art from the early 1860s through to the 1920s.

Royal Air Force Museum Hendon
Barnet NW9 5LL
(020) 8205 2266
www.rafmuseum.org
Take off to the Royal Air Force Museum, located on the former Hendon Aerodrome, and flypast the history of aviation with an exciting display of suspended aircraft, touch screen technology, simulator rides, hands-on section, film shows, licensed restaurant.

Royal Observatory Greenwich
Greenwich SE10 9NF
(020) 8858 4422
www.rmg.co.uk
Stand on the Greenwich Meridian Line, Longitude Zero, which divides East and West. Watch the time-ball fall at 1 o'clock, and explore your place in the universe at London's only planetarium.

Science Museum
Kensington and Chelsea SW7 2DD
0870 870 4868
www.sciencemuseum.org.uk
The Science Museum is world-renowned for its historic collections, awe-inspiring galleries, family activities and exhibitions - and it's free!

Somerset House
Westminster WC2R 1LA
(020) 7845 4670
www.somersethouse.org.uk
This magnificent 18th century building houses the celebrated collections of the Courtauld Institute of Art Gallery, Gilbert Collection and Hermitage Rooms. During summer months 55 fountains dance in the courtyard, and in winter you can skate on one of London's favourite ice rinks.

Southbank Centre
Lambeth SE1 8XX
(020) 7960 4200
www.southbankcentre.co.uk
A unique arts centre with 21 acres of creative space, including the Royal Festival Hall, Queen Elizabeth Hall and The Hayward.

Southwark Cathedral
Southwark SE1 9DA
(020) 7367 6700
http://cathedral.southwark.anglican.org
Oldest Gothic church in London (c.1220) with interesting memorials connected with the Elizabethan theatres of Bankside.

Tate Britain
Westminster SW1P 4RG
(020) 7887 8888
www.tate.org.uk
Presenting the world's greatest collection of British art in a dynamic series of new displays and exhibitions.

Tate Modern
Southwark SE1 9TG
(020) 7887 8888
www.tate.org.uk/modern
The national gallery of international modern art and is one of London's top free attractions. Packed with challenging modern art and housed within a disused power station on the south bank of the River Thames.

Tower Bridge Exhibition
Southwark SE1 2UP
(020) 7403 3761
www.towerbridge.org.uk
Inside Tower Bridge Exhibition you will travel up to the high-level walkways, located 140 feet above the Thames and witness stunning panoramic views of London before visiting the Victorian Engine Rooms.

Tower of London
Tower Hamlets EC3N 4AB
0844 482 7777
www.hrp.org.uk
The Tower of London spans over 900 years of British history. Fortress, palace, prison, arsenal and garrison, it is one of the most famous fortified buildings in the world, and houses the Crown Jewels, armouries, Yeoman Warders and ravens.

Victoria and Albert Museum
Kensington and Chelsea SW7 2RL
(020) 7942 2000
www.vam.ac.uk
The V&A is the world's greatest museum of art and design, with collections unrivalled in their scope and diversity.

The View from The Shard
London SE1 9QU
(08444) 997111
www.theviewfromtheshard.com
The View from The Shard is the premium visitor attraction at the top of Western Europe's tallest building, and London's newest landmark, The Shard, designed by Master Architect Renzo Piano.

Virgin Money London Marathon
April, Various venues
www.virginmoneylondonmarathon.com
Whether you run, walk or cheer from the sidelines, this is a London sporting institution you won't want to miss.

Wembley Stadium Tours

Brent HA9 0WS
0800 169 9933
www.wembleystadium.com
Until your dream comes true, there's only one way to experience what it's like winning at Wembley - take the tour.

William Morris Gallery
Lloyd Park, Forest Road, Walthamstow E17 4PP
(020) 8496 4390
www.wmgallery.org.uk
The William Morris Gallery is devoted to the life and legacy of one of Britain's most remarkable designers and is housed in the grade II listed Georgian house that was his family home in north-east London from 1848 to 1856.*

Wimbledon Lawn Tennis Championships
June - July, Wimbledon
www.wimbledon.com
The world of tennis descends on Wimbledon in South West London every summer for two weeks of tennis, strawberries and cream, and good-natured queuing.

Wimbledon Lawn Tennis Museum
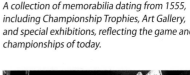
Merton SW19 5AG
(020) 8944 1066
www.wimbledon.com
A collection of memorabilia dating from 1555, including Championship Trophies, Art Gallery, and special exhibitions, reflecting the game and championships of today.

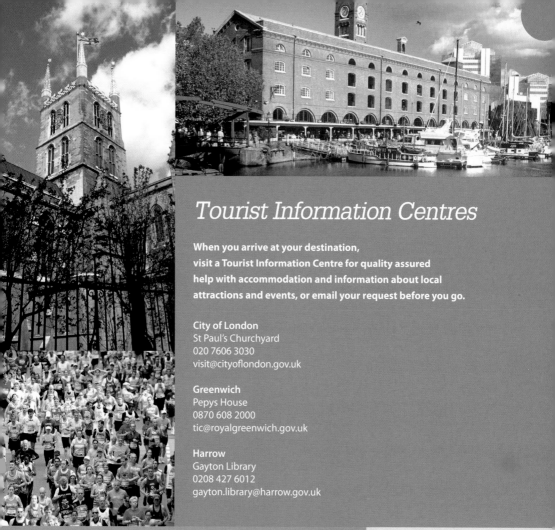

Tourist Information Centres

When you arrive at your destination,
visit a Tourist Information Centre for quality assured
help with accommodation and information about local
attractions and events, or email your request before you go.

City of London
St Paul's Churchyard
020 7606 3030
visit@cityoflondon.gov.uk

Greenwich
Pepys House
0870 608 2000
tic@royalgreenwich.gov.uk

Harrow
Gayton Library
0208 427 6012
gayton.library@harrow.gov.uk

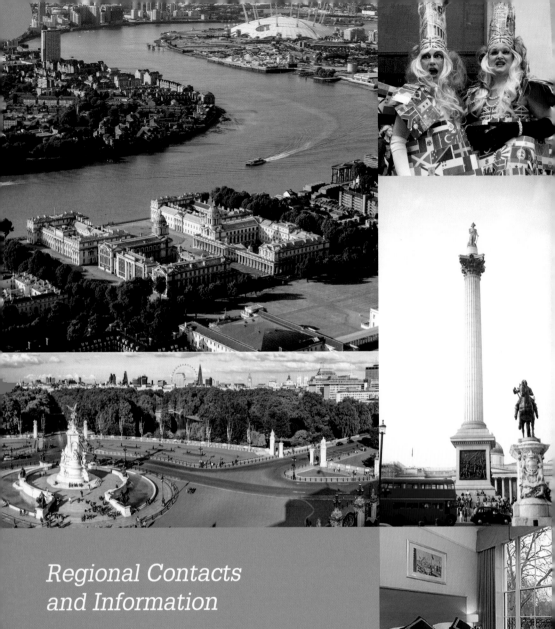

Regional Contacts and Information

Find everything you need to plan your trip on visitlondon.com, the official London website. Here you can download free London maps and guides: transport maps of London, the latest London Planner and the Welcome to London Guide. We do not mail out printed maps and guides as all our London guides, news, editorial and listings are available for free online.

For more information while you're in London, visit one of London's Tourist Information Centres or download our free Official London Cityguide App.

Travel and Transport in London
If you have questions about travelling in London, including Oyster cards, ticket prices, journey planning, booking a taxi and the congestion charge, please visit the Transport for London websitecall 0343 222 1234 or Textphone 020 7918 3015.

Stay – London

Entries appear alphabetically by town name in each county. A key to symbols appears on page 7

LONDON N4, Inner London   Map ref 2D2   SatNav N4 2LX

METRO HOTEL

B&B PER ROOM PER NIGHT
S: £50.00 - £55.00
D: £60.00 - £70.00

Kent Hall Hotel
414 Seven Sisters Road, Finsbury Park, London N4 2LX T: (020) 8802 0800
F: 020 8802 9070 E: enquiries@kenthallhotel.co.uk
W: www.kenthallhotel.co.uk £ **BOOK ONLINE**

Budget hotel located next to Manor House Station on the Piccadilly Line (Zone 2). 15 minutes from Central London by Tube. Within walking distance of Arsenal Football Stadium. Direct from Heathrow and Eurostar terminals. **Directions:** Exit 5 from Manor House station- Piccadilly Line. **Bedrooms:** All room have private bathroom, TV, fridge, WiFi **Open:** All year. 24 hours per day

Site: **P** Payment: **£** **€** Property: ⬛ ℋ ◑ Children: ⛄ Room: ⬚ ✹ ☎ 📺 ⛧

LONDON W5, Inner London   Map ref 2D2   SatNav W5 2UU

★★★
GUEST
ACCOMMODATION

B&B PER ROOM PER NIGHT
S: £65.00 - £85.00
D: £70.00 - £110.00

The Caspian
14 Haven Green, Ealing, London W5 2UU T: (02089) 973524 F: 020 8998 8236
E: caspianhtl@aol.com
W: www.caspianhotel.co.uk

A charming, cosy bed & breakfast Hotel located in the heart of Ealing Broadway – London's "Queen of Suburbs". We pride ourselves on offering a true home from home, whether you are on business, holiday or visiting family. As seen on TV-Hotel Inspector Ch 5. **Directions:** A40/M40-A406, right on Uxbridge Road (sign posted Ealing/ Southall), or left driving from M4 /A4, right at HMV / McDonald's at Spring Bridge Road into Haven Green. We are on the corner of Castlebar Road. **Bedrooms:** Single, double, triple, family and Deluxe Boutique rooms available.

Site: **P** Payment: **£** Property: ⛟ 🛏 Room: ✹ 📺

Book your accommodation online

Visit our websites for detailed information, up-to-date availability and to book your accommodation online. Includes over 20,000 places to stay, all of them star rated.

www.visitor-guides.co.uk

Temple Lodge Club Ltd
Temple Lodge, 51 Queen Caroline Street, Hammersmith, London W6 9QL
T: (02087) 488388 **E:** templelodgeclub@btconnect.com
W: www.templelodgeclub.com

B&B PER ROOM PER NIGHT
S: £58.00 – £90.00
D: £76.00 – £120.00

SPECIAL PROMOTIONS
Please see website for special promotions.

Hidden away from the hustle and bustle of central Hammersmith, yet a surprisingly short walk from its main transport hub, this listed building provides a quiet and relaxing haven after the exertions of a busy day or night out. Breakfast is hearty, vegetarian and mainly organic. Bedrooms are comfortably furnished, light and airy. Most rooms, including library, look out onto our secluded garden.

Directions: Exit Hammersmith tube towards the Apollo Theatre, turn left towards the river and Hammersmith Bridge, next door but one is Temple Lodge. Enter small courtyard, come to blue front door and ring doorbell!

Bedrooms: 5 single with companion bed if needed, 4 double (1 en suite, 1 private bathroom, 1 shower only in room, 1 facilities on corridor) 2 twin-bedded.
Open: All year

Site: ❀ Payment: 🔳 Property: ⚑ 🖥 ♟ Children: 🐾⁶ Catering: 🍴 Room: 🐾 ♨

Goodenough Club
23 Mecklenburgh Square, London WC1N 2AD **T:** (02077) 694727
E: reservations@goodenough.ac.uk
W: www.club.goodenough.ac.uk £ **BOOK ONLINE**

B&B PER ROOM PER NIGHT
S: £149.00 – £199.00
D: £155.00 – £250.00

Occupies 5 Georgian town houses in the heart of Bloomsbury, walking distance to West End, Covent Garden and the Eurostar. Luxurious Garden Suites are available and a Health club day is available charged nearby. **Bedrooms:** TV, Wi-Fi, hairdryer and hospitality tray **Open:** All year

Site: ❀ Payment: 🔳 Leisure: ⚒ Property: 🖥 ♟ ◐ Children: 🐾 🍴 Room: 🐾 ♨ ☎ 📺 ⚓

★★★ GUEST HOUSE
VisitEngland

B&B PER ROOM PER NIGHT
S: £43.00 - £48.00
D: £66.00

Woodstock Guest House

30 Woodstock Road, Croydon CR0 1JR **T:** (02086) 801489 **F:** 020 8680 1489
E: guesthouse.woodstock@gmail.com
W: www.woodstockhotel.co.uk

Victorian house located in a quiet residential area, only a five minute walk to the town centre, local amenities and East Croydon Railway Station. Well-appointed and spacious rooms. High standard of housekeeping and homely atmosphere. Wi-Fi and parking available. Single rooms from £43 to £48 per night, twin/double rooms £66 per night and family rooms £80 per night.

Directions: From East Croydon Station via George Street turn left into Park Lane. After roundabout exit A212. Woodstock Road is 2nd left off Park Lane.

Bedrooms: 4 single, 2 twin/double, 2 family.
Open: All year except Christmas and New Year.

Site: ✿ **P** **Payment:** 💳 **Leisure:** 🏊 ► **Property:** 🛏 ♨ **Children:** 🧒³ **Catering:** 🍴
Room: 🍵 🕯 🍳 TV DVD 🕯

★★★★ HOTEL
VisitEngland

B&B PER ROOM PER NIGHT
S: £90.00 - £190.00
D: £105.00 - £210.00

HB PER PERSON PER NIGHT
£110.00 - £230.00

SPECIAL PROMOTIONS
Weekend offer if you stay two or three nights. Best rate available. Prices include Breakfast, Car Parking, Wi-Fi internet and use of extensive leisure facilities including a 25m pool.

Lensbury

Broom Road, Teddington TW11 9NU **T:** (02086) 146400 **F:** 020 8614 6445
E: accommodation@lensbury.com
W: www.lensbury.com **£ BOOK ONLINE**

The Lensbury is a 4 star hotel, conference centre and premium leisure centre located in 25 acres of grounds on the banks of the river Thames at Teddington in West London. With 171 en-suite bedrooms, an excellent purpose-built conference centre and superb leisure facilities, The Lensbury is a "one stop shop" for the business or leisure visitor. Free car parking and Wi-Fi, 25 metre Swimming pool.

Directions: Near Heathrow & Gatwick Airports. Motorways: 15 minutes from the M25. 10 minutes from the M3. Rail: 35 minutes to London Waterloo. Complementary shuttle bus to local station Mon to Fri peak times.

Bedrooms: Standard Rooms, Superior, Executive, Deluxe, Disabled room and a Family room. Rooms can take up to a maximum of 4 people.
Open: All year

Site: ✿ **P** **Payment:** 💳 € **Leisure:** 🏊 ♪ ► ♺ 🎱 🎯 ♨ 🚲 ⚓ 🏹 **Property:** ◉ 🍴 🛏 🖥 ♨ ◐
Children: 🧒 🛏 ☂ **Catering:** (✕ 🍸 🍴 **Room:** 🍵 🕯 🍳 🕯 TV

If you have
access needs...

Guests with hearing, visual or mobility needs can feel confident about booking accommodation that participates in the National Accessible Scheme (NAS).

Look out for the NAS symbols which are included throughout the accommodation directory. Using the NAS could help make the difference between a good holiday and a perfect one!

For more information on the NAS and tips & ideas on holiday travel in England, go to: www.visitengland.com/accessforall

Don't Miss...

Audley End House & Gardens

Saffron Walden, Essex CB11 4JF
www.english-heritage.org.uk
At Audley End near Saffron Walden, you can discover one of England's grandest stately homes. Explore the impressive mansion house, uncover the story behind the Braybrooke's unique natural history collection, visit an exhibition where you can find out about the workers who lived on the estate in the 1800s and even try dressing the part with dressing up clothes provided.

The Broads

Norfolk
www.broads-authority.gov.uk
The Norfolk Broads with its scenic waterways, rare wildlife and rich history has National Park status. This ancient mosaic of lakes, land and rivers covering 303 square kilometres in the east of England, is the UK's largest protected wetland and boasts a variety of habitats including fen, carr woodland and grazing marshes, as well as pretty villages and no less than 11,000 species of wildlife. Walking, cycling, fishing, boating, wildlife spotting, the list of things to do here is endless and there is something for all ages to enjoy.

Kings College Cambridge

King's Parade, Cambridge CB2 1ST
(0)1223 331212
www.kings.cam.ac.uk
Founded in 1441 by Henry VI (1421-71), King's is one of the 31 colleges in the University of Cambridge. Regarded as one of the greatest examples of late Gothic English architecture, it has the world's largest fan-vault and the chapel's stained-glass windows and wooden chancel screen are considered some of the finest from their era. The chapel's choir, composed of male students at King's and choristers from the nearby King's College School, is one of the most accomplished and renowned in the world and every year on Christmas Eve the Festival of Nine Lessons and Carols is broadcast from the chapel to millions of listeners worldwide.

Holkham Hall

Wells-next- the-Sea, Norfolk, NR23 1AB
(01328) 710227
www.holkham.co.uk
Steeped in history, magnificent Holkham Hall on the North Norfolk Coast, is a stunning Palladian mansion with its own nature reserve. It is home to many rare species of flora and fauna, a deer park and one of the most beautiful, unspoilt beaches in the country. Step back in time in the Bygones Museum or explore the 18th Century walled gardens which are being restored, while the children have fun in the woodland adventure play area.

ZSL Whipsnade Zoo

Dunstable, Bedfordshire LU6 2LF
(020) 7449 6200
www.zsl.org/zsl-whipsnade-zoo
Set on 600 acres in the rolling Chiltern Hills, Whipsnade is home to more than 2500 species and you can get close to some of the world's hairiest, scariest, tallest and smallest animals here. Meet the animals, take a steam train ride, visit the Hullabazoo Farm or even be a keeper for the day.

East of England

Bedfordshire, Cambridgeshire, Essex,
Hertfordshire, Norfolk, Suffolk

Loved for its unspoiled character, rural landscape, architecture and traditions, the East of England is full of beautiful countryside, idyllic seaside, historic cities and vibrant towns. The Norfolk Broads and Suffolk Coast have always been popular with yachtsmen and the North Norfolk Coast has become a fashionable getaway in recent years. Cambridge is steeped in history and oozes sophistication, while Bedfordshire, Hertfordshire and Essex each have their own charms, with pockets of beauty and fascinating heritage. This is a diverse region where you'll find plenty to keep you busy.

Norfolk

Huntingdonshire

Cambridgeshire Suffolk

Bedfordshire

Essex

Hertfordshire

125

Explore –
East of England

Bedfordshire & Hertfordshire

History, the arts, family entertainment and relaxing, unspoilt countryside - this area has it all. Bedfordshire has plenty of attractions, from exotic animals at Whipsnade Zoo to vintage aeroplanes at The Shuttleworth Collection and notable historic houses. Woburn Abbey, the still inhabited home of the Dukes of Bedford, stands in a 3000-acre park and is part of one of Europe's largest drive-through game reserves. The 18th century mansion's 14 state apartments are open to the public and contain an impressive art collection. Luton Hoo is a fine Robert Adam designed house in a 1200-acre Capability Brown designed park.

Hertfordshire also has its fair share of stately homes, with Hatfield House, built from 1707 by Robert Cecil, first Earl of Salisbury, leading the way. Nearby Knebworth House is the venue for popular summer concerts and events.

Roman walls, mosaic floors and part of an amphitheatre are still visible at Verulanium, St Albans and Much Hadham, where the Bishops of London used to have their country seat, is a showpiece village. Welwyn Garden City, one of Britain's first 20th century new towns retains a certain art deco charm.

Cambridgeshire & Essex

Cambridge is a city of winding streets lined with old houses, world-famous colleges and churches, while the gently flowing Cam provides a serene backdrop to the architectural wonders. Kings College Chapel, started by Henry VI in 1446 should not be missed and the Fitzwilliam Museum is one of Europe's treasure houses, with antiquities from Greece and Rome. First-class shopping can be found in the quirky stores and exquisite boutiques tucked away along cobbled streets, and there's a vast choice of places to eat and drink.

Further afield, Cambridgeshire is a land of lazy waterways, rolling countryside, bustling market towns and quaint villages. Climb grand sweeping staircases in the stately homes of the aristocracy or relax as you chug along in a leisure boat, watching the wildlife in one of the wonderful nature reserves. Peterborough has a fine Norman cathedral with three soaring arches, whilst Ely has had an abbey on its cathedral site since AD 670.

Western Essex is dotted with pretty historic market towns and villages like Thaxted and Saffron Walden and plenty of historic sites. County town Colchester was founded by the Romans and its massive castle keep, built in 1067 on the site of the Roman Temple of Claudius, houses a collection of Roman antiquities. Explore the beautiful gardens and 110ft Norman Keep at Hedingham Castle, which also holds jousting and theatre performances.

Some of the region's loveliest countryside lies to the north, on the Suffolk Border around Dedham Vale where Constable and Turner painted, while further east you can find family seaside resorts such as Walton on the Naze and Clacton-on-Sea. Following the coast south, the Blackwater and Crouch estuaries provide havens for yachts and pleasure craft. Inland, Layer Marney Tower is a Tudor palace with buildings, gardens and parkland dating from 1520 in a beautiful, rural Essex setting. The county city of Chelmsford has a historic 15th century cathedral and Hylands House is a beautiful Grade II* listed neo-classical villa, set in over 500 acres of Hylands Park.

Norfolk

Norfolk is not as flat as Noel Coward would have you believe, as any cyclist will tell you, but cycling or walking is still a great way to see the county. In the west Thetford Forest is said to be the oldest in England while in the east, the county is crisscrossed by waterways and lakes known as The Broads - apparently the remains of medieval man's peat diggings!

The county town of Norfolk and unofficial capital of East Anglia is Norwich, a fine city whose cathedral walls are decorated with biblical scenes dating from 1046. There are 30 medieval churches in central Norwich and many other interesting historic sites, but modern Norwich is a stylish contemporary city with first rate shopping and cultural facilities. Sandringham, near Kings Lynn in the north west of the county, is the royal palace bought by Queen Victoria for the then Prince of Wales and where the present Queen spends many a family holiday.

The North Norfolk coast has become known as 'Chelsea-on-Sea' in recent years and many parts of the region have developed a reputation for fine dining. From Hunstanton in the west to Cromer in the east, this stretch of coastline is home to nature reserves, windswept beaches and quaint coastal villages. Wells-next-the-Sea, with its long sweeping beach bordered by pine woodland has a pretty harbour with small fishing boats where children fish for crabs.

Suffolk

Suffolk is famous for its winding lanes and pastel painted, thatched cottages. The county town of Ipswich has undergone considerable regeneration in recent years, and now boasts a vibrant waterfront and growing arts scene. For history lovers, Framlingham Castle has stood intact since the 13th century and magnificent churches at Lavenham, Sudbury and Long Melford are well worth a visit.

The Suffolk Coast & Heaths Area of Outstanding Natural Beauty has 155 square miles of unspoilt wildlife-rich wetlands, ancient heaths, windswept shingle beaches and historic towns and villages for you to explore. Its inlets and estuaries are extremely popular with yachtsmen. Gems such as Southwold, with its brightly coloured beach huts, and Aldeburgh are home to some excellent restaurants. Snape Maltings near Aldeburgh offers an eclectic programme of events including the world famous Aldeburgh Festival of music. The historic market town of Woodbridge on the River Deben, has a working tide mill, a fabulous riverside walk with an impressive view across the river to Sutton Hoo and an abundance of delightful pubs and restaurants.

In the south of the county, the hills and valleys on the Suffolk-Essex border open up to stunning skies, captured in paintings by Constable, Turner and Gainsborough. At the heart of beautiful Constable Country, Nayland and Dedham Vale Area of Outstanding Natural Beauty are idyllic places for a stroll or leisurely picnic.

Visit – East of England

 Attractions with this sign participate in the **Visitor Attraction Quality Assurance Scheme.**

Bedfordshire

Dunstable Downs Kite Festival
July, Dunstable, Bedfordshire LU6 2GY
www.dunstablekitefestival.co.uk
Enjoy a fantastic atmosphere as professional kite teams put on show-stopping diplays. With family activities, local artists and entertainment, there's something for everyone.

Luton International Carnival
May, Luton, Bedfordshire
www.luton.gov.uk
The highlight is the spectacular carnival parade – an eye-catching, breathtaking procession through the town centre, superbly reflecting the diverse mix of cultures in Luton. Enjoy the decorated floats, music and dance as you watch the parade go by.

Thurleigh Farm Centre
Thurleigh, Bedfordshire MK44 2EE
(01234) 771597
www.thurleighfarmcentre.co.uk
A wonderful working farm; have excellent fun with indoor activities including trampolines and mini quad biking, and the tea room with delightful homemade cakes.

Woburn Abbey
Woburn, Bedfordshire MK17 9WA
(01525) 290333
www.woburnabbey.co.uk
Home of the Duke of Bedford, a treasure house with outstanding collections of art, furniture, silver, gold and extensive gardens.

Woburn Safari Park
Bedfordshire MK17 9QN
(01525) 290407
www.woburnsafari.co.uk
Drive through the safari park with species such as white rhino, elephants, tigers and black bears in natural groups just a windscreen's width away, or even closer!

Wrest Park
Silsoe, Luton, Bedfordshire, MK45 4HR
(0870) 333 1181
www.english-heritage.org.uk
Enjoy a great day out exploring one of Britain's most spectacular French style mansions and 'secret' gardens. With hidden gems including a thatched-roof Bath house, ornate marble fountain, Chinese Temple and bridge and over 40 statues, as well as a kids audio trail and play area, it's popular with families and garden lovers alike.

Cambridgeshire

Cambridge Folk Festival
July, Cherry Hinton, Cambridgeshire
www.cambridgefolkfestival.co.uk
Top acts make this a must-visit event for folk fans.

Cambridge University Botanic Garden
1 Brookside, Cambridge CB2 1 JE
(01223) 336265
www.botanic.cam.ac.uk/Botanic
Opened to the public in 1846, the Cambridge University Botanic Garden develops & displays over 8,000 plant species in 40 acres of landscapes.

Duxford Air Show
September, Duxford, nr Cambridge, Cambridgeshire
www.iwm.org.uk/duxford
Set within the spacious grounds of the famous former First and Second World War airfield, the Duxford Air Show features an amazing array of aerial displays.

Elton Hall
Elton, Cambridgeshire PE8 6SH
(01832) 280468
www.eltonhall.com
Historic house with a fine collection of paintings, furniture, antiquarian books, bibles and Henry VIII's prayer book, together with beautiful ornate gardens and arboretum.

Imperial War Museum Duxford
Cambridge CB22 4QR
(01223) 835000
www.iwm.org.uk/duxford
Visit this historic airfield and museum of aviation history and discover the stories of people who lived and worked at RAF Duxford. With its air shows, unique history and atmosphere, nowhere else combines the sights, sounds and power of aircraft quite like it.

Kings College Chapel
Cambridge CB2 1ST
(01223) 331212
www.kings.cam.ac.uk
It's part of one of the oldest Cambridge colleges sharing a wonderful sense of history and tradition with the rest of the University. The Chapel is a splendid example of late Gothic architecture.

The National Stud
Newmarket, Cambridgeshire CB8 0XE
(01638) 663464
www.nationalstud.co.uk
The beautiful grounds & facilities are a renowned tourist attraction in the eastern region.

Oliver Cromwell's House
Ely, Cambridgeshire CB7 4HF
(01353) 662062
www.olivercromwellshouse.co.uk
Visit the former Lord Protector's family's home and experience an exhibition on 17th Century life, on the doorstep of Ely Cathedral.

Peterborough Dragon Boat Festival
June, Peterborough Rowing Lake,
Thorpe Meadows, Cambridgeshire
www.peterboroughdragonboatfestival.com
Teams of up to 11 people, dragon boats and all equipment provided, no previous experience required. Family entertainment and catering stalls.

The Raptor Foundation
Huntingdon, Cambridgeshire PE28 3BT
(01487) 741140
www.raptorfoundation.org.uk
Bird of prey centre, offering 3 daily flying displays with audience participation, gift shop, Silent Wings tearoom, Raptor crafts shop.

Essex

Adventure Island
Southend-on-Sea, Essex SS1 1EE
(01702) 443400
www.adventureisland.co.uk
One of the best value 'theme parks' in the South East with over 60 great rides and attractions for all ages. No admission charge, you only 'pay if you play'.

Central Museum and Planetarium
Southend-on-Sea, Essex SS2 6ES
(01702) 212345
www.southendmuseums.co.uk
An Edwardian building housing displays of archaeology, natural history, social and local history.

Clacton Airshow
August, Clacton Seafront, Essex
www.clactonairshow.com
An impressive two days of aerobatic displays taking to the skies whilst a whole host of exhibition, trade stands, food court and on-site entertainment are available at ground level.

Colchester Medieval Festival
June, Lower Castle Park, Colchester, Essex
www.oysterfayre.co.uk
With many of the peripheral activities that this major annual event of the period would have offered. It remembers a time when folk from the countryside and neighbouring villages would travel to the 'Big Fair' in the town.

Colchester Zoo
Essex CO3 0SL
(01206) 331292
www.colchester-zoo.com
As you step inside Colchester Zoo you are transported into a world full of magnificent animals waiting to be discovered. Learn about the animals as you see them up close and why not watch one of many daily displays.

Essex Country Show
September, Billericay, Essex, CM11 2UD
www.barleylands.co.uk
2016 marks the 30th anniversary of the Essex Country Show! A great range of arena shows, rural crafts, agricultural history and more.

Hedingham Castle
Essex CO9 3DJ
(01787) 460261
www.hedinghamcastle.co.uk
Standing in 160 acres of spectacular landscape, Hedingham Castle is a 900 year old Normal castle filled with romance, heritage and history.

Maldon Mud Race
May, Maldon, Essex
www.maldonmudrace.com
The annual Maldon Mud Race is a wacky fun competition in which participants race to become the first to finish a 400m dash over the bed of the River Blackwater.

RHS Garden Hyde Hall
Chelmsford, Essex CM3 8AT
(01245) 400256
www.rhs.org.uk/hydehall
A garden of inspirational beauty with an eclectic range of horticultural styles from traditional to modern providing year round interest.

Royal Gunpowder Mills
Waltham Abbey, Essex EN9 1JY
(01992) 707370
www.royalgunpowdermills.com
A spectacular 170-acre location for a day of family fun. Special events including Spitfire flypast, award winning Secret History exhibition, tranquil wildlife walks, guided land train tours and rocket science gallery.

Sea-Life Adventure
Southend-on-Sea, Essex SS1 2ER
(01702) 442200
www.sealifeadventure.co.uk
With more than 30 display tanks and tunnels to explore, there are loads of fishy residents to discover at Sea-Life Adventure.

Southend Carnival
August, Southend-on-Sea, Essex
www.southendcarnival.weebly.com
A wide range of exciting and enjoyable events for everyone held over eight days. Now one of the largest community events in South East Essex, and includes a thrilling fun fair and the colourful carnival procession along Southend Seafront!

Hertfordshire

Ashridge Gardens
Berkhamsted, Hertfordshire HP4 1NS
(01442) 841300
www.ashridgehouse.org.uk
Originally designed by Humphry Repton in the early 19th century, Ashridge Gardens are 190 acres of pure beauty and tranquillity. Please contact for advice on tours.

Cathedral and Abbey Church of St Alban
St. Albans, Hertfordshire AL1 1BY
(01727) 860780
www.stalbanscathedral.org
St Alban is Britain's first Christian martyr and the Cathedral, with its shrine, is its oldest place of continuous worship. The building's amazing mix of architectural styles bears witness to the many centuries of its life, first as a monastic Abbey and now as a Cathedral.

Chilli Festival
August, Benington Lordship Gardens,
Stevenage, Hertfordshire
www.beningtonlordship.co.uk
A popular family event attracting thousands of visitors over two days, offering a chance to buy Chilli plants, products and sample foods from around the world.

Hertfordshire County Show
May, Redbourn, Hertfordshire
www.hertsshow.com
County show with Trade Stands, Award Winning Food Hall, exclusive 'Made in Hertfordshire' marquee, Countryside Arena, and much much more.

Knebworth House
Hertfordshire SG3 6PY
(01438) 812661
www.knebworthhouse.com
Historic house, home to the Lytton family since 1490. Knebworth Park offers a great day out for all the family, with fun activities for children and lots to do for all ages, including Adventure Playground, Dinosaur Trail, a walk through history in Knebworth House and Gardens and special events throughout the summer.

Potters Bar Museum
Hertfordshire EN6 4HN
(01707) 654179
www.pottersbar.org
Go back in time at Potters Bar Museum with pottery and artefacts revealing history from Potters Bar and the surrounding area. See fossils, stones, and even parts of a Zeppelin that crashed into Potters Bar in 1916.

Norfolk

Banham Zoo
Norwich, Norfolk NR16 2HE
(01953) 887771
www.banhamzoo.co.uk
A 50-acre wildlife spectacular which will take you on a journey to experience tigers, leopards and zebra plus some of the world's most exotic, rare and endangered animals.

Blickling Hall, Gardens and Park
Norwich, Norfolk NR11 6NF
(01263) 738030
www.nationaltrust.org.uk/blickling-estate
A Jacobean redbrick mansion with a garden, orangery, parkland and lake. Spectacular long gallery, plasterwork ceilings and fine collections of furniture, pictures and books. You can walk across much of the 950 acres of woodland, parkland and historic countryside using waymarked routes and the estate also connects with other national paths.

Bressingham Steam and Gardens
Low Rd, Bressingham, Norfolk IP22 2AA
(01379) 686900
www.bressingham.co.uk
Where world renowned gardener and horticulturist Alan Bloom combined his passion for plants and gardens with his love of steam to create a truly unique experience for all the family.

Cromer Pier
Cromer, Norfolk NR27 9HE
www.cromer-pier.com
Cromer Pier is a Grade II listed, 12 year old, award winning, seaside pier on the north coast of Norfolk. The pier is the home of the Cromer Lifeboat Station and the Pavilion Theatre and absolutely the best crab fishing spot on the coast.

Fritton Lake Country World
Great Yarmouth, Norfolk NR31 9HA
(01493) 488288
A woodland and lakeside haven with a children's assault course, putting, an adventure playground, golf, fishing, boating, wildfowl, heavy horses, cart rides, falconry and flying displays.

Great Yarmouth Maritime Festival
September, Great Yarmouth, Norfolk
www.great-yarmouth.co.uk/maritime-festival
A mix of traditional and modern maritime vessels will be moored on South Quay for visitors to admire and go aboard.

Norwich Castle Museum and Art Gallery
Norfolk NR1 3JU
(01603) 493649
www.museums.norfolk.gov.uk
One of Norwich's most famous landmarks, the ancient Norman keep dominates the city and is one of the most important buildings of its kind in Europe. Explore the Castle's history as a palace and later as a prison, and enjoy the fabulous collections of fine art.

Royal Norfolk Show
June, Norwich, Norfolk
www.royalnorfolkshow.co.uk
The Royal Norfolk Show celebrates everything that's Norfolk. It offers 10 hours of entertainment each day from spectacular grand ring displays, traditional livestock and equine classes, to a live music stage, celebrity guests and over 650 stands.

Sainsbury Centre for Visual Arts
UEA, Norwich, Norfolk NR4 7TJ
(01603) 593199
www.scva.ac.uk
Containing a collection of world art, it was one of the first major public buildings to be designed by the architect Norman Foster.

Sandringham
King's Lynn, Norfolk PE35 6EN
(01485) 545400
www.sandringhamestate.co.uk
The Norfolk country retreat of H.M. The Queen and HRH The Duke of Edinburgh. A fascinating house, an intriguing museum and the best of the Royal gardens.

Suffolk

Aldeburgh Music Festival
June, Snape Maltings, Suffolk IP17 1SP
www.aldeburgh.co.uk
The Aldeburgh Festival of Music and the Arts offers an eclectic mix of concerts, operas, masterclasses, films and open air performances at different venues in the Aldeburgh/Snape area in Suffolk.

Gainsborough's House
Sudbury, Suffolk CO10 2EU
(01787) 372958
www.gainsborough.org
Gainsborough's House is the only museum situated in the birthplace of a great British artist. The permanent collection is built around the works of leading English painter Thomas Gainsborough, alongside other temporary exhibitions.

Go Ape! High Wire Forest Adventure - Thetford
Suffolk IP27 0AF (0845) 643 9215
www.goape.co.uk
Experience an exhilarating course of rope bridges, tarzan swings and zip slides... all set high in the trees above the forest floor.

Ickworth House, Park and Gardens
Bury St. Edmunds, Suffolk IP29 5QE
(01284) 735270
www.nationaltrust.org.uk/ickworth
Fine paintings, a beautiful collection of Georgian silver, an Italianate garden and stunning parkland.

Latitude Festival
July, Southwold, Suffolk
www.latitudefestival.com
Primarily a music festival but also has a full spectrum of art including film, comedy, theatre, cabaret, dance and poetry.

National Horseracing Museum and Tours
Newmarket, Suffolk CB8 8JH
(01638) 667333
www.nhrm.co.uk
Family-friendly venue embracing fine and decorative art, social history, archive material and photos. Discover the stories of racing from its early origins at Newmarket to its modern-day heroes.

RSPB Minsmere Nature Reserve
Saxmundham, Suffolk IP17 3BY
(01728) 648281
www.rspb.org.uk/minsmere
One of the UK's premier nature reserves, offering excellent facilities for people of all ages and abilities.

Smiths Row
Bury St Edmunds, Suffolk IP33 1BT
(01284) 762081
www.smithsrow.org
A contemporary art gallery and craft workshop; relax in The Art Lounge with an exhibition book, or take part in a workshop to develop your crafting skills.

Somerleyton Hall and Gardens
Lowestoft, Suffolk NR32 5QQ
(01502) 734901
www.somerleyton.co.uk
12 acres of landscaped gardens to explore including our famous 1864 Yew hedge maze. Guided tours of the Hall.

Suffolk Show
June, Ipswich, Suffolk
www.suffolkshow.co.uk
Animals, food and drink, shopping…there's lots to see and do at this popular county show.

Sutton Hoo
Woodbridge, Suffolk IP12 3DJ
(01394) 389700
www.nationaltrust.org.uk
Anglo-Saxon burial site set on a stunning 255 acre estate with breathtaking views over the River Debe.

Tourist Information Centres

When you arrive at your destination, visit the Tourist Information Centre for quality assured help with accommodation and information about local attractions and events, or email your request before you go.

Aldeburgh	48 High Street	01728 453637	atic@suffolkcoastal.gov.uk
Aylsham	Bure Valley Railway Station	01263 733903	aylsham.tic@broadland.gov.uk
Beccles	The Quay	01502 713196	admin@beccles.info
Bedford	St Pauls Square	01234 718112	touristinfo@bedford.gov.uk
Bishop's Stortford	2 Market Square	01279 655831	tic@bishopsstortford.org
Brentwood	Town Hall	01277 312500	
Burnham Deepdale	Deepdale Information	01485 210256	info@deepdalefarm.co.uk
Bury St Edmunds	6 Angel Hill	01284 764667	tic@stedsbc.gov.uk
Cambridge	Peas Hill	0871 226 8006	info@visitcambridge.org
Clacton-on-Sea	Town Hall	01255 686633	clactontic@tendringdc.gov.uk
Colchester	1 Queen Street	01206 282920	vic@colchester.gov.uk
Cromer	Louden Road	0871 200 3071	cromerinfo@north-norfolk.gov.uk
Diss	Meres Mouth	01379 650523	dtic@s-norfolk.gov.uk
Dunstable	Priory House	01582 891420	tic@dunstable.gov.uk
Ely	Oliver Cromwell's House	01353 662062	tic@eastcambs.gov.uk
Felixstowe	91 Undercliff Road West	01394 276770	ftic@suffolkcoastal.gov.uk
Great Yarmouth	25 Marine Parade	01493 846346	gab@great-yarmouth.gov.uk
Hertford	10 Market Place	01992 584322	tic@hertford.gov.uk
Holt	3 Pound House	0871 200 3071 / 01263 713100	holtinfo@north-norfolk.gov.uk
Hoveton	Station Road	01603 782281	hovetontic@broads-authority.gov.uk
Hunstanton	Town Hall	01485 532610	info@visithunstanton.info
Ipswich	St Stephens Church	01473 258070	tourist@ipswich.gov.uk
King's Lynn	The Custom House	01553 763044	kings-lynn.tic@west-norfolk.gov.uk
Lavenham	Lady Street	01787 248207	lavenhamtic@babergh.gov.uk
Letchworth Garden City	33-35 Station Road	01462 487868	tic@letchworth.com
Lowestoft	East Point Pavilion	01502 533600	touristinfo@waveney.gov.uk
Luton	Luton Central Library	01582 401579	tourist.information@lutonculture.com
Maldon	Wenlock Way	01621 856503	tic@maldon.gov.uk
Newmarket	63 The Guineas	01638 719749	tic.newmarket@forest-heath.gov.uk
Norwich	The Forum	01603 213999	tourism@norwich.gov.uk
Peterborough	9 Bridge Street	01733 452336	tic@peterborough.gov.uk
Saffron Walden	1 Market Place	01799 524002	tourism@saffronwalden.gov.uk
Sandy	Rear of 10 Cambridge Road	01767 682 728	tourism@sandytowncouncil.gov.uk
Sheringham	Station Approach	01263 824329	sheringhaminfo@north-norfolk.gov.uk
Skegness	Embassy Theatre	0845 6740505	skegnessinfo@e-lindsey.gov.uk
Southend-on-Sea	Pier Entrance	01702 215620	vic@southend.gov.uk
Southwold	69 High Street	01502 724729	southwold.tic@waveney.gov.uk
St Albans	Old Town Hall	01727 864511	tic@stalbans.gov.uk
Stowmarket	The Museum of East Anglian Life	01449 676800	tic@midsuffolk.gov.uk
Sudbury	Sudbury Library	01787 881320 / 372331	sudburytic@sudburytowncouncil.co.uk
Swaffham	The Shambles	01760 722255	swaffham@eetb.info
Waltham Abbey	6 Highbridge Street	01992 660336	tic@walthamabbey-tc.gov.uk
Wells-Next-The-Sea	Staithe Street	0871 200 3071 / 01328 710885	wellsinfo@north-norfolk.gov.uk
Whitlingham	Whitlingham Country Park	01603 756094	whitlinghamtic@broads-authority.gov.uk
Wisbech	2-3 Bridge Street	01945 583263	tourism@fenland.gov.uk
Witham	61 Newland Street	01376 502674	tic@witham.gov.uk
Woodbridge	Woodbridge Library	01394 446510 / 276770	felixstowetic@suffolkcoastal.gov.uk
Wymondham	Market Cross	01953 604721	wymondhamtic@btconnect.com

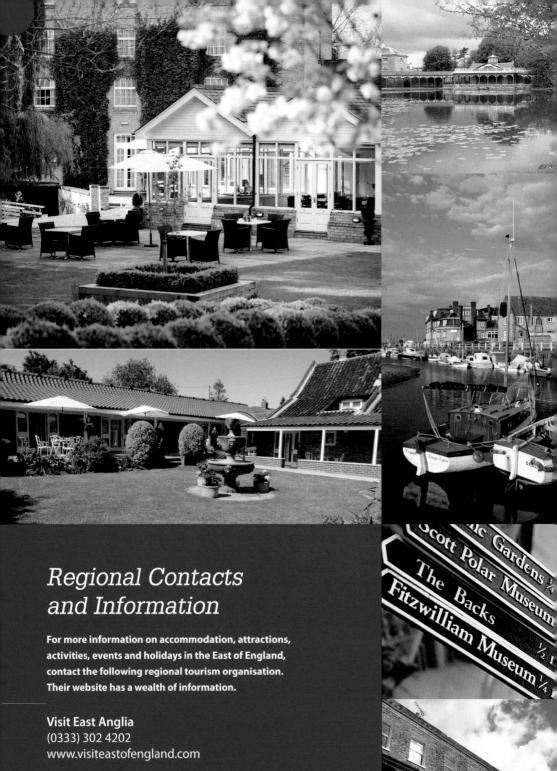

Regional Contacts and Information

For more information on accommodation, attractions, activities, events and holidays in the East of England, contact the following regional tourism organisation. Their website has a wealth of information.

Visit East Anglia
(0333) 302 4202
www.visiteastofengland.com

Stay –
East of England

Entries appear alphabetically by town name in each county. A key to symbols appears on page 7

CAMBRIDGE, Cambridgeshire   Map ref 2D1   SatNav CB25 9AF H

Cambridge Quy Mill Hotel and Spa

Church Road, Stow-cum-Quy, Cambridge, Cambridgeshire CB25 9AF
T: (01223) 293383 **F:** 01223 293770 **E:** qmh.reception@cambridgequymill.co.uk
W: www.cambridgequymill.co.uk £ BOOK ONLINE

B&B PER ROOM PER NIGHT
S: £82.50 - £222.50
D: £95.00 - £255.00
EVENING MEAL PER PERSON
£30.00 - £46.00

On the outskirts of Cambridge with easy access from the A14. Enjoy award winning 2 AA Rosette food in the informal Mill House Restaurant or bar meals in the Orangery. The Celtic Bar and Lounge features real ales and over 40 whiskies. **Directions:** Please see website. **Bedrooms:** 24 hour reception, 24 hour porter service, express check out, dry cleaning and laundry service, room service menus, wake up calls, overnight shoe shine service **Open:** All year

Site: ❋ P Payment: 🖃 Leisure: 🏌 ⚽ 🎯 Property: ⓦ 🍽 💻 🖥 🦽 ◑ Children: 🚼 Catering: ⊗ 🍴 Room: 🖤 ☕ 📞 📺 📀 🍳 🧺

CAMBRIDGE, Cambridgeshire   Map ref 2D1   SatNav CB4 1DE B

Southampton Guest House

7 Elizabeth Way, Cambridge CB4 1DE **T:** (01223) 357780 **F:** 01223 314297
E: southamptonhouse@btinternet.com
W: www.southamptonguesthouse.com

B&B PER ROOM PER NIGHT
S: £40.00 - £55.00
D: £60.00 - £65.00

Victorian property with friendly atmosphere, only 15 minutes walk along riverside to city centre, colleges and shopping mall. **Directions:** Please contact us for directions. **Bedrooms:** 1 single, 1 double, 3 family **Open:** All year

Site: P Payment: € Property: 💻 Children: 🚼 🧒 Room: 🖤 ☕ 📞 📺 🍳

COLCHESTER, Essex Map ref 3B2 SatNav CO6 4PZ H

Stoke by Nayland Hotel, Golf & Spa
Keepers Lane, Leavenheath, Colchester, Essex CO6 4PZ T: (01206) 265835
F: 01206 265840 E: sales@stokebynayland.com
W: www.stokebynayland.com £ BOOK ONLINE

B&B PER ROOM PER NIGHT
S: £76.00
D: £86.00

SPECIAL PROMOTIONS
For current special offers please see our website or call 01206 265835.

In secluded tranquility yet only 10 minutes from Colchester, this multi award-winning, family-owned hotel is situated in 300 acres of stunning "Constable Country". Two championship golf courses, 2 AA Rosette Lakes Restaurant, extensive spa facilities, indoor pool, gym, free car parking and free hi-speed Wi-Fi.

Directions: Situated North of Colchester on the Essex/Suffolk border just off the A134, only an hour from London via the A12.

Bedrooms: 80 ensuite bedrooms including club rooms, golf doubles, golf deluxes and junior suites. Flat screen TVs, in-room safes, air conditioning and free WiFi.
Open: All Year

Site: P Payment: Leisure: Property: Children: Catering: Room:

ORSETT, Essex Map ref 3B3 SatNav RM16 3LJ B

Jays Lodge
Chapel Farm, Baker Street, Orsett, Grays RM16 3LJ T: (01375) 891663
E: info@jayslodge.co.uk
W: www.jayslodge.co.uk

B&B PER ROOM PER NIGHT
S: £35.00 - £47.50
D: £50.00 - £65.00

Barn conversion to provide twelve rooms all with en suite, mini kitchen facility, colour television with Freeview and free Wi-Fi access. Ample, free and secure car parking available. Directions: Please contact us for directions. Bedrooms: 2 single, 2 double, 8 twin Open: All year

Site: P Payment: Leisure: Property: Catering: Room:

WEST MERSEA, Essex Map ref 3B3 SatNav CO5 8LS B

Victory at Mersea
Coast Road, Mersea Island, Colchester CO5 8LS T: (01206) 382907
E: info@victoryatmersea.com
W: www.victoryatmersea.com £ BOOK ONLINE

B&B PER ROOM PER NIGHT
S: £70.00 - £95.00
D: £80.00 - £120.00
EVENING MEAL PER PERSON
£12.00 - £22.00

The Victory is situated on the Mersea waterfront. We have 7 really comfortable, superior quality rooms, individually decorated with a personal touch, some with fantastic estuary views.
Directions: Mersea is clearly signposted from the A12 and you'll find us on the outskirts of the village centre, right on the waterfront. Bedrooms: 5 double, 1 twin, 1 family. Open: All year

Site: P Payment: Leisure: Property: Children: Catering: Room:

ST. ALBANS, Hertfordshire Map ref 2D1   SatNav AL3 4RY H

St Michael's Manor Hotel

St Michael's Village, Fishpool Street, St Albans, Hertfordshire AL3 4RY **T:** (01727) 864444
F: 01727 848909 **E:** reservations@stmichaelsmanor.com
W: www.stmichaelsmanor.com £ **BOOK ONLINE**

B&B PER ROOM PER NIGHT
S: £125.00
D: £135.00 - £305.00
EVENING MEAL PER PERSON
£18.00 - £34.00

SPECIAL PROMOTIONS
Please check website
for details.

Close to the city centre of St Alban's Hertfordshire, formerly the ancient Roman city of Verulanium, and near the famous Abbey Cathedral you will find this lovely manor house hotel. Set in five acres of beautiful private English country gardens with its own one acre lake this country-style venue is, surprisingly, only 20 minutes by train from London. The original house dates back over 500 years and was converted into a hotel in the early 1960s by the Newling Ward family. They still remain as private owners and managers, which gives the hotel its unique flavour. Bedroom prices start from £125, including breakfast. Evening meal prices based on The Lake Menu. Please see website for A la Carte, Sunday Lunch and Afternoon Tea menus.

Directions: Please see
www.stmichaelsmanor.com/find-us

Bedrooms: Premier, Luxury, Deluxe, Suites & Accessible. Most rooms have garden views. All have tea/coffee making facilities, biscuits/sweets, bottled water.
Open: All year

Site: P Payment: Leisure: Property: Children: Catering: Room:

AYLSHAM, Norfolk Map ref 3B1   SatNav NR11 6BY B

The Old Pump House

Holman Road, Aylsham, Norwich NR11 6BY **T:** (01263) 733789
E: theoldpumphouse@btconnect.com
W: www.theoldpumphouse.com

B&B PER ROOM PER NIGHT
S: £85.00 - £100.00
D: £100.00 - £125.00

Beautiful Georgian home located a short walk from the market place with 5 tastefully furnished, comfortable bedrooms. Delicious breakfasts served in the Georgian room overlooking the garden. Situated within easy reach of the North Norfolk coast, the cathedral city of Norwich and several National Trust houses, Blickling Hall being just 1.5 miles away. Free Wi-Fi. **Bedrooms:** 1 double, 2 king size, 2 twin family. All rooms are en suite. **Open:** All year except Christmas & New Year.

Site: P Payment: Leisure: Property: Children: Room:

FAKENHAM, Norfolk Map ref 3B1   SatNav NR21 0AW B

Abbott Farm B&B

Walsingham Road, Binham, Fakenham NR21 0AW **T:** (01328) 830519
E: abbot.farm@btinternet.com
W: www.abbottfarm.co.uk

B&B PER ROOM PER NIGHT
S: £30.00 - £45.00
D: £60.00 - £80.00

A 190-acre arable farm. Rural views of North Norfolk including the historic Binham Priory. Liz and Alan offer a warm welcome to their guest house. **Directions:** Please refer to website. **Bedrooms:** 1 double (en suite), 1 twin (en suite) **Open:** All year except Christmas

Site: P Payment: € Leisure: Property: Children: Catering: Room:

East of England - Norfolk

Burlington Palm Hotel

North Drive, Great Yarmouth NR30 1EG **T:** (01493) 844568 **F:** 01493 331848
E: enquiries@burlington-hotel.co.uk
W: www.burlington-hotel.co.uk **£ BOOK ONLINE**

B&B PER ROOM PER NIGHT
S: £55.00 - £120.00
D: £80.00 - £160.00
EVENING MEAL PER PERSON
£18.50 - £34.00

SPECIAL PROMOTIONS
Nightly discounts for
extended stays. Check
website for special
offers.

Seafront Hotel overlooking Great Yarmouth's Golden Sands. We are a short walk from all the main attractions and 1.5 miles from the train station. We are also the only Hotel in Great Yarmouth with a heated indoor swimming pool. Catering for Old and Young, Private, Business and Groups customers. Free Off Road Car Parking for all.

Directions: From the A12 or A47 follow signs for Seafront turn left, we are on North Drive about 600 Yards north of the Britannia Pier.

Bedrooms: 7 single, 22 double, 21 twin, 18 family
Open: All year except 28th December - 2nd January

Site: **P** Payment: 🖪 Leisure: ♪ ▶ ◕ ⌇ Property: ♟ 🚇 🏛 Children: ⛄ 🛏 ⚲ Catering: (✗ ♨ 🍽
Room: 🖥 ✆ 📺 🔔

For **key to symbols** see page 7

GREAT YARMOUTH, Norfolk   Map ref 3C1   SatNav NR31 9AB B

VisitEngland ★★★★ GUEST ACCOMMODATION

VisitEngland Gold AWARD

Decoy Barn

Beccles Road, Fritton, Great Yarmouth, Norfolk NR31 9AB **T:** (01493) 488222
E: decoybarn@yahoo.co.uk
W: www.decoybarn.co.uk **£ BOOK ONLINE**

B&B PER ROOM PER NIGHT
S: £60.00 - £65.00
D: £75.00 - £85.00

Decoy Barn is a 200 year old converted barn and stables with a warm, welcoming atmosphere. All rooms are elderly/level one disabled friendly, on the ground floor, and have lovely views across the patio, gardens and Fritton Lake Country Park. **Directions:** We are located on the A143 Beccles Road in Fritton opposite the Decoy Tavern and a few hundred yards from Fritton lake country park. **Bedrooms:** U/floor heating, en suite, flat screen tv,tea/coffee. **Open:** All year

 Site: ✿ **P** **Payment:** 💳 € **Leisure:** ▸ ∪ **Property:** ⍭ 🏨 **Catering:** 🍴 **Room:** ☎ 🖊 📺 ⛶

HEACHAM, Norfolk   Map ref 3B1   SatNav PE31 7HB B

VisitEngland ★★★★ GUEST HOUSE

VisitEngland Silver AWARD

St Anne's Guest House

53 Neville Road, Heacham, Norfolk PE31 7HB **T:** (01485) 570021
E: jeannie@stannesguesthouse.co.uk
W: www.stannesguesthouse.co.uk

B&B PER ROOM PER NIGHT
S: £45.00 - £50.00
D: £75.00 - £80.00

A Victorian family-run guest house in the quiet village of Heacham near Hunstanton, we offer a relaxed informal atmosphere for a peaceful enjoyable break. Rooms: 2 single, 1 with ensuite, 1 family with ensuite, 1 twin with ensuite, 3 double with ensuite. Family room available from £100 per night. **Bedrooms:** Flatscreen TV, tea and coffee in rooms. **Open:** All Year

 Site: ✿ **Payment:** 💳 **Property:** 🖥 ♫ **Children:** ⛄ ⚲ **Catering:** 🍴 **Room:** ☎ 🖊 📺

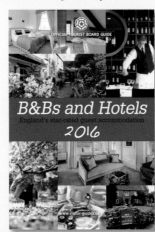
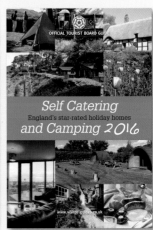

MUNDESLEY, Norfolk   Map ref 3C1
SatNav NR11 8DB **B**

Overcliff Lodge
46 Cromer Road, Mundesley, Norfolk NR11 8DB **T:** (01263) 720016
E: enquiries@overclifflodge.co.uk
W: www.overclifflodge.co.uk **£ BOOK ONLINE**

B&B PER ROOM PER NIGHT
S: £50.00 - £65.00
D: £70.00 - £105.00

Overcliff Lodge is a large Victorian house, situated just a few minutes walk from the Blue Flag sandy beach and village centre. The house offers spacious, comfortable accommodation and has a fully enclosed small rear garden.
Directions: Overcliff Lodge is situated at the junction of Gimingham Road and Cromer Road just west of Mundesley.
Bedrooms: All rooms are en suite with tea and coffee **Open:** All year except 3 weeks in January

Site: ❀ **P** Payment: 🖃 Leisure: ▶ ♒ Property: 🛏 ♨ ⌀ Catering: 🍴 Room: ☎ ♨ 📺 📷

NORWICH, Norfolk   Map ref 3C1
SatNav NR12 7BG **H**

Old Rectory Hotel
North Walsham Road, Crostwick, Norwich, Norfolk NR12 7BG **T:** (01603) 738513
F: 01603 738712 **E:** info@oldrectorycrostwick.com
W: www.oldrectorycrostwick.com **£ BOOK ONLINE**

B&B PER ROOM PER NIGHT
S: £40.00 - £77.00
D: £60.00 - £97.00

EVENING MEAL PER PERSON
£9.50 - £35.50

SPECIAL PROMOTIONS
Discounted two night midweeks stays. Mon - Thurs min, 2 night stay, excluding bank hol

Ideal location for Norwich and Broads. This family run hotel offers excellent facilities and service in a beautiful setting in rural Norfolk. All rooms are ground floor, en suite and very well equipped. It also boasts 3.5 acres of gardens, patio seating, bar, restaurant, heated outdoor pool and ample free parking.
Perfect for a short break or relaxing holiday.

Directions: B1150 North Walsham Rd out of Norwich off the outer ring-road travel 4-miles. The Old Rectory is situated 200m past the Spixworth turning.

Bedrooms: 6 dble, 8 twin, 1 family, 1 suite
Open: All year

Site: ❀ **P** Payment: 🖃 Leisure: ⚴ ♩ ▶ ♒ ⚘ Property: 🦮 🐴 🚃 🖥 Children: 🐕 🛏 🎠
Catering: (🗙 🍷 🍴 Room: ☎ ♨ ☏ 📻 📺 📷

RACKHEATH, Norfolk   Map ref 3C1
SatNav NR13 6NN **B**

Barn Court
6 Back Lane, Rackheath, Norwich NR13 6NN **T:** (01603) 782536
E: barncourtbb@hotmail.com

B&B PER ROOM PER NIGHT
S: £30.00 - £35.00
D: £55.00 - £65.00

Barn Court is a spacious, friendly and comfortable B&B 5 miles from the centre of Norwich and 2 miles from Wroxham, in a traditional barn conversion built around a courtyard. Good variety of breakfasts provided. **Directions:** From Norwich, take A1151 towards Wroxham, Back Lane is 3.5 miles from ring road on left, and Barn Court is first driveway on right. **Bedrooms:** 2 double, 1 twin **Open:** All year except Christmas and New Year

Site: ❀ **P** Leisure: ⚴ ♩ ▶ ♒ Property: 🐴 🚃 Children: 🐕¹ 🛏 🎠 Catering: 🍴
Room: ♨ ☏ 📺 📷

COUNTRY HOUSE HOTEL
★★★
VisitEngland

Broom Hall Country Hotel

Richmond Road, Saham Toney, Thetford IP25 7EX **T:** (01953) 882125 **F:** 01953 885325
E: enquiries@broomhallhotel.co.uk
W: www.broomhallhotel.co.uk **£ BOOK ONLINE**

B&B PER ROOM PER NIGHT
S: £75.00 - £110.00
D: £85.00 - £185.00
EVENING MEAL PER PERSON
£9.15 - £30.00

SPECIAL PROMOTIONS
Two night breaks,
dinner B&B, priced per
couple for two nights.
Winter from £238.00,
summer from £275.00.

Family-run, Victorian country house offering peace and tranquillity in 15 acres of garden and
parkland. Open fire warms winter evenings. After a swim in heated indoor pool, enjoy a cream tea
on the terrace or in the conservatory or relax in the Rose Room Bar. Purpose-built, ground-floor,
disabled rooms. Restaurant or bar meals are available lunchtimes and evenings.

Directions: From A11, take A1075 to Watton.
Left at lights, 0.5m right at roundabout. From
A47, take A1065 Newmarket, left onto B1108, left
at roundabout.

Bedrooms: 9 double, 4 twin, 2 family all en suite,
ground floor disabled access rooms.
Open: All year except Christmas and New Year.

Site: ✿ P **Payment:** 💷 **Leisure:** ♿ ♪ ▶ ᴜ ♨ 🎿 **Property:** 🍴 🐕 🛏 📷 🎱 🚲 **Children:** 🚼 🎮 🎎
Catering: 🍽 🍷 **Room:** 🖂 💧 ☎ 📺 🔌 🛁

Book your accommodation online

Visit our websites for detailed
information, up-to-date availability and
to book your accommodation online.
Includes over 20,000 places to stay,
all of them star rated.

www.visitor-guides.co.uk

VisitEngland ★★★★ INN

SPECIAL PROMOTIONS
3 nights stay for £175.

Chequers Inn

Griston Road, Thompson IP24 1PX **T:** (01953) 483360
E: richard@thompsonchequers.co.uk
W: www.thompsonchequers.co.uk

The Chequers is a 16th century village inn with a thatched roof, still retaining all of its original character. A true country retreat in the heart of Breckland. Local produce and fresh fish a speciality. Local real ales include Wolf, Wherry, Adnams and Greene King IPA to name a few. Please contact for 2016 Rates.

Directions: Twelve miles north east of Thetford, just off the A1075. Snetterton Race Track just a short drive away.

Bedrooms: 2 double, 1 twin
Open: All year

Site: ✿ P Payment: 💷 Leisure: ♪ ▶ Property: 🐾 🖼 Children: ↻ ★ Catering: ♟ 🍽
Room: 📶 ☕ 📞 🅰 📺 ♿

VisitEngland ★★★★ GUEST ACCOMMODATION

B&B PER ROOM PER NIGHT
D: £75.00 - £120.00

f

Arch House Bed and Breakfast

50 Mill Road, Wells-Next-The-Sea, Norfolk NR23 1DB **T:** (01328) 710112
E: enquiries@archhouse.co.uk
W: www.archhouse.co.uk £ BOOK ONLINE

Arch House is a distinguished Grade II listed Bed & Breakfast with large car park, just a short walk from the centre of Wells-next-the-Sea with its excellent restaurants, pubs, quirky shops and bustling fishing quay. Situated a mile from the stunning Holkham Estate and The Norfolk Coastal Path, Arch House is the perfect base to explore this Area of Outstanding Natural Beauty.
Bedrooms: Accommodates up to 24 guests in 11 ensuite rooms
Open: All year except Christmas

Site: ✿ P Payment: 💷 Property: 🖼 Children: ↻⁴ Catering: 🍽 Room: 📶 ☕ 📺 ☕ ♿ 🚪

For **key to symbols** see page 7

WIGHTON, Norfolk   Map ref 3B1   SatNav NR23 1PF   B

Meadow View Guest House

53 High Street, Wighton, Wells-next-The-Sea, Norfolk NR23 1PF **T:** (01328) 821527
F: 01328 821527 **E:** booking@meadow-view.net
W: www.meadow-view.net **£ BOOK ONLINE**

B&B PER ROOM PER NIGHT
S: £90.00
D: £100.00 - £120.00

SPECIAL PROMOTIONS
Oct/Nov stay for 3
nights pay for 2 nights

A 5 star Gold award guest house awaits you with a warm, friendly welcome in the centre of Wighton, 3 miles from Wells, a busy coastal resort on the North Norfolk coast.

Directions: From B1105 Wighton is situated just off the B1105, accessible from the A149 coast road.

Bedrooms: 1 double, 1 twin, 3 suite
Open: All year

Site: ❀ P Payment: 🖭 Leisure: ♿ ✦ Property: 🛏 ⌂ Catering: 🍽 🍴 Room: 🔌 ♨ 🛎 📺 📀 🔥

BURY ST. EDMUNDS, Suffolk   Map ref 3B2   SatNav IP28 6EY   B

West Stow Hall

Icklingham Road, West Stow, Bury St. Edmunds IP28 6EY **T:** (01284) 728127
E: eileengilbert54@aol.com
W: www.weststowhall.com

B&B PER ROOM PER NIGHT
S: £70.00 - £75.00
D: £120.00 - £130.00
EVENING MEAL PER PERSON
£15.00 - £30.00

Enjoy the tranquility and beauty of this historic hall set in six acres of lovely grounds. Large comfortable bedrooms, great breakfasts and a warm welcome are guaranteed. The Studio, with ground floor access, is ideally suited for less mobile guests. **Directions:** M11 to A11 direction Mildenhall. Before Mildenhall take A1101 to Bury St Edmunds, left turn West Stow. The hall is clearly signposted on the left. **Bedrooms:** 2 double, 1 twin, 1 family. **Open:** All year except Christmas.

Site: ❀ P Payment: 🖭 € Leisure: ♿ ✦ ▶ ♲ Property: 🛏 🚬 📱 Children: 🛝 🎠 Catering: 🍴
Room: 🔌 ♨ 🛎 📶 🔥

ELMSWELL, Suffolk   Map ref 3B2   SatNav IP30 9QR   B

Kiln Farm Guest House

Kiln Lane, Elmswell, Bury St Edmunds, Suffolk IP30 9QR **T:** (01359) 240442
E: davejankilnfarm@btinternet.com

B&B PER ROOM PER NIGHT
S: £40.00 - £50.00
D: £80.00 - £100.00
EVENING MEAL PER PERSON
£12.50

Welcoming Victorian farmhouse with courtyard of converted barns in secluded location just off A14. Licensed bar with conservatory for breakfasts and pre-booked evening meals. Ideal for exploring Suffolk. Businessmen welcome. **Directions:** A14 jct47. Travelling East Kiln Lane is right off exit slip road. From West, turn right over to roundabout, third exit. 50 yards on left. **Bedrooms:** 5 double, 1 twin, 2 family **Open:** All year

Site: ❀ P Payment: 🖭 € Property: 🐕 🚬 Children: 🛝 🍽 🎠 Catering: 🍷 🍴 Room: 🔌 ♨ 📺 🔥

FRAMLINGHAM, Suffolk   Map ref 3C2
SatNav IP13 9PD **B**

VisitEngland ★★★★ FARMHOUSE

High House Farm

Cransford, Woodbridge, Suffolk IP13 9PD **T:** (01728) 663461 **E:** info@highhousefarm.co.uk
W: www.highhousefarm.co.uk

A warm welcome awaits you in our beautifully restored 15th century farmhouse, featuring exposed beams, inglenook fireplaces and attractive gardens. Situated midway between Framlingham and Saxmundham. **Directions:** Please refer to website address.
Bedrooms: 1 double, 1 family **Open:** All year

B&B PER ROOM PER NIGHT
S: £46.00 - £60.00
D: £70.00 - £95.00

Site: ✿ P Leisure: ☕ ♪ ▶ ♫ Property: ↖ ☷ ♨ ∅ Children: ☇ ▦ ⚲ Catering: ⊌ Room: ⚲ ♨ ☏ TV

HITCHAM, Suffolk   Map ref 3B2
SatNav IP7 7NY **B**

VisitEngland ★★★★ FARMHOUSE

Stanstead Hall

Buxhall Road, Hitcham, Ipswich IP7 7NY **T:** (01449) 740270 **E:** stanstead@btinternet.com
W: www.stansteadcamping.co.uk

Very friendly Moated Farmhouse standing off the road in the quiet open countryside. Large garden to relax in under a glass verandah. In easy reach of Lavenham, Long Melford, Bury St Edmunds and central to many of Suffolk's beauty spots. **Directions:** Directions on website. **Bedrooms:** Large rooms, with shower, TV and tea/coffee.
Open: All year

B&B PER ROOM PER NIGHT
S: £40.00
D: £70.00

Site: ✿ P Leisure: ☕ ♪ ♫ Property: ↖ ☷ Room: ⚲ ♨ ☏ TV

NEWMARKET, Suffolk   Map ref 3B2
SatNav CB8 7BX **H**

AA
★★★★

Bedford Lodge Hotel & Spa

Bury Road, Newmarket, Suffolk CB8 7BX **T:** (01638) 663175 **F:** 01638 667391
E: info@bedfordlodgehotel.co.uk
W: www.bedfordlodgehotel.co.uk **£ BOOK ONLINE**

The four red star Bedford Lodge Hotel & Spa was originally an 18th century Georgian Hunting Lodge. Today, we offer the best in modern comfort. Our stylish hotel retains the charm and character of its country house beginnings. **Directions:** Between Cambridge and Bury St. Edmunds; in Newmarket and is easily accessible by road, rail and air with the A14 and A11 dual carriageways close by.
Bedrooms: Flat screen tv, tea and coffee, safe and cooler
Open: All Year

B&B PER ROOM PER NIGHT
S: £109.00 - £350.00
D: £120.00 - £350.00

Site: ✿ P Payment: ☷ Leisure: ▶ ⚹ ♨ ⚡ ⚘ Property: ⊛ ⚲ ☷ ♨ ◐ ∅ Children: ☇
Catering: ⚱ ⊌ Room: ⚲ ♨ ☎ ☏ TV ♿

STOWMARKET, Suffolk   Map ref 3B2
SatNav IP14 5EU **B**

VisitEngland ★★★★ GUEST ACCOMMODATION

Three Bears Cottage

Mulberry Tree Farm, Middlewood Green, Stowmarket IP14 5EU **T:** (01449) 711707
F: 01449 711707 **E:** gbeckett01@aol.com
W: www.3bearscottagesuffolk.co.uk **£ BOOK ONLINE**

Self-contained converted barn offering comfort, privacy & country views. Lounge with TV, kitchenette, a substantial continental breakfast available. Ground floor bedroom, shower/bathroom sleeps 6. Well behaved dogs accepted, many bridalway walks at the back of the cottage. Within easy reach of Bury St Edmunds, Ipswich Cambridge & Suffolk coast. **Directions:** A14, A1120 through Stowupland turn into Saxham St, 1st right 1m, right into Blacksmiths Lane **Bedrooms:** 1 King size, 1 family **Open:** All year

B&B PER ROOM PER NIGHT
S: £30.00
D: £60.00

Site: ✿ P Leisure: ☕ ♪ ▶ ♫ Property: ↖ ♨ Children: ☇ Catering: ⊌ Room: ⚲ ♨ ☏ TV ♿ ⊞

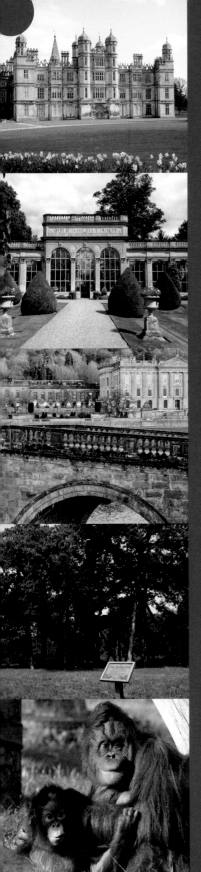

Don't Miss...

Burghley House

Stamford, Lincolnshire PE9 3JY
(01780) 752451
www.burghley.co.uk

Used in films Pride and Prejudice and The Da Vinci Code, the house boasts eighteen magnificent State Rooms and a huge collection of works and art, including one of the most important private collections of 17th century Italian paintings, the earliest inventoried collection of Japanese ceramics in the West and wood carvings by Grinling Gibbons and his followers.

Castle Ashby Gardens

Northamptonshire NN7 1LQ
(01604) 695200
www.castleashbygardens.co.uk

A haven of tranquility and beauty in the heart of Northamptonshire. Wander through these beautiful gardens, open 365 days of the year, and you are taking a walk through history. Set in the heart of a 10,000-acre estate, the 35 acres of extensive gardens are a combination of several styles including the romantic Italian Gardens, the unique Orangery and impressive Arboretum. The full Castle Ashby experience also involves a menagerie, children's play area, plant centre, tea room and gift shop.

Chatsworth

Bakewell, Derbyshire DE45 1PP
(01246) 565300
www.chatsworth.org

Chatsworth is a spectacular historic house set in the heart of the Peak District in Derbyshire, on the banks of the river Derwent. There are over 30 rooms to explore, including the magnificent Painted Hall and Sculpture Gallery. In the garden, discover water features, giant sculptures and beautiful flowers set in one of Britain's most well-known historic landscapes.

Sherwood Forest

Sherwood Forest Visitor Centre,
Edwinstowe, Nottinghamshire NG21 9HN
www.nottinghamshire.gov.uk

Once part of a royal hunting forest and legendary home of Robin Hood, Sherwood Forest National Nature Reserve covers 450 acres of ancient woodlands where veteran oaks over 500 years old grow, as well as being home to a wide variety of flora and fauna. Follow the waymarked trails amongst the leafy glades and spot birds including nightjars, woodlarks, hawfinches, marsh and willow tits. Marvel in the shadow of the historic Major Oak, browse the Visitor Centre shops or relax with a coffee in the Forest Table Restaurant.

Twycross Zoo

Hinckley, Leicestershire CV9 3PX
(01827) 880250
www.twycrosszoo.org

Set in more than 80 acres and renowned as a World Primate Centre, Twycross Zoo has around 500 animals of almost 150 species, including many endangered animals and native species in the Zoo's Nature Reserve. Pay a visit to meet the famous orangutans, gorillas and chimpanzees plus many other mammals, birds and reptiles.

East Midlands

Derbyshire, Leicestershire, Lincolnshire, Northamptonshire, Nottinghamshire, Rutland

The East Midlands is a region of historic castles and cathedrals, lavish houses, underground caves, a rich industrial heritage and spectacular countryside including the Peak District and the Lincolnshire Wolds. Climb to enchanting hilltop castles for breathtaking views. Explore medieval ruins and battlefields. Discover hidden walks in ancient forests, cycle across hills and wolds, or visit one of the regions many events and attractions.

Lincolnshire

Derbyshire

Nottinghamshire

Rutland

Leicestershire

Northamptonshire

Explore – East Midlands

Derbyshire

'There is no finer county in England than Derbyshire. To sit in the shade on a fine day and look upon verdure is the most perfect refreshment' according to Jane Austen. Derbyshire is the home of the UK's first National Park, the Peak District, which has been popular with holidaymakers for centuries. It forms the beginning of the Pennine Chain and its reservoirs and hills are second to none in beauty. This is excellent walking, riding and cycling country and contains plenty of visitor attractions and historic sites such as Gullivers Theme Park at Matlock Bath and the 17th century Palladian Chatsworth, seat of the Duke of Devonshire.

Leicestershire & Rutland

Leicester is a cathedral city with a 2000-year history, now host to a modern university and the county's pastures fuel one of its main exports: cheese. Foxton Locks is the largest flight of staircase locks on the English canal system with two 'staircases' of five locks bustling with narrowboats. Belvoir Castle in the east dominates its vale. Rockingham Castle at Market Harborough was built by William the Conqueror and stands on the edge of an escarpment giving dramatic views over five counties and the Welland Valley below. Quietly nestling in the English countryside, England's smallest county of Rutland is an idyllic rural destination with an array of unspoilt villages and two charming market towns, packed with rich history and character.

Lincolnshire

Lincolnshire is said to produce one eighth of Britain's food and its wide open meadows are testament to this. Gothic triple-towered Lincoln Cathedral is visible from the Fens for miles around, while Burghley House hosts the famous annual Horse Trials and is a top tourist attraction. The Lincolnshire Wolds, a range of hills designated an Area of Outstanding Natural Beauty and the highest area of land in eastern England between Yorkshire and Kent, is idyllic walking and cycling country. Also perfect for bird watchers and nature lovers, Lincolnshire's Natural Coast is one of this region's best kept secrets!

Northamptonshire

County town Northampton is famous for its shoe making, celebrated in the Central Museum and Art Gallery, and the county also has its share of stately homes and historic battlefields. Silverstone in the south is home to the British Grand Prix. Althorp was the birthplace and is now the resting place of the late Diana Princess of Wales.

Nottinghamshire

Nottingham's castle dates from 1674 and its Lace Centre illustrates the source of much of the city's wealth, alongside other fine examples of Nottinghamshire's architectural heritage such as Papplewick Hall & Gardens. Legendary tales of Robin Hood, Sherwood Forest and historic battles may be what the county is best known for, but it also hosts world class sporting events, live performances and cutting edge art, and there's plenty of shopping and fine dining on offer too. To the north, the remains of Sherwood Forest provide a welcome breathing space and there are plenty of country parks and nature reserves, including the beautiful lakes and landscape of the National Trust's Clumber Park.

Visit – East Midlands

 Attractions with this sign participate in the Visitor Attraction Quality Assurance Scheme.

Derbyshire

Buxton Festival
July, Buxton, Derbyshire
www.buxtonfestival.co.uk
A summer celebration of the best opera, music and literature, at the heart of the beautiful Peak District.

Creswell Crags
Chesterfield, Derbyshire S80 3LH
(01909) 720378
www.creswell-crags.org.uk
A world famous archaeological site, honeycombed with caves and smaller fissures. Stone tools and remains of animals found in the caves by archaeologists provide evidence for a fascinating story of life during the last Ice Age between 50,000 and 10,000 years ago. It is also home to Britain's only known Ice Age cave art.

Derby Museum and Art Gallery
Derby DE1 1BS
(01332) 641901
www.derbymuseums.org
Derby Museum and Art Gallery holds collections and displays relating to the history, culture and natural environment of Derby and its region.

Derbyshire Food & Drink Fair
May, Derby, Derbyshire
www.derbyshirefoodanddrinkfair.co.uk
Over 150 stalls will showcase the best local produce from Derbyshire and the Peak District region, as well as unique and exotic foods from further afield.

Gulliver's Kingdom Theme Park
Matlock Bath, Derbyshire DE4 3PG
(01629) 580540
www.gulliversfun.co.uk
With more than 40 rides & attractions, Gulliver's provides the complete family entertainment experience. Fun & adventure with Gully Mouse, Dora the explorer, Diego and "The Lost World".

Haddon Hall
Bakewell, Derbyshire DE45 1LA
(01629) 812855
www.haddonhall.co.uk
Haddon Hall is a stunning English Tudor and country house on the River Wye at Bakewell in Derbyshire, Haddon Hall is one of England's finest examples of a medieval manor.

Hardwick Hall
Chesterfield, Derbyshire S44 5QJ
(01246) 850430
www.nationaltrust.org.uk/hardwick
Owned by the National Trust, Hardwick Hall is one of Britain's greatest Elizabethan houses. The water-powered Stainsby Mill is fully functioning and the Park has a fishing lake and circular walks.

Heights of Abraham
Matlock, Derbyshire DE4 3NT
(01629) 582365
www.heightsofabraham.com
Country park and famous show caverns set in 60 acres of woodland and reached by cable car over deep limestone gorge in the Peak District.

Kedleston Hall
Derby DE22 5JH
(01332) 842191
www.nationaltrust.org.uk/kedleston-hall
A fine example of a neo-classical mansion built between 1759-65 by the architect Robert Adam and set in over 800 acres of parkland and landscaped pleasure grounds. Administered by The National Trust.

Renishaw Hall and Gardens
Dronfield, Derbyshire S21 3WB
(01246) 432310
www.renishaw-hall.co.uk
The Gardens are Italian in design and were laid out over 100 years ago by Sir George Sitwell. The garden is divided into 'rooms' with yew hedges, flanked with classical statues.

The Silk Mill - Museum of Industry and History
Derby DE1 3AF
(01332) 255308
www.derbymuseums.org
The Silk Mill was completed around 1723 and the re-built Mill now contains displays on local history and industry.

Speedwell Cavern and Peak District Cavern
Castleton, Hope Valley, Derbyshire S33 8WA
(01433) 623018
www.speedwellcavern.co.uk
Speedwell Cavern and Peak District Cavern offer the chance for amazing adventures in the heart of the Peak District, with unusual rock formations, the largest natural cave entrance in the British Isles and an incredible underground boat trip.

Sudbury Hall
Ashbourne, Derbyshire DE6 5HT
(01283) 585305
www.nationaltrust.org.uk/sudburyhall/
Explore the grand 17th Century hall with its richly decorated interior and see life below stairs. Learn about George Vernon, the young man who built the hall you see today at Sudbury in 1660.

Leicestershire & Rutland

Artisan Cheese Fair
April / May, Melton Mowbray, Leicestershire
www.artisancheesefair.co.uk
A chance to taste the huge range of cheeses that are made locally and further afield. Visitors to the Artisan Cheese Fair can sample and purchase many of the 250 popular and rare cheeses on show from 50 exhibitors including the leading names in UK artisan cheese production.

Ashby-de-la-Zouch Castle
Leicestershire LE65 1BR
(01530) 413343
www.english-heritage.org.uk/daysout/properties/ashby-de-la-zouch-castle
Visit Ashby-de-la-Zouch Castle where you will see the ruins of this historical castle, the original setting for many of the scenes of Sir Walter Scott's classic tale 'Ivanhoe'.

Bosworth Battlefield Heritage Centre
Market Bosworth, Leicestershire CV13 0AD
(01455) 290429
www.bosworthbattlefield.com
Delve into Leicestershire's fascinating history at Bosworth Battlefield Country Park - the site of the 1485 Battle of Bosworth.

Conkers Discovery Centre
Ashby-de-la-Zouch, Leicestershire DE12 6GA
(01283) 216633
www.visitconkers.com/thingstodo/discoverycentre
Enjoy the great outdoors and explore over 120 acres of the award winning parkland.

Easter Vintage Festival
March, Great Central Railway, Leicestershire
www.gcrailway.co.uk
A real treat for all this Easter with traction engines, classic cars and buses, fairground rides, trade stands, a beer tent as well as lots of action on the double track.

Great Central Railway
Leicester LE11 1RW
(01509) 632323
www.gcrailway.co.uk
The Great Central Railway is Britain's only double track main line steam railway. Enjoy an exciting calendar of events, a footplate ride or dine in style on board one of the steam trains.

Lincoln Castle
Castle Hill, Lincoln LN1 3AA
(01522) 554559
www.lincolncastle.com
Discover a site steeped in history spanning the centuries and experience nearly 1000 years of jaw-dropping history, from battles to the hanging of criminals and ghostly tales.

National Space Centre
Leicester LE4 5NS
(0845) 605 2001
www.spacecentre.co.uk
The award winning National Space Centre is the UK's largest attraction dedicated to space. From the moment you catch sight of the Space Centre's futuristic Rocket Tower, you'll be treated to hours of breathtaking discovery & interactive fun.

Rutland Water
Egleton, Oakham, Rutland LE15 8BT
(01572) 770651
www.rutlandwater.org.uk
There's plenty to keep everyone entertained at Rutland Water, with a huge range of watersports, fantastic fishing, an outdoor adventure centre and nature reserves teeming with wildlife.

Twinlakes Theme Park
Melton Mowbray, Leicestershire LE14 4SB
(01664) 567777
www.twinlakespark.co.uk
Twinlakes Theme Park - packed with variety, fun and endless adventures for every member of your family.

Lincolnshire

Ayscoughfee Hall Museum and Gardens
Spalding, Lincolnshire PE11 2RA
(01775) 764555
www.ayscoughfee.org
Ayscoughfee Hall Museum is housed in a beautiful wool merchant's house built in 1451 on the banks of the River Welland.

Belton House
Belton, Lincolnshire NG32 2LS
(01476) 566116
www.nationaltrust.org.uk/belton-house
Belton, is a perfect example of an English Country House. The mansion is surrounded by formal gardens and a series of avenues leading to follies within a larger wooded park.

Burghley Horse Trials
September, Burghley House, Lincolnshire
www.burghley-horse.co.uk
One of the most popular events in the British equestrian calendar.

Doddington Hall
Lincoln LN6 4RU
(01522) 694308
www.doddingtonhall.com
A Elizabethan mansion by the architect Robert Smythson. The hall stands today as it was completed in 1600 with walled courtyards, turrets and gatehouse.

Hardys Animal Farm
Ingoldmells, Lincolnshire PE25 1LZ
(01754) 872267
www.hardysanimalfarm.co.uk
Learn about the countryside and how a farm works. There are animals for the children to enjoy as well as the history and traditions of the countryside.

Lincolnshire Show
June, Lincolnshire Showground
www.lincolnshireshow.co.uk
Agriculture remains at the heart of the Lincolnshire Show with livestock and equine competitions, machinery displays and the opportunity to find out where your food comes from and to taste it too!

Lincolnshire Wolds Walking Festival
May, Louth, Lincolnshire
www.woldswalkingfestival.co.uk
Over 90 walks and bike rides, taking place in an Area of Outstanding Natural Beauty and surrounding countryside.

Normanby Hall Museum and Country Park
Scunthorpe, Lincolnshire DN15 9HU
(01724) 720588
xwww.normanbyhall.co.uk
Normanby Hall is a classic English mansion set in 300 acres of gardens, parkland, deer park, woods, ornamental and wild birds.

Tattershall Castle
Lincolnshire LN4 4LR
(01526) 342543
www.nationaltrust.org.uk/tattershall-castle
Tattershall Castle was built in the 15th Century to impress and dominate by Ralph Cromwell, one of the most powerful men in England. The castle is a dramatic red brick tower.

Northamptonshire

78 Derngate
Northampton NN1 1UH
(01604) 603407
The only house in England designed by Charles Rennie Mackintosh is ow a multi award-winning visitor attraction offering an unforgettable day out.

Althorp
Northampton NN7 4HQ
(01604) 770107
www.spencerofalthorp.com
One of England's finest country houses, and ancestral home of Diana, Princess of Wales.

British Grand Prix
July, Silverstone, Northamptonshire
www.silverstone.co.uk
The only place in the UK to see the world's best Formula One drivers in action.

Coton Manor Garden
Nr Guilsborough, Northants NN6 8RQ
(01604) 740219
www.cotonmanor.co.uk
A beautiful Old English garden with luxuriant borders, rose gardens, herb gardens, woodland and water gardens enclosed by old yew and holly hedges.

Lamport Hall and Gardens
Northamptonshire NN6 9HD
(01604) 686272
www.lamporthall.co.uk
Grade 1 listed building that was home to the Isham family and their collections for over four centuries.

National Waterways Museum -
Stoke Bruerne
Towcester, Northamptonshire NN12 7SE
(01604) 862229
www.canalrivertrust.org.uk
Stoke Bruerne is an ideal place to explore the story of our waterways.

Prebendal Manor Medieval Centre
Nassington, Northamptonshire PE8 6QG
(01780) 782575
www.prebendal-manor.co.uk
Visit a unique medieval manor and enjoy the largest recreated medieval gardens in Europe.

Rockingham Castle
Market Harborough, Northamptonshire LE16 8TH
(01536) 770240
www.rockinghamcastle.com
Rockingham Castle stands on the edge of an escarpment giving dramatic views over five counties and the Welland Valley below.

Salcey Forest
Hartwell, Northamptonshire NN17 3BB
(01780) 444920
www.forestry.gov.uk/salceyforest
Wildlife and history are in abundance at Salcey, so come and discover this ancient semi-natural woodland and get a birds eye view on the tremendous Tree Top Way.

Sulgrave Manor
Northamptonshire OX17 2SD
(01625) 822447
www.sulgravemanor.org.uk
Sulgrave Manor is the ancestral home of George Washington's family with authentic furniture shown by friendly guides.

Wicksteed Park
Kettering, Northamptonshire NN15 6NJ
(01536) 512475
www.wicksteedpark.co.uk
Wicksteed Park remains Northamptonshire's most popular attraction and entertainment venue.

Nottinghamshire

Armed Forces Weekend
June, Wollaton Park, Nottingham, Nottinghamshire
www.experiencenottinghamshire.com
Nottingham welcomes the annual national event celebrating our Armed Forces past and present.

Attenborough Nature Centre
Attenborough, Nottingham, NG9 6DY
(01159) 721777
www.attenboroughnaturecentre.co.uk
With a visionary eco-design, set against the backdrop of the beautiful Attenborough Nature Reserve, the Attenboroudgh Nature Centre provides a place for visitors to look, learn and refresh.

Festival of Words
October, Nottingham, Nottinghamshire
www. nottwords.org.uk
Celebrating Nottingham's love of words, this dazzling line up of events and diverse range of host venues pay a fitting tribute to Nottinghamshire's rich literary heritage.

Galleries of Justice Museum
Nottingham NG1 1HN
(0115) 952 0555
www.galleriesofjustice.org.uk
There are many ways to explore the museum of Crime and Punishment, with free exhibitions, audio and performance-led tours plus an on-site café and gift shop. You will be delving in to the dark and disturbing past of crime and punishment.

Holme Pierrepont Country Park
Newark, Nottinghamshire NG24 1BG
(01636) 655765
www.nwscnotts.com
Set in 270 acres of beautiful parkland and home to the National Watersports Centre. With excellent water sports facilities, Family Fun Park, Life Fitness Gym and marvellous nature trails for cycling and walking.

Newark Air Museum
Nottinghamshire NG24 2NY
(01636) 707170
www.newarkairmuseum.org
The air museum is located on part of the former World War Two airfield of RAF Winthorpe. Displaying aircraft, helicopters, aeroplanes, aero engines and aviation exhibits. The museum is open to the public every day except December 24th, 25th, 26th and January 1st.

Newark Castle
Holme Pierrepont, Nottinghamshire NG12 2LU
(0115) 982 1212
www.newark-sherwooddc.gov.uk
At the heart of the town for many centuries the castle has played an important role in historical events. The gardens are pretty, formal gardens bordered by the remaining walls of Newark Castle.

The Newark International Antiques and Collectors Fair
February, Newark, Nottinghamshire NG24 2NY
www.iacf.co.uk/newark
(01636) 702 326
The largest event of its kind in Europe. It is the ultimate treasure hunting ground with 2,500 stands attracting thousands of dealers and buyers from around the globe.

Nottingham Castle
Nottingham NG1 6EL
(0115) 915 3700
www.nottinghamcastle.org.uk
Situated on a high rock, commanding spectacular views over the city and once rivalled the great castles of Windsor and the Tower of London.

Nottinghamshire County Show
May, Newark Showground, Nottinghamshire
www.newarkshowground.com
Promoting farming, food, rural life and heritage in Nottinghamshire and beyond.

Papplewick Hall & Gardens
Nottinghamshire NG15 8FE
(0115) 963 3491
www.papplewickhall.co.uk
A fine Adam house, built in 1787 and Grade I listed building with a landscape park, surrounded by tree belts and a woodland garden.

Robin Hood Beer Festival
October, Nottingham Castle, Nottinghamshire
www.beerfestival.nottinghamcamra.org
Set in the stunning grounds of Nottingham Castle, the Robin Hood Beer Festival offers the world's largest selection of real ales and ciders.

Robin Hood Festival
August, Sherwood Forest, Nottinghamshire
www.experiencenottinghamshire.com
Celebrate our most legendary outlaw in Sherwood Forest's medieval village with jousting tournaments, story tellers, comedy acts amd more.

Sherwood Forest Country Park
Nottinghamshire NG21 9HN
(01623) 823202
www.nottinghamshire.gov.uk/sherwoodforestcp
Sherwood Forest Country Park covers 450 acres and incorporates some truly ancient areas of native woodland.

Sherwood Pines Forest Park
Edwinstowe, Nottinghamshire NG21 9JL
(01623) 825411
www.forestry.gov.uk/sherwoodpines
The largest forest open to the public in the East Midlands and centre for outdoor activities.

Tourist Information Centres

When you arrive at your destination, visit the Tourist Information Centre for quality assured help with accommodation and information about local attractions and events, or email your request before you go.

Ashbourne	13 Market Place	01335 343666	ashbourneinfo@derbyshiredales.gov.uk
Ashby-de-la-Zouch	North Street	01530 411767	ashby.tic@nwleicestershire.gov.uk
Bakewell	Old Market Hall	01629 813227	bakewell@peakdistrict.gov.uk
Boston	Boston Guildhall	01205 356656 / 720006	ticboston@boston.gov.uk
Buxton	The Pavilion Gardens	01298 25106	tourism@highpeak.gov.uk
Castleton	Buxton Road	01433 620679	castleton@peakdistrict.gov.uk
Chesterfield	Rykneld Square	01246 345777	tourism@chesterfield.gov.uk
Derby	Assembly Rooms	01332 643411	tourism@derby.gov.uk
Glossop	Glossop One Stop Shop	0845 1297777	
Grantham	The Guildhall Centre, Council Offices	01476 406166	granthamtic@southkesteven.gov.uk
Horncastle	Wharf Road	01507 601111	horncastle.info@cpbs.com
Kettering	Municipal Offices	01536 315115	tic@kettering.gov.uk
Leicester	51 Gallowtree Gate	0844 888 5181	info@goleicestershire.com
Lincoln Castle Hill	9 Castle Hill	01522 545458	visitorinformation@lincolnbig.co.uk
Loughborough	Loughborough Town Hall	01509 231914	loughborough@goleicestershire.com
Louth	Cannon Street	01507 601111	louth.info@cpbs.com
Mablethorpe	Louth Hotel, Unit 5	01507 474939	mablethorpeinfo@e-lindsey.gov.uk
Melton Mowbray	The Library, Wilton Road	0116 305 3646	
Newark	Keepers Cottage, Riverside Park	01636 655765	newarktic@nsdc.info
Northampton	Sessions House, County Hall	01604 367997/8	tic@northamptonshire.gov.uk
Nottingham City	1-4 Smithy Row	08444 775 678	tourist.information@nottinghamcity.gov.uk
Retford	40 Grove Street	01777 860780	retford.tourist@bassetlaw.gov.uk
Rutland Water	Sykes Lane	01780 686800	tic@anglianwater.co.uk
Sherwood	Sherwood Heat	01623 824545	sherwoodtic@nsdc.info
Silverstone	Silverstone Circuit	0844 3728 200	Elicia.Bonamy@silverstone.co.uk
Spalding	South Holland Centre	01775 725468 / 764777	touristinformationcentre@sholland.gov.uk
Stamford	Stamford TI Arts Centre	01780 755611	stamfordtic@southkesteven.gov.uk
Swadlincote	Sharpe's Pottery Museum	01283 222848	gail.archer@sharpespotterymusuem.org.uk
Woodhall Spa	The Cottage Museum	01526 353775	woodhall.spainfo@cpbs.com

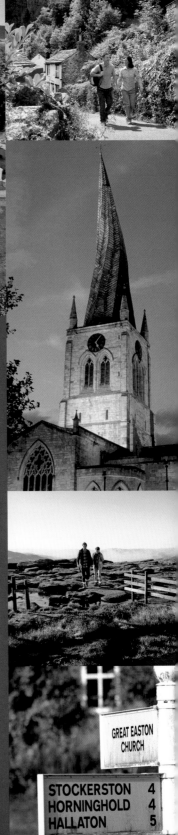

Regional Contacts and Information

For more information on accommodation, attractions, activities, events and holidays in the East Midlands, contact one of the following regional or local tourism organisations. Their websites have a wealth of information and many produce free publications to help you get the most out of your visit.

East Midlands Tourism
www.eastmidlandstourism.com

Experience Nottinghamshire
www.experiencenottinghamshire.com

Peak District and Derbyshire
www.visitpeakdistrict.com

Discover Rutland
(01572) 722577
www.discover-rutland.co.uk

Lincolnshire
(01522) 545458
www.visitlincolnshire.com

VisitNorthamptonshire
www.visitnorthamptonshire.co.uk

Leicestershire
0844 888 5181
www.goleicestershire.com

Stay – East Midlands

Entries appear alphabetically by town name in each county. A key to symbols appears on page 7

ASHBOURNE, Derbyshire   Map ref 4B2
SatNav DE6 1QU [B]

B&B PER ROOM PER NIGHT
S: £61.00 - £83.00
D: £66.00 - £88.00

Peak District Spa
Buxton Road, Nr Alsop en le Dale, Ashbourne, Derbyshire DE6 1QU **T:** (01335) 310100
F: 01335 310100 **E:** PeakDistrictSpa@rivendalecaravanpark.co.uk
W: www.peakdistrictspa.co.uk **£ BOOK ONLINE**

Occupying a secluded location on part of Rivendale's 37 acre site with its own parking, terrace and garden with superb views over Eaton Dale. Ideal for cycling, walking & outdoor pursuits (fly fishing lake on site). Convenient Chatsworth, Alton Towers, Carsington Water. All rooms with en suites, oak or travertine floors, under floor heating. Ground floor rooms accessible for wheelchairs M1/M2.

Directions: Travelling north from Ashbourne towards Buxton on the A515, find Rivendale on the RHS.

Bedrooms: 2 double, 2 twin. Ground floor rooms with wheelchair access & shower room wet rooms en suite. 1st floor rooms with over bath showers en suite
Open: All year except closes 2nd Jan - 31st Jan

Site: ✿ P Payment: 💳 Leisure: ♿ ♪ ⛳ ♻ Property: 🛏 ⬛ ⌀ Children: 🐴 🛏 ✦ Catering: 🍷 🍽
Room: 📞 ☕ 🎧 📺 🛁 🖨

BAMFORD, Derbyshire   Map ref 4B2
SatNav S33 0AZ [B]

B&B PER ROOM PER NIGHT
S: £55.00 - £70.00
D: £70.00 - £120.00

EVENING MEAL PER PERSON
£8.95 - £14.00

SPECIAL PROMOTIONS
Go to our website to see the latest offers available. Discounts for 3 or more nights. For those that would like to stay longer we also have 5* self catering apartments.
www.ladybowerapartments.co.uk.

Yorkshire Bridge Inn
Ashopton Road, Bamford in the High Peak, Hope Valley S33 0AZ **T:** (01433) 651361
F: 01433 651361 **E:** info@yorkshire-bridge.co.uk
W: www.yorkshire-bridge.co.uk **£ BOOK ONLINE**

This famous inn enjoys an idyllic setting near the beautiful reservoirs of Ladybower, Derwent and Howden in the Peak District, and was voted one of the top six freehouses of the year for all-year-round excellence. Superb, en suite rooms, lovely bar and dining areas offering excellent cuisine. Brochure available.

Directions: M1 jct 29, Chesterfield - Baslow - Calver - Hathersage - Bamford. A6013 through Bamford. After 0.5 miles on left-hand side.

Bedrooms: 10 double, 2 twin, 2 family.
Open: All year except Christmas Day.

Site: ✿ P Payment: 💳 Leisure: ♪ ⛳ ♻ Property: 🐴 🛏 Children: 🐴 🛏 ✦ Catering: ✗ 🍷 🍽
Room: 📞 ☕ 📞 🎧 📺 🛁 🖨

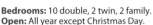

East Midlands - Derbyshire

Biggin Hall Hotel

Biggin by Hartington, Buxton SK17 0DH **T:** (01298) 84451 **E:** enquiries@bigginhall.co.uk
W: www.bigginhall.co.uk

B&B PER ROOM PER NIGHT
S: £80.00 - £132.00
D: £90.00 - £142.00

EVENING MEAL PER PERSON
£25.00

SPECIAL PROMOTIONS
Available throughout
the year. See website
www.bigginhall.co.uk

Biggin Hall in the Peak District National Park is the ideal base for cycling and walking and for exploring stunning landscapes and glimpses of past grandeurs – including Chatsworth, Haddon Hall, Kedleston etc - and bold enterprises now preserved as industrial archaeology. The 17th century Grade II* listed main house oozes character and charm. 21st century comforts and Classical English cuisine.

Directions: Half a mile off the A515, midway between Ashbourne and Buxton.

Bedrooms: 1 single, 8 double, 9 twin, 3 suites.
Open: All year

Site: ❀ **Payment:** 💷 € **Leisure:** ♿ ♪ ☋ **Property:** ♟ ♞ 🖼 **Children:** 🐾12 **Catering:** ♟ 🍴
Room: ♨ ♨ ☏ 🖥 📺 ♿ 🚪

Alison Park Hotel

3 Temple Road, Buxton, Derbyshire SK17 9BA **T:** (01298) 22473 **F:** 01298 72709
E: reservations@alison-park-hotel.co.uk
W: www.alison-park-hotel.co.uk **£ BOOK ONLINE**

B&B PER ROOM PER NIGHT
S: £54.00 - £60.00
D: £108.00 - £120.00
EVENING MEAL PER PERSON
£16.00 - £18.50

An Edwardian arts and crafts house, set within its own grounds in quiet location, just out of the town centre. The family management of the hotel ensures a warm welcome. **Bedrooms:** 3 single, 7 double, 3 twin, 2 family **Open:** All year

Site: ❀ **Payment:** 💷 **Leisure:** ♿ ♪ **Property:** ♟ ♞ 🖼 **Children:** 🐾 🛏 🚲 **Catering:** ♟ 🍴 **Room:** ♨ ♨ ☏ 🖥 📺 ♿

Looking for something else?

The official and most comprehensive guide to independently inspected, quality-assessed accommodation.

• **B&Bs and Hotels**
• **Self Catering and Camping**

Now available in all good bookshops and online at
www.hudsons.co.uk/shop

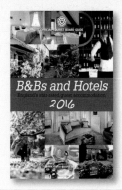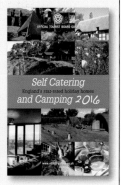

East Midlands - Derbyshire

Old Hall Hotel

The Square, Buxton SK17 6BD **T:** (01298) 22841 **F:** 01298 72437
E: reception@oldhallhotelbuxton.co.uk
W: www.oldhallhotelbuxton.co.uk **£ BOOK ONLINE**

B&B PER ROOM PER NIGHT
S: £65.00 - £75.00
D: £79.00 - £165.00
EVENING MEAL PER PERSON
£20.00 - £28.00

SPECIAL PROMOTIONS
Chatsworth House
Breaks, Theatre Breaks
and Special
promotions available
throughout the year.

This historic hotel, reputedly the oldest in England, offers a warm and friendly service. Ideally located opposite Pavillion Gardens and Edwardian opera house, we serve pre and post theatre dinner in our restaurant and wine bar. Rooms available on B&B and half-board basis. The perfect Peak District base.

Directions: Map available, please see our website for full directions.

Bedrooms: 14 classic double and twin bedrooms, 11 standard doubles, 6 executive doubles and twins, 4 four poster beds, 2 singles and a flat
Open: All year

Site: ❋ **Payment:** 🔲 **Leisure:** 🏊 ♪ ↑ ⛹ **Property:** ♞ 🐾 🖥 🛎 🎂 ◐ **Children:** 🐴 🛏 🧍
Catering: (✗ 🍷 🍴 **Room:** 🍵 ♨ 📞 ⊕ 📺 📠

Causeway House B&B

Back Street, Castleton, Hope Valley S33 8WE **T:** (01433) 623291
E: info@causewayhouse.co.uk
W: www.causewayhouse.co.uk **£ BOOK ONLINE**

B&B PER ROOM PER NIGHT
S: £35.00 - £42.50
D: £75.00 - £85.00

A Former Cruck cottage from the 14th century with oak beams and low ceilings. Heart of the Peak district Castleton is renowned for its Hiking and Cycling trails. **Directions:** Castleton, Hope Valley Derbyshire. Nearest station Hope Derbyshire. Bus depot in the village. **Bedrooms:** 2 single, 1 double, 2 family **Open:** All year

Site: ❋ **P Payment:** 🔲 **Leisure:** 🏊 ♪ ↑ ⛹ **Property:** 🐾 🖥 **Children:** 🐴1 🛏 🧍
Catering: 🍴 **Room:** 🍵 ♨ 📺 🎂 📠

Abigails Guest House

62 Brockwell Lane, Chesterfield S40 4EE **T:** (01246) 279391 **F:** 01246 854468
E: gail@abigails.fsnet.co.uk
W: www.abigailsguesthouse.co.uk

B&B PER ROOM PER NIGHT
S: £38.00
D: £58.00

Relax taking breakfast in the conservatory overlooking Chesterfield and surrounding moorlands. Garden with pond, private car park. Best B&B winners 2000. Free Wi-Fi. **Directions:** Please contact us for directions. **Bedrooms:** 2 single, 3 double, 2 twin **Open:** All year

Site: ❋ **P Payment:** 🔲 **Leisure:** ♪ ↑ 🎣 ⚲ **Property:** 🐾 🖥 🛎 **Children:** 🐴 🛏 🧍 **Catering:** 🍴
Room: 🍵 ♨ 📞 ⊕ 🎂 📠 🖨

★★★
HOTEL

Supreme Inns

Bicker Bar, Bicker, Boston PE20 3AN **T:** (01205) 822804 **E:** enquiries@supremeinns.co.uk
W: www.supremeinns.co.uk **£ BOOK ONLINE**

B&B PER ROOM PER NIGHT
S: £60.50 - £68.00
D: £60.50 - £68.00

EVENING MEAL PER PERSON
£12.00 - £25.00

SPECIAL PROMOTIONS
Dinner, Bed & Breakfast
£99 based on 2 people
sharing.

Situated in Bicker Bar near Boston in Lincolnshire, the Boston Supreme Inn hotel has 55 large and
well equipped bedrooms all with en suite facilities. All rooms have internet access, telephone
points, flat screen televisions. We have a modern, relaxing bar area, serving homemade bar meals
all day, every day. The award winning Haven restaurant is also open in the evenings.

Directions: Located on the junction between
the A17/A52.

Bedrooms: 32 dbl, 21 twin, 2 suite.
Open: All year

Site: ✿ **Payment:** 🖃 **Leisure:** ♪ ➤ **Property:** ♟ 🖃 🗄 ◐ **Children:** 🛏 🏠 ⚹ **Catering:** ♟ 🍴
Room: 🖥 ✦ ☎ ⬚ 📺 🖴

★★★★
BED & BREAKFAST

Gold
AWARD

Glebe House Muston

Glebe House, 26 Church Lane, Muston, Nottingham NG13 0FD **T:** (01949) 842993
E: glebehouse@glebehousemuston.co.uk
W: www.glebehousemuston.co.uk **£ BOOK ONLINE**

B&B PER ROOM PER NIGHT
S: £70.00 - £90.00
D: £90.00 - £130.00

EVENING MEAL PER PERSON
£20.00 - £30.00

This fine Georgian house, a former rectory, lies in 16 acres of parkland in the tranquil Vale of Belvoir.
Glebe House is a spacious, comfortable home with every modern convenience, wi-fi etc, yet it
retains all its original 18C architectural details along with period furniture, four-poster beds, log fires
and grand reception rooms. If you require an evening meal please arrange by telephone in
advance.

Directions: From A1 near Grantham take A52
towards Nottingham for 4 miles. After
Leicestershire sign turn left at The Gap Inn (sign
post Muston). Glebe House is 300 yds down the
road on the left by the lamp post.

Bedrooms: Two en suite double bedrooms, and
option of either a twin or further four-poster
with private bathroom. Wi-fi, TVs, hairdryer and
Tea/coffee facilities.
Open: Open All Year

Site: ✿ **P** **Payment:** € **Property:** ♟ 🐕 🖃 🏠 ⊘ **Children:** 🛏 🏠 ⚹ **Catering:** (✗ ♟ 🍴
Room: 🖥 ✦ 📺 🖴

East Midlands - Lincolnshire

Branston Hall Hotel

Branston Park, Lincoln Road, Branston LN4 1PD **T:** (01522) 793305 **F:** 01522 790734
E: info@branstonhall.com
W: www.branstonhall.com **£ BOOK ONLINE**

B&B PER ROOM PER NIGHT
S: £89.00 - £105.00
D: £115.00 - £139.00
EVENING MEAL PER PERSON
£32.50

SPECIAL PROMOTIONS
For best offers and promotions check our website which is updated constantly with new promotions and offers.

Country house elegance.

Branston Hall is situated just 3 miles away from the centre of Lincoln. It sits within 88 acres of idyllic grounds, has ample free parking and offers luxurious accommodation coupled with award winning food.

It boasts individually styled rooms including 4 posters, family rooms and honeymoon suites as well as an indoor swimming pool, sauna and Jacuzzi and gym.

Directions: GPS: 53.194389, -0.482629. Visit our website for more details.

Bedrooms: A selection of doubles, twins, family rooms, honeymoon suites and 4 poster beds all en suite, sky TV and wifi available at great prices
Open: Every day 24hrs per day

Site: P Leisure: Property: Catering: Room:

LINCOLN, Lincolnshire   Map ref 4C2
SatNav LN6 9BT **B**

Redhouse Farm Bed & Breakfast & Self-Catering

Thorpe Road, Whisby, Lincoln, Lincolnshire LN6 9BT **T:** (01522) 695513
E: reservations@redhousefarmbnb.com
W: www.redhousefarmbnb.com **£ BOOK ONLINE**

B&B PER ROOM PER NIGHT
S: £43.00 - £48.00
D: £58.00 - £70.00

Redhouse Farm is a delightful old farmhouse with a separate ground floor guest annexe with private parking, overlooking pony paddocks. Situated approx 2 miles off the A46 giving easy access to the historical Cathedral City of Lincoln. **Directions:** At Whisby roundabout on A46 near The Pride of Lincoln pub take exit onto Whisby Road towards Whisby/Eagle, then take the first left onto Thorpe Road. **Bedrooms:** Ground floor, en suite, TV, free Wi Fi and refreshments **Open:** All year

Site: P Leisure: Property: Children: Room:

LINCOLN, Lincolnshire   Map ref 4C2
SatNav LN6 9PF **B**

Welbeck Cottage Bed and Breakfast

19 Meadow Lane, South Hykeham, Lincoln LN6 9PF **T:** (01522) 692669
E: maggied@hotmail.co.uk
W: www.welbeckcottagelincoln.com **£ BOOK ONLINE**

B&B PER ROOM PER NIGHT
S: £38.00
D: £58.00

We offer a warm welcome to our home set in a quiet village location, with access to Lincoln, Newark and many local attractions. Children and pet friendly. Off-road parking. Please contact us for prices. **Directions:** Map and directions supplied on request. **Bedrooms:** 2 double, 1 twin. All en-suite, TV, tea and coffee. **Open:** All year except Christmas and New Year.

 Site: P Leisure: Property: Children: Catering: Room:

LOUTH, Lincolnshire   Map ref 4D2
SatNav LN11 8NU **B**

The Old Rectory

Muckton, Louth, Lincolnshire LN11 8NU **T:** (01507) 480608 **E:** franciswarr@btinternet.com
W: www.theoldrectorylouth.co.uk

B&B PER ROOM PER NIGHT
S: £40.00
D: £60.00

Situated on the edge of the Wolds, this Georgian house offers a quiet rural retreat. Guests' sitting room with open fire, TV etc. Non smoking establishment offers a warm friendly welcome. **Bedrooms:** 2 double en suites and twin with private bathroom. **Open:** All year

Site: P Leisure: Property: Children: Catering: Room:

SKEGNESS, Lincolnshire   Map ref 4D2
SatNav PE25 2TY **B**

Stepping Stones

4 Castleton Boulevard, Skegness PE25 2TY **T:** (01754) 765092
E: info@stepping-stones-hotel.co.uk
W: www.stepping-stones-hotel.co.uk **£ BOOK ONLINE**

B&B PER ROOM PER NIGHT
D: £51.00 - £57.00

Small and friendly we are 50 yards from the prom and all its attractions, including Natureland, bowling greens and the theatre. Within walking distance of town centre. Breakfast menu. **Directions:** A158 head straight through all lights towards sea. A52 south turn right at Ship Inn. A52 north, 2nd right (Scarborough Ave.) until pier, left, left. **Bedrooms:** 3 double, 1 twin, 2 family **Open:** All year except Christmas.

Site: P Payment: Children: Catering: Room:

Petwood Hotel

Stixwould Road, Woodhall Spa LN10 6QG **T:** (01526) 352411 **F:** 01526 353473
E: reception@petwood.co.uk
W: www.petwood.co.uk **£ BOOK ONLINE**

B&B PER ROOM PER NIGHT
S: £75.00
D: £130.00

SPECIAL PROMOTIONS
Book 2 nights Dinner, B&B and get the third night B&B free valid Sunday to Thursday.

Friendly service, excellent food and a perfect location for exploring Lincolnshire. Enjoy stunning gardens, cosy log fires and a historical setting linked to the 'Dambusters'. Mid-week special offers available. Rates are from £70 for single rooms and from £125 for double/twin rooms. Upgrade charges apply to executive and four poster rooms.

Directions: From Lincoln take the A15 south to Metheringham (from Sleaford take the A15 north to Metheringham) then take the B1191 to Woodhall Spa. Upon entering Woodhall Spa, continue to the roundabout and turn left (Petwood Hotel is signposted). The hotel is situated 500m on the right.

Bedrooms: 6 singles, 21 doubles, 13 twins, 10 executives, 3 four posters. Half board prices (per room per night) singles £100, doubles £190-£230
Open: All year

Site: ✿ **P** **Payment:** 💷 **Leisure:** ♿ 🏌 ► ♒ 🎱 ✎ **Property:** ⊛ 🐾 🛏 ⊟ 🏢 🛗 ◐ ∅ **Children:** 🚼 🛏 🅰
Catering: (✕ 🍽 🍴 **Room:** 🍵 🕯 ☎ 🎬 📺 🚿 🛏

Village Limits Country Pub, Restaurant & Motel

Stixwould Road, Woodhall Spa, Lincolnshire LN10 6UJ **T:** (01526) 353312
E: info@villagelimits.co.uk
W: www.villagelimits.co.uk **£ BOOK ONLINE**

B&B PER ROOM PER NIGHT
S: £52.00 - £60.00
D: £85.00 - £90.00
EVENING MEAL PER PERSON
£8.50 - £25.00

SPECIAL PROMOTIONS
15% discount for 4 nights or more. Other low season special offers available.

Select Lincolnshire Food & Accommodation Winners 2006-2013. Free WiFi throughout. All rooms en suite with hairdryers & Sealy mattresses. Peaceful location. Air-conditioning in bar. Delicious, home-cooked pub food available. Ample parking.

Directions: On Stixwould Road, next to Woodhall Country Park. 500m past Petwood Hotel. 1 mile to Woodhall Spa centre. 1.5 miles to Woodhall Spa Golf Club.

Bedrooms: 8 twin.
Open: Open all year except New Year.

Site: ✿ **P** **Payment:** 💷 **Property:** 🛏 **Children:** 🚼 🅰 **Catering:** (✕ 🍽 🍴 **Room:** 🍵 🕯 📺 🚿

NEWARK, Nottinghamshire   Map ref 4C2
SatNav NG24 1RZ [H]

The Grange Hotel

73 London Road, Newark NG24 1RZ **T:** (01636) 703399 **F:** 01636 702328
E: info@thegrangenewark.co.uk
W: www.grangenewark.co.uk **£ BOOK ONLINE**

B&B PER ROOM PER NIGHT
S: £85.00 - £120.00
D: £120.00 - £165.00
EVENING MEAL PER PERSON
£23.50 - £35.00

Stylish Victorian hotel with tranquil landscaped gardens, sympathetically refurbished, retaining many of its original features. Located in a quiet residential area less than one mile from the town centre, it is owned and personally managed by Tom and Sandra Carr who will offer you a warm welcome and attentive service. **Directions:** Hotel approx 2m from A1 (follow Newark signs, through Balderton). Hotel approx 1m from town centre (follow signs for Balderton/Grantham). **Bedrooms:** 3 single, 13 dbl, 3 twin. All rooms en suite **Open:** All year except Christmas and New Year

Site: ❀ Leisure: ♪ Property: ▦ ▣ Children: ⋯ Catering: ♟ ▩ Room: ℺ ⬥ ☎ ⧗

OAKHAM, Rutland   Map ref 4C3
SatNav LE15 8AH [H]

Barnsdale Lodge Hotel

The Avenue, Rutland Water, Oakham LE15 8AH **T:** (01572) 724678 **F:** 01572 724961
E: reception@barnsdalelodge.co.uk
W: www.barnsdalelodge.co.uk

SPECIAL PROMOTIONS
Special promotions always available, please see our website for full details.

Enjoy a relaxing break on the beautiful north shore of Rutland Water. We offer you anything from a wedding to an intimate dinner for two. Our informal dining areas are reflected in our seasonal bistro menu. Our bedrooms are all comfortably and individually decorated and have garden or countryside views.

Directions: Please see our website for map and full directions.

Bedrooms: 7 single, 27 double, 9 twin, 1 family
Open: All year

Site: ❀ Payment: ▦ Leisure: ⬥ ♪ ⚲ Property: ♟ ⚲ ▦ ▣ Children: ⋯ Catering: ♟ ▩ Room: ℺ ⬥ ☎ ⧗

Don't Miss...

Dudley
Zoological Gardens
Dudley, West Midlands DY1 4QB
(01384) 215313
www.dudleyzoo.org.uk
DZG is unique - a zoo with hundreds of animals set around an
11th century castle incorporating the world's largest single collection
of Tecton buildings and the country's only vintage chairlift – all sited
on a 40-acre wooded hillside with a rich geological history. From lions
and tigers to snakes and spiders, animal feeding, face painting, land
train and fair rides, there's something for everyone.

Iron Bridge and Toll House ✿
Telford, Shropshire TF8 7DG
(01952) 433424
www.ironbridge.org.uk
The Ironbridge Gorge is a remarkable and beautiful insight into the
region's industrial heritage. Ten award-winning Museums spread along
the valley beside the wild River Severn - still spanned by the world's first
Iron Bridge, where you can peer through the railings and conjure a
vision of sailing vessels heading towards Bristol and the trading markets
of the world.

The Potteries Museum & Art Gallery
Stoke-on-Trent ST1 3DW
(01782) 232323
www.stokemuseums.org.uk/visit/pmag
Travel back in time and discover the history of The Potteries including
the world's greatest collection of Staffordshire ceramics, a World War II
Spitfire, decorative arts and natural history. A warm and friendly
welcome awaits at one of Britain's leading museums where the
unique combination of 'product and place' is celebrated in its
outstanding displays.

Shakespeare's
Birthplace Trust ✿
Stratford-upon-Avon, Warwickshire CV37 6QW
www.shakespeare.org.uk
A unique Shakespeare experience with outstanding archive and library
collections, inspiring educational and literary event programmes.
Discover the Tudor town house that was Shakespeare's Birthplace.
Visit Mary Arden's Farm, the childhood home of Shakespeare's mother.
Explore the lavish rooms and tranquil gardens of Hall's Croft. Fall in
love with romantic Anne Hathaway's Cottage, the quintessentially
English thatched family home of Shakespeare's wife. Take in the period
splendour of Nash's House and learn about Shakespeare's final
home at New Place where he died in 1616.

Warwick Castle
Warwickshire CV34 4QU
0871 265 2000
www.warwick-castle.co.uk
Battlements, towers, turrets, History, magic, myth and adventure -
Warwick Castle is a Scheduled Ancient Monument and Grade 1 listed
building packed with things to do, inside and out.

Heart of England

Herefordshire, Shropshire,
Staffordshire, Warwickshire,
West Midlands, Worcestershire

The Heart of England: a name that defines this lovely part of the country so much better than its geographical name: The Midlands. Like a heart it has many arteries and compartments, from the March counties of Shropshire and Herefordshire, through Birmingham and the West Midlands, birthplace of the Industrial revolution. It is a region rich in history and character and you'll find pretty villages, grand castles and plenty of canals and waterways to explore.

Staffordshire

Shropshire

West
Midlands

Warwick-   Worcester-
shire   shire

Herefordshire

Explore –
Heart of England

Coventry & Warwickshire

From castles and cathedrals to art galleries, museums and exciting events, this region captivates visitors from all over the world.

A beautifully preserved Tudor town on the banks of the Avon and Warwickshire's most visited, Stratford-upon-Avon is the bard's birthplace with numerous theatres playing Shakespeare and other dramatists' work. The city of Warwick is dominated by its 14th century castle and its museums, and plenty of family activities are staged throughout the year. Historic Coventry has over 400 listed buildings and is most famous for its cathedrals, with the modern Church of St Michael sitting majestically next to the 'blitzed' ruins of its 14th century predecessor.

Herefordshire

Herefordshire's ruined castles in the border country and Iron Age and Roman hill-forts recall a turbulent battle-scarred past. Offa's Dyke, constructed by King Offa of Mercia in the 8th century marks the border with Wales but today the landscape is peaceful, with delightful small towns and villages and Hereford cattle grazing in pastures beside apple orchards and hop gardens.

Hereford has an 11th century cathedral and the Mappa Mundi while in the west, the Wye meanders through meadows and valleys. Hay-on-Wye is now best known for its annual Book Festival and plethora of second hand bookshops.

Shropshire

Tucked away on the England/Wales border, Shropshire is another March county that saw much conflict between English and Welsh, hostilities between warring tribes and invading Romans.

The Wrekin and Stretton Hills were created by volcanoes and in the south the Long Mynd rises to 1700 ft with panoramic views of the Severn plain. Ironbridge, near Telford, is said to be where the Industrial Revolution started. County town Shrewsbury was an historic fortress town built in a loop of the river Severn and these days joins Ludlow, with its 11th century castle, as one of the gastronomic high spots of Britain.

There are many splendid historic and architectural gems in Shropshire, from Jacobean coaching inns in the heart of picturesque market towns to Elizabethan manor houses such as the 16th Century Upton Cressett Hall, with its restored Great Hall dining room and spectacular gatehouse, set in the remote and unspoilt Shropshire countryside.

Staffordshire

Staffordshire, squeezed between the Black Country to the south and Manchester to the north, conceals many heritage treasures and an exciting industrial history. It is home to the Potteries, a union of six towns made famous by Wedgwood, Spode and other ceramic designers, celebrated at the many museums and visitor centres.

Lichfield, just north of Birmingham is the birthplace of Samuel Johnson and has a magnificent three-spired 13th century cathedral, while some of England's finest houses and most beautiful gardens are also to be found in the county. Fabulous examples include the award-winning landscaped gardens on the Trentham Estate and the 'Capability' Brown parklands at Weston Park, on the border with Shropshire. Meanwhile, the unspoilt ancient heathland of Cannock Chase, leafy woodlands of the National Forest and secluded byways of South Staffordshire all offer the chance to further enjoy the great outdoors.

West Midlands

The Industrial revolution of the 19th century led to the growth of Birmingham into Britain's second city - the city of a thousand trades. Its prosperity was based on factories, hundreds of small workshops and a network of canals, all of which helped in the production of everything from needles and chocolate to steam engines and bridges. Nowadays the city has one of the best concert halls in Europe, excellent shopping and a regenerated waterside café culture.

The West Midlands is an urban area which still represents the powerhouse of Central Britain. Wolverhampton has been called Capital of the Black Country, made famous through its ironwork and Walsall, birthplace of Jerome K Jerome, has three museums. Affluent Sutton Coldfield and Solihull have proud civic traditions and a number of pretty parks. Many of Solihull's rural villages sit along the Stratford-upon-Avon canal and offer plenty of picturesque pubs along the tow path from which to watch the gentle meander of passing narrow boats.

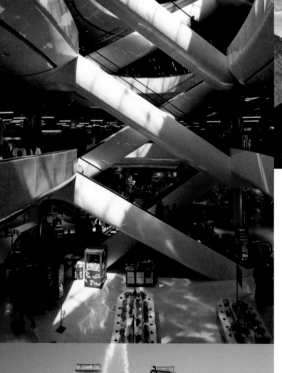

Worcestershire

The beautiful county of Worcestershire has a fantastic selection of historic houses and gardens to discover and Worcester itself has a famous cathedral, cricket ground, and 15th century Commandery, now a Civil war museum.

Great Malvern, still a Spa town, is famous as the birthplace of Sir Edward Elgar, who drew much of his inspiration from this countryside and who is celebrated at the annual Malvern Festival. The old riverside market town of Evesham is the centre of the Vale of Evesham fruit and vegetable growing area which, with the tranquil banks of the river Avon and the undulating hills and peaceful wooded slopes of the Cotswolds, offers some of the prettiest landscapes in the country.

Droitwich, known in Roman times as Salinae, still has briny water in its spa baths and can trace the origins of salt extraction in the area back to prehistoric times, it even holds an annual Salt Festival to celebrate this unique heritage.

Visit – Heart of England

Coventry & Warwickshire

Coventry Cathedral - St Michael's
West Midlands CV1 5AB
(024) 7652 1257
www.coventrycathedral.org.uk
Glorious 20th century Cathedral, with stunning 1950's art & architecture, rising above the stark ruins of the medieval Cathedral destroyed by air raids in 1940.

Compton Verney
Stratford-upon-Avon CV35 9HZ
(01926) 645500
www.comptonverney.org.uk
Award-winning art gallery housed in a grade I listed Robert Adam mansion.

Godiva Festival
July, Coventry, Warwickshire
www.godivafestival.com
The Godiva Festival is the UK's biggest free family festival held over a weekend in the War Memorial Park, Coventry. The event showcases some of the finest local, national and International artists, live comedy, family entertainment, Godiva Carnival, and lots more.

Heart Park
Fillongley, Warwickshire CV7 8DX
(01676) 540333
www.heartpark.co.uk
"We believe that the heart of our Park is the beach and lake. But for those of you who'd like to try out a few 'different' activities - we've got a great assortment for you to try."

Heritage Open Days
September, Coventry, Warwickshire
www.heritageopendays.org.uk
Celebrating England's architecture and culture by allowing visitors free access to interesting properties that are either not usually open or would normally charge an entrance fee. Also including tours, events and activities that focus on local architecture and culture.

Kenilworth Castle and Elizabethan Garden
Warwickshire CV8 1NE
(01926) 852078
www.english-heritage.org.uk/kenilworth
One of the most spectacular castle ruins in England.

Packwood House
Solihull, Warwickshire B94 6AT
(01564) 782024
www.nationaltrust.org.uk/packwood-house
Restored tudor house, park and garden with notable topiary.

Ragley Hall
Stratford-upon-Avon, Warwickshire B49 5NJ
(01789) 762090
www.ragley.co.uk
Ragley Hall is set in 27 acres of beautiful formal gardens. If a fun family day out is what you're looking for then Ragley Hall, Park & Gardens really does have something for everyone!

Ryton Pools Country Parks
Coventry, Warwickshire CV8 3BH
(024) 7630 5592
www.warwickshire.gov.uk/parks
The 100 acres of Ryton Pools Country Park are just waiting to be explored. The many different habitats are home to a wide range of birds and other wildlife.

Stratford River Festival
July, Stratford, Warwickshire
www.stratfordriverfestival.co.uk
The highly successful Stratford-upon-Avon River Festival brings the waterways of Stratford alive, with boatloads of family fun, on the first weekend of July.

Three Counties Show
June, Malvern, Warwickshire
www.threecounties.co.uk
Three jam-packed days of family entertainment and fun, all in celebration of the great British farming world and countryside.

Herefordshire

Eastnor Castle

Ledbury, Herefordshire HR8 1RL
(01531) 633160
www.eastnorcastle.com
Fairytale Georgian Castle dramatically situated in the Malvern Hills. Surrounded by a beautiful deer park, arboretum and lake, this award winning tourist attraction is a fun filled family day out.

Goodrich Castle

Ross-on-Wye, Herefordshire HR9 6HY
(01600) 890538
www.english-heritage.org.uk/goodrich
Come and relive the turbulent history of Goodrich Castle with our free audio and then climb to the battlements for breathtaking views over the Wye Valley.

The Hay Festival

May / june, Hay-on-Wye, Herefordshire
www.hayfestival.com
Some five hundred events see writers, politicians, poets, scientists, comedians, philosophers and musicians come together on a greenfield site for a ten day fesitval of ideas and stories at the Hay Festival.

Hereford Cathedral

Herefordshire HR1 2NG
(01432) 374202
www.herefordcathedral.org
Some of the finest examples of architecture from Norman times to the present day. Its most famous treasure is Mappa Mundi, a mediaeval map of the world dating from the 13th century.

Hereford Museum and Art Gallery

Herefordshire HR4 9AU
(01432) 260692
www.herefordshire.gov.uk
Hereford Museum and Art Gallery, housed in a spectacular Victorian gothic building, has been exhibiting artefacts and works of fine and decorative art connected with the local area since 1874. The Art Gallery hosts regularly changing exhibitions of contemporary and historic art and themed object displays

Hergest Croft Gardens

Kington, Herefordshire HR5 3EG
(01544) 230160
www.hergest.co.uk
The gardens extend over 50 acres, with more than 4000 rare shrubs and trees. With over 60 champion trees and shrubs it is one of the finest collections in the British Isles. With a Gift Shop and Tearooms the Gardens are the perfect place to explore and relax.

Ledbury Heritage Centre

Herefordshire, HR8 1DN
(01432) 260692
www.herefordshire.gov.uk
The story of Ledbury's past displayed in a timber-framed building in the picturesque lane leading to the church. Learn about the poets John Masefeild and Elizabeth Barrett Browning and try your hand at timber framing.

Shropshire

Bridgnorth Cliff Railway

Bridgnorth, Shropshire, WV16 4AH
(01746) 762124
www.bridgnorthcliffrailway.co.uk
Take a journey on the oldest and steepest funicular inland electric cliff railway in the country between High Town and Low Town. Visit spectacular shops, gardens, and enjoy the views that Charlies I named the finest in his kingdom.

The British Ironwork Centre

Oswestry, Shropshire SY11 4JH
(0800) 6888386
www.britishironworkcentre.co.uk
A treasure trove of magnificent animal sculptures and decorations, including of a 13ft-high gorilla made from an incredible 40,000+ spoons donated by people from all over the world.

Darby Houses (Ironbridge)

Telford, Shropshire TF8 7EW
(01952) 433424
www.ironbridge.org.uk
The Darby Houses are one of the ten Ironbridge Gorge Museums. Experience the everyday life of Coalbrookdale's ironmasters in the former homes of the Darby family.

Enginuity
Telford, Shropshire TF8 7DG
(01952) 433424
www.ironbridge.org.uk
Enginuity is one of the ten Ironbridge Gorge Museums. Enjoy a fun-filled family day out at this science and technology centre. At Enginuity you can turn the wheels of your imagination, test your horse power and discover how good ideas are turned in to real things.

English Haydn Festival
June, Bridgnorth, Shropshire
www.englishhaydn.com
Focusing on Joseph Haydn's music and his life in Vienna, in particular during the years leading up to his death in 1809 and his friendship and influence on Beethoven and Schubert, performed in St. Leonards Church, Bridgnorth.

Ludlow Food Festival
September, Ludlow, Shropshire
www.foodfestival.co.uk
More than 160 top quality independent food and drink producers inside Ludlow Castle.

Much Wenlock Priory
Shropshire TF13 6HS
(01952) 727466
www.english-heritage.org.uk/wenlockpriory
Wenlock Priory, a ruined 12th century monastery, with its stunning clipped topiary, has a pastoral setting on the edge of lovely Much Wenlock.

RAF Cosford Air Show
June, Shifnal, Shropshire
www.cosfordairshow.co.uk
This RAF-organised show usually features all the airshow favourites, classic and current British and foreign aircraft, exhibits and trade stalls all on this classic RAF airbase.

Royal Air Force Museum Cosford
Shifnal, Shropshire TF11 8UP
(01902) 376200
www.rafmuseum.org
The award winning museum houses one of the largest aviation collections in the United Kingdom along with being home to the National Cold War Exhibition. FREE Admission.

Severn Valley Railway – The Engine House
Highley, Shropshire
www.svr.co.uk/EngineHouse
The stunning Engine House Centre at Highley takes you on a fascinating journey behind the scenes. Marvel at the massive locomotives, delve into the intriguing history of Britain's railways, enjoy themed exhibitions and meet the engine that collided with a camel!

Shrewsbury Folk Festival
August, Shrewsbury, Shropshire
www.shrewsburyfolkfestival.co.uk
Shrewsbury Folk Festival has a reputation for delivering established artists from the UK alongside acts celebrating folk traditions from across the world who will take you on a voyage of discovery, bringing you ever-changing musical colours with their breath-taking performances.

Stokesay Castle
Craven Arms, Shropshire SY7 9AH
(01588) 672544
www.english-heritage.org.uk/stokesaycastle
Stokesay Castle, nestles in peaceful South Shropshire countryside near the Welsh Border. It is one of more than a dozen English Heritage properties in the county.

V Festival
August, Weston Park, Shropshire
www.vfestival.com
Legendary rock and pop festival held annually during the penultimate weekend in August.

Wenlock Olympian Games
July, Much Wenlock, Shropshire
www.wenlock-olympian-society.org.uk
The games that inspired the modern Olympic Movement.

Wroxeter Roman City
Shrewsbury, Shropshire SY5 6PH
(01743) 761330
www.english-heritage.org.uk/wroxeter
Wroxeter Roman City, or Viroconium, to give it its Roman title, is thought to have been one of the largest Roman cities in the UK with over 200 acres of land, 2 miles of walls and a population of approximately 5,000.

Staffordshire

Abbots Bromley Horn Dance
September, Abbots Bromley, Staffordshire
www.abbotsbromley.com
Ancient ritual dating back to 1226. Six deer-men, a fool, hobby horse, bowman and Maid Marian perform to music provided by a melodian player.

Aerial Extreme Trentham
Staffordshire ST4 8AX
0845 652 1736
www.aerialextreme.co.uk/index.php/courses/trentham-estate
Our tree based adventure ropes course, set within the tranquil grounds of Trentham Estate is a truly spectacular journey. All ages are guaranteed a bucket load of fun.

Etruria Industrial Museum
Staffordshire ST4 7AF
(01782) 233144
www.stokemuseums.org.uk
Discover how they put the 'bone' in bone china at the last working steam-powered potters mill in Britain. Includes a Bone and Flint Mill and family-friendly interactive exhibition.

Leek Food Festival
March, Staffordshire, ST13 5HH
www.leekfoodanddrink.co.uk
The Leek Food Festival is host over 70 stalls and hot vendors, a beer festival tent, and experience Leek's fabulous shops and pubs at the same time.

Lichfield Cathedral
Staffordshire WS13 7LD
(01543) 306100
www.lichfield-cathedral.org
A medieval Cathedral, one of the oldest places of Christian worship in Britain, with 3 spires in the heart of an historic City set in its own serene Close.

Midlands Grand National
March, Uttoxeter Racecourse, Staffordshire
www.uttoxeter-racecourse.co.uk
The biggest fixture in Uttoxeter's calendar and the second longest Steeplechase in the country at 4 miles and 1 1/2 furlongs.

National Memorial Arboretum
Lichfield, Staffordshire DE13 7AR
(01283) 792333
www.thenma.org.uk
150 acres of trees and memorials, planted as a living tribute to those who have served, died or suffered in the service of their Country.

The Roaches
Upper Hulme, Leek, Staffordshire ST13 8UB
www.staffsmoorlands.gov.uk
The Roaches (or Roches) is a wind-carved outcrop of gritstone rocks that rises above the waters or Tittesworth reservoir, between Leek in Staffordshire and Buxton in Derbyshire. It's impressive gritstone edges and craggy rocks are loved by walkers and climbers alike.

Stone Food & Drink Festival
October, Stone, Staffordshire
www.stonefooddrink.org.uk
Growing from humble beginnings in the town's Georgian High Street into one of the Midlands' biggest and busiest food festivals.

Tamworth Castle
Staffordshire B79 7NA
(01827) 709629
www.tamworthcastle.co.uk
The number one Heritage attraction located in the town. Explore over 900 years of history in the magnificent Motte and Bailey Castle.

Trentham Gardens
Stoke-on-Trent, Staffordshire, ST4 8JG
(01782) 646646
www.trentham.co.uk/trentham-gardens
Enjoy beautiful show gardens; take a woodland stroll along the mile-long lake, or get active in the adventure playground.

World of Wedgwood
Stoke-on-Trent, Staffordshire ST12 9ER
(01782) 282986
www.worldofwedgwood.com
Enjoy the past, buy the present and treasure the experience. The World of Wedgwood offers a unique chance to immerse yourself in the heritage of Britain's greatest ceramics company.

West Midlands

Barber Institute of Fine Arts
Edgbaston, West Midlands B15 2TS
(0121) 414 7333
www.barber.org.uk
British and European paintings, drawings and sculpture from the 13th century to mid 20th century, including Old Master and Impressionist collections. The Barber Institute also hosts an impressive range of concert programmes throughout the year.

Bewdley Museum
Bewdley, DY12 2AE
(01299) 403573
www.bewdleymuseum.co.uk
Set in a historic Butchers Shambles, Bewdley Museum offers a fascinating insight to the history of Bewdley with gardens, interesting displays and demonstrations using craft.

Birmingham Botanical Gardens
Edgbaston, Birmingham B15 3TR
(0121) 454 1860
www.birminghambotanicalgardens.org.uk
Visit the ornamental gardens and glasshouses spaning from tropical rainforest to arid desert climates. A lively birdhouse, wildlife trails and a seasonal butterfly house also sit attractively amongst the fifteen acres of flourishing gardens and foliage.

Birmingham Literature Festival
October, Birmingham, West Midlands
www.visitbirmingham.com
Celebrating the city's literature scene, the Birmingham Literature Festival takes places every year with its trademark mix of literature events, talks and workshops.

Birmingham International Jazz and Blues Festival
July, Birmingham, West Midlands
www.visitbirmingham.com
The festival presents around 175 performances each year in around 40 venues. Musicians and fans come to the city from every corner of the UK as well as from further afield and significantly, almost all of the events are free to the public.

Black Country Living Museum
Dudley, West Midlands DY1 4SQ
(0121) 557 9643
www.bclm.co.uk
Britain's friendliest open-air museum - visit original shops and houses, ride on fair attractions, take a look down the underground coalmine.

Frankfurt Christmas Market & Craft Fair
November-December, Birmingham, West Midlands
www.visitbirmingham.com
The largest authentic German market outside Germany and Austria and the centrepiece of the city's festive event calendar.

Great Malvern Priory
Malvern, WR14 2AY
(01684) 561020
www.greatmalvernpriory.org.uk
Great Malvern Priory was founded as Benedictine Priory in 1085 and has been changing and developing for centuries. See different stages of life and appreciate the beautiful architecture in this parish church dedicated to St Mary and St Michael.

Ikon Gallery
Brindley Place, Birmingham B1 2HS
(0121) 248 0708
www.ikon-gallery.org
Ikon is an internationally acclaimed contemporary art venue housed in the Grade II listed, neo-gothic former Oozells Street Board School, designed by John Henry Chamberlain in 1877.

Moseley Folk Festival
September, Birmingham, West Midlands
www.visitbirmingham.com
Offering an inner city Shangri-la bringing together people from all ages and backgrounds to witness folk legends playing alongside their contemporaries.

Thinktank-Birmingham Science Museum
West Midlands B4 7XG
(0121) 348 8000
www.thinktank.ac
Thinktank is Birmingham's science museum where the emphasis is firmly on hands on exhibits and interactive fun.

Worcestershire

The Almonry Museum & Heritage Centre
Evesham, Worcestershire WR11 4BG
(01386) 446944
www.almonryevesham.org
The 14th century house has 12 rooms of exhibits from 2000 years of Evesham history and pleasant gardens to the rear.

Greyfriars House
Worcester WR1 2LZ
(01905) 23571
www.nationaltrust.org.uk
The National Trust's Greyfriars House and Garden, Worcestershire, built in 1480 by a wealthy merchant, is a fine timbered Medieval merchants house and walled garden.

Hanbury Hall
Droitwich Spa, Worcestershire WR9 7EA
(01527) 821214
www.nationaltrust.org.uk/hanburyhall
Early 18th century house, garden & park owned by the Vernon family for nearly 300 years. Choose from one of the scenic walks and make the most of your day by exploring the estate and surrounding countryside.

West Midland Safari and Leisure Park
Bewdley, Worcestershire DY12 1LF
(01299) 402114
www.wmsp.co.uk
Are you ready to SAFARI and come face to face with some of the fastest, tallest, largest and cutest animals around? The park is home to some of the world's most beautiful and endangered exotic animal species. The leisure park features 28 rides and attractions, there is something here to suit the whole family.

Worcester Cathedral
Worcestershire WR1 2LA
(01905) 732900
www.worcestercathedral.co.uk
Worcester Cathedral is one of England's most magnificent and inspiring buildings, as it rises majestically above the River Severn. It has been place of prayer and worship for 14 centuries.

Worcester City Art Gallery & Museum
Worcestershire WR1 1DT
(01905) 25371
www.whub.org.uk
The art gallery & museum runs a programme of exhibitions/events for all the family. Explore the fascinating displays, exhibitions, café, shop and Worcestershire Soldier Galleries. The collections and exhibitions are many and varied, covering centuries of the county's history right up to the present day.

Tourist Information Centres

When you arrive at your destination, visit the Tourist Information Centre for quality assured help with accommodation and information about local attractions and events, or email your request before you go.

Bewdley	Load Street	0845 6077819	bewdleytic@wyreforestdc.gov.uk
Bridgnorth	The Library	01746 763257	bridgnorth.tourism@shropshire.gov.uk
Bromyard	The Bromyard Centre	01885 488133	enquiries@bromyard-live.org.uk
Church Stretton	Church Street	01694 723133	churchstretton.scf@shropshire.gov.uk
Droitwich Spa	St Richard's House	01905 774312	heritage@droitwichspa.gov.uk
Ellesmere, Shropshire	The Boathouse Visitor Centre	01691 622981	ellesmere.tourism@shropshire.gov.uk
Evesham	The Almonry	01386 446944	tic@almonry.ndo.co.uk
Hereford	1 King Street	01432 268430	reception@visitherefordshire.co.uk
Ironbridge	Museum of The Gorge	01952 433424 / 01952 435900	tic@ironbridge.org.uk
Kenilworth	Kenilworth Library	0300 5558171	kenilworthlibrary@warwickshire.gov.uk
Ledbury	38 The Homend	0844 5678650	info@vistledbury.info
Leek	1 Market Place	01538 483741	tourism.services@staffsmoorlands.gov.uk
Leominster	1 Corn Square	01568 616460	leominstertic@herefordshire.gov.uk
Lichfield	Lichfield Garrick	01543 412112	info@visitlichfield.com
Ludlow	Castle Street	01584 875053	ludlow.tourism@shropshire.gov.uk
Malvern	21 Church Street	01684 892289	info@visitthemalverns.org
Market Drayton	49 Cheshire Street	01630 653114	marketdrayton.scf@shropshire-cc.gov.uk
Much Wenlock	The Museum - Visitor Information Centre	01952 727679 / 01743 258891	muchwenlock.tourism@shropshire.gov.uk
Newcastle-Under-Lyme	Newcastle Library	01782 297313	tic.newcastle@staffordshire.gov.uk
Nuneaton	Nuneaton Library	0300 5558171	nuneatonlibrary@warwickshire.gov.uk
Oswestry (Mile End)	Mile End	01691 662488	oswestrytourism@shropshire.gov.uk
Oswestry Town	The Heritage Centre	01691 662753	ot@oswestry-welshborders.org.uk
Redditch	Palace Theatre	01527 60806	info.centre@bromsgroveandredditch.gov.uk
Ross-on-Wye	Market House	01989 562768 / 01432 260675	visitorcentreross@herefordshire.gov.uk
Royal Leamington Spa	Royal Pump Rooms	01926 742762	vic@warwickdc.gov.uk
Rugby	Rugby Art Gallery Museum	01788 533217	visitor.centre@rugby.gov.uk
Shrewsbury	Barker Street	01743 281200	visitorinformation@shropshire.gov.uk
Solihull	Central Library	0121 704 6130	artscomplex@solihull.gov.uk
Stafford	Stafford Gatehouse Theatre	01785 619619	tic@staffordbc.gov.uk
Stoke-On-Trent	Victoria Hall, Bagnall Street	01782 236000	stoke.tic@stoke.gov.uk
Stratford-Upon-Avon	Bridge Foot	01789 264293	tic@discover-stratford.com
Tamworth	Philip Dix Centre	01827 709581	tic@tamworth.gov.uk
Telford	The Telford Shopping Centre	01952 238008	tourist-info@telfordshopping.co.uk
Upton Upon Severn	The Heritage Centre	01684 594200	upton.tic@malvernhills.gov.uk
Warwick	Visit Warwick	01926 492212	info@visitwarwick.co.uk
Whitchurch (Shropshire)	Whitchurch Heritage Centre	01948 664577	heritage@whitchurch-shropshire-tc.gov.uk
Worcester	The Guildhall	01905 726311 / 722561	touristinfo@visitworcester.com
Coventry	St Michael's Tower, Coventry Cathedral Ruins	024 7622 5616	tic@coventry.gov.uk

Regional Contacts and Information

For more information on accommodation, attractions, activities, events and holidays in the Heart of England, contact one of the following regional or local tourism organisations. Their websites have a wealth of information and many produce free publications to help you get the most out of your visit.

Marketing Birmingham
(0844) 888 3883
www.visitbirmingham.com

Visit Coventy & Warwickshire
(024) 7622 5616
www.visitcoventryandwarwickshire.co.uk

Visit Herefordshire
(01432) 268430
www.visitherefordshire.co.uk

Shakespeare Country
(0871) 978 0800
www.shakespeare-country.co.uk

Shropshire Tourism
(01743) 261919
www.shropshiretourism.co.uk

Destination Staffordshire
(01785) 277397
www.enjoystaffordshire.com

Stoke-on-Trent
(01782) 236000
www.visitstoke.co.uk

Destination Worcestershire
(0845) 641 1540
www.visitworcestershire.org

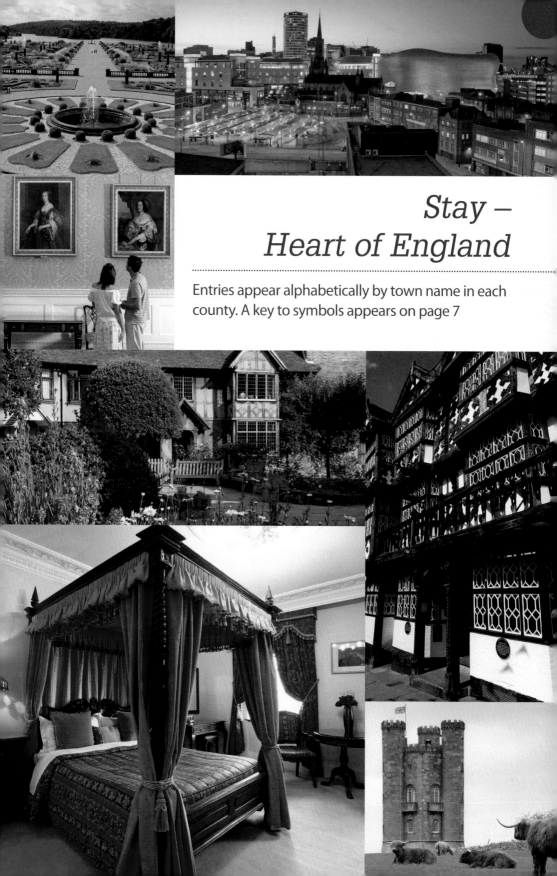

Stay –
Heart of England

Entries appear alphabetically by town name in each county. A key to symbols appears on page 7

HEREFORD, Herefordshire   Map ref 2A1   SatNav HR2 7BP   H

B&B PER ROOM PER NIGHT
S: £69.00 - £85.00
D: £84.00 - £100.00
EVENING MEAL PER PERSON
£14.95 - £35.00

Three Counties Hotel

Belmont Road, Hereford HR2 7BP   **T:** (01432) 299955   **F:** 01432 275114
E: enquiries@threecountieshotel.co.uk
W: www.threecountieshotel.co.uk   £ BOOK ONLINE

Excellently appointed hotel set in 3.5 acres. Emphasis on traditional, friendly service. Tasteful bedrooms, restaurant and bar offer today's guests all modern comforts. Free Wi-Fi in all public areas and selected bedrooms. Town centre 1.5 miles. **Directions:** Please see website. **Bedrooms:** 18 dbl, 42 twin. **Open:** All year

Site: ✿ Payment: 💳 Property: 🐕 🚭 🌙 Children: 🚼 🎮 ♿ Catering: 🍷 🍽 Room: 📶 ♨ 📞 📺 🛏

BROSELEY, Shropshire   Map ref 4A3   SatNav TF12 5EW   B

B&B PER ROOM PER NIGHT
S: £45.00 - £55.00
D: £75.00 - £90.00

Broseley House

1 The Square, Broseley, Ironbridge TF12 5EW   **T:** (01952) 882043
E: info@broseleyhouse.co.uk
W: www.broseleyhouse.co.uk

Period townhouse, one mile Ironbridge. Unique, comfortable bedrooms with Wi-Fi, freeview, plus many thoughtful extras and close good local amenities. Walkers, cyclists welcome. Self catering also available. **Directions:** Refer to the website or call for directions. **Bedrooms:** 3 double, 1 twin, 2 family **Open:** All year

 Site: ✿ Payment: 💳 Property: 🚭 🌙 Children: 🚼5 Catering: 🍽 Room: 📶 ♨ 📺 📀 🛏

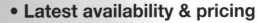

CLUN, Shropshire Map ref 4A3 — SatNav SY7 8JA **B**

*** INN

B&B PER ROOM PER NIGHT
S: £40.00 - £42.50
D: £65.00 - £70.00

EVENING MEAL PER PERSON
£7.95 - £18.95

The White Horse Inn
The Square, Clun, Shropshire SY7 8JA T: (01588) 418 161 E: room@whi-clun.co.uk
W: www.whi-clun.co.uk £ BOOK ONLINE

Small, friendly, 'Good Pub Guide' listed pub with well-appointed, en suite family bedrooms in traditional style. Wide-ranging menu available in dining room. Specialising in Real Ales with own micro-brewery **Directions:** In the centre of Clun. **Bedrooms:** 2 twin, 2 double. **Open:** All year except Christmas.

Site: Payment: Leisure: Property: Children: Catering: Room:

LUDLOW, Shropshire Map ref 4A3 — SatNav SY8 1AA **H**

*** HOTEL

B&B PER ROOM PER NIGHT
S: £90.00 - £120.00
D: £130.00 - £220.00

EVENING MEAL PER PERSON
£32.00 - £39.95

The Feathers Hotel
Bull Ring, Ludlow SY8 1AA T: (01584) 875261 F: 01584 876030
E: enquiries@feathersatludlow.co.uk
W: www.feathersatludlow.co.uk £ BOOK ONLINE

At the heart of the ancient market town of Ludlow with Jacobean architecture and a medieval heritage. Recently refurbished. Award winning restaurant. High standard of food and service. **Directions:** From A49 follow signs to Ludlow town centre. We are situated on the brow of the hill, near a pedestrian crossing. **Bedrooms:** 3 single, 23 dbl, 12 twin, 2 family. **Open:** All year

Site: Payment: Leisure: Property: Children: Catering: Room:

TELFORD, Shropshire Map ref 4A3 — SatNav TF6 6BE **B**

**** GUEST ACCOMMODATION

B&B PER ROOM PER NIGHT
S: £45.00 - £50.00
D: £60.00 - £70.00

The Mill House B&B
Shrewsbury Road, High Ercall, Telford TF6 6BE T: (01952) 770394 E: Judy@ercallmill.co.uk
W: www.ercallmill.co.uk

The Mill House; an 18th Century converted water mill, is situated beside the River Roden. Located in the village of High Ercall, it is halfway between the historic county town of Shrewsbury and the new town of Telford. Wi-Fi and EV charging. **Directions:** 1 mile South West of High Ercall on B5062. **Bedrooms:** All rooms en suite, Wi-Fi,TV tea & coffee in rooms. **Open:** All Year

Site: P Payment: Leisure: Property: Children: Catering: Room:

Sign up for our newsletter
Visit our website to sign up for our e-newsletter and receive regular information on events, articles, exclusive competitions and new publications.
www.visitor-guides.co.uk

TELFORD, Shropshire   Map ref 4A3

SatNav TF1 2HA   **B**

VisitEngland
★★★★★
INN

B&B PER ROOM PER NIGHT
S: £65.00 - £125.00
D: £89.00 - £145.00
EVENING MEAL PER PERSON
£12.00 - £35.00

SPECIAL PROMOTIONS
Stay & Eat offer
(DBB for £125.00 per
couple).

Wrekin Weekend
(3 nights DBB plus
extras £375.00).

The Old Orleton Inn

378 Holyhead Road, Wellington, Telford, Shropshire TF1 2HA **T:** (01952) 255011
E: info@theoldorleton.com
W: www.theoldorleton.com **£ BOOK ONLINE**

Contemporary Styled 17th Century Coaching Inn facing the famous Wrekin Hill. The Old Orleton Inn, Wellington, Shropshire is a charming retreat for both work and pleasure.

Directions: 7 miles from Shrewsbury, 4 miles from Ironbridge, M54 (exit 7), 400yds on the left towards Wellington.

Bedrooms: 1 single, 7 double, 2 twin.
Open: Closed for two weeks in January.

Site: ✿ **P Payment:** 🖃 **Leisure:** ♿ ♪ ▶ ♺ **Property:** ◉ ♟ 🖥 🗄 ⌀ **Catering:** (✕ ♟ 🍴
Room: 🗞 ♨ ☎ 🖵 📺 🖨

CHEADLE, Staffordshire   Map ref 4B2

SatNav ST10 1RA   **B**

VisitEngland
★★★★
FARMHOUSE

B&B PER ROOM PER NIGHT
S: £30.00
D: £55.00

Rakeway House Farm B&B

Rakeway Road, Cheadle, Alton Towers Area ST10 1RA **T:** (01538) 755295
E: rakewayhousefarm@btinternet.com
W: www.rakewayhousefarm.co.uk

Charming farmhouse and gardens. Fantastic views over Cheadle and surrounding countryside. Alton Towers 15 minutes drive. Good base for Peak District and Potteries. First-class accommodation, excellent menu, superb hospitality. **Bedrooms:** 1 double, 1 family
Open: All year

Site: ✿ **P Leisure:** ♿ ♪ ▶ ♺ **Property:** 🖥 **Children:** ⅄ **Catering:** 🍴 **Room:** 🗞 ♨ ☎ 📺 ♿ 🖨

Colton House

Bellamour Way, Colton, Rugeley, Staffs. WS15 3LL **T:** (01889) 578580
F: 01889 578580 **E:** mail@coltonhouse.com
W: coltonhouse.com **£ BOOK ONLINE**

B&B PER ROOM PER NIGHT
S: £76.00 - £120.00
D: £98.00 - £214.00
EVENING MEAL PER PERSON
£15.00

Colton House, winner of The Best B&B in England, set in 1.5 acre garden. Beautifully restored Grade II* property, in picturesque village of Colton on the edge of Cannock Chase. **Directions:** M6 Toll Jct 7, A460 to Rugeley then B5013 towards Uttoxeter, after 2 miles, right into Colton. Colton House is 0.25 miles on the right. **Bedrooms:** 10 double, 1 twin **Open:** All year

Site: ❀ P Payment: 🔲 Property: 🍷 🖥 📷 🍴 Catering: (X 🍷 🍽 Room: 📶 🌢 📺 📠

Wyndale Guest House

199 Corporation Street, Stafford ST16 3LQ **T:** (01785) 223069 **E:** wyndale@aol.com
W: www.wyndaleguesthouse.co.uk **£ BOOK ONLINE**

B&B PER ROOM PER NIGHT
S: £37.00 - £48.00
D: £60.00 - £70.00
EVENING MEAL PER PERSON
£7.00 - £20.00

SPECIAL PROMOTIONS
Offers are available, please ring 01785 223069 for more information.

Wyndale is a comfortable Victorian house conveniently Situated 0.25 miles from town centre, with easy access to Stafford university, the M6, Stafford train station and Stafford record office. We are on route to county show ground, hospitals & business parks. Local attractions including Shugborough, Trentham Gardens & Amerton Farm. Enjoy home made preserves and locally sourced meat for breakfast.

Directions: Please go to our web site where we have full direction & maps. www.wyndaleguesthouse.co.uk.

Bedrooms: We offer 2 single, 2 double, 2 twin and 2 family rooms. Twin rooms have the capability of being used as double rooms. 5 en suite rooms.
Open: All year except Christmas.

Site: ❀ P Payment: 🔲 Property: 🐾 🖥 Children: 🧒 🛏 🎯 Catering: (X 🍽 Room: 📶 🌢 📡 📺 📠

Adelphi Guest House

39 Grove Road, Stratford-upon-Avon, Warwickshire CV37 6PB **T:** (01789) 204469
E: info@adelphi-guesthouse.com
W: www.adelphi-guesthouse.com

B&B PER ROOM PER NIGHT
S: £47.50 - £75.00
D: £85.00 - £105.00

Breakfasts are popular, as are the home baked cakes. The rooms are decorated in period style. The bedding is pure cotton. The house over looks the Fir Gardens and is minutes from the train station, town centre, Shakespeare sites, and theatres. **Directions:** From the A3400 turn onto the A4390 which becomes Grove Road at the next crossroads. The Adelphi is approx 200m on the right as is a lane to parking. **Bedrooms:** Rooms have luxury toiletries and hospitality tray **Open:** All year

Site: P Payment: 🔲 Property: 🖥 Catering: 🍽 Room: 📶 🌢 📺 📠

VisitEngland
GUEST HOUSE
★★★★

Avonlea

47 Shipston Road, Stratford-Upon-Avon CV37 7LN   **T:** (01789) 205940
E: enquiries@avonlea-stratford.co.uk
W: www.avonlea-stratford.co.uk

B&B PER ROOM PER NIGHT
S: £45.00 - £55.00
D: £75.00 - £90.00

SPECIAL PROMOTIONS
£5 Discount on stays of 4 or more nights. 50% off Sunday when booking 3 or more nights, subject to T&C.

Avonlea is the winner of the coveted Pride of Stratford 'Hospitality Business of the Year Award 2015.

The stylish Victorian town-house is located to the south of the River Avon, just a five minute walk from the town centre and its cultural attractions including the Royal Shakespeare Theatre and Shakespeare's Birthplace.

Directions: A3400 Shipston Road, 100m from Clopton Bridge.

Bedrooms: 2 single, 2 double, 2 twin/superking, 2 family (1 Double 1 Single bed)
Open: All year except Mid December till end of January

Site: ✿ P **Payment:** 🖃 **Leisure:** ✇ ♪ ▸ **Property:** 🛏 **Children:** ⚊ **Catering:** 🍴 **Room:** ✇ ♨ 📺 ⚊

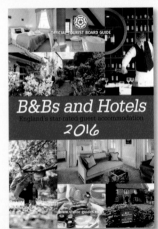
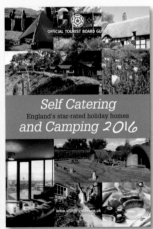

WARWICK, Warwickshire   Map ref 2B1   SatNav CV34 5QR B

B&B PER ROOM PER NIGHT
S: £40.00 - £45.00
D: £60.00 - £65.00

Jersey Villa Guest House, Warwick

69 Emscote Road, Warwick CV34 5QR **T:** (01926) 730336 / 07929 338321
E: info@jerseyvillaguesthouse.co.uk
W: www.jerseyvillaguesthouse.co.uk

Jersey Villa Guest House is located on the borders of Warwick and Royal Leamington Spa. The guest house offers quality bed and breakfast accommodation. Both towns are within walking distance, Warwick Castle is a mere 15 minute walk. **Directions:** Warwick Railway Station, come out onto Broad Street, turn left into Emscote Road, continue for 5 minutes, turn left into Jersey Villa Guest House. **Bedrooms:** Family room sleeps up to 5. Doubles, singles and twins. All rooms large, with en suite, welcome tray etc. **Open:** All year

Site: **P** Leisure: 🦽 ♪ ▶ ৬ Property: 🛏 Children: ᗰ5 ⅋ Catering: 🍴 Room: 🔌 ♨ 📺 📀 ⚘

BIRMINGHAM, West Midlands   Map ref 4B3   SatNav B26 1DD B

Central Guest House

1637 Coventry Road, Yardley, Birmingham B26 1DD **T:** (0121) 706 7757
E: stay@centralguesthouse.com
W: www.centralguesthouse.com **£ BOOK ONLINE**

We are a small, family run guest house. A home from home, close to all local facilities. A full English breakfast is included in the price. Parking available. Ironing facilities and TV in all rooms. Telephone available. Children welcome. All our rooms are non-smoking. Please contact for 2016 Rates. **Directions:** Please contact. **Bedrooms:** All rooms en suite, apart for single room with private facilities. Tea & coffee making facilities. Hairdryer in all rooms. **Open:** All Year

Site: **P** Payment: 💷 Property: 🛏 Children: ᗰ Room: 🔌 ♨ 📞 📺

WORCESTER, Worcestershire   Map ref 2B1   SatNav WR5 2JT B

B&B PER ROOM PER NIGHT
S: £45.00
D: £55.00 - £59.00

Holland House

210 London Road, Worcester WR5 2JT **T:** (01905) 353939 **F:** 01905 353939
E: beds@holland-house.me.uk
W: www.holland-house.me.uk **£ BOOK ONLINE**

A warm welcome awaits you at this Victorian mid-terrace house, situated within easy reach of M5 Jct 7 and walking distance of the cathedral. It retains many original features and offers fully en suite rooms throughout. **Directions:** We are situated on A44 approximately half way between M5/J7 and the cathedral. **Bedrooms:** 2 double, 1 twin **Open:** All year

Payment: 💷 Property: 🛏 Children: ᗰ 🍳 Catering: 🍴 Room: 🔌 ♨ 📱 📺 📀

Need more information?

Visit our websites for detailed information, up-to-date availability and to book your accommodation online. Includes over 20,000 places to stay, all of them star rated.

www.visitor-guides.co.uk

Don't Miss...

Castle Howard
Malton, North Yorkshire YO60 7DA
(01653) 648444
www.castlehoward.co.uk
A magnificent 18th century house situated in breathtaking parkland, dotted with temples, lakes statues and fountains; plus formal gardens, woodland garden and ornamental vegetable garden. Inside the House guides share stories of the house, family and collections, while outdoor-guided tours reveal the secrets of the architecture and landscape.

National Media Museum
Bradford, West Yorkshire BD1 1NQ
0870 701 0200
www.nationalmediamuseum.org.uk
The National Media Museum is a fabulous free museum in Bradford, West Yorkshire devoted to film, photography & TV. Journey through popular photography, discover the past, present and future of television in Experience TV, watch your favourite film and TV moments in the BFI Mediatheque, play with light, lenses and colour in the Magic Factory, explore the world of animation and get gaming in the Games Lounge! The National Media Museum is also home to Yorkshire's only IMAX cinema, for an eye-opening, jaw-dropping 3D cinema experience.

National Railway Museum
York, North Yorkshire YO26 4XJ
0844 815 3139
www.nrm.org.uk
A fantastic day out for the whole family in York with over 300 years of fascinating history in York's only National Museum. Explore giant halls full of trains, railway legends including the majestic Duchess of Hamilton and the futuristic Japanese Bullet Train and marvel at the stunning opulence of the Royal Trains. Watch engineers at work in The Workshop, uncover hidden treasures in The Warehouse and make tracks to the outdoor area where children can let off steam in the play area or take a trip on the miniature railway rides.

The Deep
Hull, East Riding of Yorkshire HU1 4DP
(01482) 381000
www.thedeep.co.uk
Full with over 3500 fish and more than 40 sharks, The Deep tells the amazing story of the world's oceans through stunning marine life, interactives and audio-visual presentations making it a fun-filled family day out for all ages.

Yorkshire Sculpture Park
West Bretton, West Yorkshire WF4 4LG
(01924) 832631
www.ysp.co.uk
Showing work by British and international artists, including Henry Moore and Barbara Hepworth the Yorkshore Sculpture Park is an extraordinary place that sets out to challenge, inspire, inform and delight.

Yorkshire

Yorkshire, the largest county in England, is one of the most popular and boasts award-winning culture, heritage and scenery. There's cosmopolitan Leeds, stylish Harrogate and rural market towns full of charm and character. The wild moors and deserted dales of the Yorkshire Dales and North York Moors National Parks are majestic in their beauty and the county has a spectacular coastline of rugged cliffs and sandy beaches. The region also has a wealth of historic houses, ruined castles, abbeys and fortresses for visitors to discover.

Yorkshire

Explore – Yorkshire

North Yorkshire

Steeped in history, North Yorkshire boasts some of the country's most splendid scenery. Wherever you go in The Dales, you'll be faced with breathtaking views and constant reminders of a historic and changing past. In medieval days, solid fortresses like Richmond and Middleham were built to protect the area from marauding Scots. Ripley and Skipton also had their massive strongholds, while Bolton Castle in Wensleydale once imprisoned Mary, Queen of Scots. The pattern of history continues with the great abbeys, like Jervaulx Abbey, near Masham, where the monks first made Wensleydale cheese and the majestic ruins of Fountains Abbey in the grounds of Studley Royal. Between the Dales and the North York Moors, Herriot Country is named for one of the world's best loved writers, James Herriot, who made the area his home for more than 50 years and whose books have enthralled readers with tales of Yorkshire life.

Escape to the wild, deserted North York Moors National Park with its 500 square miles of hills, dales, forests and open moorland, neatly edged by a spectacular coastline. Walking, cycling and pony trekking are ideal ways to savour the scenery and there are plenty of greystone towns and villages dotted throughout the Moors that provide ideal bases from which to explore. From Helmsley, visit the ruins of Rievaulx Abbey, founded by Cistercian monks in the 12th century or discover moorland life in the Ryedale Folk Museum at Hutton-le-Hole. The Beck Isle Museum in Pickering provides an insight into the life of a country market town and just a few miles down the road you'll find Malton, once a Roman fortress, and nearby Castle Howard, the setting for Brideshead Revisited.

York

Wherever you turn within the city's medieval walls, you will find glimpses of the past. The splendours of the 600-year old Minster, the grim stronghold of Clifford's Tower, the National Railway Museum, the medieval timbers of the Merchant Adventurers' Hall and the fascinating Jorvik Viking Centre all offer an insight into the history of this charming city.

Throughout the city, statues and monuments remind the visitor that this was where Constantine was proclaimed Holy Roman Emperor, Guy Fawkes was born and Dick Turpin met his end.

Modern York is has excellent shopping, a relaxed cafe culture, first class restaurants and bars, museums, tours and attractions. Whether you visit for a romantic weekend or a fun-filled family holiday, there really is something for everyone.

Leeds & West Yorkshire

For centuries cloth has been spun from the wool of the sheep grazing in the Pennine uplands and the fascinating story of this industrial heritage can be seen in the numerous craft centres and folk museums throughout West Yorkshire.

Bradford was a major industrial centre and this can be seen in the number of converted wool, cotton and other textile mills in the area. Salts Mill is a Grade II Listed historic mill building built in 1853 by Sir Titus Salt along with the village to house his workers, in what is now an area of architectural and historical interest. Not far from Haworth is Bingley, where the Leeds & Liverpool canal makes its famous uphill journey, a route for the coal barges in days gone by, nowadays replaced by holidaymakers in gaily painted boats. Leeds itself is a vibrant city with its Victorian shopping arcades, Royal Armories Museum and lively arts scene.

Yorkshire Coastline

The Yorkshire coastline is one of the UK's most naturally beautiful and rugged, where pretty fishing villages cling to rocky cliffs, in turn towering over spectacular beaches and family-friendly seaside destinations.

At the northern end of the coastline, Saltburn is a sand and shingle beach popular with surfers and visitors can ride the Victorian tram from the cliff to the promenade during the summer. Whitby is full of quaint streets and bestowed with a certain Gothic charm. At Scarborough, one of Britain's oldest seaside resorts, the award-winning North Bay and South Bay sand beaches are broken by the rocky headland, home to the historic Scarborough Castle. Filey, with its endless sands, has spectacular views and a 40-mile stretch of perfect sandy beach sweeps south from the dramatic 400 ft high cliffs at Flamborough Head. Along this coastline you can find the boisterous holiday destination of Bridlington, or a gentler pace at pretty Hornsea and Withernsea.

East Yorkshire

From cosmopolitan Hull to the hills and valleys of the Yorkshire Wolds, East Yorkshire is wonderfully diverse. A landscape of swirling grasslands, medieval towns, manor houses and Bronze Age ruins contrasting with the vibrant energy and heritage of the Humber. The Wolds are only a stones throw from some great seaside resorts and Beverley, with its magnificent 13th century minster and lattice of medieval streets, is just one of the many jewels of architectural heritage to be found here. Hull is a modern city rebuilt since the war, linked to Lincolnshire via the impressive 1452 yd Humber Bridge.

South Yorkshire

The historic market town of Doncaster was founded by the Romans and has a rich horseracing and railway heritage. The area around Sheffield - the steel city - was once dominated by the iron and steel industries and was the first city in England to pioneer free public transport. The Industrial Museum and City Museum display a wide range of Sheffield cutlery and oplate. Today, Meadowhall shopping centre, with 270 stores under one roof, is a must-visit for shopaholics.

Visit – Yorkshire

 Attractions with this sign participate in the Visitor Attraction Quality Assurance Scheme.

North Yorkshire

Flamingo Land Theme Park and Zoo
Malton, North Yorkshire YO17 6UX
0871 911 8000
www.flamingoland.co.uk
One-price family funpark with over 100 attractions, 5 shows and Europe's largest privately-owned zoo.

The Forbidden Corner
Middleham, Leyburn, North Yorkshire DL8 4TJ
(01969) 640638
www.theforbiddencorner.co.uk
The Forbidden Corner is a unique labyrinth of tunnels, chambers, follies and surprises created within a four acre garden in the heart of Tupgill Park and the Yorkshire Dales.

Grassington Festival
June - July, Grassington, North Yorkshire
www.grassington-festival.org.uk
15 days of music and arts in the Yorkshire Dales.

Malton Food Lovers Festival
May, Malton, North Yorkshire
www.maltonyorkshire.co.uk
Fill up on glorious food and discover why Malton is considered 'Yorkshire's Food Town' with mountains of fresh produce.

North Yorkshire Moors Railway
Pickering, North Yorkshire YO18 7AJ
(01751) 473799
www.nymr.co.uk
Take a classic steam train from Pickering to Grosmont on the famous North Yorkshire Moors Railway for breathaking scenery.

Ripon International Festival
September, Ripon, North Yorkshire
www.riponinternationalfestival.com
A festival packed with music events, solo dramas, intriguing theatre, magic, fantastic puppetry, literary celebrities, historical walks - and more!

Scarborough Castle
Scarborough, North Yorkshire YO11 1HY
www.english-heritage.org.uk
(01723) 372451
One of the finest tourist attractions in Yorkshire, with its 3,000 year history, stunning location and panoramic views over the dramatic Yorkshire coastline.

Scarborough Jazz Festival
September, Scarborough, North Yorkshire
www.jazz.scarboroughspa.co.uk
A variety and range of jazz acts with a balanced programme of predominantly British musicians, with the addition of a few international stars.

Scarborough Seafest
July, Scarborough, North Yorkshire
www.discoveryorkshirecoast.com
Celebrating Scarborough's maritime heritage with seafood kitchen cooking demonstrations, exhibitor displays and musical performances.

Swaledale Festival
May - June, Various locations, North Yorkshire
www.swaledale-festival.org.uk
The award-winning Festival is an annual celebration of music and arts in the beautiful landscape of the three northernmost Yorkshire Dales - Swaledale, Wensleydale and Arkengarthdale. A Varied programme of top-quality events, individually ticketed, realistically priced, and spread over two glorious weeks.

The Walled Garden at Scampston
Malton, North Yorkshire YO17 8NG
(01944) 759111
www.scampston.co.uk
Set within the 18th century walls of the original kitchen garden for Scampston Hall, an exciting 4 acre contemporary garden. Created by Piet Oudolf, with striking perennial meadow planting as well as traditional spring/autumn borders.

Whitby Abbey
Whitby, North Yorkshire, YO22 4JT
(01947) 603568
www.english-heritage.org.uk/whitbyabbey
Perched high on a cliff, it's easy to see why the haunting remains of Whitby Abbey were inspiration for Bram Stoker's gothic tale of 'Dracula'. Recently named Britain's most romantic ruin, Whitby Abbey is bursting with history just waiting to be explored.

York

Fairfax House
York, North Yorkshire, YO1 9RN
(01904) 655543
www.fairfaxhouse.co.uk
Fairfax House is one of the finest Georgian houses in England, ready to transport you straight back to Georgian England with magnificent architect designed John Carr, changing exhibitions and a range of special events.

JORVIK Viking Centre
York, North Yorkshire YO1 9WT
(01904) 615505
www.jorvik-viking-centre.co.uk
Travel back 1000 years on board your time machine through the backyards and houses to the bustling streets of Jorvik. JORVIK Viking Centre also offers four exciting exhibitions and the chance to actually come face to face with a 'Viking'.

York Early Music Festival
July, York, North Yorkshire
www.ncem.co.uk
The 2015 festival takes as its starting point the 600th anniversary of the Battle of Agincourt and features cross-currents between France and England from the Middle Ages through to the Baroque.

York Boat Guided River Trips
North Yorkshire YO1 7DP
(01904) 628324
www.yorkboat.co.uk
Sit back, relax and enjoy a drink from the bar as the sights of York city and country sail by onboard a 1 hour Guided River Trip along the beautiful River Ouse with entertaining live commentary delivered by the local and knowledgeable skippers.

York Minster
York, North Yorkshire YO1 7JN
(0)1904 557200
www.yorkminster.org
Regularly voted one of the most popular things to do in York, the Minster is not only an architecturally stunning building but is a place to discover the history of York over the centuries, its artefacts and treasures.

Yorkshire Air Museum
York, North Yorkshire YO41 4AU
(01904) 608595
www.yorkshireairmuseum.org
The Yorkshire Air Museum is based on a unique WWII Bomber Command Station with fascinating exhibits and attractive award-winning Memorial Gardens. In addition to its role as a history of aviation museum, the Yorkshire Air Museum is also home to The Allied Air Forces Memorial.

Leeds & West Yorkshire

The Bronte Parsonage Museum
Haworth, West Yorkshire BD22 8DR
(01535) 642323
www.bronte.org.uk
Stop off at Haworth, home of the Bronte sisters, to visit The Bronte Parsonage museum and experience the rugged atmosphere of Wuthering Heights.

Eureka! The National Children's Museum
Halifax, West Yorkshire HX1 2NE
(01422) 330069
www.eureka.org.uk
Eureka! The National Children's Museum is a magical place where children play to learn and grown-ups learn to play.

Harewood House
Leeds, West Yorkshire LS17 9LG
(0113) 218 1010
www.harewood.org
Harewood House, Bird Garden, Grounds and Adventure Playground - The Ideal day out for all the family.

Haworth 1940's Weekend
May, Haworth, West Yorkshire
www.haworth1940sweekend.co.uk
A fabulous weekend celebrating and comemorating the 1940s.

The Henry Moore Institute
Leeds, LS1 3AH
(0113) 246 7467
www.henry-moore.org/hmi
Discover sculpture in Leeds. Feel inspired in three beautiful gallery spaces with an ever-changing programme of exhibitions accompanied by tours, talks and events which explore sculpture from ancient to modern.

Leeds City Museum
Leeds, LS2 8BH
(0113) 224 3732
www.leeds.gov.uk/museumsandgalleries/Pages/Leeds-City-Museum
Leeds City Museums offers six galleries to visit and lots of fun, interactive learning for all the family.

Leeds Festival
August, Wetherby, Leeds
www.leedsfestival.com
From punk and metal, through rock, alternative and indie to dance, Leeds offers music fans a chance to see hot new acts, local bands, huge stars and exclusive performances.

Lotherton Hall & Gardens
Leeds, West Yorkshire LS25 3EB
(0113) 378 2959
www.leeds.gov.uk/lothertonhall
Lotherton is a charming Edwardian house and country estate set in beautiful grounds.

National Coal Mining Museum for England
Wakefield, West Yorkshire WF4 4RH
(01924) 848806
www.ncm.org.uk
Based at the site of Caphouse Colliery in Overton the National Coal Mining Museum offers an exciting and enjoyable insight into the working lives of miners through the ages.

Pontefract Liquorice Festival
July, Wakefield, West Yorkshire
www.yorkshire.com
The festival celebrates this unusual plant, the many wonderful products created from it and its historic association with the town.

Royal Armouries Museum
Leeds, West Yorkshire LS10 1LT
(0133) 220 1999
www.royalarmouries.org
Over 8,000 objects displayed in five galleries - War, Tournament, Oriental, Self Defence and Hunting. Among the treasures are Henry VIII's tournament armour and the world record breaking elephant armour. Regular jousting and horse shows.

Salt's Mill
Saltaire, West Yorkshire BD18 3LA
(01274) 531163
www.saltsmill.org.uk
Shopping, dining and art in one glorious building... Salt's Mill is an art gallery, shopping and restaurant complex inside a converted former mill, built by Sir Titus Salt.

Xscape Castleford

Castleford, West Yorkshire WF10 4TA
(01977) 664 794
www.xscape.co.uk
The ultimate family entertainment awaits! Dine, bowl, snow, skate, climb, movies, shop, dance on ice!

York Gate Garden

Leeds LS16 8DW
0113 267 8240
www.perennial.org.uk/garden/york-gate-garden
Tucked away behind the ancient church in Adel, on the northern outskirts of Leeds, York Gate is a garden of immense style and craftsmanship, widely recognised as one of the most innovative small gardens of the period.

East Yorkshire

East Riding Rural Life Museum

Beverley, East Yorkshire HU16 5TF
(01482) 392780
www.museums.eastriding.gov.uk
Working early 19th century four-sailed Skidby Windmill, the last working mill in Yorkshire, plus Museum of East Riding Rural Life.

RSPB Bempton Cliffs Reserve

Bridlington, East Riding of Yorkshire YO15 1JF
(01262) 422212
www.rspb.org.uk
A family favourite, and easily the best place in England to see, hear and smell seabirds! More than 200,000 birds (from April to August) make the towering chalk cliffs seem alive.

Skipsea Castle

Hornsea, East Riding of Yorkshire YO15 3NP
0870 333 1181
www.english-heritage.org.uk/daysout/properties/skipsea-castle/
The remaining earthworks of a motte-and-bailey castle dating from before 1086 and among the first raised in Yorkshire.

Treasure House and Art Gallery

Beverley, East Riding of Yorkshire HU17 8HE
(01482) 392790
www.museums.eastriding.gov.uk/treasure-house-and-beverley-art-gallery
Art gallery and museum with historic exhibitions. The Treasure House tower provides splendid views over the rooftops of Beverley.

Wilberforce House

Hull, East Riding of Yorkshire HU11NQ
(01482) 300300
www.hullcc.gov.uk/museums
Slavery exhibits, period rooms and furniture, Hull silver, costume, Wilberforce and abolition.

South Yorkshire

Barnsley Market

Barnsley, South Yorkshire, S70 1SX
(01226) 772238
www.barnsley.gov.uk
Barnsley Markey boats over 300 stalls including local butchers, fishmongers and grocers and a huge variety of craft, cosmetics, antiques and much more. Every day except Thursdays.

Brodsworth Hall and Gardens
Doncaster, South Yorkshire DN5 7XJ
(01302) 722598
www.english-heritage.org.uk/brodsworth
One of England's most complete surviving Victorian houses. Inside many of the original fixtures & fittings are still in place, although faded with time. Outside the 15 acres of woodland & gardens have been restored to their 1860's heyday.

Cannon Hall Farm
Barnsley, South Yorkshire, S75 4AT
(01226) 790427
www.cannonhallfarm.co.uk
Cannon Hall Farm is a family-run farm filled with animal magic. Watch out for special events, new arrivals, and one of the best farm shops around with both local and worldwide produce.

Doncaster Racecourse
Leger Way, Doncaster DN2 6BB
(01302) 304200
www.doncaster-racecourse.co.uk
The St Leger at Doncaster Racecourse is the oldest classic horse race in the world, and the town celebrates in style with a whole festival of events.

Magna Science Adventure Centre
Rotherham, South Yorkshire S60 1DX
(01709) 720002
www.visitmagna.co.uk
Magna is the UK's 1st Science Adventure Centre set in the vast Templeborough steelworks in Rotherham. Fun is unavoidable here with giant interactives.

RSPB Old Moor Nature Reserve
Barnsley, South Yorkshire S73 0YF
(01226) 751593
www.rspb.org.uk
Whether you're feeling energetic or just fancy some time out visit Old Moor to get closer to the wildlife.

Sheffield Botanical Gardens
South Yorkshire S10 2LN
(0114) 268 6001
www.sbg.org.uk
Extensive gardens with over 5,500 species of plants, Grade II Listed garden pavillion.

Sheffield: Millennium Gallery
South Yorkshire S1 2PP
(0114) 278 2600
www.museums-sheffield.org.uk
One of modern Sheffield's landmark public spaces, the Gallery always has something new to offer.

Tourist Information Centres

When you arrive at your destination, visit the Tourist Information Centre for quality assured help with accommodation and information about local attractions and events, or email your request before you go.

Aysgarth Falls	Aysgarth Falls National Park Centre	01969 662910	aysgarth@yorkshiredales.org.uk
Beverley	34 Butcher Row	01482 391672	beverley.tic@eastriding.gov.uk
Bradford	Brittainia House	01274 433678	bradford.vic@bradford.gov.uk
Bridlington	25 Prince Street	01262 673474 / 01482 391634	bridlington.tic@eastriding.gov.uk
Brigg	The Buttercross	01652 657053	brigg.tic@northlincs.gov.uk
Cleethorpes	Cleethorpes Library	01472 323111	cleetic@nelincs.gov.uk
Danby	The Moors National Park Centre	01439 772737	moorscentre@northyorkmoors.org.uk
Doncaster	Blue Building	01302 734309	tourist.information@doncaster.gov.uk
Filey	The Evron Centre	01723 383637	fileytic2@scarborough.gov.uk
Grassington	National Park Centre	01756 751690	grassington@yorkshiredales.gov.uk
Halifax	The Piece Hall	01422 368725	halifax@ytbtic.co.uk
Harrogate	Royal Baths	01423 537300	tic@harrogate.gov.uk
Hawes	Dales Countryside Museum	01969 666210	hawes@yorkshiredales.org.uk
Haworth	2/4 West Lane	01535 642329	haworth.vic@bradford.gov.uk
Hebden Bridge	New Road	01422 843831	hebdenbridge@ytbtic.co.uk
Holmfirth	49-51 Huddersfield Road	01484 222444	holmfirth.tic@kirklees.gov.uk
Hornsea	Hornsea Museum	01964 536404	hornsea.tic@eastriding.gov.uk
Horton-in-Ribblesdale	Pen-y-ghent Cafe	01729 860333	mail@pen-y-ghentcafe.co.uk
Huddersfield	Huddersfield Library	01484 223200	huddersfield.information@kirklees.gov.uk

Hull	1 Paragon Street	01482 223559	tourist.information@hullcc.gov.uk
Humber Bridge	North Bank Viewing Area	01482 640852	humberbridge.tic@eastriding.gov.uk
Ilkley	Town Hall	01943 602319	ilkley.vic@bradford.gov.uk
Ingleton	The Community Centre Car Park	015242 41049	ingleton@ytbtic.co.uk
Knaresborough	9 Castle Courtyard	01423 866886	kntic@harrogate.gov.uk
Leeds	The Arcade	0113 242 5242	tourinfo@leedsandpartners.com
Leeming Bar	The Yorkshire Maid, 88 Bedale Road	01677 424262	thelodgeatleemingbar@btconnect.com
Leyburn	The Dales Haven	01969 622317	
Malham	National Park Centre	01969 652380	malham@ytbtic.co.uk
Otley	Otley Library & Tourist Information	01943 462485	otleytic@leedslearning.net
Pateley Bridge	18 High Street	0845 389 0177	pbtic@harrogate.gov.uk
Reeth	Hudson House, The Green	01748 884059	reeth@ytbtic.co.uk
Richmond	Friary Gardens	01748 828742	hilda@richmondtouristinformation.co.uk
Ripon	Minster Road	01765 604625	ripontic@harrogate.gov.uk
Rotherham	40 Bridgegate	01709 835904	tic@rotherham.gov.uk
Scarborough	Brunswick Shopping Centre	01723 383636	scarborough2@scarborough.gov.uk
Scarborough (Harbourside)	Harbourside TIC	01723 383636	scarborough2@scarborough.gov.uk
Selby	Selby Library	0845 034 9540	selby@ytbtic.co.uk
Settle	Town Hall	01729 825192	settle@ytbtic.co.uk
Sheffield	Unit 1 Winter Gardens	0114 2211900	visitor@marketingsheffield.org
Skipton	Town Hall	01756 792809	skipton@ytbtic.co.uk
Sutton Bank	Sutton Bank Visitor Centre	01845 597426	suttonbank@northyorkmoors.org.uk
Todmorden	15 Burnley Road	01706 818181	todmorden@ytbtic.co.uk
Wakefield	9 The Bull Ring	0845 601 8353	tic@wakefield.gov.uk
Wetherby	Wetherby Library & TIC	01937 582151	wetherbytic@leedslearning.net
Whitby	Langborne Road	01723 383637	whitbytic@scarborough.gov.uk
Withernsea	Withernsea Lighthouse Museum	01964 615683 / 01482 486566	withernsea.tic@eastriding.gov.uk
York	1 Museum Street	01904 550099	info@visityork.org

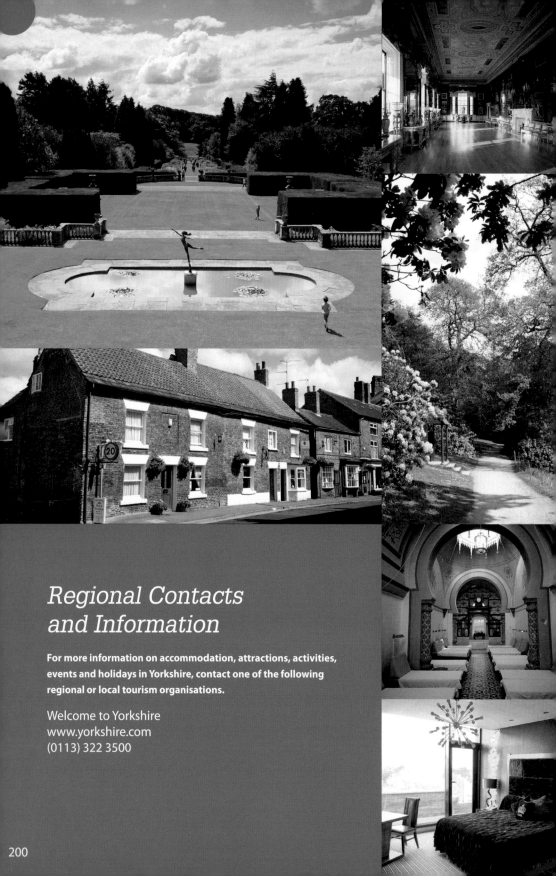

Regional Contacts and Information

For more information on accommodation, attractions, activities, events and holidays in Yorkshire, contact one of the following regional or local tourism organisations.

Welcome to Yorkshire
www.yorkshire.com
(0113) 322 3500

Stay – Yorkshire

Entries appear alphabetically by town name in each county. A key to symbols appears on page 7

BEVERLEY, East Yorkshire   Map ref 4C1   SatNav HU17 8EG B

BED & BREAKFAST
★★★★★

B&B PER ROOM PER NIGHT
S: £60.00
D: £80.00 - £120.00

Newbegin B&B

Newbegin House, 10 Newbegin, Beverley, East Yorkshire HU17 8EG **T:** (01482) 888880
E: wsweeney@wsweeney.karoo.co.uk
W: www.newbeginhousebbbeverley.co.uk

Beverley's only 5 Star B&B. Warm welcome in beautiful Georgian mansion 100 metres from Saturday Market. Three luxurious en suite guest bedrooms, including one family room, king sized beds; splendid dining room; free parking. We also appear in the latest edition of the Good Hotel Guide. **Directions:** 100 metres on foot from Saturday Market. By car, approach from Westwood Road and go down Newbegin (one way) to number 10 on left.
Bedrooms: 2 double, 1 family suite **Open:** All year

Site: ✿ P Leisure: ⏵ ∪ Property: 🖵 🖵 Children: ⿻ Catering: 🍴 Room: 🖉 ⬤ 📺

BEVERLEY, East Yorkshire   Map ref 4C1   SatNav HU17 9SH H

HOTEL
★★★

B&B PER ROOM PER NIGHT
S: £97.00 - £160.00
D: £130.00 - £200.00
EVENING MEAL PER PERSON
£30.00 - £45.00

Tickton Grange Hotel & Restaurant

Tickton, Near Beverley, East Yorkshire HU17 9SH **T:** (01964) 543666 **F:** 01964 542556
E: info@ticktongrange.co.uk
W: www.ticktongrange.co.uk **£ BOOK ONLINE**

Set within 4 acres of grounds our beautiful country house offers bedrooms a million miles away from formulaic sameness. Dine in our award winning restaurant Hide & enjoy dishes prepared with ingredients supplied by local artisan producers. **Directions:** Two miles outside of Beverley on the A1035. **Bedrooms:** En suite, tv, tea, coffee and homemade flapjack. **Open:** All year

Site: ✿ P Payment: 🔢 Property: 🍷 🐾 🖵 ◑ ⌀ Children: ⿻ ⼊ Catering: (✕ 🍷 🍴 Room: 🖉 ⬤ 📞 🔥 ☕

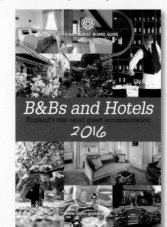
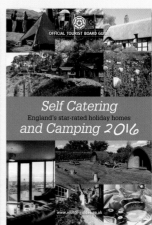

Cairn Hotel

Ripon Road, Harrogate, North Yorkshire HG1 2JD **T:** (01423) 504005 **F:** 01423 500056
E: salescairn@strathmorehotels.com
W: www.strathmorehotels.com **£ BOOK ONLINE**

B&B PER ROOM PER NIGHT
S: £50.00 - £130.00
D: £80.00 - £180.00
HB PER PERSON PER NIGHT
£60.00 - £150.00

SPECIAL PROMOTIONS
Free child places 0-4
years. Half-price 5-14
years. Christmas and
New Year breaks
available. Special last
minute breaks. See
website.

Built during Harrogate's period as a spa town, stylish and comfortable decor goes hand in hand with gracious hospitality to offer a welcome that is second to none. This charming hotel is only five minutes walk from the town centre - ideal for leisure breaks, meetings/conferences and exhibitions.

Directions: By car: 7 miles off the north/south A1 and 17 miles from the M1/M62. By rail: Harrogate station. By air: Leeds/Bradford airport (12 miles).

Bedrooms: 13 single, 48 double, 65 twin, 8 family, 1 suite
Open: All year

Site: ❀ **Payment:** 🖃 **Leisure:** 🏃 **Property:** 🍷 🖳 ◗ **Children:** 🐾 🛏 🎠 **Catering:** 🍷 🍽
Room: 🛁 📞 🔊 📺 ♨ 🖥 🖨

The Station Hotel

Station Road, Birstwith, Harrogate, North Yorkshire HG3 3AG **T:** (01423) 770254
E: admin@station-hotel.net
W: www.station-hotel.net **£ BOOK ONLINE**

B&B PER ROOM PER NIGHT
S: £70.00 - £80.00
D: £80.00 - £120.00

Situated in the beautiful Nidderdale village of Birstwith, just 5 miles from Harrogate. Our location provides excellent access to the Yorkshire Dales, Ripon, Knaresborough and the spa town of Harrogate.

We have five fantastic guest bedrooms which are all furnished to a very high standard with traditional oak furniture, comfortable beds and luxury en-suites.

We look forward to welcoming you!

Open: All Year

Site: ❀ **P** **Payment:** 🖃 **Property:** 🖳 ⊘ **Children:** 🎠 **Catering:** 🍴 🍷 🍽 **Room:** 🔊 🛁 🔊 🖨

KIRKBY MALZEARD, North Yorkshire   Map ref 5C3   SatNav HG4 3SR B

B&B PER ROOM PER NIGHT
S: £55.00 - £70.00
D: £80.00 - £95.00

Cowscot House

Back Lane, Kirkby Malzeard, Ripon, N. Yorkshire HG4 3SR **T:** (01765) 658181
E: liz@cowscothouse.co.uk
W: www.cowscothouse.co.uk **£ BOOK ONLINE**

Cowscot House offers a high standard of accommodation in a sympathetically converted stone barn and stables on the edge of a popular village. All the en suite bedrooms are on the ground floor in a peaceful setting. **Directions:** From Ripon direction enter Kirkby Malzeard and continue down Main Street. Take right turn just after Highside Butchers turning immediately left into Back Lane.
Bedrooms: 3 double, 1 twin **Open:** All year

Site: ❀ **P** Payment: 💳 Leisure: ♪ ⌿ ♃ Property: 🏠 Children: 🚼 ⚡ Catering: 🍴 Room: 🍵 ♿ 📶 📺 🚿

MALTON, North Yorkshire   Map ref 5D3   SatNav YO17 7EG B

B&B PER ROOM PER NIGHT
S: £85.00 - £96.00
D: £120.00 - £145.00

Old Lodge Malton

Old Maltongate, Malton YO17 7EG **T:** (01653) 690570 **F:** 01653 690652
E: info@theoldlodgemalton.com
W: www.theoldlodgemalton.com **£ BOOK ONLINE**

Tudor mansion with luxurious four-poster bedrooms. Great restaurant serving freshly prepared, locally-sourced food. All-day Yorkshire Sunday lunch. All-day tea, coffee & clotted cream scones. Super gardens. Great for weddings & celebrations. **Directions:** Take the Malton exit from the A64. We are approx. 250 yards from the town centre, towards Old Malton. We're behind a big, old wall.
Bedrooms: 20 double (onsite), 8 double (offsite). **Open:** All year

Site: ❀ **P** Payment: 💳 € Leisure: ⛵ ♪ ⌿ ♃ ♋ Property: 🍷 🐾 🖥 🕐 🌙 🍴 Children: 🚼 🛏 ⚡ Catering: (✕ 🍷 🍴 Room: 🍵 ♿ 📞 📺 📀 🚿 📠

RIPON, North Yorkshire   Map ref 5C3   SatNav HG43NJ B

B&B PER ROOM PER NIGHT
S: £45.00
D: £90.00

Holme Grange Farm

Galphay, Ripon, North Yorkshire HG4 3NJ **T:** (01765) 658718
E: b.c.stonard@btinternet.com
W: www.holmegrangefarm.co.uk

Beautiful unique wheelhouse B & B accommodation on small working farm within the Nidderdale AONB. Close to Fountains Abbey and Ripon. The large circular room has exposed beams and its own access. A minute's walk away from the village pub.
Directions: Located in the centre of the village, opposite the flagpole on the village green. **Bedrooms:** 2 king, 1 double, 1 x 2 bedroom cottage. **Open:** All year

Site: ❀ **P** Leisure: ⌿ Property: 🖥 Children: 🚼5 Room: 🍵 ♿ 📺 🚿

SALTBURN-BY-THE-SEA, North Yorkshire   Map ref 5C3   SatNav TS12 2QX B

B&B PER ROOM PER NIGHT
S: £45.00 - £60.00
D: £70.00 - £80.00

SPECIAL PROMOTIONS
Check website for
special offers.

The Arches Country House

Low Farm, Ings Lane, Brotton, Salturn-By-The-Sea, North Yorkshire TS12 2QX
T: (01287) 677512 **F:** 01287 677150 **E:** sales@gorallyschool.co.uk
W: www.thearcheshotel.co.uk **£ BOOK ONLINE**

The Arches Country House is an independent, family owned and run accommodation located not far from Saltburn in North Yorkshire. We pride ourselves on our relaxed and informal atmosphere. We offer bed and breakfast. We also offer functions and a conference facility. Licenced to hold Civil Ceremony Weddings.

Directions: From North A1(M) Jct 60, A689 to A19 for Thirsk. From A19 to A174 toward Redcar, through Saltburn & Brotton. Stay on main road, 2nd left to St Margarets Way, past houses, past golf club, turn right.

Bedrooms: All rooms en suite. Flat screen TV, tea & coffee making facilities. Four poster room, family, single, double, twin rooms, ground floor available.
Open: All Year except Christmas and New Year.

Site: ❀ P Payment: 🖭 Leisure: ► Property: ❦ 🐾 🖼 Children: ⛲ 🎠 ⚹ Catering: ❢
Room: 📺 ♨ 📺 💈 📶

SCARBOROUGH, North Yorkshire   Map ref 5D3   SatNav YO11 1XX B

B&B PER ROOM PER NIGHT
S: £28.00
D: £56.00

Empire Guesthouse

39 Albemarle Crescent, Scarborough YO11 1XX **T:** (01723) 373564
E: gillian@empire1939.wanadoo.co.uk
W: www.empireguesthouse.co.uk

The Empire overlooks pleasant gardens located in the centre of town, ideally situated for all Scarborough's many attractions and town centre amenities. Every effort made to make your visit enjoyable. Evening meals available from Easter until the end of September. **Directions:** The Empire is 5mins from bus & rail terminals. We extend a very warm welcome to all our guests. **Bedrooms:** 2 single, 1 double, 1 twin, 1 family, 3 suite. **Open:** All year except Christmas and New Year.

Property: 🖼 🗟 🖾 Children: ⛲ 🎠 ⚹ Catering: (✗ ❢ 🍴 Room: 📺 ♨ ◉ 📺

SCARBOROUGH, North Yorkshire   Map ref 5D3   SatNav YO12 7HU B

B&B PER ROOM PER NIGHT
D: £54.00 - £86.00

Howdale

121 Queen's Parade, Scarborough YO12 7HU **T:** (01723) 372696
E: mail@howdalehotel.co.uk
W: www.howdalehotel.co.uk/ve **£ BOOK ONLINE**

A cosy stay at the Howdale ensures your visit to Scarborough is perfect! Close to town. Stunning views over Scarborough North Bay & Castle. Fantastic delicious breakfast. Spotless, comfortable, friendly, efficient! Free parking. **Directions:** At traffic lights opposite railway station turn left. Next traffic lights turn right. At 1st roundabout turn left. Property is 0.5 miles on the right. **Bedrooms:** 11 double, 2 twin **Open:** March to October

Site: ❀ P Payment: 🖭 Property: 🐾 🖼 🖾 Children: ⛲ 🎠 ⚹ Room: 📺 ♨ 📺

SCARBOROUGH, North Yorkshire   Map ref 5D3   SatNav YO11 3TP B

Killerby Cottage Farm

Killerby Cottage Farm, Killerby Lane, Cayton, Scarborough YO11 3TP **T:** (01723) 581236
E: val@killerbycottagefarm.co.uk
W: www.killerbycottagefarm.co.uk **£ BOOK ONLINE**

B&B PER ROOM PER NIGHT
S: £48.00 - £50.00
D: £78.00 - £85.00

EVENING MEAL PER PERSON
£15.00 - £25.00

Killerby Cottage Farm is halfway between Scarborough and Filey just 1 ½ miles from beautiful Cayton Bay. Our rooms have every facility to ensure a comfortable stay. Our award winning breakfasts are served overlooking the beautiful garden. **Directions:** Situated just off the B1261 between Cayton and Lebberston **Bedrooms:** 2 double, 1 twin/double **Open:** All year except Christmas and New Year

Site: ✿ P Payment: £ € Property: 🖻 ⚔ ∂ Catering: 🍴 Room: ☏ ♨ 🄰 📺 📀

SCARBOROUGH, North Yorkshire   Map ref 5D3   SatNav YO12 7HY B

AA
★★★★
Guest Accommodation

The Whiteley

99-101 Queens Parade, Scarborough YO12 7HY **T:** (01723) 373514 **F:** 01723 373007
E: thewhiteley@gmail.com
W: www.yorkshirecoast.co.uk/whiteley

B&B PER ROOM PER NIGHT
S: £36.50 - £38.00
D: £60.00 - £72.00

SPECIAL PROMOTIONS
Oct-May inclusive (excl Bank Holidays): reduction of £1.50pppn when staying 2 nights or more.

Small, family-run, non-smoking, licensed guest accommodation located in an elevated position overlooking the North Bay, close to the town centre and ideally situated for all amenities. The bedrooms are well co-ordinated and equipped with useful extras, many with sea views. Good home cooking is served in the traditional dining room.

Directions: Left at traffic lights near railway station, right at next lights, Castle Road to roundabout. Left onto North Marine Road. 2nd right onto Queens Parade.

Bedrooms: 7 double, 3 family.
Open: Closed December & January.

Site: ✿ P Payment: £ Property: 🖻 ⚔ Children: 🧒3 Catering: 🍷 🍴 Room: ☏ ♨ ℃ 📺 ♿

SKIPTON, North Yorkshire   Map ref 4B1   SatNav BD23 4EA H

The Coniston Hotel, Country Estate & Spa

Coniston Cold, Skipton BD23 4EA **T:** (01756) 748080 **F:** 01756 749487
E: reservations@theconistonhotel.com
W: www.theconistonhotel.com **£ BOOK ONLINE**

B&B PER ROOM PER NIGHT
S: £89.00 - £189.00
D: £99.00 - £249.00

EVENING MEAL PER PERSON
£9.95 - £39.95

Set in 1400 acre estate with stunning views, warm friendly welcome awaits, perfect location as a base to explore the Dales. Estate activities include clay pigeon shooting, Kubota RTV and off road experience, archery, falconry and new for 2015, state of the art spa and leisure facilities. **Directions:** On the A65 between Skipton (7 miles) and Settle (9 miles) at Coniston Cold. Just 8 miles from Malham. **Bedrooms:** 65 double, 6 family.
Open: All year

Site: ✿ P Payment: 💷 € Leisure: ⚓ ♪ ▶ ♻ 🎿 Property: ⊛ 🐕 🍴 🖥 ☐ 🅿 ❶ ⌀ Children: 🍼 🛏 🧍 Catering: (✕ ☎ 🍽 Room: 📶 🛀 📞 ☐ 📺 📀 🔌

THIRSK, North Yorkshire   Map ref 5C3   SatNav YO7 1PQ B

The Gallery Bed & Breakfast

18 Kirkgate, Thirsk, North Yorkshire YO7 1PQ **T:** (01845) 523767
E: kathryn@gallerybedandbreakfast.co.uk
W: www.gallerybedandbreakfast.co.uk

B&B PER ROOM PER NIGHT
S: £50.00
D: £70.00 - £75.00

The Gallery Bed & Breakfast is Grade II Listed and full of charm, located close to Thirsk Market Square and opposite The World of James Herriot. 3 en-suite rooms, serving award winning locally sourced breakfasts. **Directions:** From the Market Square turn down Kirkgate and we are 50 yards on the right. **Bedrooms:** All rooms en-suite, tv/dvd, wi-fi, tea/coffee etc. **Open:** All year except Christmas and New Year.

  Payment: 💷 Leisure: ⚓ ♪ ▶ ♻ Property: 🖥 Catering: 🍽 Room: 📶 🛀 📺 📀

WEST WITTON, North Yorkshire   Map ref 5B3   SatNav DL8 4LU B

The Old Star

Main Street, West Witton, Leyburn, North Yorkshire DL8 4LU **T:** (01969) 622949
E: enquiries@theoldstar.com
W: www.theoldstar.com

B&B PER ROOM PER NIGHT
S: £32.00 - £45.00
D: £58.00 - £66.00

Former 18th century inn in the heart of Wensleydale, good views, oak beams, log fire, cycle store, cottage gardens and a friendly atmosphere. Excellent centre for walking and exploring the Dales. Two nearby pubs serve good food and ale. **Directions:** West Witton is on the A684, 4 miles west of Leyburn. Northallerton is our nearest station, there is a bus from Northallerton to West Witton via Bedale. **Bedrooms:** 4 double, 1 twin, 2 flexible/family, 5 are en suite. **Open:** All year except Christmas.

Site: ✿ P Payment: 💷 € Leisure: ♪ Property: 🍴 🖥 ☐ 🅿 ⌀ Children: 🍼 🛏 🧍 Catering: 🍽 Room: 📶 🛀 📺 🔌

WHITBY, North Yorkshire   Map ref 5D3   SatNav YO21 1QL H

Bagdale Hall, No. 4 & Lodge

1 Bagdale, Whitby YO21 1QL **T:** (01947) 602958 **F:** 01947 820714
E: bagdale@btconnect.com
W: www.bagdale.co.uk

B&B PER ROOM PER NIGHT
S: £70.00 - £130.00
D: £90.00 - £240.00

EVENING MEAL PER PERSON
£9.95 - £40.00

Whitby, Yorkshire. Bagdale Hall is an old Tudor Manor House dating back to 1516. No.4 Bagdale is a Georgian town house built around 1790. Bagdale Lodge is a large detached Georgian house circa 1770. **Directions:** Bagdale Hall is located in the centre of town a 2 minute walk to Whitby Harbour. **Bedrooms:** 21 double, 2 twin, 4 suite **Open:** All year

Site: P Payment: 💷 Leisure: ⚓ ♪ ▶ ♻ Property: 🍴 🖥 ☐ 🅿 Children: 🍼 🛏 🧍 Catering: (✕ ☎ 🍽 Room: 📶 🛀 📞 ☐ 📺 🔌

Yorkshire - North Yorkshire

WHITBY, North Yorkshire   Map ref 5D3

SatNav YO21 3QN **B**

B&B PER ROOM PER NIGHT
S: £44.95
D: £89.90
EVENING MEAL PER PERSON
£10.00

SPECIAL PROMOTIONS
Sunday to Thursday
from 1 November - 24
March - 3 nights B&B
£121 per person
(based on 2 people
sharing: £131 for single
occupancy). Supper
included on one
evening. Disabled
access available.

Sneaton Castle Centre

Castle Road, Whitby YO21 3QN **T:** (01947) 600051 **F:** 01947 603490
E: reception@sneatoncastle.co.uk
W: www.sneatoncastle.co.uk

Set in the stunning grounds and gardens of Sneaton Castle, on the outskirts of Whitby and on the edge of the North York Moors and near the seashore. We offer high quality en suite accommodation and an excellent Yorkshire breakfast. Ample free and safe parking.

Directions: Please refer to website.

Bedrooms: 1 double, 8 twin and 3 family
Open: All year except Christmas and New Year

Site: ✿ P Payment: 🖃 Leisure: ♪ ↾ ↻ ✎ Property: 🖳 🗐 Children: 🚲 🛏 ⅍ Catering: ⅋ 🍴
Room: 📶 ✇ 🖨

YORK, North Yorkshire   Map ref 4C1

SatNav YO23 1NX **B**

B&B PER ROOM PER NIGHT
S: £46.00 - £50.00
D: £80.00 - £95.00

Avondale Guest House

61 Bishopthorpe Road, York, North Yorkshire YO23 1NX **T:** (01904) 633989 / 07958 021024
E: kaleda@avondaleguesthouse.co.uk
W: www.avondaleguesthouse.co.uk **£ BOOK ONLINE**

Avondale, a lovely Victorian home, short walk to medieval walls, city, attractions, river walks, racecourse and station. Comfortable en suite rooms with award winning fresh breakfast menu, try our Whisky Porridge.

Directions: Short walk from train/bus station. Drive from south A19, A1 or A64, from north A19 or A59. Find us easily from instructions on website.

Bedrooms: 1 single, 3 double, 1 twin/king, 1 family
Open: All year except Christmas

Site: P Payment: 🖃 Property: 🖳 Children: 🚲 🛏 ⅍ Catering: 🍴 Room: 📶 ✇ 📺

The Official Tourist Board Guide to **B&Bs and Hotels 2016**

YORK, North Yorkshire Map ref 4C1 SatNav YO23 2RB B

Bracken Lodge Bed & Breakfast

10 Main Street, Bishopthorpe, York YO23 2RB T: (01904) 500703
E: stay@bracken-lodge.co.uk
W: www.brackenlodgeyork.co.uk £ BOOK ONLINE

B&B PER ROOM PER NIGHT
S: £65.00 - £80.00
D: £80.00 - £90.00

Bracken Lodge Bed and Breakfast is situated in Bishopthorpe, 3 miles from York and has 3 rooms, 1 x king size double/twin, 1 x king size double and 1 x double all with en suite. Private car parking, quiet location, close to York racecourse. **Directions:** From A64 take exit toward York (West)/A1036 follow signs to Bishopthorpe. From Sim Balk Lane turn left on to Main St, Bracken Lodge is on right. **Bedrooms:** En suite, flat screen TV, tea & coffee in Rooms. **Open:** All Year except Christmas and New Year

Site: P Leisure: Room:

YORK, North Yorkshire Map ref 4C1 SatNav YO30 7BT B

Georgian House and Mews

35 Bootham, York YO30 7BT T: (01904) 622874 F: 01904 623823 E: york1e45@aol.com
W: www.georgianhouse.co.uk £ BOOK ONLINE

B&B PER ROOM PER NIGHT
S: £40.00 - £48.00
D: £60.00 - £90.00

City centre guesthouse, 100 yards from City walls and 350 yards from York Minster. This is the best located guesthouse in York and we have a mixture of 3 and 4 star accommodation between Georgian House and Georgian Mews and are the cheaper option to the hotels in the area. Parking is available nearby for £4.50 per day. Please note, smoking is not allowed anywhere on the premises

Directions: By car, enter York by the A19 Thirsk roundabout and we are situated on the left after about 2.1 miles.

Bedrooms: All rooms are en suite with flat screen tv, tea making, hairdryer etc
Open: All year except Christmas

Payment: Leisure: Property: Children: Catering: Room:

YORK, North Yorkshire Map ref 4C1 SatNav YO1 6DH H

The Queens Hotel

Queens Staith Road, Skeldergate, York YO1 6DH T: (01904) 611321 F: 01904 611388
E: sales@queenshotel-york.com
W: www.queenshotel-york.com

B&B PER ROOM PER NIGHT
S: £85.00 - £120.00
D: £95.00 - £130.00
EVENING MEAL PER PERSON
£10.25 - £27.00

Ideally located on the banks of the river in the heart of the city of York, The Queens Hotel offers quality accommodation for leisure, families and groups. The restaurant is open daily and serves breakfast and dinner. A warm welcome awaits.
Bedrooms: 30 double, 25 twin, 23 family. **Open:** All year

Payment: Property: Children: Catering: Room:

The Earl of Doncaster Hotel

The Earl of Doncaster Hotel, Bennetthorpe, Doncaster, South Yorkshire DN2 6AD
T: (01302) 361371 **F:** 01302 321858 **E:** reception@theearl.co.uk
W: www.theearl.co.uk **£ BOOK ONLINE**

B&B PER ROOM PER NIGHT
S: £70.00 - £150.00
D: £87.50 - £250.00
EVENING MEAL PER PERSON
£12.95 - £30.00

SPECIAL PROMOTIONS
For the best rates
please book direct at
www.theearl.co.uk or
call 01302 361371

The Earl of Doncaster Hotel is superbly located within 500 metres of Doncaster Racecourse and the town centre, offering Wi-Fi throughout and free onsite parking. This impressive Art Deco 4 Star Hotel has beautifully designed Executive Bedrooms, a stylish Cafe Bar Concerto Restaurant, two traditional Function Suites and a unique Boutique Ballroom. The Earl – one of Doncaster's best kept secrets.

Directions: Follow the signs for Doncaster Racecourse, at the roundabout take the A638 (Bennetthorpe) towards the town centre, the hotel is located on the left and car park is situated at the rear of the hotel.

Bedrooms: En suite, flat screen TVs, Wi-Fi, tea & coffee facilities, desk and chair, 24 hour room service, climate control, iron & ironing board.
Open: All year

Site: P Payment: Leisure: Property: Children: Catering: Room:

SHEFFIELD, South Yorkshire   Map ref 4B2   SatNav S6 6HE   **B**

BED & BREAKFAST

B&B PER ROOM PER NIGHT
S: £40.00 - £65.00
D: £65.00 - £90.00

Padley Farm B & B

Dungworth Green, Dungworth, Bradfield, Sheffield, South Yorkshire S6 6HE
T: (0114) 285 1427 **E:** lindabestall@sky.com
W: www.padleyfarm.co.uk **£ BOOK ONLINE**

Set in the peaceful village of Dungworth, each room boasts wonderful panoramic views over the countryside and to Sheffield. The 17th century building has been converted to facilitate all today's comforts with en suite showers. Free Wifi **Directions:** A6101 through Hillsbrough. Take 3rd exit at Mailin Bridge to Loxley B6077. Left at Dam Flask then left up Briers house lane B6070. Next left.
Bedrooms: All rooms have freeview, DVD TVs & hairdryers
Open: All year except New Year

Site: ✿ P Payment: 💳 Leisure: ♪ ⊳ ∪ Property: 🛏 💺 ⛪ Children: 🎠 🎮 ☂ Catering: 🍴 Room: 🕸 ☕ TV DVD 🖨

HAWORTH, West Yorkshire   Map ref 4B1   SatNav BD22 8EZ   **B**

GUEST HOUSE

B&B PER ROOM PER NIGHT
S: £75.00 - £250.00
D: £99.00 - £250.00
EVENING MEAL PER PERSON
£15.00 - £45.00

SPECIAL PROMOTIONS
Book one night and receive your 2nd night half price, QUOTE VISIT16 for this special offer exclusive to Visit England subscribers. *on selected dates, subject to availability.

Ashmount Country House

Mytholmes Lane, Haworth BD22 8EZ **T:** (01535) 645726 **E:** info@ashmounthaworth.co.uk
W: www.ashmounthaworth.co.uk **£ BOOK ONLINE**

Our Victorian house, built by Dr Ingham the Bronte family's physician, offers luxury bed & breakfast accommodation with a fantastic AA awarded restaurant; the 'Drawing Room'. With many original features and antique furniture, fabulous gardens, wonderful views and private parking. We provide a romantic retreat with hot tub rooms available and we cater for intimate Weddings and private parties.

Bedrooms: All rooms are en suite and with flat screen tvs, some with four-poster beds, feature baths and hot tubs in selected rooms
Open: All year

Site: ✿ P Payment: 💳 Property: 🛏 🐾 💺 ⛪ ∅ Children: 🎠 Catering: ⍓ ☕ 🍴
Room: 🕸 ☕ TV DVD 🖨 🖥

HAWORTH, West Yorkshire   Map ref 4B1   SatNav BD22 9SG   **B**

GUEST ACCOMMODATION

B&B PER ROOM PER NIGHT
S: £55.00 - £65.00
D: £70.00 - £80.00

Leeming Wells

Long Causeway, Oxenhope, Keighley, West Yorkshire BD22 9SG **T:** (01535) 646757
F: 01535 648992 **E:** info@leemingwells.co.uk
W: www.leemingwells.co.uk

Leeming Wells offers 4* accommodation in an amazing setting in Oxenhope, near Haworth. With beautiful en suite bedrooms you can relax in our Swimming Pool with the backdrop of Yorkshire rolling countryside. Breakfast at Dog & Gun next door.
Directions: By car: Haworth 9 minutes. Skipton Market Town 30 minutes. Bradford Alhambra Theatre 20 minutes. **Bedrooms:** En suite, flat screen TV, tea/coffee and biscuit tray **Open:** All year

Site: ✿ P Payment: 💳 Leisure: ⊳ ♨ 🏊 Property: 🛏 🐾 💺 ⛪ Children: 🎠 🎮 Catering: ⍓ ☕
Room: 🕸 ☕ 📞 TV 🖨

Don't Miss...

Blackpool Illuminations
Sept-Nov, Blackpool
www.illuminations.visitblackpool.com
This world famous display lights up Blackpool's promenade with over
1 million glittering lights that will make you oooh and aaah in wonder.
Head for the big switch on or buy tickets for the Festival Weekend.
There's also Blackpool Zoo, the Pleasure Beach Resort and fabulous
entertainment at the Blackpool tower. Whether you're nine or 90, there
are plenty of things to do in Blackpool day and night, all year round.

Chester Zoo
Cheshire CH2 1LH
(01244) 380280
www.chesterzoo.org
Over 12000 animals and 400 different species, including some of the
most exotic and endangered species on the planet in 125 acres of award-
winning zoological gardens. Chester Zoo is one of the world's top zoos,
and the UK's number one wildlife attraction, with over the 1.4 million
visitors every year..

Jodrell Bank Discovery Centre
Macclesfield, Cheshire SK11 9DL
(01477) 571766
www.jodrellbank.net
A great day out for all the family, explore the wonders of the universe
and learn about the workings of the giant Lovell Telescope. Start your
visit in the Planet Pavillion by exploring our place in the universe with
the clockwork Orrery. Discover how Jodrell Bank scientists use radio
telescopes to learn more about distant objects in space in the Space
Pavilion exhibition, listen to the sound of the Big Bang, and find out
about 'Big Telescopes' via a range of hands-on activities.

Muncaster Castle
Ravenglass, Cumbria CA18 1RQ
(01229) 717614
www.muncaster.co.uk
Medieval Muncaster Castle is a treasure trove of paintings,
silver, embroideries and more in acres of Grade 2 woodland gardens,
famous for rhododendrons and breathtaking views of the
Lake District. The Great Hall, octagonal library and elegant dining room
must not be missed. Elegant rooms, historic furnishings, superb works of
art, yet still a lived-in home. The audio tour, narrated by the Pennington
family, whose ancestors have been at Muncaster for 8 centuries, enlivens
the castle, bringing the past to the present.

Tate Liverpool
Merseyside L3 4BB
(0151) 702 7400
www.tate.org.uk/liverpool
Housing the national collection of modern art in the North in beautiful
light filled galleries, Tate Liverpool is one of the largest galleries of
modern and contemporary art outside London. Major exhibitions in
recent years have included the work of Jackson Pollock, Andy Warhol
and René Magritte. Free to visit except for special exhibitions. The Tate
Liverpool café offers a range of refreshments with views of the historic
Albert Dock.

North West

Cheshire, Cumbria, Lancashire,
Greater Manchester, Merseyside

The breathtaking scenery of the Lake District dominates the North West, but urban attractions such as cosmopolitan Manchester and Liverpool, with its grand architecture and cultural credentials, have much to recommend them. Further afield, you can explore the Roman and Medieval heritage of Chester, discover Lancashire's wealth of historic houses and gardens, or make a date for one of the huge variety of events that take place in this region throughout the year.

Cumbria

Lancashire

Greater Manchester

Merseyside

Cheshire

Explore – North West

Cheshire

The charms of the old walled city of Chester and the picturesque villages that dot Cheshire's countryside contrast sharply with the industrial towns of Runcorn and Warrington. Iron age forts, Roman ruins, Medieval churches, Tudor cottages and elegant Georgian and Victorian stately homes are among the many attractive sights of the county. South Cheshire, like Cumbria to the north, has long been the home of the wealthy from Manchester and Liverpool and boasts a huge selection of of excellent eateries. It also has peaceful, pretty countryside, and is within easy reach of the wilder terrain of the Peak District and North Wales.

Cumbria

In this lovely corner of England, there is beauty in breathtaking variety. The area is loved by many who come back time and again to its inspirational magic, brilliant blue lakes and craggy mountain tops. The central Lake District with its mountains, lakes and woods is so well known that there is a tendency to forget that the rest of Cumbria contains some of the most varied and attractive landscape in Britain. In the east of the county, the peaceful Eden Valley is sheltered by the towering hills of the Pennines, with charming little red sandstone villages and reminders of the Roman occupation everywhere. Alston, with its cobbled streets is the highest town in England, and has been used for numerous TV location sets.

Cumbria's long coastline is full of variety with rocky cliffs, sea birds, sandy estuaries, miles of sun-trap sand dunes and friendly harbours. In Autumn the deciduous woodlands and bracken coloured hillsides glow with colour. In Winter, the snow covered mountain tops dazzle magnificently against blue skies. In Spring, you can discover the delights of the magical, constantly changing light and the joy of finding carpets of wild flowers.

The Lake District is an outdoor enthusiasts paradise offering everything from walking and climbing to orienteering, potholing, cycling, riding, golf, sailing, sailboarding, canoeing, fishing and waterskiing. A great way to take in the beauty of this unique area is to plan your own personal route on foot, or cycle one of the many formal trails such as the Cumbria Cycle Way.

The Cumbrian climate is ideal for gardens and the area is famous for the rhododendrons and azaleas which grow here in abundance.

If you fancy a break from the great outdoors there is a wealth of historic houses, from small cottages where famous writers have lived to stately homes, that have seen centuries of gracious living and architectural importance.

Lancashire

Lancashire's Forest of Bowland is an area of outstanding natural beauty with wild crags, superb walks, streams, valleys and fells.

Blackpool on the coast has been the playground of the North West for many years and still draws millions of holiday makers every year, attracted to its seven miles of beach, illuminations, Pleasure Beach Amusement Park and golf. Morecambe, Southport, Lytham St Annes and Fleetwood also offer wide beaches, golf and bracing walks.

Lancaster, a city since Roman times, has fine museums, a castle and an imitation of the Taj Mahal, the Ashton Memorial.

Manchester

Manchester's prosperity can be traced back to the 14th century when Flemish weavers arrived to transform a market town into a thriving boom city at the forefront of the Industrial Revolution.

Now known as The Capital of the North, the city is rich in culture with plenty of galleries, museums, libraries and theatres. The City Art Gallery displays its famous pre-Raphaelite collection while the Halle Orchestra regularly fills the Bridgewater Hall.

At Granada Studios you can still tour the set of Coronation Street and you can find quality shopping locations and sporting (particularly football) traditions. Cosmopolitan Manchester makes a great place to stay for a spot of retail therapy too!

Merseyside

Liverpool was an important city long before The Beatles emerged from their Cavern in the Swinging Sixties. It grew from a village into a prosperous port, where emigrants sailed for the New World and immigrants arrived from Ireland. Today the ocean going liners are fewer, but the revitalised dock complex ensures that the city is as vibrant as ever. Liverpool's waterfront regeneration flagship is the Albert Dock Village, which includes the Maritime Museum and Tate Gallery Liverpool. The city has two modern cathedrals, a symphony orchestra, plenty of museums and Britain's oldest repertory theatre The Playhouse.

In recent years, Liverpool has seen the opening of an extensive range of cafés, restaurants and accommodation to suit all tastes and budgets, as well as becoming a mecca for serious shoppers with locations such as the Metquarter and Liverpool ONE, the huge open-air shopping district that is home to more than 160 famous high street shops, cool independent boutiques, cafés and restaurants in the heart of the city centre.

Visit – North West

 Attractions with this sign participate in the Visitor Attraction Quality Assurance Scheme.

Cheshire

Anson Engine Museum
Macclesfield, Cheshire SK12 1TD
(01625) 874426
www.enginemuseum.org
Recognised as one of the Country's leading specialist museums; see exhibitions of engines of all sizes, as well as craft demonstrations, working machinery and local history exhibitions. A must-see for both enthusiasts and non-enthusiasts.

Arley Hall & Gardens
Northwich, Cheshire CW9 6NA
(01565) 777353
www.arleyhallandgardens.com
The Gardens are outstanding for their vitality, variety and historical interest and are particularly celebrated for the magnificent double herbaceous border. The Hall is an impressive example of a Victorian country house built in the Elizabethan style.

Catalyst Science Discovery Centre
Widnes, Cheshire WA8 0DF
(0151) 420 1121
www.catalyst.org.uk
Interactive science centre whose aim is to make science exciting and accessible to people of all ages.

Chester Cathedral
Cheshire CH1 2HU
(01244) 324756
www.chestercathedral.com
A must-see for Chester, a beautiful cathedral with a fascinating history.

Cholmondeley Castle Gardens
Malpas, Cheshire SY14 8AH
(0182) 720383
www.cholmondeleycastle.com
Visitors can enjoy the tranquil Temple Water Garden, Ruin Water Garden, memorial mosaic, Rose garden & many mixed borders.

Forest Live
July, Delamere Forest Cheshire, CW8 2JD
www.forestry.gov.uk
Hosted in seven different forest venues, Forest Live hosts some of the biggest names in the music industry. A fantastic outdoor concert for any music lover.

Go Ape! Hire Wire Forest Adventure -.Delamere
Northwich, Cheshire CW8 2JD
(0845) 643 9215
www.goape.co.uk
Take to the trees and experience an exhilarating course of rope bridges, tarzan swings and zip slides.

Grosvenor Park Open Air Theatre
July-August, Grosvenor Park, Chester, Cheshire
www.grosvenorparkopenairtheatre.co.uk
The award winning Grosvenor Park Open Air Theatre is the greatest open air theatre experience outside of London. 2016 guarantees another summer of exciting performances.

Hare Hill Gardens
Macclesfield, Cheshire SK10 4PY
(01625) 584412
www.nationaltrust.org.uk/harehill
A small but perfectly formed and tranquil woodland garden, surrounded by parkland, with a delightful walled garden at its heart.

National Waterways Museum
Ellesmere Port, Cheshire CH65 4FW
(0151) 335 5017
www.canalrivertrust.org.uk
Unlock the wonders of our waterways at the National Waterways Museum, a fun and informative day out for all ages.

RHS Flower Show Tatton Park
July, Tatton Park, Knutsford, Cheshire
www.rhs.org.uk
A fantastic display of flora and fauna and all things garden related in stunning Cheshire countryside.

Cumbria

Great North Swim
June, Windermere, Cumbria
www.greatswim.org
Europe's biggest open water swim series comes to the Lake District.

Grizedale Forest Visitor Centre
Hawkshead, Cumbria LA22 0QJ
(01229) 860010
www.forestry.gov.uk/northwestengland
Grizedale Forest offers a range of activities for all ages through the year, from mountain biking to relaxing walks, Go-Ape to the sculpture trails.

Holker Hall & Gardens
Grange-over-Sands, Cumbria LA11 7PL
(01539) 558328
www.holker.co.uk
Home to Lord and Lady Cavendish, Victorian wing, glorious gardens, parkland and woodlands.

Hutton-in-the-Forest
Penrith, Cumbria CA11 9TH
(017684) 84449
www.hutton-in-the-forest.co.uk
A beautiful house surrounded by magnificent woodland of the medieval forest of Inglewood. Both the interior and exterior show a wide variety of architectural and decorative styles from the 17th century to the present day.

Museum of Lakeland Life
Kendal, Cumbria LA9 5AL
(01539) 722464
www.lakelandmuseum.org.uk
This award-winning museum takes you and your family back through time to tell the story of the Lake District and its inhabitants.

Penrith Castle
Cumbria CA11 7HX
(01912) 691200
www.english-heritage.org.uk/daysout/properties/penrith-castle/
The mainly 15th Century remains of a castle begun by Bishop Strickland of Carlisle and developed by the Nevilles and Richard III.

Ravenglass & Eskdale Railway
Cumbria CA18 1SW
(01229) 717171
www.ravenglass-railway.co.uk
Heritage steam engines haul open-top and covered carriages from the Lake District coastal village of Ravenglass to the foot of England's highest mountains.

South Lakes Safari Zoo
Dalton-in-Furness, Cumbria LA15 8JR
(01229) 466086
www.southlakessafarizoo.com
The ultimate interactive animal experience. Get close to wildlife at Cumbria's top tourist attraction.

Ullswater Steamers
Cumbria CA11 0US
(01768) 482229
www.ullswater-steamers.co.uk
The 'Steamers' create the opportunity to combine a cruise with some of the spectacular walks in the lake District.

Windermere Lake Cruises, Lakeside
Newby Bridge, Cumbria LA12 8AS
(01539) 443360
www.windermere-lakecruises.co.uk
Steamers and launches sail daily between Ambleside, Bowness and Lakeside.

The World of Beatrix Potter
Bowness, Cumbria LA23 3BX
(01539) 488444
www.hop-skip-jump.com
A magical indoor attraction that brings to life all 23 Beatrix Potter's Peter Rabbit tales.

Lancashire

Blackpool Dance Festival
May, Blackpool, Lancashire
www.blackpooldancefestival.com
The world's first and foremost festival of dancing.

Blackpool Pleasure Beach
Blackpool, Lancashire FY4 1EZ
(0871) 222 1234
www.blackpoolpleasurebeach.com
The UK's most ride intensive theme park and home to the legendary Big One and Valhalla.

The Blackpool Tower
Blackpool, Lancashire FY1 4BJ
(0871) 222 9929
www.theblackpooltower.com
Built in 1894, The Blackpool Tower is one of Britain's best loved landmarks. There are plenty of experiences on offer at The Blackpool Tower to ensure you have an unparalleled Blackpool experience.

Clitheroe Food Festival
August, Clitheroe, Lancashire
www.clitheroefoodfestival.com
Celebrating the very finest Lancashire food and drink produces. Includes chef demos, tastings and cookery workshops.

Farmer Ted's Farm Park
Ormskirk, Lancashire L39 7HW
(0151) 526 0002
www.farmerteds.com
An interactive children's activity park, sited on a working farm within the beautiful Lancashire countryside.

Garstang Walking Festival
May, Garstang, Lancashire
www.visitlancashire.com
A celebration of springtime in the stunning countryside of Garstang and the surrounding area. Guided walks and activities for all the family.

Lytham Proms Festival
August, Lytham & St Annes, Lancashire
www.visitlancashire.com
Summer proms spectacular with shows from leading performers.

Ribchester Roman Museum
Preston, Lancashire PR3 3XS
(01254) 878261
www.ribchesterromanmuseum.org
Lancashire's only specialist Roman museum, located on the North bank of the beautiful River Ribble.

Sandcastle Waterpark
Blackpool, Lancashire FY4 1BB
(01253) 343602
www.sandcastle-waterpark.co.uk
The UK's Largest Indoor Waterpark and with 18 slides and attractions.

Thornton Hall Farm Country Park
Lancashire BD23 3TS
(01282) 841148
www.thorntonhallcountrypark.co.uk
Come rain or shine, a fun filled family day out is always guaranteed at Thornton Hall Farm. Get involved with hands-on activities, make friends with the farm animals and visit the new tearoom while the little ones burn off the remainder of their energy in the huge fun filled Wizzick Play Barn.

Wyre Estuary Country Park
Thornton Lancashire FY5 5LR
(01253) 863100
www.wyre.gov.uk
The award winning Wyre Estuary Country Park offers year-round activities and events for all the family including ranger-led walks, environmentally themed activities and annual events like the Family Sculpture Day.

Manchester

East Lancashire Railway
Bury, Greater Manchester BL9 0EY
(0161) 764 7790
www.eastlancsrailway.org.uk
The beautifully restored East Lancashire Railway takes you on a captivating journey to discover the region's rich transport heritage.

Greater Manchester Marathon in Trafford
April, Trafford, Manchester
www.greatermanchestermarathon.com
The UK's flattest, fastest and friendliest Marathon with a superfast course, great entertainment, outstanding crowd support and glorious finish at Manchester United Football Club.

The Lowry
Pier 8, Salford Quays M50 3AZ
(0843) 208 6000
www.thelowry.com
Set in a stunning waterside location at the heart of the redeveloped Salford Quays in Greater Manchester, The Lowry is an architectural gem that brings together a wide variety of performing and visual arts, including the works of LS Lowry and contemporary exhibitions.

Manchester Art Gallery
Greater Manchester M2 3JL
(0161) 235 8888
www.manchestergalleries.org
Houses one of the country's finest art collections in spectacular Victorian and Contemporary surroundings. With changing exhibitions and a programme of events and a host of free family friendly resources.

Manchester Histories Festival
June, Various city centre locations
www.manchesterhistoriesfestival.org.uk
The ten-day MHF celebrates the heritage and history of Manchester across numerous city centre venues. The festival offers a fantastic opportunity to explore and learn this great city and is a great event for old and young alike.

Manchester Museum
Greater Manchester M13 9PL
(0161) 275 2648
www.manchester.ac.uk/museum
Found on Oxford Road, on The University of Manchester campus (in a very impressive gothic-style building). Highlights include Stan the T.rex, mummies, live animals such as frogs and snakes, object handling and a varied programme of events.

Manchester United Museum & Tour Centre
Greater Manchester M16 0RA
(0161) 868 8000
www.manutd.com
The story of Manchester United is unlike any other club in the world. Beginning more than a century ago, it combines eras of total English and European domination. The official museum and tour offers every football fan a unique insight into Manchester United Football Club and a fantastic day out.

National Football Museum
Urbis Building, Manchester M4 3BG
0161 605 8200
www.nationalfootballmuseum.com
The world's biggest and best football museum. Drama, History, Skill, Art, Faith, Style, Passion is what we're all about at the National Football Museum. More than 140,000 football-related items plus a kids' discovery zone and skills-testing simulators.

People's History Museum
Greater Manchester M3 3ER
(0161) 838 9190
www.phm.org.uk
National centre for the collection, conservation, interpretation and study of material relating to the history of working people in Britain.

Ramsbottom Chocolate Festival
March / April, Ramsbottom, Greater Manchester
www. ramsbottomchocolatefestival.com
Two-day chocolate market, with interactive workshops, activities for adults and children, music, competitions, Giant Easter Egg display, and much more.

Saddleworth and District Whit Friday Brass Band Contest
May, Oldham, Greater Manchester
www.whitfriday.brassbands.saddleworth.org
Brass bands compete in contests at venues scattered around the moorland villages and towns on the western edge of the Pennines.

Whitworth Art Gallery
Manchester M15 6ER
(0161) 275 7450
www.manchester.ac.uk/whitworth
Home to an famous collection of British watercolours, textiles and wallpapers.

Merseyside

'Another Place' by Antony Gormley
Crosby Beach, Liverpool L23 6SX
www.antonygormley.com
100 cast-iron, life-size figures spread out along three kilometres of the foreshore on Crosby beach in Liverpool, stretching almost one kilometre out to sea. The spectacular sculptures - each one weighing 650 kilos - are made from casts of the artist's own body standing on the beach, all of them looking out to sea, staring at the horizon in silent expectation.

Beatles Story
Liverpool, Merseyside L3 4AD
(0151) 709 1963
www.beatlesstory.com
A unique visitor attraction that transports you on an enlightening and atmospheric journey into the life, times, culture and music of the Beatles.

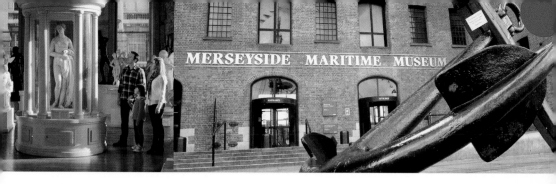

Birkenhead Festival of Transport
September, Birkenhead, Merseyside
www.bheadtransportfest.com
A fantastic week-end of activities for all the family. Featuring classic cars, steam engines and other modes of vintage transport.

Croxteth Hall & Country Park
Liverpool, Merseyside L12 0HB
(0151) 233 3020
www.liverpoolcityhalls.co.uk/croxteth-hall/
Situated in a beautiful Country Park setting and one of Liverpool's most important heritage sites. The Country Park is also home to a real working Home Farm, a Victorian Walled Garden and a 500 acre nature reserve - all open to the public.

The Gallery Liverpool
Merseyside L8 5RE
(0151) 709 2442
www.thegalleryliverpool.co.uk
Set in the heart of Liverpool's Independent Cultural District, the gallery occupies the entire upper floor of the industrial premises of John O'Keeffe and Son Ltd.

Grand National
April, Aintree, Merseyside
www.aintree.co.uk
The most famous horse race over jumps takes place over the challenging Aintree fences.

Knowsley Safari Park
Merseyside L34 4AN
(0151) 430 9009
www. knowsleysafariexperience.co.uk
Enjoy a 5 mile safari through 450 acres of parkland.

Liverpool Football Club
Merseyside L4 0TH
(0151) 260 6677
www.liverpoolfc.com
Meet an LFC Legend; get your photograph with one of our many trophies or indulge yourself in one of our award winning Experience Days.

Liverpool Sound City
May, Bramley Moore Dock, Liverpool
www.liverpoolsoundcity.co.uk
A 3-day festival of incredible live music and arts.

Mersey Ferries
Woodside Ferry Terminal, Merseyside, L3 1DP
(0151) 330 1444
www.merseyferries.co.uk
Step aboard to see Liverpool's stunning waterfront. The decks of the Mersey Ferry offer the best way to see the city's world-famous skyline. Our River Explorer Cruise takes you on a 50 minute trip where you'll be captivated by Liverpool's fascinating history.

Merseyside Maritime Museum
Liverpool Waterfront, Liverpool L3 4AQ
www.liverpoolmuseums.org.uk
(0151) 478 4499
Discover objects rescued from the Titanic among the treasures, one of the venues of the National Museums Liverpool, a group of free museums and galleries.

Speke Hall, Gardens & Estate
Liverpool, Merseyside L24 1XD
(0151) 427 7231
www.nationaltrust.org.uk/spekehall
One of the most famous half timbered houses in Britain. The Great Hall and priest hole date from Tudor times, while the Oak Parlour and smaller rooms, some with William Morris wallpapers, illustrates the Victorian desire for privacy and comfort.

Walker Art Gallery
Liverpool, Merseyside L3 8EL
(0151) 478 4199
www.liverpoolmuseums.org.uk/walker
Home to outstanding works by Rubens, Rembrandt, Poussin, Gainsborough and Hogarth, the Walker Art Gallery is one of the finest art galleries in Europe

Wirral Folk on the Coast Festival
June, Wirral, Merseyside
www.wirralfolkonthecoast.com
All-on-one-site friendly festival at Whitby Sports & Social Club, with fine music real ale and good food being served plus many more visitor attractions.

World Museum Liverpool
Merseyside L3 8EN
(0151) 478 4393
www.liverpoolmuseums.org.uk/wml
Extensive collections from the Amazonian Rain Forest to the mysteries of outer space.

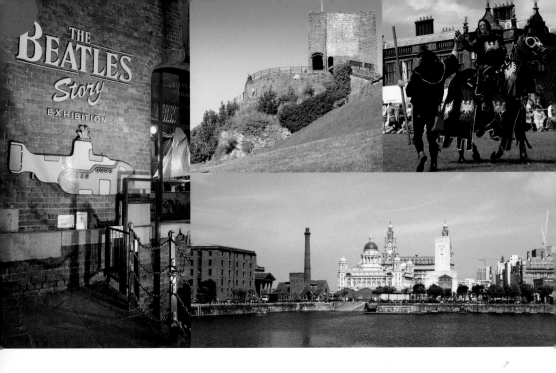

Tourist Information Centres

When you arrive at your destination, visit the Tourist Information Centre for quality assured help with accommodation and information about local attractions and events, or email your request before you go.

Accrington	Town Hall	01254 380293	information@leisureinhyndburn.co.uk
Alston Moor	Town Hall	01434 382244	alston.tic@eden.gov.uk
Altrincham	20 Stamford New Road	0161 912 5931	tourist.information@trafford.gov.uk
Ambleside	Central Buildings	015394 32582	tic@thehubofambleside.com
Appleby-in-Westmorland	Moot Hall	017683 51177	tic@applebytown.org.uk
Barnoldswick	Post Office Buildings	01282 666704 / 661661	tourist.info@pendle.gov.uk
Barrow-in-Furness	Forum 28	01229 876543	touristinfo@barrowbc.gov.uk
Blackburn	Blackburn Market	01254 688040	visit@blackburn.gov.uk
Blackpool	Festival House, The People's Promenade	01253 478222	tic@blackpool.gov.uk
Bolton	Central Library Foyer	01204 334321 / 334271	tourist.info@bolton.gov.uk
Bowness	Glebe Road	015394 42895	bownesstic@lakedistrict.gov.uk
Brampton	Moot Hall	016977 3433 / 01228 625600	bramptontic@gmail.co.uk
Broughton-in-Furness	Town Hall	01229 716115	broughtontic@btconnect.com
Burnley	Regeneration and Planning Policy	01282 477210	tic@burnley.gov.uk
Bury	The Fusilier Museum	0161 253 5111	touristinformation@bury.gov.uk
Carlisle	Old Town Hall	01228 625600	tourism@carlisle.gov.uk
Chester (Town Hall)	Town Hall	0845 647 7868	welcome@chestervic.co.uk
Clitheroe	Platform Gallery & VIC	01200 425566	tourism@ribblevalley.gov.uk
Cockermouth	4 Old Kings Arms Lane	01900 822634	cockermouthtouristinformationcentre@btconnect.com
Congleton	Town Hall	01260 271095	congletontic@cheshireeast.gov.uk
Coniston	Ruskin Avenue	015394 41533	mail@conistontic.org
Discover Pendle	Boundary Mill Stores	01282 856186	discoverpendle@pendle.gov.uk
Egremont	12 Main Street	01946 820693	lowescourt@btconnect.com

Ellesmere Port	McArthur Glen Outlet Village	0151 356 5562	enquiries@cheshiredesigneroutlet.com
Garstang	1 Cherestanc Square	01995 602125	garstangtic@wyrebc.gov.uk
Glennridding Ullswater	Bekside Car Park	017684 82414	ullswatertic@lakedistrict.gov.uk
Grange-Over-Sands	Victoria Hall	015395 34026	council@grangeoversands.net
Kendal	25 Stramongate	01539 735891	info@kendaltic.co.uk
Keswick	Moot Hall	017687 72645	keswicktic@lakedistrict.gov.uk
Kirkby Stephen	Market Square	017683 71199	visit@uecp.org.uk
Lancaster	The Storey	01524 582394	lancastervic@lancaster.gov.uk
Liverpool Albert Dock	Anchor Courtyard	0151 233 2008	jackie.crawford@liverpool.gov.uk
Liverpool John Lennon Airport	Information Desk	0151 907 1058	information@liverpoolairport.com
Lytham St Annes	c/o Town Hall	01253 725610	touristinformation@fylde.gov.uk
Macclesfield	Town Hall	01625 378123 / 378062	karen.connon@cheshireeast.gov.uk
Manchester	45-50 Piccadilly Plaza	0871 222 8223	touristinformation@visitmanchester.com
Maryport	The Wave Centre	01900 811450	info@thewavemaryport.co.uk
Millom	Millom Council Centre	01946 598914	millomtic@copelandbc.gov.uk
Morecambe	Old Station Buildings	01524 582808	morecambevic@lancaster.gov.uk
Nantwich	Civic Hall	01270 537359	nantwichtic@cheshireeast.gov.uk
Northwich	Information Centre	01606 288828	infocentrenorthwich@ cheshirewestandchester.gov.uk
Oldham	Oldham Library	0161 770 3064	tourist@oldham.gov.uk
Pendle Heritage Centre	Park Hill	01282 677150	pendleheritagecentre@htnw.co.uk
Penrith	Middlegate	01768 867466	pen.tic@eden.gov.uk
Preston	The Guildhall	01772 253731	tourism@preston.gov.uk
Rheged	Redhills	01768 860015	tic@rheged.com
Rochdale	Touchstones	01706 924928	tic@link4life.org
Rossendale	Rawtenstall Queens Square	01706 227911	rawtenstall.library@lancashire.gov.uk
Saddleworth	Saddleworth Museum	01457 870336	saddleworthtic@oldham.gov.uk
Salford	The Lowry, Pier 8	0161 848 8601	tic@salford.gov.uk
Sedbergh	72 Main Street	015396 20125	tic@sedbergh.org.uk
Silloth-on-Solway	Solway Coast Discovery Centre	016973 31944	sillothtic@allerdale.gov.uk
Southport	112 Lord Street	01704 533333	info@visitsouthport.com
Stockport	Staircase House	0161 474 4444	tourist.information@stockport.gov.uk
Ulverston	Coronation Hall	01229 587120 / 587140	ulverstontic@southlakeland.gov.uk
Windermere	Victoria Street	015394 46499	info@ticwindermere.co.uk

Regional Contacts and Information

For more information on accommodation, attractions, activities, events and holidays in North West England, contact one of the following regional or local tourism organisations. Their websites have a wealth of information and many produce free publications to help you get the most out of your visit.

Visit Chester
www.visitchester.com

Cumbria Tourism
T (01539) 822 222
E info@cumbriatourism.org
www.golakes.co.uk

Visit Lancashire
T (01257) 226600 (Brochure request)
E info@visitlancashire.com
www.visitlancashire.com

Visit Manchester
T 0871 222 8223
E touristinformation@visitmanchester.com
www.visitmanchester.com

Visit Liverpool
T (0151) 233 2008 (information enquiries)
T 0844 870 0123 (accommodation booking)
E info@visitliverpool.com (accommodation enquiries)
E liverpoolvisitorcentre@liverpool.gov.uk
(information enquiries)
www.visitliverpool.com

Stay – North West

Entries appear alphabetically by town name in each county. A key to symbols appears on page 7

CHESTER, Cheshire   Map ref 4A2
SatNav 28CH4 8JQ **B**

Mitchell's of Chester Guest House
28 Hough Green, Chester CH4 8JQ **T:** (01244) 679004
E: welcome@mitchellsofchester.com
W: www.mitchellsofchester.com **£ BOOK ONLINE**

B&B PER ROOM PER NIGHT
S: £70.00 - £110.00
D: £94.00 - £110.00

Highly recommended by good guides. Relax in this tastefully restored Victorian residence with rooms having hospitality tray, clock/radio, TV, free Wi Fi, hairdryer and many other comforts. Easy 20 minutes walking to city. Off-road car park. **Directions:** Leave south side of Chester on A483, turn right on to A5104 (Saltney). This is Hough Green. We are 300m along on the right. **Bedrooms:** 3 doubles en-suite. Can be let as singles. **Open:** All year except Christmas and New Year.

Site: **P** Payment: Leisure: **▶** Property: Catering: Room:

TARPORLEY, Cheshire   Map ref 4A2
SatNav CW6 0AX **B**

Foresters Arms
92 -94 High Street, Tarporley CW6 0AX **T:** (01829) 733151 **F:** 01829 730020
E: foresters-arms@btconnect.com
W: www.theforesters.co.uk

B&B PER ROOM PER NIGHT
S: £45.00
D: £65.00
EVENING MEAL PER PERSON
£6.50 - £25.00

A country public house on the edge of Tarporley, offering a homely and friendly service.
With recently refurbished comfortable rooms.
Directions: Situated at the bottom end of the village, opposite the Spar Petrol Station. **Bedrooms:** On Suite facilities, flat screen TV's, tea & coffee **Open:** All year round.

Site: **P** Payment: Leisure: Property: Catering: Room:

AMBLESIDE, Cumbria   Map ref 5A3
SatNav LA22 0BH **B**

Churchill Inn
33 Lake Road, Ambleside, Cumbria LA22 0BH **T:** (01539) 433192 **F:** 015394 34900
E: churchill.hotel@btconnect.com
W: www.churchillhotel.uk.com **£ BOOK ONLINE**

SPECIAL PROMOTIONS
Book by telephone for best rates.

The Churchill Inn is situated at the heart of the picturesque South Lakeland town of Ambleside. Charming shops, cafes and galleries are nestled around the Inn. Come and enjoy walking the local fells, sailing on Windermere or just relax and soak up the atmosphere of Ambleside and the surrounding area. To make your stay as comfortable as possible, all of our rooms have en suite bathroom, tea/coffee making facilities, LCD television with multiple channels and free Wi-Fi. We welcome all visitors equally, however, we do not accept bookings from Hen or Stag parties. Parking in Ambleside or any town centre is of a premium and the Churchill Inn is unique in that regard, having its own car park. The entrance is quite narrow but accessible, or if you would prefer to park off site, there are numerous car parks within a five minute walk of the Inn.

Directions: Leave the M6 at J36, Ambleside approx 18 miles. Go past Market Place on to Lake Road. The Churchill Inn is on the right immediately after Church Street

Bedrooms: 16 rooms, all recently refurbished to a high standard, many with wonderful scenic views of the local fells.

Site: **P** Property: Children: Catering: Room:

AMBLESIDE, Cumbria   Map ref 5A3 | SatNav LA22 0EP | B

VisitEngland
★★★★
INN

B&B PER ROOM PER NIGHT
S: £49.00 - £70.00
D: £84.00 - £185.00

EVENING MEAL PER PERSON
£11.00 - £25.00

Wateredge Inn

Waterhead Bay, Ambleside, Cumbria LA22 0EP **T:** (015394) 32332 **F:** 015394 31878
E: stay@wateredgeinn.co.uk
W: www.wateredgeinn.co.uk **£ BOOK ONLINE**

Delightfully situated 22 bedroom Inn on the shores of Windermere at Waterhead Bay. Enjoy country Inn style dining, freshly prepared bar meals, real ales and fine wines all served overlooking the lake. **Directions:** From M6 jct 36 follow A591 through to Ambleside. At Waterhead bear left at traffic lights, Wateredge is on left at end of promenade. **Bedrooms:** Lake & Fell Views, Wi-Fi, TV, tea & coffee. **Open:** All year except Christmas.

Site: ✿ P Payment: 💷 Leisure: ♪ Property: 🐾 🖥 ⌀ Children: 👶 🛏 ☂ Catering: ⓧ 🍷 🍴 Room: ☕ ♨ 📺 📶

APPLEBY-IN-WESTMORLAND, Cumbria   Map ref 5B3 | SatNav CA16 6JH | B

VisitEngland
★★★★
BED & BREAKFAST

B&B PER ROOM PER NIGHT
S: £45.00 - £55.00
D: £75.00 - £90.00

SPECIAL PROMOTIONS
10% discount to
walkers & cyclists.

The Hollies

Roman Road, Appleby in Westmorland, Cumbria CA16 6JH **T:** (01768) 352553
E: stay@theholliesappleby.co.uk
W: www.TheHolliesAppleby.co.uk **£ BOOK ONLINE**

Blending homely Victorian elegance with modern facilities and 'green' credentials. Situated in the historic county town of Appleby between The Lakes & The Dales we provide the perfect base to explore by foot cycle or car.
A relaxing base within 3 acres of woodland & wild flowers.
Start your day with our locally sourced Westmorland breakfast.
1 dog per room welcome. Boot room & secure cycle store.

Directions: M6J40 - A66 - Appleby exit keep right -T junct. Roman Road, T Rt We are 1/2 ml on left. A66 East or M6J38 - From Appleby centre ,T Rt past station, at T Junct. T Lft under A66 We are 1/4 mile on Rt.

Bedrooms: Ensuite with power shower, flat screen tv, tea and coffee in rooms, superb beds & quality linen & towels.
Open: All Year

Site: ✿ P Leisure: ♪ Property: 🐾 🖥 Children: ☂ Catering: 🍴 Room: ☕ ♨ 📺

BOWNESS-ON-WINDERMERE, Cumbria   Map ref 5A3 | SatNav LA23 3HH | H

VisitEngland
★★★
COUNTRY HOUSE HOTEL

B&B PER ROOM PER NIGHT
S: £80.00 - £125.00
D: £95.00 - £185.00

EVENING MEAL PER PERSON
£27.50 - £45.00

Burn How Garden House Hotel

Back Belsfield Road, Bowness-on-Windermere, Windermere, Cumbria LA23 3HH
T: (015394) 46226 **F:** 015394 47000 **E:** info@burnhow.co.uk
W: www.burnhow.co.uk **£ BOOK ONLINE**

The unique Burn How Hotel has individually designed rooms set in the privacy of our gardens. An oasis in the middle of bustling Bowness but only a 2 minute stroll to the village or lake Windermere. **Open:** All year except 15th Dec to 27th Dec

Site: ✿ P Payment: 💷 Leisure: ⚡ Property: 🖥 🏛 Children: 👶 🛏 ☂ Catering: ⓧ 🍷 Room: ☕ ♨ 📞 📺 ♨ 📶

BUTTERMERE, Cumbria Map ref 5A3   SatNav CA13 9XA B

★★★★ INN

B&B PER ROOM PER NIGHT
S: £55.00 - £65.00
D: £100.00 - £120.00
EVENING MEAL PER PERSON
£8.00 - £15.75

The Fish Inn
Buttermere, Nr Cockermouth CA13 9XA **T:** (017687) 70253 **F:** 017687 70287
E: info@fishinnbuttermere.co.uk
W: www.fishinnbuttermere.co.uk

Set in unbeatable surroundings a short stroll from Buttermere and Crummock waters. The Inn is comfortable and informal serving traditional food alongside local real ales, assuring you a warm welcome. **Directions:** At M6 J40 take A66 to Keswick, continue towards Cockermouth, 9 miles after Keswick roundabout turn left, follow signs B5289 Lorton and Buttermere. **Bedrooms:** 7 double (2 are superior), 2 twin, 1 family.

Site: ❀ P Payment: 💷 Leisure: 🎣 Children: 🚼 🏛 🎠 Catering: 🍴 🍽 Room: 🗄 🐾 📞

CARLISLE, Cumbria Map ref 5A2   SatNav CA1 1HR B

★★★★ GUEST HOUSE

B&B PER ROOM PER NIGHT
S: £30.00 - £41.00
D: £70.00 - £77.00
EVENING MEAL PER PERSON
£5.00 - £25.00

Langleigh House
6 Howard Place, Carlisle, Cumbria CA1 1HR **T:** (01228) 530440 **E:** langleighhouse@aol.com
W: www.langleighhouse.co.uk **£ BOOK ONLINE**

Situated in a quiet conservation area with private car park, just five minutes walk from the city centre, this delightful period property dressed tastefully in Victorian style has been awarded the prestigious TripAdvisor 2015 "Certificate of Excellence" Be assured of a warm and friendly welcome. We look forward to greeting you.

Directions: Junction 43 off the M6. Drive along Warwick Road and we are the third turning on the right after St. Aidans church.

Bedrooms: Free WiFi, Flat screen TV's, welcome tray
Open: All year except Christmas and New Year

Site: ❀ P Payment: 💷 Leisure: 🚲 ⚑ Property: 📺 📶 Children: 🚼 🏛 🎠 Catering: 🍴✗ 🍽 Room: 🗄 🐾 📺 🍳

CARLISLE, Cumbria   Map ref 5A2
SatNav CA1 2HH **B**

University of Cumbria - Carlisle
Fusehill Street, Carlisle, Cumbria CA1 2HH **T:** (01228) 616317 **F:** 01228 616235
E: conferences.carlisle@cumbria.ac.uk
W: www.cumbria.ac.uk/conferences

BED ONLY PER NIGHT
£20.00 - £48.00

Comfortable, modern, en suite rooms (summer only) in which to relax and unwind at the end of a busy day. Each flat has internet access and a fully equipped kitchen, plus laundry and drying facilities and a gym on site. The campus is situated just a short walk from the city centre. Within easy reach of the motorway, Hadrian's Wall and the Lake District. Ideally placed for cycling & walking routes. **Directions:** Please refer to website. **Bedrooms:** 85 single ensuites (2 can be twinned) in 13 flats.

Site: ✿ **Payment:** 💷 **Leisure:** 🏃 **Property:** 🍴 🖥 📠 **Children:** 👶 🎒 **Catering:** ✗ 🍴 🍷 **Bedroom:** ☕ 🍵 🖳

CLIFTON, Cumbria   Map ref 5B2
SatNav CA10 2ER **B**

George and Dragon
Clifton, Penrith, Cumbria CA10 2ER **T:** (01768) 865381
E: enquiries@georgeanddragonclifton.co.uk
W: www.georgeanddragonclifton.co.uk **£ BOOK ONLINE**

B&B PER ROOM PER NIGHT
S: £85.00 - £119.00
D: £95.00 - £155.00

EVENING MEAL PER PERSON
£13.50 - £25.00

The George and Dragon is a stylish and welcoming country inn with a lovely restaurant, cosy bar and 11 elegant yet comfortable en suite bedrooms. A great foodie destination where the menu changes seasonally and the specials daily. **Directions:** Just a few miles from Penrith and junction 40 of the M6 in Clifton village. By direct train, Penrith is just three hours from London.
Bedrooms: En suite, flat screen tv, bath or shower **Open:** All year (closed on Boxing Day)

Site: ✿ **P** **Payment:** 💷 **Leisure:** 🏊 **Property:** 🐾 🖥 🍴 **Children:** 👶 🛏 🎒 **Catering:** ✗ 🍷 🍴 **Room:** 🍵 🕭 📺 📀

GRANGE-OVER-SANDS, Cumbria   Map ref 5A3
SatNav LA11 7HQ **H**

Clare House
Park Road, Grange-over-Sands, Cumbria LA11 7HQ **T:** (01539) 533026
E: info@clarehousehotel.co.uk
W: www.clarehousehotel.co.uk

HB PER PERSON PER NIGHT
£93.00 - £102.00

SPECIAL PROMOTIONS
Early-season terms in April, mid-summer and autumn. Special 4-day breaks available all season.

Charming hotel in its own grounds, with well-appointed bedrooms, pleasant lounges and superb bay views, offering peaceful holidays to those who wish to relax and be looked after. Delightful meals, prepared with care and pride from fresh local produce, will add greatly to the enjoyment of your stay.

Directions: From M6 jct 36 follow A590 through Grange, keep alongside sea. Clare House is on Park Road next to bandstand, between sea and road.

Bedrooms: 4 single, 2 double, 12 twin
Open: Mid March to mid December

Site: ✿ **P** **Payment:** 💷 **Property:** 🖥 🍴 🚭 **Children:** 👶 **Catering:** ✗ 🍷 🍴 **Room:** 🍵 ☕ 📞 📺 🛁

★★★
HOTEL

B&B PER ROOM PER NIGHT
S: £40.00 - £100.00
D: £60.00 - £150.00

HB PER PERSON PER NIGHT
£50.00 - £120.00

SPECIAL PROMOTIONS
Free child places 0-4
years. Half-price 5-14
years. Murder Mystery
and themed
weekends. Christmas
and New Year breaks.

Cumbria Grand Hotel

Lindale Road, Grange-over-Sands, Cumbria LA11 6EN   **T:** (01539) 532331   **F:** 01539 534534
E: salescumbria@strathmorehotels.com
W: www.strathmorehotels.com   £ BOOK ONLINE

Set in 20 acres of private gardens and woodlands, and overlooking the stunning Morecambe Bay,
you will receive a warm and friendly welcome at this charming Victorian hotel. Only a short drive
from Lake Windermere, there is much to see and do in the beautiful surrounding area.

Directions: By car: 15 minutes from the M6. By
train: connections to Grange-over-Sands station
from London, Birmingham, Leeds, Glasgow and
Edinburgh.

Bedrooms: 14 single, 31 dbl, 66 twin, 10 family,
3 suite. Bay view room upgrades available.
Open: All year

Site: ❀ Payment: 💷 Leisure: ♪ ▶ ♨ ⚲ Property: 🐾 🐕 🖥 🌙 Children: 🐴 🛏 🚼 Catering: 🍽 🍴
Room: 🚿 📞 ☕ 📺 💈 📠

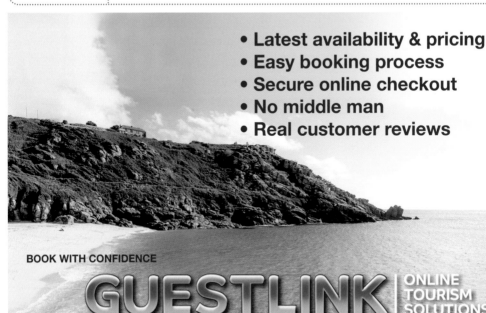

• Latest availability & pricing
• Easy booking process
• Secure online checkout
• No middle man
• Real customer reviews

BOOK WITH CONFIDENCE

GUESTLINK | ONLINE TOURISM SOLUTIONS

www.visitor-guides.co.uk • www.roomcheck.co.uk
www.ukgreatbreaks.com • and many more!

Crosslands Farm
Rusland, Hawkshead, Cumbria LA22 8JU **T:** (01229) 860242
E: enquiries@crosslandsfarm.co.uk
W: www.crosslandsfarm.co.uk

B&B PER ROOM PER NIGHT
S: £50.00
D: £80.00 - £86.00

EVENING MEAL PER PERSON
£20.00

Crosslands Farm is a early 17th century Lakeland Farmhouse set in the beautiful Rusland Valley 5 miles south of Hawkshead & near Grizedale Forest. It has delightful bedrooms, lovely bathrooms and a cosy lounge with log fire. Breakfast is served in the dining room converted from the old dairy with original slate flag floors and beams. It is an ideal base for walking and biking. Private parking.

Directions: Take the M6 at J36 follow the A590 until Newby Bridge past The Steam Railway turn right & follow the signs for Grizedale. At 4 miles turn right at y junction. Go up the little hill to the Farmhouse.

Bedrooms: 3 rooms, 1 double with en suite shower room and window seat, twin room with private bathroom & underfloor heating, 1 double room and en suite bathroom
Open: All year except Christmas. Restrictions at New Year

Site: ✿ **P Payment:** 💷 **Leisure:** 🚲 ♪ ∪ **Property:** 🐾 🖥 ⌂ ∅ **Children:** ⛱ 🛏 ♿ **Catering:** (✗ 🍴 **Room:** 📶 🛁 📻 📺

Yewfield Vegetarian Guest House
Hawkshead Hill, Hawkshead, Ambleside LA22 0PR **T:** (01539) 436765
E: derek.yewfield@btinternet.com
W: www.yewfield.co.uk

B&B PER ROOM PER NIGHT
S: £60.00 - £88.00
D: £90.00 - £130.00

SPECIAL PROMOTIONS
3 night mid week break that includes 2x3 course dinners at our award winning restaurants in Ambleside:\from £345.00 per couple.

Yewfield is an impressive country house set in over 80 acres of private grounds, a peaceful and quiet retreat with lovely walks straight from the grounds. Following recent refurbishments, Yewfield was awarded a 5 stars VisitBritain award. We also host classical concert evenings with exceptional musicians from around the world.

Directions: One mile from Hawkshead, 4 miles from Ambleside, 2 miles past The Drunken Duck. See website for map.

Bedrooms: 8 double, 4 twin, 3 suite & 3 Apartments.
Open: Closed December and January.

Site: ✿ **P Payment:** 💷 **Leisure:** ∪ **Property:** 🖥 **Children:** ⛱⁹ **Catering:** 🍴 **Room:** 📶 🛁 📻 📺 🔌 🚪

HEADS NOOK, Cumbria Map ref 5B2
SatNav CA8 9EG **B**

VisitEngland
★★★★
GUEST
ACCOMMODATION

B&B PER ROOM PER NIGHT
S: £45.00 - £69.00
D: £60.00 - £100.00
EVENING MEAL PER PERSON
£8.50 - £17.95

String of Horses Inn
Faugh, Heads Nook, Brampton, Carlisle CA8 9EG **T:** (01228) 670297
E: info@stringofhorses.com
W: www.stringofhorses.com **£ BOOK ONLINE**

Dating from 1659, this traditional coaching inn is set in quiet country village only 10 minutes from Carlisle and Junction 43 of the M6 motorway. Near Hadrian's Wall and The Lake District. With great food, oak beams and panelling, real ales, log fires, free Wi-Fi and all rooms en suite. Pets are not permitted. **Directions:** A69 from J43 M6-Newcastle. 5 m right at Lights Corby Hill/Warwick Bridge at BP Station. 1 m through Heads Nook, left into Faugh. **Bedrooms:** 9 dbl, 1 twin, 1 family **Open:** All year

Site: **P Payment:** Leisure: **Property:** Children: Catering: Room:

KENDAL, Cumbria Map ref 5B3
SatNav LA9 4JW **B**

VisitEngland
★★★★
BED & BREAKFAST

B&B PER ROOM PER NIGHT
S: £38.00 - £45.00
D: £64.00 - £85.00

Hillside Bed & Breakfast
4 Beast Banks, Kendal, Cumbria LA9 4JW **T:** (01539) 722836 **E:** info@hillside-kendal.co.uk
W: www.hillside-kendal.co.uk **£ BOOK ONLINE**

A warm welcome awaits you at this 4 Star B&B, just 2 mins walk to town centre. Located in a quiet conservation area, close to golf course, Brewery Arts Centre, museums, restaurants and shops. Ideally placed for exploring the Lakes and Dales **Directions:** 10 mins drive from M6 motorway, within easy walking distance to Kendal train and bus stations **Bedrooms:** En suite, LCD TV, free Wi-Fi and hospitality tray. **Open:** All Year

Site: **P Payment:** Leisure: **Property:** Catering: Room:

KESWICK, Cumbria Map ref 5A3
SatNav CA12 4LJ **B**

VisitEngland
★★★★
BED & BREAKFAST

B&B PER ROOM PER NIGHT
D: £64.00 - £80.00

Ash Tree House
Penrith Road, Keswick CA12 4LJ **T:** (01768) 772203 **E:** peterredfearn@aol.com
W: www.ashtreehouse.co.uk

Family run Bed and Breakfast in a former farm house built in 1841 with garden. Comfortable en suite rooms and full English breakfast. Plenty of off road parking. **Directions:** 15 minute walk from town centre and a good base for all Lake District attractions. Detailed directions on our web site www.ashtreehouse.co.uk. **Bedrooms:** 1 double, 1 twin **Open:** All year except Christmas

Site: **P** Leisure: **Property:** Children: Catering: Room:

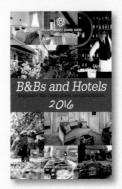
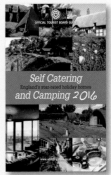

Burleigh Mead

The Heads, Keswick CA12 5ER **T:** (01768) 775935 **E:** info@burleighmead.co.uk
W: www.burleighmead.co.uk **£ BOOK ONLINE**

Conveniently situated between town centre and Derwentwater, our charming Victorian house offers excellent accommodation with outstanding views of surrounding fells. **Directions:** Once in Keswick follow signs for Lake and Borrowdale. The Heads is across from Central Car Park, we are 100 yards up road on right.
Bedrooms: All en suite with fantastic views and all mod cons
Open: March to November

B&B PER ROOM PER NIGHT
D: £80.00 - £110.00

Site: ❀ P **Leisure:** ♪ ▶ ∪ **Property:** 🖥 ⎚ **Children:** 🐾10 **Catering:** 🍴 **Room:** 🕾 ♨ 📺

Charnwood Guest House

6 Eskin Street, Keswick CA12 4DH **T:** (01768) 774111 **E:** sue.banister@gmail.com
W: www.charnwoodkeswick.co.uk

Elegant listed building. Close to lake and fells and in a quiet street. A warm welcome and really good food can be found at Charnwood. We cater for vegetarians. **Directions:** From A66 join the A591 to town centre and before the traffic lights turn left into Greta Street which leads to Eskin Street. **Bedrooms:** 2 double, 3 family **Open:** All year except Christmas

B&B PER ROOM PER NIGHT
S: £45.00
D: £35.00 - £40.00

Payment: 💷 **Property:** 🖥 **Children:** 🐾5 **Catering:** 🍴 **Room:** 🕾 ♨ 🔌 📺 🔥 🖥 🗒

Greystones

Ambleside Road, Keswick, Cumbria CA12 4DP **T:** (017687) 73108 **F:** 017687 73108
E: info@greystoneskeswick.co.uk
W: www.greystoneskeswick.co.uk **£ BOOK ONLINE**

Greystones enjoys an enviable location with splendid views of the surrounding mountains yet is only a 3 minute walk to the shops, restaurants and pubs in the historic Market Square of Keswick. Private parking, secure cycle storage, drying room.
Bedrooms: 5 x double & 2 x twin en suite rooms, flat screen TVs, tea & coffee, hairdryer, free Wi-Fi **Open:** 1st March - 31st November

B&B PER ROOM PER NIGHT
D: £78.00 - £80.00

Site: P **Payment:** 💷 **Property:** 🖥 ⎚ **Catering:** 🍴 **Room:** 🕾 ♨ 📺

Lane Head Farm Country Guest House

Troutbeck, Nr. Keswick, Cumbria CA11 0SY **T:** (01768) 779220 **E:** info@laneheadfarm.co.uk
W: www.laneheadfarm.co.uk **£ BOOK ONLINE**

Charming 18thC former farmhouse, close to Keswick & Ullswater. Set amid panoramic views of surrounding fells. Individually designed en-suite rooms, guest lounge, free onsite car parking, dogs welcome, cycle storage & free WiFi.
Open: All year except Christmas

B&B PER ROOM PER NIGHT
S: £40.00 - £45.00
D: £70.00 - £80.00
EVENING MEAL PER PERSON
£15.00 - £20.00

Site: ❀ P **Payment:** 💷 **Leisure:** ♪ ▶ ∪ **Property:** 🐾 🖥 ⎚ 🐕 **Children:** 🐾10 **Catering:** (✗ 🍷 🍴 **Room:** 🕾 ♨ 📺 🔥 🖥

KESWICK, Cumbria Map ref 5A3 — SatNav CA12 4DX [B]

Lindisfarne House

21 Church Street, Keswick, Cumbria CA12 4DX T: (017687) 73218
E: info@lindisfarne-keswick.co.uk
W: www.lindisfarne-keswick.co.uk

B&B PER ROOM PER NIGHT
S: £36.50
D: £82.00

Lindisfarne is a victorian house quietly situated, but within a few minutes walk to the town centre, lakes, parks and theatre by the lake. We offer clean and comfortable accommodation in our four star guest house, with a hearty breakfast. **Directions:** A66 into Keswick, take Southey Street, 3rd turning on left into Church Street. **Bedrooms:** 2 single standard, 1 single en suite (£41 prpn), 3 double en suites, 1 family (£73 prpn)/twin room **Open:** All year

Site: P Payment: 🏧 Leisure: 🚲 ♪ ► ∪ Property: 🛏 Children: 👶5 Catering: 🍴 Room: 📶 ♿ 📺 ☕

KIRKBY LONSDALE, Cumbria Map ref 5B3 — SatNav LA6 2AU [B]

Copper Kettle Restaurant & Guest House

3-5 Market Street, Kirkby Lonsdale LA6 2AU T: (015242) 71714 F: 015242 71714
E: gamble_p@btconnect.com

B&B PER ROOM PER NIGHT
S: £39.00
D: £55.00 - £65.00
EVENING MEAL PER PERSON
£9.00 - £12.00

Building was built in 1610-1640. Lovely restaurant on site. In town there is Ruskin's View with the river and Devil's Bridge. Lots of good walking and plenty of shops and pubs in the nearby town. Prices include breakfast. **Directions:** M6, exit 36, follow road for 5 miles. Turn into Kirkby Lonsdale on Market Street. **Bedrooms:** 2 single, 3 double, 3 twin, 2 family **Open:** All year

Site: P Payment: 🏧 € Leisure: ♪ ► Property: 🐕 Children: 👶 🛏 🎮 Catering: 🍷 🍴 Room: ♿ 📼 📺

ROSTHWAITE, *Cumbria* Map ref 5A3

SatNav CA12 5XB **H**

★★★ HOTEL

Gold AWARD

B&B PER ROOM PER NIGHT
S: £65.00 - £105.00
D: £130.00 - £210.00
EVENING MEAL PER PERSON
£17.95 - £45.00

SPECIAL PROMOTIONS
Spring, summer, autumn and winter breaks available throughout the year. Please call or check the website for details.

Scafell Hotel
Rosthwaite, Borrowdale, Keswick CA12 5XB **T:** (01768) 777208 **F:** 01768 777280
E: info@scafell.co.uk
W: www.scafell.co.uk

The Scafell Hotel is in the heart of Borrowdale Valley, considered by many to be England's finest valley. Situated almost at the foot of Great Gable and Scafell Massif, the hotel is an excellent centre for walking. Recently refurbished, the Scafell boasts great food, great service and a great atmosphere. AA Rosette, Dining Award, Gold Award and Breakfast Award. Individual and Independent for 45yrs.

Directions: From jct 40 (Penrith) of the M6 follow A46 to Keswick. From Keswick follow the B5298 for Borrowdale. Travel 6.5 miles to Rosthwaite.

Bedrooms: 3 single, 9 dble, 7 twin, 3 family, 1 suite
Open: All year

Site: ✿ **Payment:** ⊞ € **Leisure:** ⅍ ♩ **Property:** ♄ ▯ **Children:** ⋈ ▥ ⚥ **Catering:** ☺ ⅏
Room: ⒟ ⚲ ☎ ◉ TV ⚄

TROUTBECK, *Cumbria* Map ref 5A2

SatNav CA11 0SJ **B**

★★★★ INN

B&B PER ROOM PER NIGHT
S: £55.00
D: £75.00 - £85.00
EVENING MEAL PER PERSON
£14.75 - £35.00

Troutbeck Inn
Troutbeck, Penrith CA11 0SJ **T:** (01768) 483635 **F:** 01768 483639
E: info@troutbeckinn.co.uk
W: www.thetroutbeckinn.co.uk **£ BOOK ONLINE**

Country hotel/inn with open fire, bar, lounge, restaurant. Quality food, wines & real ales. Dogs welcome in our bedrooms & cottages. Close to Penrith, Keswick & Ullswater. **Directions:** From J40 on M6 travel west towards Keswick. After 8 miles exit onto the A5091 to Ullswater. Troutbeck Inn is on the left. **Bedrooms:** 1 single, 4 double, 1 twin, 1 family. **Open:** All year

Site: ✿ **P** **Payment:** ⊞ **Leisure:** ∪ **Property:** ♄ ▭ ▯ **Children:** ⋈ **Catering:** ☺ ⅏ **Room:** ⒟ ⚲ ◉ TV

ULVERSTON, *Cumbria* Map ref 5A3

SatNav LA12 7HD **B**

★★★★ GUEST ACCOMMODATION

B&B PER ROOM PER NIGHT
S: £50.00
D: £80.00
EVENING MEAL PER PERSON
£25.00

St Marys Mount
Belmont, Ulverston LA12 7HD **T:** (01229) 583372 **E:** gerry.bobbett@virgin.net
W: www.stmarysmount.co.uk

Guest house overlooking Morecambe Bay in own grounds. 5 minutes walk to Ulverston town centre at the foot of the Hoad Monument. Peaceful surroundings and guests can enjoy homecooked food.
Evening meals by request.
Directions: Follow the A590 into Ulverston, pass Booths. At next major roundabout take the 3rd exit onto Fountain Street. At mini roundabout take a sharp right. **Bedrooms:** 4 double, 2 twin
Open: All year

Site: ✿ **P** **Payment:** ⊞ **Leisure:** ⅍ ♩ ▶ ∪ **Property:** ▭ ▯ **Children:** ⋈ ▥ **Catering:** ⅏ **Room:** ⒟ ⚲ TV ⚄

WINDERMERE, Cumbria   Map ref 5A3   SatNav LA23 3JY B

Bowfell Cottage

Middle Entrance Drive, Storrs Park, Bowness-on-Windermere, Cumbria LA23 3JY
T: (01539) 444835 **E:** annetomlinson45@btinternet.com
W: www.bowfell-cottage.co.uk

B&B PER ROOM PER NIGHT
S: £32.00 - £35.00
D: £60.00 - £70.00

Cottage in a delightful setting, about 1mile south of Bowness off A5074, offering traditional Lakeland hospitality with comfortable accommodation and good home-cooking. Secluded parking in own grounds surrounding the property. **Directions:** From Bowness opposite church, take A5074 Kendal Rd for 1.2 miles. Turn right into Middle Entrance Drive, entrance 100 yards down Lane on left. **Bedrooms:** 1 double,en-suite 1 twin, 1 family\ flat screen tv **Open:** All year except Christmas

Site: ❖ P Leisure: 🚲 ♪ ▶ ∪ Property: 🐾 🖥 🗄 Children: 🧸 Catering: (✗ 🍴 Room: 🔌 💧 ☕ 📺

WINDERMERE, Cumbria   Map ref 5A3   SatNav LA23 2EQ B

Glenville House

Lake Road, Windermere, Cumbria LA23 2EQ **T:** (015394) 43371 **F:** 015394 48457
E: mail@glenvillehouse.co.uk
W: www.glenvillehouse.co.uk **£ BOOK ONLINE**

B&B PER ROOM PER NIGHT
S: £68.00 - £80.00
D: £70.00 - £110.00

Adults only.
With a relaxed tranquil atmosphere, this Victorian residence is situated a short walk from both Windermere and Bowness at the heart of the English Lake District. We are also AA 4* Rated. **Directions:** Please see website for directions **Bedrooms:** The guest house offers seven luxurious en suite rooms with colour flat screen TV's, iPod docking stations and free Wi-Fi **Open:** All year

Site: ❖ P Payment: 💷 Leisure: 🚲 ▶ 🏃 Property: 🖥 Catering: 🍴 Room: 🔌 💧 📺 🛏

WINDERMERE, Cumbria   Map ref 5A3   SatNav LA23 3JF H

Lindeth Howe Country House Hotel

Lindeth Drive, Longtail Hill, Bowness-on-Windermere, Windermere, Cumbria LA23 3JF
T: (015394) 45759 **F:** 015394 46368 **E:** hotel@lindeth-howe.co.uk
W: www.lindeth-howe.co.uk

B&B PER ROOM PER NIGHT
S: £75.00 - £105.00
D: £119.00 - £199.00
EVENING MEAL PER PERSON
£46.50

Idyllic secluded retreat with superb views over Lake Windermere & fells, once owned by Beatrix Potter. Boasts beautiful bedrooms, cosy lounges, a 2 AA Rosette restaurant and leisure facilities with holistic treatments. **Directions:** From the M6 j36 take the A591 following signs for Bowness On Windermere, then take the A592 turning left turn up Longtail hill, hotel is on the left. **Bedrooms:** En Suite, Flat Screen TV, Tea & Coffee **Open:** All year

Site: ❖ P Payment: 💷 Leisure: 🚲 ▶ 🏃 ⛳ 🎣 Property: 🐕 🐾 🖥 🔥 🌙 🎨 Children: 🧸 🍴 🏀 Catering: (✗ 🍷 🍴 Room: 🔌 💧 ☕ 📺 💿 🛏 🖨

WINDERMERE, Cumbria   Map ref 5A3   SatNav LA23 1AE B

Southview House & Indoor Pool

Cross Street, Windermere, Cumbria LA23 1AE **T:** (01539) 442951
E: admin@southview.co.uk
W: www.southview.co.uk

B&B PER ROOM PER NIGHT
S: £52.00 - £62.00
D: £33.00 - £60.00

A warm welcome awaits you at Southview Guest House situated in the heart of Windermere in the Lake District National Park. We offer high quality bed and breakfast accommodation with our own indoor heated swimming pool and bar, exclusively for the use of our guests. **Directions:** M6, Jct 36, take A590 which turns into A591 and follow signs for Windermere. **Bedrooms:** All en suite bedrooms, 1 single, 2 classic doubles, 1 classic twin, 6 luxurious superior rooms, 1 contemporary four poster room

Site: ❖ P Payment: 💷 Leisure: 🚲 ▶ ∪ 🎣 Property: 🖥 🔥 Catering: 🍷 🍴 Room: 🔌 💧 📺 💿 🖨

BLACKBURN, Lancashire   Map ref 4A1   SatNav BB2 7NP H

Stanley House Hotel & Spa

Further Lane, Mellor, Blackburn BB2 7NP T: (01254) 769200 F: 01254 769206
E: info@stanleyhouse.co.uk
W: www.stanleyhouse.co.uk £ BOOK ONLINE

B&B PER ROOM PER NIGHT
S: £155.00 - £205.00
D: £185.00 - £285.00
HB PER PERSON PER NIGHT
£135.00 - £150.00

Stanley House is an award-winning hotel, with 30 first-class bedrooms, unrivalled wedding and conference facilities, the stylish Grill on the Hill restaurant, the hugely popular Mr Fred's and a world-class spa, truly a hotel like no other. **Directions:** Located on the A677, 4 miles from the M6/M65. Preston station 6 miles. Blackpool International Airport 25 miles. Manchester International Airport 40 miles. **Open:** All year

Site: ❀ P Payment: 🏧 Leisure: ♪ ↑ 🎿 ✗ 🏊 Property: ◉ ☎ ⌨ 🗐 ♨ ◐ Children: ⛁ 🛏 🎠 Catering: (✗ 🍷 🍽 Room: 🗝 ⚤ 📞 🕘 📺 🛁 🍳

BLACKPOOL, Lancashire   Map ref 4A1   SatNav FY1 6BP B

4 Star Phildene Blackpool

5-7 St. Chads Road, Blackpool, Lancashire FY1 6BP T: (01253) 346141 F: 01253 345243
E: info@4starblackpool.co.uk
W: www.4starblackpool.co.uk £ BOOK ONLINE

B&B PER ROOM PER NIGHT
S: £45.00 - £65.00
D: £75.00 - £99.00
EVENING MEAL PER PERSON
£15.00 - £25.00

We are ideally located 25 metres from Blackpool seafront, opposite St Chad's Headland. Just a short walk from the centre of Blackpool and all major attractions. Perfectly suited for both business and leisure guests. Child free property 18+. **Directions:** The easiest directions to give you are to make your way on to the Promenade Blackpool. St Chads Road is halfway between Central Pier and South Pier. **Bedrooms:** 5 Single, 6 Doubles, 2 Premier & 1 Superior Suite. **Open:** All year Except Christmas & New Year

Site: ❀ Payment: 🏧 € Leisure: ♿ ♪ ↑ ♻ Property: ⌨ ♨ Catering: 🍷 🍽 Room: 🗝 ⚤ 📞 📺 🛁

Arabella

102 Albert Road, Blackpool, Lancashire FY1 4PR **T:** (01253) 623189
E: graham.waters3@virgin.net
W: www.thearabella.co.uk

SPECIAL PROMOTIONS
We charge per person
not per room. Price
starts at £25 per
person and all prices
are based on two
adults sharing.

B&B: 4 night stay for
two people £152.
BB&EM: 4 night stay for
two people £208.

We provide clean and comfortable accommodation within a family friendly atmosphere. Home cooking, dietary needs catered for, rooms are serviced daily, few minutes walk from the winter gardens, 10 minutes from the Tower and sea front. We do not take stag or hen parties. Specials available Mon - Fri. Prices on application. We also have a licensed bar, free car park & Wi-Fi.

Directions: Contact our website for google map directions.

Bedrooms: All rooms have En-suites, central heating, tea & coffee facilities, flat screen tv'
Open: All year

Site: ✿ P **Payment:** ⊞ **Property:** ☷ **Children:** ⛎ ⌸ ♣ **Catering:** ♟ ⛾ **Room:** ⍷ ✹ ⊕ ℡

Doric Hotel

48-52 Queens Promenade, Blackpool FY2 9RP **T:** (01253) 352640 **F:** 01253 596842
E: info@dorichotel.co.uk
W: www.dorichotel.co.uk

B&B PER ROOM PER NIGHT
S: £32.00 - £55.00
D: £64.00 - £125.00

HB PER PERSON PER NIGHT
£34.00 - £60.00

Situated on Queens Promenade with breathtaking views over the Irish Sea. The Doric has become popular offering a wide range of facilities and good-value holidays for all. **Directions:** Exit M55 signposted Fleetwood A585 onto Promenade B5265 approximately 0.5miles on the right hand side. **Bedrooms:** 10 single, 20 double, 13 twin, 47 family, 13 suite **Open:** All year

Site: ✿ **Payment:** ⊞ € **Leisure:** ⚲ ⚒ **Property:** ♟ ☷ ◗ **Children:** ⛎ ⌸ ♣ **Catering:** ♟ ⛾ **Room:** ⍷ ✹ ℡ ⌕

Elgin Hotel

36-42 Queens Promenade, Blackpool FY2 9RW **T:** (01253) 353535 **F:** 01253 353790
E: info@elginhotel.com
W: www.elginhotel.com **£ BOOK ONLINE**

B&B PER ROOM PER NIGHT
S: £50.00 - £66.00
D: £70.00 - £100.00

EVENING MEAL PER PERSON
£11.95 - £15.00

The Elgin is a family run hotel situated near to the Cliffs overlooking the Blackpool sands. This 89 bedroom Hotel offers 5 room types, Lift to all floors, exciting entertainment and car parking. TripAdvisor Winner of 'Certificate of Excellence Award 2014' & 'Large Hotel of the Year 2015 - Finalist - Lancashire Tourism Awards'.
Directions: One mile north of Blackpool Tower on the promenade facing sea. **Bedrooms:** 2 single, 24 double, 25 twin and 38 family
Open: All year.

Site: ✿ **Payment:** ⊞ **Leisure:** ♿ ⚲ ▶ ∪ **Property:** ♟ ⛾ ☷ ◗ **Children:** ⛎ ⌸ ♣ **Catering:** ♟ ⛾
Room: ⍷ ✹ ⊕ ℡ ⌕ ⛏ ⌕

VisitEngland
★★
HOTEL

B&B PER ROOM PER NIGHT
S: £28.00 - £122.00
D: £35.00 - £128.00
HB PER PERSON PER NIGHT
£39.00 - £64.00

SPECIAL PROMOTIONS
Big Reductions Early
Season

Lyndene Hotel

305-315 Promenade, Blackpool FY1 6AN **T:** (01253) 346779 **F:** 01253 346466
E: enquiries@lyndenehotel.com
W: www.lyndenehotel.com **£ BOOK ONLINE**

Situated between Tower/Pleasure Beach, the Lyndene is an ideal location from which to enjoy all the resort has to offer. 140 comfortable bedrooms makes us the right choice for your stay in Blackpool. Three lifts access all floors inc. ground floor rooms. Three bars, two air conditioned sea-view Cabaret lounges (entertainment nightly). Two restaurants with choice of cuisine. Bar snacks served daily.

Directions: See web page for directions.   **Bedrooms:** 1 single, 52 dble, 21 twin, 66 family.
Open: All year round.

Site: ❀ Payment: 🖽 Property: 🖥 🖺 ◗ Children: 🚲5 Catering: 🍴 🍽 Room: 🖐 🗑 📞 ▣ 📺 🖳 🗲

Need more information?

Visit our websites for detailed information, up-to-date availability and to book your accommodation online. Includes over 20,000 places to stay, all of them star rated.

www.visitor-guides.co.uk

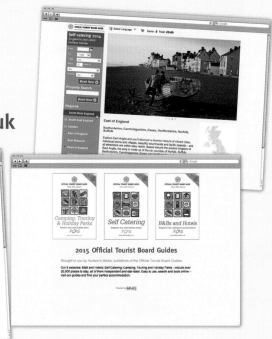

2015 Official Tourist Board Guides

Brought to you by Hudson's Media, publishers of the Official Tourist Board Guides.

Our 3 websites: B&B and Hotels; Self Catering; Camping, Touring and Holiday Parks - include over 20,000 places to stay, all of them independent and star rated. Easy to use, search and book online - visit our guides and find your perfect accommodation.

BLACKPOOL, Lancashire   Map ref 4A1

SatNav FY1 2HA

Park House Hotel

308 North Promenade, Blackpool FY1 2HA **T:** (01253) 620081 **F:** 01253 290181
E: enquiries@blackpoolparkhousehotel.com
W: www.blackpoolparkhousehotel.com **£ BOOK ONLINE**

Ideally situated on north promenade within walking distance of town centre and all major attractions. Fabulous cuisine. Entertainment seven nights a week in our ballroom or bar lounge. **Directions:** End of M55 along Yeadon Way onto Promenade from A584 heading north approximately 1 mile. **Bedrooms:** 12 single, 34 double, 33 twin, 20 family, 4 suites **Open:** All year

B&B PER ROOM PER NIGHT
S: £32.00 - £55.00
D: £64.00 - £120.00
EVENING MEAL PER PERSON
£14.95

Site: ✿ Payment: 🔲 Property: 🍷 🖥 ◑ Children: 👶 🛏 🚶 Catering: 🍴 🍽 Room: 📶 👤 ☎ 📺

BLACKPOOL, Lancashire   Map ref 4A1

SatNav FY1 4PW

Ruskin Hotel

55-61 Albert Road, Blackpool FY1 4PW **T:** (01253) 624063 **F:** 01253 623571
E: reception@ruskinhotel.com
W: www.ruskinhotel.com

Centrally located. Conference facilities, fabulous food and nightly entertainment (in season). Four bars, three dance floors, public bar and bistro. Cabaret weekends available. **Bedrooms:** 5 single, 29 dble, 24 twin, 13 family **Open:** All year

B&B PER ROOM PER NIGHT
S: £35.00 - £79.00
D: £60.00 - £88.00
HB PER PERSON PER NIGHT
£31.00 - £71.00

Site: ✿ Payment: 🔲 Leisure: ♿ ♪ ▶ Property: 🍷 🐾 🖥 📷 ◑ Children: 👶 🛏 🚶 Catering: 🍴 🍽
Room: 📶 👤 ☎ 📺 ♿

LYTHAM ST. ANNES, Lancashire   Map ref 4A1

SatNav FY8 1HN

Clifton Park Hotel

299-301 Clifton Drive South, St Annes-on-Sea, Lytham St Annes, Lancashire FY8 1HN
T: (01253) 725801 **F:** 01253 721735 **E:** info@cliftonpark.co.uk
W: www.cliftonpark.co.uk **£ BOOK ONLINE**

Just 10 mins from Blackpool's bustling centre the Clifton Park Hotel is situated in the popular seaside resort of Lytham St Annes. The hotel boasts excellent facilities and a warm friendly atmosphere. **Directions:** From the end of the M55, follow signs for Lytham St.Annes. We are situated 150 yards on your left after St.Annes Square. **Bedrooms:** All our rooms vary in shapes, sizes & styles. **Open:** All Year Round

B&B PER ROOM PER NIGHT
S: £30.00 - £75.00
D: £60.00 - £150.00
EVENING MEAL PER PERSON
£15.00 - £22.50

Site: ✿ P Payment: 🔲 Leisure: ▶ 🎿 🎣 Property: 🍷 🖥 📷 🍴 ◑ Catering: (✗ 🍴 🍽 Room: 📶 👤 ☎ 📺 ♿

SALE, Greater Manchester   Map ref 4A2

SatNav M33 2AE

Belforte House

7-9 Broad Road, Sale, Manchester M33 2AE **T:** (01619) 738779 **F:** 01619 738779
E: belfortehousehotel@aol.co.uk
W: www.belfortehousehotel.co.uk **£ BOOK ONLINE**

Privately owned hotel with a personal, friendly approach. Ideally located for Manchester Airport, the Metrolink and the city centre. Situated directly opposite Sale Leisure Centre. **Directions:** 1 mile from Junction 6 M60. 200 metres from Tram Station. **Bedrooms:** 14 single, 4 double, 2 twin, 3 family **Open:** All year except Christmas and New Year

B&B PER ROOM PER NIGHT
S: £38.00 - £49.95
D: £65.00
EVENING MEAL PER PERSON
£6.95 - £13.95

Site: ✿ P Payment: 🔲 Leisure: ♪ ⛳ Property: 🐾 🖥 📷 Children: 👶 🛏 🚶 Catering: 🍴 🍽 Room: 📶 👤 ☎ 📻 📺 ♿

LIVERPOOL, Merseyside   Map ref 4A2   SatNav L20 3AW B

Breeze Guest House

237 Hawthorne Road, Bootle L20 3AW **T:** (0151) 933 2576 **E:** breezegh@googlemail.co.uk
W: www.breezeguesthouse.co.uk **£ BOOK ONLINE**

The Breeze Guesthouse is a luxury townhouse located in Bootle Village, 3 miles away from vibrant city of Liverpool home of the Beatles, Liverpool & Everton stadia & Aintree Race Course.
Directions: Conveniently located for all modes of transport to/from Liverpool city centre, Crosby or Southport including bus, train and motorway. **Bedrooms:** 1 single, 8 twin, 1 family
Open: All year except Christmas

B&B PER ROOM PER NIGHT
S: £35.00 - £50.00
D: £70.00 - £80.00
EVENING MEAL PER PERSON
£5.00 - £10.00

Site: P Payment: ⊞ **Property:** 🐾 🖾 **Children:** 🚼 ⛺ 🚼 **Catering:** 🍴 **Room:** 🔌 🕯 📺 📀 🔌 🌀

LIVERPOOL, Merseyside   Map ref 4A2   SatNav L1 9DA H

Hope Street Hotel

40 Hope Street, Liverpool, Merseyside L1 9DA **T:** (0151) 7093000 **F:** 0151 7092454
E: sleep@hopestreethotel.co.uk
W: www.hopestreethotel.co.uk **£ BOOK ONLINE**

B&B PER ROOM PER NIGHT
S: £102.00 - £507.00
D: £114.00 - £519.00
EVENING MEAL PER PERSON
£25.00 - £55.00

SPECIAL PROMOTIONS
Lazy Sunday Package - from £149 for two. Stay Sunday, enjoy a two course dinner in The London Carriage Works followed by a full Liverpool breakfast and a late check out of 12 noon on the Monday.

Liverpool's original boutique hotel, in the centre of the city's Georgian quarter, is surrounded by cathedrals, theatres, an international concert hall, a National Trust house, and several infamous hostelries. The style is chic with original warehouse features. The hotel's restaurant, The London Carriage Works, is a destination in its own right and a consistent 2 AA Rosette holder.

Directions: From M62, continue to end of motorway, follow signs for cathedrals (approx 3 miles). Hope Street links the two cathedrals and Hope Street Hotel is in the middle opposite the Philharmonic Hall.

Bedrooms: Oversized beds with white Egyptian cotton, solid birch and oak floors, bespoke furniture, original beams and brickwork, REN toiletries and free Wi-Fi
Open: All Year

Site: P Payment: ⊞ **Leisure:** ✶ **Property:** ⊛ 🍸 🐾 🖾 🖥 🏛 ◑ **Children:** 🚼 🚼 🚼 **Catering:** (✗ 🍷 🍴
Room: 🔌 🕯 ☎ 📀 📺 📀 🔌

LIVERPOOL, Merseyside   Map ref 4A2   SatNav L1 9JG B

International Inn

4 South Hunter Street, Liverpool L1 9JG **T:** (0151) 709 8135 **F:** 0151 709 8135
E: info@internationalinn.co.uk
W: www.internationalinn.co.uk **£ BOOK ONLINE**

Tourist hostel, located in the heart of the city centre, near to theatres, cathedrals and nightlife. With a variety of dormitory sizes, Free tea/coffee, toast. No curfew, bedding provided. Free Wi-Fi.
Directions: Check out our web site for full directions. We have great connections from all transport links. **Bedrooms:** 3 double, 4 twin **Open:** All year except Christmas

BED ONLY PER NIGHT
£17.00

Payment: ⊞ **Leisure:** 🔦 **Property:** ⊛ 🍸 🖾 📀 📺 📀 🗄 **Children:** 🚼 🚼 🚼 **Room:** 🔌 🌀 **Bedroom:** 🔌 🖥

National Accessible Scheme

Finding suitable accommodation is not always easy, especially if you have to seek out rooms with level entry or large print menus. Use the National Accessible Scheme to help you make your choice.

Additional help and guidance on accessible tourism can be obtained from the national charity Tourism for All:

Tourism for All

Tourism for All UK
7A Pixel Mill
44 Appleby Road
Kendal, Cumbria LA9 6ES

Information helpline
0845 124 9971
(lines open 9-5 Mon-Fri)
E info@tourismforall.org.uk
W www.tourismforall.org.uk
www.openbritain.net

Proprietors of accommodation taking part in the National Accessible Scheme have gone out of their way to ensure a comfortable stay for guests with hearing, visual or mobility needs. These exceptional places are full of extra touches to make everyone's visit trouble-free, from handrails, ramps and step-free entrances (ideal for buggies too) to level-access showers and colour contrast in the bathrooms. Members of staff may have attended a disability awareness course and will know what assistance will really be appreciated.

Appropriate National Accessible Scheme symbols are included in the guide entries (shown opposite). If you have additional needs or specific requirements, we strongly recommend that you make sure these can be met by your chosen establishment before you confirm your reservation. The index at the back of the guide gives a list of accommodation that has received a National Accessible Scheme rating.

For more information on the NAS and tips and ideas on holiday travel in England go to: **www.visitengland.com/accessforall**

The criteria VisitEngland has adopted does not necessarily conform to British Standards or to Building Regulations. They reflect what the organisation understands to be acceptable to meet the practical needs of guests with mobility or sensory impairments and encourage the industry to increase access to all.

England

Mobility Impairment Symbols

Older and less mobile guests
Typically suitable for a person with sufficient mobility to climb a flight of steps but who would benefit from fixtures and fittings to aid balance.

Part-time wheelchair users
Typically suitable for a person with restricted walking ability and for those who may need to use a wheelchair some of the time and can negotiate a maximum of three steps.

Independent wheelchair users
Typically suitable for a person who depends on the use of a wheelchair and transfers unaided to and from the wheelchair in a seated position. This person may be an independent traveller.

Assisted wheelchair users
Typically suitable for a person who depends on the use of a wheelchair and needs assistance when transferring to and from the wheelchair in a seated position.

Access Exceptional is awarded to establishments that meet the requirements of independent wheelchair users or assisted wheelchair users shown above and also fulfil more demanding requirements with reference to the British Standards BS8300.

Visual Impairment Symbols

Typically provides key additional services and facilities to meet the needs of visually impaired guests.

Typically provides a higher level of additional services and facilities to meet the needs of visually impaired guests.

Hearing Loss Symbols

Typically provides key additional services and facilities to meet the needs of guests with hearing loss.

Typically provides a higher level of additional services and facilities to meet the needs of guests with hearing loss.

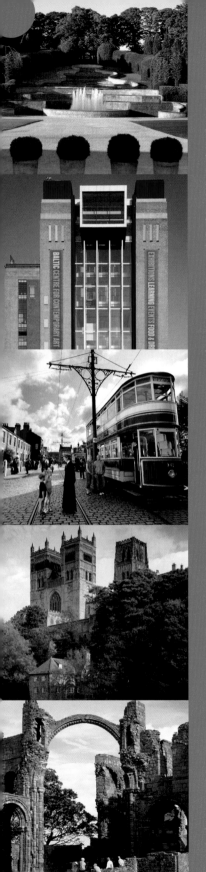

Don't Miss...

The Alnwick Garden
Alnwick, Northumberland NE66 1YU
(01665) 511350
www.alnwickgarden.com
Be inspired by the most exciting contemporary garden developed in
the last century, The Alnwick Garden. The inspiration of the Duchess
of Northumberland, this fascinating garden features the Grand Cascade
as its centrepiece to create spellbinding water displays. Explore the Rose
Garden, Ornamental Garden, Serpent Garden with eight water sculptures
nestling in the coils of a topiary serpent, Bamboo Labyrinth and don't miss
the Poison Garden which holds dangerous plants and their stories. The
garden is also home to the and one of the world's largest tree houses,
with rope bridges, walkways in the sky and a fantastic place to eat.

BALTIC Centre for Contemporary Art
Gateshead, Tyne and Wear NE8 3BA
(01914) 781810
www.balticmill.com
Housed in a landmark industrial building on the south bank of the River
Tyne in Gateshead, BALTIC is a major international centre for contemporary
art and is the biggest gallery of its kind in the world. It presents a
dynamic, diverse and international programme of contemporary visual
art, ranging from blockbuster exhibitions to innovative new work and
projects created by artists working within the local community.

Beamish Museum
County Durham DH9 0RG
(01913) 704000
www.beamish.org.uk
Beamish - The Living Museum of the North, is a world-famous open air
museum vividly recreating life in the North East in the early 1800's and 1900's.
It tells the story of the people of North East England during the Georgian,
Victorian, and Edwardian periods through a costumed cast, engaging
exhibits and an exciting programme of events including The Great North
Festival of Transport, a Georgian Fair, The Great North Festival of Agriculture.

Durham Cathedral
County Durham DH1 3EH
(0191) 3864266
www.durhamcathedral.co.uk
Durham Cathedral is perhaps the finest example of Norman church
architecture in England or even Europe. Set grandly on a rocky
promontory next to the Castle with the medieval city huddled
below and the river sweeping round, it is a World Heritage Site and
houses the tombs of St Cuthbert and The Venerable Bede.

Lindisfarne Priory
Holy Island, Northumberland TD15 2RX
(01289) 389200
www.english-heritage.org.uk/lindisfarnepriory
Lying just a few miles off the beautiful Northumberland coast, Holy Island
contains a wealth of history and is home to one of the region's most revered
treasures, Lindisfarne Priory. The epicentre of Christianity in Anglo Saxon
times and once the home of St Oswald, it was the birthplace of the Lindisfarne
Gospels, one of the world's most precious books and remains a place of
pilgrimage today. NB: watch the tides as the causeway is only open at low tide.

North East

County Durham, Northumberland,
Tees Valley, Tyne & Wear

The North East contains two Areas of Outstanding Natural Beauty, a National Park, Hadrian's Wall, the dynamic city of Newcastle, and County Durham, with its fine cathedral and castle. This region is awash with dramatic hills, sweeping valleys, vast expanses of dune-fringed beaches and ragged cliffs with spectacular views. Littered with dramatic castles, ruins and historic houses, there are plenty of exciting family attractions and walking routes galore.

Northumberland

Tyne & Wear

County Durham

Tees Valley

245

Explore – North East

County Durham & Tees Valley

Durham Cathedral, the greatest Norman building in England, was once a prison and soars grandly above the Medieval city and surrounding plain. Famed for its location as much as for its architecture, it is the burial place of both St Cuthbert, a great northern saint, and the Venerable Bede, author of the first English history.

The Vale of Durham is packed full of award-winning attractions including Locomotion: The National Railway Museum at Shildon and Beamish – The Living Museum of the North, the country's largest open air museum. Auckland Castle was the palace of Durham's unique Prince Bishops for more than 900 years. Part of the North Pennines Area of Outstanding Natural Beauty, the Durham Dales including Teesdale and Weardale, is a beautiful landscape of hills, moors, valleys and rivers, with numerous picturesque villages and market towns.

Comprising miles of stunning coastline and acres of ancient woodland, Tees Valley covers the lower, flatter area of the valley of the River Tees. This unique part of the UK, split between County Durham and Yorkshire, has nearly a hundred visitor attractions, including Preston Hall and Saltholme Nature Reserve, which can both be found in Stockton-on-Tees.

The Durham Heritage Coast, from Sunderland to Hartlepool, is one of the finest in England. The coastal path that runs along much of its length takes you on a spectacular journey of natural, historical and geological interest, with dramatic views along the shore and out over the North Sea. The historic port city of Hartlepool has award-winning attractions, a fantastic marina, beaches and countryside.

Newcastle & Tyne And Wear

Newcastle-upon-Tyne, once a shipbuilding centre, is a rejuvenated city of proud civic tradition with fine restaurants, theatres, and one of the liveliest arts scenes outside London. As well as the landmark Baltic, there's the Laing Art Gallery, the Great North Museum and The Sage concert venue. The Theatre Royal is the third home of the Royal Shakespeare Company and a venue for major touring companies. The Metro Centre in neighbouring Gateshead attracts shoppers from all over the country with more than 300 outlets and 11 cinema screens.

Northumberland

Northumbria, to use its ancient name, is an undiscovered holiday paradise where the scenery is wild and beautiful, the beaches golden and unspoiled, and the natives friendly. The region is edged by the North Sea, four national parks and the vast Border Forest Park. Its eastern sea boundary makes a stunning coastline, stretching 100 miles from Staithes on the Cleveland boundary, to Berwick-on-Tweed, England's most northerly town, frequently fought over and with the finest preserved example of Elizabethan town walls in the country. In between you'll find as many holiday opportunities as changes of scenery.

Step back in time 2,000 years along Hadrian's Wall, explore the hills, forests and waterfalls of the National Parks, and discover historic castles, splendid churches and quaint towns. Visitors can trace man's occupation of the region from prehistoric times through rock carvings, ancient hill forts, Saxon churches, Norman priories, medieval castles, and a wealth of industrial archaeology. Housesteads Roman Fort at Haydon Bridge is the most complete example of a British Roman fort. It features magnificent ruins and stunning views of the countryside surrounding Hadrian's Wall.

The region has a rich maritime heritage too. Ruined coastal fortifications such as Dunstanburgh and fairy-tale Lindisfarne are relics of a turbulent era. Agriculture is also one of the region's most important industries. Take a trip on the Heatherslaw Light Railway, a narrow gauge line operating from Etal Village to Heatherslaw Mill, a restored waterdriven corn mill and agricultural museum near the delightful model village of Ford.

Visit – North East

 Attractions with this sign participate in the Visitor Attraction Quality Assurance Scheme.

County Durham & Tees Valley

Adventure Valley
Durham, County Durham DH1 5SG
(01913) 868291
www.adventurevalley.co.uk
Split into six Play Zones (with three under cover), you'll find the very best in family fun come rain or shine.

Billingham International Folklore Festival
August, Billingham, County Durham
www.billinghamfestival.co.uk
A festival of traditional and contemporary world dance, music and arts.

Bishop Auckland Food Festival
April, Bishop Auckland, County Durham
www.bishopaucklandfoodfestival.co.uk
Be inspired by cookery demonstrations and entertained by performers.

The Bowes Museum
Barnard Castle, County Durham DL12 8NP
(01833) 690606
www.thebowesmuseum.org.uk
A collection of outstanding European fine and decorative arts offering an acclaimed exhibition programme, special events and children's activities.

Durham Book Festival
October/November, Durham, County Durham
www.durhambookfestival.com
With writers covering everything from politics to poetry, and fiction to feminism, there's something for everyone at the Durham Book Festival. See website for dates and full programme.

Durham Castle
County Durham DH1 3RW
(01913) 343800
www.durhamworldheritagesite.com
Durham Castle is part of the Durham City World Heritage Site and has enjoyed a long history of

continuous use. Along with Durham Cathedral, it is among the greatest monuments of the Norman Conquest of Britain and is now home to students of University College, Durham. Entrance is by guided tour only, please telephone opening and tour times.

East Durham Heritage and Lifeboat Centre
County Durham, SR7 7EE
www.seahamlifeboats.oneuk.com
Take a look at exhibitions with themed displays on the area's maritime, industrial and social heritage dating back from before the 8th Century.

Hall Hill Farm
Durham, County Durham DH7 0TA
(01388) 731333
www.hallhillfarm.co.uk
Award-winning farm attraction set in attractive countryside, see and touch the animals at close quarters.

Hamsterley Forest
Bishop Auckland, County Durham DL13 3NL
(01388) 488312
www.forestry.gov.uk/hamsterleyforest
A 5,000 acre mixed woodland open to the public all year.

Hartlepool Art Gallery
Hartlepool, Tees Valley TS24 7EQ
(01429) 869706
www.hartlepool.gov.uk
Former church building also includes the TIC and a bell tower viewing platform looking over Hartlepool.

Hartlepool's Maritime Experience
Tees Valley TS24 0XZ
(01429) 860077
www.hartlepoolsmaritimeexperience.com
A superb re-creation of an 18th century seaport and a fantastic place to visit. It brings to life the time of Nelson, Napoleon and the Battle of Trafalgar.

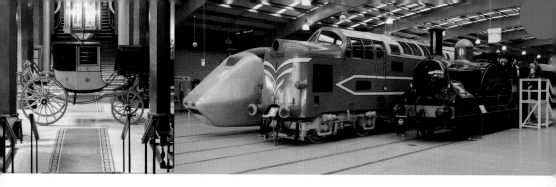

Hartlepool Museum
Maritime Avenue, Hartlepool TS24 0XZ
(01429) 860077
www.hartlepoolsmaritimeexperience.com
Situated beside Hartlepool Historic Quay, includes local historical exhibits, PSS Wingfield Castle and the original lighthouse light.

Head of Steam
Tees Valley DL3 6ST
(01325) 405060
www.darlington.gov.uk/Culture/headofsteam/welcome
Restored 1842 station housing a collection of exhibits relating to railways in the North East of England, including Stephenson's Locomotion, call for details of events.

High Force Waterfall
Middleton-in-Teesdale, County Durham DL12 0XH
(01833) 622209
www.highforcewaterfall.com
Discover the force of nature at High Force, one of the most spectacular waterfalls in England. Enjoy a picnic or take a walk along many way marked routes.

HMS Trincomalee
Hartlepool, Tees Valley TS24 0XZ
(01429) 223193
www.hms-trincomalee.co.uk
HMS Trincomalee, built in 1817, is one of the oldest ship afloat in Europe. Come aboard for a unique experience of Navy life two centuries ago.

Killhope, The North of England
Lead Mining Museum
Bishop Auckland, County Durham DL13 1AR
(01388) 537505
www.killhope.org.uk
Fully restored Victorian lead mine and the most complete lead mining site in Great Britain.

Locomotion: The National Railway Museum at Shildon
Shildon, County Durham DL4 1PQ
(01388) 931232
www.nrm.org.uk/locomotion
The first National Museum in the North East. Free admission. View over 60 vehicles, children's play area and interactive displays.

mima
Middlesbrough, Tees Valley TS1 2AZ
(01642) 726720
www.visitmima.com
mima, Middlesbrough Institute of Modern Art, is a £14.2m landmark gallery in the heart of Middlesbrough. mima showcases an international programme of fine art and applied art from the 1900s to the present day.

Preston Hall Museum and Park
Stockton-on-Tees, Tees Valley TS18 3RH
(01642) 527375
www.prestonparkmuseum.co.uk
A Georgian country house set in beautiful parkland overlooking the River Tees. A Museum of social history with a recreated Victorian street and working craftsmen.

Raby Castle
Staindrop, County Durham DL2 3AH
(01833) 660202
www.rabycastle.com
Home of Lord Barnard's family since 1626, includes a 200 acre deer park, gardens, carriage collection, adventure playground, shop and tearoom.

Saltburn Smugglers Heritage Centre
Saltburn-by-the-Sea, Tees Valley TS12 1HF
(01287) 625252
www.thisisredcar.co.uk/visit/saltburn-smugglers-heritage-centre
Step back into Saltburn's past and experience the authentic sights, sounds and smells.

Saltholme Wildlife Reserve
Middlesbrough, Tees Valley TS2 1TU
(01642) 546625
www.rspb.org.uk/reserves/guide/s/saltholme
An amazing wildlife experience in the Tees Valley.

Weardale Railway
County Durham, DL13 2YS
(01388) 526203
www.weardale-railway.org.uk
The Weardale Railway follows the path of the River Wear and passes through spectacular scenery. A good time is to be had by all on these heritage locomotives.

Newcastle & Tyne And Wear

Arbeia Roman Fort and Museum
South Shields, Tyne and Wear NE33 2BB
(01912) 771410
www.twmuseums.org.uk/arbeia
Arbeia is the best reconstruction of a Roman fort in Britain and offers visitors a unique insight into the every day life of the Roman army, from the soldier in his barrack room to the commander in his luxurious house.

BBC Tours Newcastle
Newcastle upon Tyne, NE2 4NS
www.bbc.co.uk/showsandtours/tours/newcastle
Take a tour of the broadcasting house for an in depth behind the scenes look into what it's like to be a director and presenter for the BBC. Take a seat in the director's chair, or ask questions that have always been a mystery.

Centre for Life
Newcastle-upon-Tyne, Tyne and Wear NE1 4EP
(01912) 438210
www.life.org.uk
The Centre for Life is an award-winning science centre where imaginative exhibitions, interactive displays and special events promote greater understanding of science and provoke curiosity in the world around us.

Discovery Museum
Newcastle-upon-Tyne, Tyne and Wear NE1 4JA
(01912) 326789
www.twmuseums.org.uk/discovery
A wide variety of experiences for all the family to enjoy.

Evolution Emerging
May, Newcastle, Tyne and Wear
www.evolutionemerging.com
The North East's premier music event, taking place over a Bank Holiday.

Great North Museum: Hancock
Newcastle-upon-Tyne, Tyne and Wear NE2 4PT
(0191) 208 6765
www.twmuseums.org.uk/great-north-museum
See major new displays showing the wonder of the animal and plant kingdoms, objects from the Ancient Greeks and a planetarium and a life-size T-Rex.

Hatton Gallery
Newcastle-upon-Tyne, Tyne and Wear NE1 7RU
(01912) 226059
www.twmuseums.org.uk/hatton
Temporary exhibitions of contemporary and historical art. Permanent display of Kurt Schwitters' Merzbarn.

Laing Art Gallery
Newcastle-upon-Tyne, Tyne and Wear NE1 8AG
(01912) 327734
www.twmuseums.org.uk/laing
The Laing Art Gallery is home to an important collection of 18th and 19th century painting, which is shown alongside temporary exhibitions of historic and contemporary art.

Namco Funscape
Gateshead, Tyne and Wear, NE11 9XY
(0191) 406 1066
Find fun in 38, 000 sq ft of state-of-the-art arcade games, tenpin bowling, fantastic bars and the fastest dodgem track in Europe.

National Glass Museum
Liberty Way, Sunderland, SR6 0GL
(01915) 155555
www.nationalglasscentre.com
Overlooking the River Wear, enjoy an ever-changing programme of exhibitions, live glass blowing, and banqueting and a stunning restaurant.

Newcastle Theatre Royal
Newcastle upon Tyne NE1 6BR
(0844) 811 2121
www.theatreroyal.co.uk
The Theatre Royal is a Grade I listed building situated on historic Grey Street in Newcastle-upon-Tyne. It hosts a variety of shows, including ballet, contemporary dance, drama, musicals and opera in a restored 1901 Frank Matcham Edwardian interior.

Sage Gateshead
Gateshead Quays, Gateshead NE8 2JR
(0191) 443 4661
www.sagegateshead.com
A concert venue and centre for musical education on the south bank of the River Tyne. It stages a varied and eclectic programme in state-of-the-art halls.

Segedunum Roman Fort, Baths & Museum
Wallsend, Tyne and Wear NE28 6HR
(0191) 278 4217
www.twmuseums.org.uk/segedunum
*Segedunum Roman Fort is the gateway to
Hadrian's Wall. Explore the excavated fort site, visit
reconstructions of a Roman bath house, learn about
the history of the area in the museum and enjoy the
view from the 35 metre viewing tower.*

Tyneside Cinema
Newcastle upon Tyne, Tyne and Wear NE1 6QG
(0191) 227 5500
www.tynesidecinema.co.uk
*Showing the best films in beautiful art deco
surroundings, Tyneside Cinema's programme ranges
from mainstream to arthouse and world cinema. As
the last surviving Newsreel theatre still operating
full-time in the UK, this Grade II-listed building is a
must-visit piece of lovingly restored heritage.*

WWT Washington Wetland Centre
Washington, Tyne and Wear NE38 8LE
(01914) 165454
www.wwt.org.uk/visit/washington
*45 hectares of wetland, woodland and wildlife reserve.
Home to wildfowl, insects and flora with lake-side hides,
wild bird feeding station, waterside cafe, picnic areas,
sustainable garden, playground and events calendar.*

Northumberland

Alnwick Beer Festival
September, Alnwick, Northumberland
www.alnwickbeerfestival.co.uk
*If you enjoy real ale, or simply want to enjoy a
fantastic social event, then make sure you pay this
festival a visit.*

Alnwick Castle
Northumberland NE66 1NQ
(01665) 511100
www.alnwickcastle.com
*A significant visitor attraction with lavish State
Rooms and superb art collections, as well as
engaging activities and events for all ages, and all
set in beautiful landscape by Northumberland-
born 'Capability' Brown. Potter fans will recognise
Alnwick as Hogwarts from the Harry Potter films.*

Bailiffgate Museum
Alnwick, Northumberland NE66 1LX
(01665) 605847
www.bailiffgatemuseum.co.uk
*Bailiffgate Museum brings to life the people and places
of North Northumberland in exciting interactive style.*

Bamburgh Castle
Northumberland NE69 7DF
(01668) 214515
www.bamburghcastle.com
*A spectacular castle with fantastic coastal views.
The stunning Kings Hall and Keep house collections
of armour, artwork, porcelain and furniture.*

Belsay Hall, Castle & Gardens
Nr Morpeth, Northumberland NE20 0DX
(01661) 881636
www.english-heritage.org.uk
*Lose yourself at Belsay with its unique combination
of Grecian architecture, medieval ruins, formal
terraces and lush jungle-esque Quarry Garden. Enjoy
wonderful views from the top of the castle tower and
a tasty treat at the tempting Victorian tearoom.*

Chillingham Castle
Northumberland, NE66 5NJ
01668 215359
www.chillingham-castle.com
*A remarkable Medieval fortress with Tudor additions,
torture chamber, shop, dungeon, tearoom, woodland
walks, furnished rooms and topiary garden.*

Cragside House, Gardens & Estate
Morpeth, Northumberland NE65 7PX
(01669) 620333
www.nationaltrust.org.uk/cragside/
Built on a rocky crag high above Debdon Burn, the house is crammed with ingenious gadgets and was the first in the world to be lit electrically. The gardens are breathtaking with 5 lakes, one of Europe's largest rock gardens, and over 7 million trees and shrubs.

Haydon Bridge Festival
July, Haydon Bridge, Northumberland
www.haydonbridgefestival.co.uk
Annual celebration of the finest real ales and wines.

Hexham Abbey Festival
September-October, Hexham, Northumberland
www.hexhamabbey.org.uk
An exciting array of events to capture the imagination, bringing the very best world-class musicians and artists to Hexham.

Hexham Old Gaol
Northumberland NE46 1XD
(01670) 624523
www.hexhamoldgaol.org.uk
Step into the oldest purpose-built prison in England. *Tour the Old Gaol, 1330AD, by glass lift. Meet the gaoler to learn about the treatment of criminals then put yourself in the prisoners' shoes and try on costumes.*

Kielder Castle Forest Park Centre
Northumberland NE48 1ER
(01434) 250209
www.forestry.gov.uk/kielder
Features include forest shop, information centre, tearoom and exhibitions. Bike hire available.

Lindisfarne Castle
Northumberland TD15 2SH
(01289) 389244
www.nationaltrust.org.uk/lindisfarne-castle/
Rising from the sheer rock face at the tip of Holy Island off the Northumberland coast, Lindisfarne Castle was built to defend a harbour sheltering English ships during skirmishes with Scotland.

Northumberland National Park
Northumberland, NE66 4LT
(01665) 578890
www.northumberlandnationalpark.org.uk
Covering 405 acres of breathtaking landscape rich in wildlife, heritage and picturesque valleys.

RNLI Grace Darling Museum
Bamburgh, Northumberland NE69 7AE
(01668) 214910
www.rnli.org.uk/gracedarling
A museum dedicated to Grace Darling and her family, as well as all those who Save Lives at Sea.

Warkworth Castle
Warkworth, Northumberland NE65 0UJ
(01665) 711423
www.english-heritage.org.uk/warkworthcastle
This hill-top fortress and hermitage offers a fantastic family day out. The magnificent cross-shaped keep was once home to 'Harry Hotspur', immortalised as a rebel lord by Shakespeares.

Whalton Manor Gardens
Northumberland, NE61 3UT
(01670) 775205
www.whaltonmanor.co.uk
Experience a first-hand insight into nature's true beauty with a guided tour from the owner. Why not stay for home-cooked lunch and a cream tea as well?

Tourist Information Centres

When you arrive at your destination, visit the Tourist Information Centre for quality assured help with accommodation and information about local attractions and events, or email your request before you go.

Alnwick	2 The Shambles	01670 622152 / 01670 622151	alnwick.tic@northumberland.gov.uk
Amble	Queen Street Car Park	01665 712313	amble.tic@northumberland.gov.uk
Bellingham	Station Yard	01434 220616	bellinghamtic@btconnect.com
Berwick-Upon-Tweed	106 Marygate	01670 622155 / 625568	berwick.tic@northumberland.gov.uk
Bishop Auckland	Town Hall Ground Floor	03000 269524	bishopauckland.touristinfo@durham.gov.uk
Corbridge	Hill Street	01434 632815	corbridge.tic@northumberland.gov.uk
Craster	Craster Car Park	01665 576007	craster.tic@northumberland.gov.uk
Darlington	Central Library	01325 462034	crown.street.library@darlington.gov.uk
Durham Visitor Contact Centre	1st Floor	03000 262626	visitor@thisisdurham.com
Gateshead	Central Library	0191 433 8420	libraries@gateshead.gov.uk
Guisborough	Priory Grounds	01287 633801	guisborough_tic@redcar-cleveland.gov.uk
Haltwhistle	Westgate	01434 322002	haltwhistle.tic@northumberland.gov.uk
Hartlepool	Hartlepool Art Gallery	01429 869706	hpooltic@hartlepool.gov.uk
Hexham	Wentworth Car Park	01434 652220	hexham.tic@northumberland.gov.uk
Middlesbrough	Middlesbrough Info. Centre & Box Office	01642 729900	tic@middlesbrough.gov.uk
Middleton-in-Teesdale	10 Market Place	01833 641001	tic@middletonplus.myzen.co.uk
Morpeth	The Chantry	01670 623455	morpeth.tic@northumberland.gov.uk
North Shields	Unit 18	0191 2005895	ticns@northtyneside.gov.uk
Once Brewed	National Park Centre	01434 344396	tic.oncebrewed@nnpa.org.uk
Otterburn	Otterburn Mill	01830 521002	tic@otterburnmill.co.uk
Saltburn by Sea	Saltburn Library	01287 622422 / 623584	saltburn_library@redcar-cleveland.gov.uk
Seahouses	Seafield Car Park	01665 720884 / 01670 625593	seahouses.tic@northumberland.gov.uk
South Shields	Haven Point	0191 424 7788	tourism@southtyneside.gov.uk
Stockton-On-Tees	High Street	01642 528130	visitorinformation@stockton.gov.uk
Whitley Bay	York Road	0191 6435395	susan.clark@northtyneside.gov.uk
Wooler	The Cheviot Centre	1668 282123	wooler.tic@northumberland.gov.uk

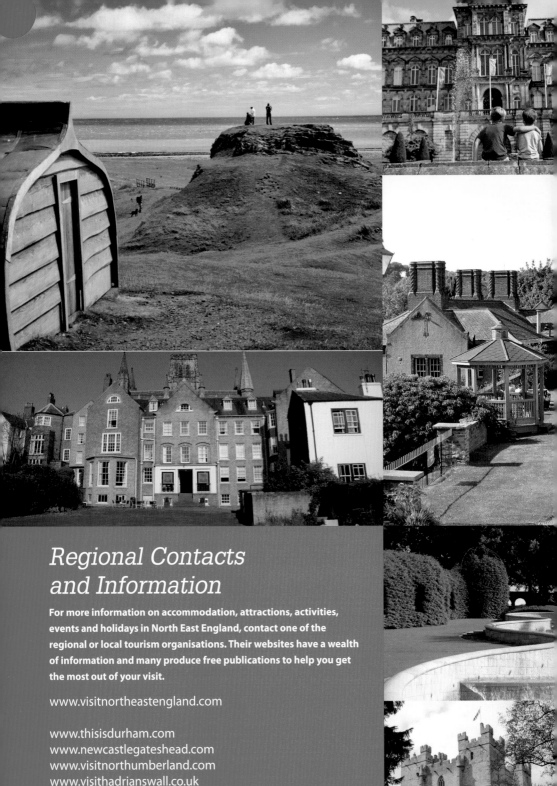

Regional Contacts
and Information

For more information on accommodation, attractions, activities, events and holidays in North East England, contact one of the regional or local tourism organisations. Their websites have a wealth of information and many produce free publications to help you get the most out of your visit.

www.visitnortheastengland.com

www.thisisdurham.com
www.newcastlegateshead.com
www.visitnorthumberland.com
www.visithadrianswall.co.uk
www.visitnorthtyneside.com
www.visitsouthtyneside.co.uk
www.seeitdoitsunderland.co.uk

Stay – North East

Entries appear alphabetically by town name in each county. A key to symbols appears on page 7

DURHAM, Co Durham   Map ref 5C2   SatNav DH1 4PS B

Castle View Guest House

4 Crossgate, Durham DH1 4PS T: (0191) 3868852 E: castle_view@hotmail.com
W: www.castle-view.co.uk

B&B PER ROOM PER NIGHT
D: £100.00 - £130.00

Two hundred and fifty year old listed building in the heart of the old city, with woodland and riverside walks and magnificent views of the cathedral and castle. Complimentary parking.
Directions: From A1(M) take junction 62, follow signs A690 Crook until river crossing. At traffic lights turn left into Crossgate, next to St Margarets Church. **Bedrooms:** 3 double, 2 twin **Open:** All year except Christmas and New Year

Site: ✿ Payment: 🖭 Property: 🚗 Children: 🐴2 Catering: 🍴 Room: 🔌 ☕ 📺 🛁

DURHAM, Co Durham   Map ref 5C2   SatNav DH1 3RH B

St Chad's College

18 North Bailey, Durham DH1 3RH T: (01913) 343358 F: 01913 343371
E: chads@durham.ac.uk
W: www.dur.ac.uk/chads/

B&B PER ROOM PER NIGHT
S: £35.00 - £40.00
D: £60.00 - £75.00
EVENING MEAL PER PERSON
£15.00 - £35.00

In the heart of historic Durham, adjacent to the World Heritage Site and next to the Cathedral, St Chad's provides comfortable modern accommodation, supported by friendly service, in its range of listed buildings - a spectacular location. Group bookings welcome.

Directions: Follow the A1(M) until the A690, direct to Durham, towards Cathedral. The college lies opposite of Durham Cathedral.

Bedrooms: Over 150 en suite and standard bedrooms. Evening meals pre book only.
Open: Easter/Summer student vacations.

Site: ✿ Payment: 🖭 Leisure: 🎵 🏃 Property: 🏠 Children: 🐾 🖾 🎏 Catering: 🍷 🍴 Room: 🛁

DURHAM, Co Durham   Map ref 5C2
SatNav DH1 3RJ **B**

★★★
GUEST ACCOMMODATION

B&B PER ROOM PER NIGHT
S: £35.00
D: £62.00

St John's College
3 South Bailey, Durham DH1 3RJ **T:** (0191) 3343877 **E:** s.l.hobson@durham.ac.uk
W: www.durham.ac.uk/st-johns.college

Located in the heart of Durham City alongside the cathedral, St John's offers accommodation in distinctive, historic buildings with riverside gardens. **Directions:** Take A1(M) motorway junction 62, dual carriageway A690 Gilesgate roundabout. Take third exit, second left exit, then left to Market Square, 200 yards to College.
Bedrooms: 66 single, 15 double, 2 twin
Open: Summer vacations only

Site: ❀ Payment: 💳 Property: 🖥 🔲 Children: 🧸 🛝 Catering: 🍴 Room: 🛁 🧺

ALNWICK, Northumberland   Map ref 5C1
SatNav NE66 2HJ **B**

★★★
GUEST ACCOMMODATION

B&B PER ROOM PER NIGHT
S: £44.00 - £55.00
D: £59.00 - £120.00

EVENING MEAL PER PERSON
£15.00 - £30.00

SPECIAL PROMOTIONS
Stay Mon-Thu get Thursday Half Price. Stay Fri & Sat get Sunday Half Price, Ex Bk Hols. Adaptable family rooms.

Alnwick Lodge
West Cawledge Park, Alnwick NE66 2HJ
T: (01665) 604363 / (01665) 603377 / 07881 696769 **E:** bookings@alnwicklodge.com
W: www.alnwicklodge.com **£ BOOK ONLINE**

Lonely Planet recommended and Trip Advisor 4* rated accommodation in beautiful Northumberland. A unique creation AD1650-2012. Alnwick Lodge, West Cawledge Park is a combination of history and rural charm with an air of sophistication, whilst linked to technology. Fascinating, uncomparable accommodation for business, pleasure, conferences, film crews and parties. Antique galleries and log fires.

Directions: 1 mile south of Alnwick. Direct access from A1 (trunk road) highway signposted to West Cawledge Park (chair on the roof).

Bedrooms: 4 single, 4 double, 3 twin and 4 family. Glamping - Foresters Wagon, Shepherds Hut, Gypsy Caravans.
Open: All year

Site: ❀ P Payment: 💳 Leisure: 🎿 🎵 ▶ ∪ Property: 🐕 🖥 Children: 🧸 🎮 🛝 Catering: 🍴
Room: 🍵 🛁 📺 🧺 🛋 🖨

AMBLE, Northumberland   Map ref 5C1
SatNav NE65 0AL **B**

★★★
GUEST HOUSE

Amble Guesthouse
16 Leazes Street, Amble NE65 0AL **T:** (01665) 714661 **E:** stephmclaughlin@aol.com
W: www.ambleguesthouse.co.uk

A family run 4 bedroom guest house. All rooms en suite. In picturesque fishing port of Amble. Ten+ golf courses within twelve mile radius. Please contact us for prices. **Directions:** From main A1 follow signposts to Amble. Will supply more concise details on request by e-mail or phone. **Bedrooms:** 1 single, 1 double, 1 twin, 1 family **Open:** All year except Christmas and New Year

Payment: 💳 Leisure: 🎿 🎵 ▶ Property: 🐕 🖥 Children: 🧸12 Room: 🍵 🛁 📻 📺

Alannah House

84 Church Street, Berwick upon Tweed, Northumberland TD15 1DU **T:** (01289) 307252
E: info@alannahhouse.com
W: www.alannahhouse.com

B&B PER ROOM PER NIGHT
S: £50.00 - £65.00
D: £75.00 - £80.00

Georgian town house, situated in town centre within the famous Elizabethan town walls. We have a well maintained walled garden and patio area for guests' use. Parking permits available. All rooms en suite and have digital TV. **Directions:** Enter Berwick town centre, head for town hall turn immediately left behind the hall, 400yds on the right past the police station. **Bedrooms:** 1 double, 1 triple, 1 family. All en suite **Open:** All year

Site: ✿ Leisure: ♪ ▸ Property: 🖥 🗎 Children: 🐾 🛏 🎠 Catering: 🍽 Room: 🔌 🖐 🔟 📺

Fenham Farm Coastal Bed & Breakfast

Beal, Berwick-upon-Tweed TD15 2PL **T:** (01289) 381245 **E:** stay@fenhamfarm.co.uk
W: www.fenhamfarm.co.uk **£ BOOK ONLINE**

B&B PER ROOM PER NIGHT
S: £72.00 - £85.00
D: £95.00 - £105.00

Quality Bed & Breakfast accommodation in converted farm outbuildings on a beautiful coastal spot overlooking the Holy Island of Lindisfarne. 7 warm & comfortable en suite bedrooms. Delicious breakfasts served in the farmhouse. **Directions:** Fenham Farm is on the coast approximately 1.5 miles off the A1, 10 miles south of Berwick upon Tweed and 6 miles north of Belford. **Bedrooms:** 6 double/ twin, 1 family **Open:** Easter until November

Site: **P** Payment: 💷 Leisure: ▸ Property: 🍴 🖥 🎱 ∅ Children: 🐾 🛏 🎠
Catering: 🍽 Room: 🔌 🖐 📺 ♨

HEXHAM, Northumberland Map ref 5B2

Langley Castle Hotel
Langley-on-Tyne, Hexham NE47 5LU T: (01434) 688888 F: 01434 684019
E: manager@langleycastle.com
W: www.langleycastle.com £ BOOK ONLINE

B&B PER ROOM PER NIGHT
S: £129.50 - £219.50
D: £159.00 - £279.00
EVENING MEAL PER PERSON
£49.50 - £65.00

SPECIAL PROMOTIONS
Reserve a castle-view room and we will upgrade to a 'castle' room (if available at check-in), at no extra charge.

A genuine 14th Century Castle set in woodland estate. All rooms with facilities, some with window seats set into seven foot thick walls. Sauna, four poster beds. The magnificent drawing room, with blazing log fire, complements intimate Josephine Restaurant. Perfect to explore Hadrian's Wall, Northumberland, Bamburgh Castle, Holy Island and Borders.

Directions: Half an hour drive from Newcastle airport. From A69 take A686 for 2 miles.

Bedrooms: 27 rooms in total
Open: All year

Site: ✿ P Payment: 💳 Leisure: ♨ 🏌 ♨ Property: ◉ 🍴 🐾 ▦ 🖥 🅿 ❶ ∅ Children: 🧒1 🛏 🪑 Catering: (✗ 🍴 🍽 Room: 📶 🛗 ☎ ⏰ 📺 🔌 🎧

HEXHAM, Northumberland Map ref 5B2

Loughbrow House
Dipton Mill Road NE46 1RS T: (01434) 603351 E: patriciaclark351@btinternet.com
W: www.loughbrow.fsnet.co.uk

B&B PER ROOM PER NIGHT
S: £50.00 - £60.00
D: £110.00 - £150.00
HB PER PERSON PER NIGHT
£80.00 - £100.00

A mansion house built in 1780 set in 9 acres of garden, surrounded by own farm land looking up the North Tyne valley. Situated 1 mile from Hexham. Ample parking. **Directions:** From Hexham take B6306. After 0.25 miles take right-hand fork, Dipton Mill Road, for further 0.25 miles. Turn into drive gates, house is 0.5 miles. **Bedrooms:** 2 single, 1 double, 2 twin with ensuit £100 - £140 prpn, with private bathroom £95 - £120 prpn. **Open:** All year except Christmas and New Year

Site: ✿ P Leisure: ▶ Property: 🖥 Children: 🧒5 Catering: 🍽 Room: 📶 🛗 📺

Sign up for our newsletter
Visit our website to sign up for our e-newsletter and receive regular information on events, articles, exclusive competitions and new publications.
www.visitor-guides.co.uk

For **key to symbols** see page 7

Riverdale Hall Hotel

Bellingham, Hexham, Northumberland NE48 2JT **T:** (01434) 220254 **F:** 01434 700002
E: reservations@riverdalehallhotel.co.uk
W: www.riverdalehallhotel.co.uk **£ BOOK ONLINE**

B&B PER ROOM PER NIGHT
S: £55.00 - £74.00
D: £98.00 - £128.00
EVENING MEAL PER PERSON
£9.90 - £21.40

Country House Hotel with swimming pool, cricket field and salmon river. 28 rooms all with en suite facilities. Award winning restaurant (Les routiers Gold plate award), bar with open log fire, cask ales and good wines, swimming pool and sauna. Four self-catering apartments. Perfect situation for walkers on Hadrian's Wall and Pennine Way. Bellingham's 18 hole golf course opposite. Nearest hotel to Northumberland International Dark Sky Park, Kielder Water and Forest. Private salmon fishing.

Directions: Please see our website for a map and route planner.

Bedrooms: Spacious, all en suite some with balconies or patios looking south over the North Tyne River. Free wi-fi
Open: All year

Site: **P** Leisure: ♪ ▶ ♨ ❀ Property: ♟ 🐾 🚼 🖥 Children: 🧍 Catering: ⊗ 🍴 Room: 📶 🛁 📞 📺 🔌 ✉

Little Haven Hotel

River Drive, South Shields NE33 1LH **T:** (01914) 554455 **F:** 01914 554466
E: info@littlehavenhotel.com
W: www.littlehavenhotel.com **£ BOOK ONLINE**

B&B PER ROOM PER NIGHT
S: £85.00 - £220.00
D: £85.00 - £220.00

SPECIAL PROMOTIONS
Please visit our website for special offers and forthcoming events. Book online for advance purchase rates.

Uniquely situated at the gateway of the River Tyne, Little Haven Hotel boasts extensive views of the river and Little Haven Beach. Within 15 minutes of both Newcastle and Sunderland. Enjoy a varied and exciting wining and dining experience in the Boardwalk restaurant, fashionably set in the conservatory overlooking the historical River Tyne with a view to Little Haven Beach and the lively waterfront.

Directions: Please contact us for directions.

Bedrooms: 33 double, 14 twin, 4 family, 8 executive & 3 penthouse suites
Open: All year

Site: ❁ Payment: 💳 Leisure: ♿ ♪ ▶ ∪ Property: ♟ 🐾 🚼 🖥 ◑ Children: 🎮 🧍 Catering: 🍴 🍽 Room: 📶 🛁 📞 🔌 📺

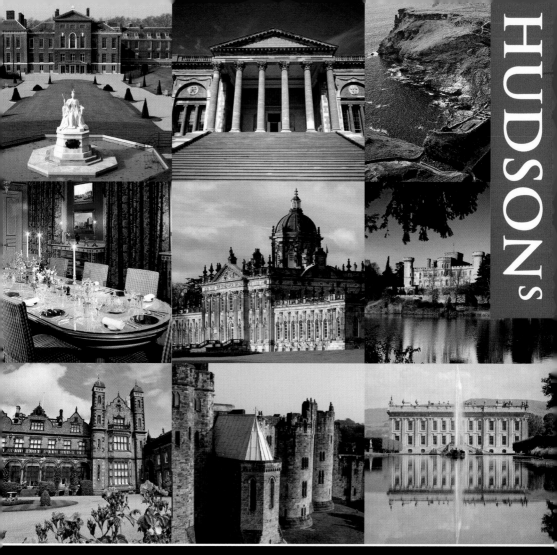

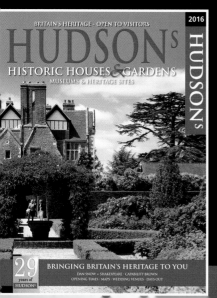

Map 1

Location
Maps

Every place name featured in the regional accommodation sections of this guide has a map reference to help you locate it on the maps which follow. For example, to find Colchester, Essex, which has 'Map ref 3B2', turn to Map 3 and refer to grid square B2.

All place names appearing in the regional sections are shown with orange circles on the maps. This enables you to find other places in your chosen area which may have suitable accommodation – the place index (at the back of this guide) gives page numbers.

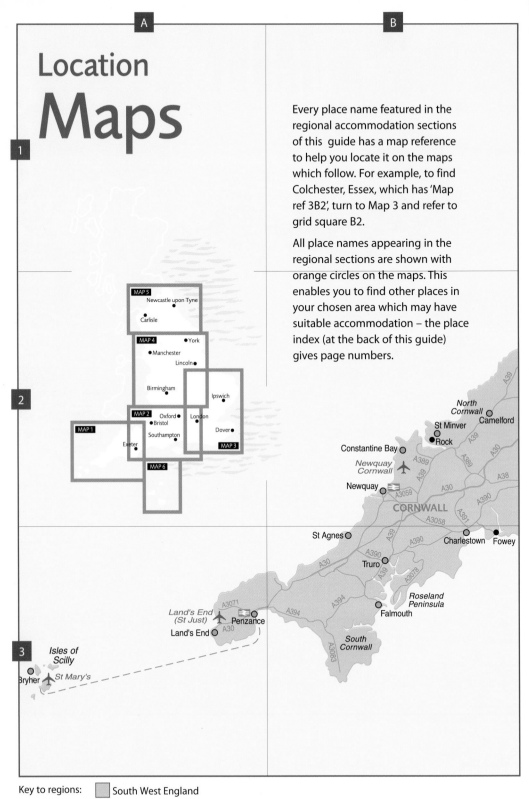

Key to regions: South West England

Map 1

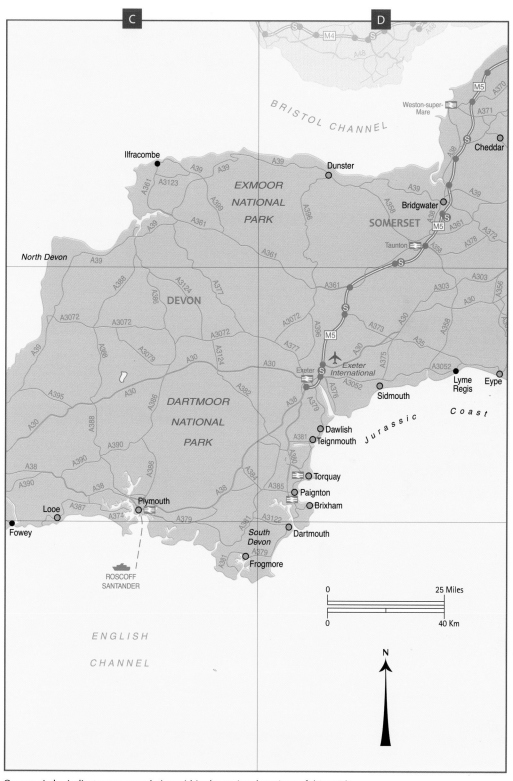

Orange circles indicate accommodation within the regional sections of this guide

Map 2

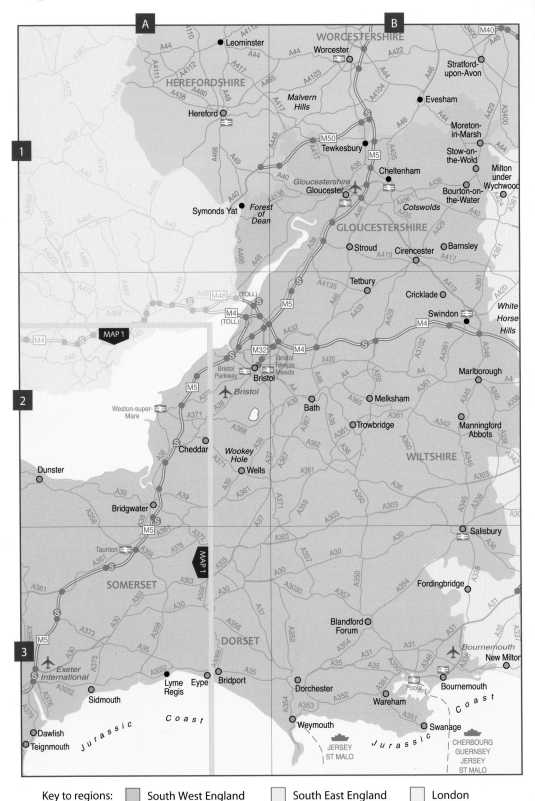

Key to regions: South West England South East England London

264

Map 2

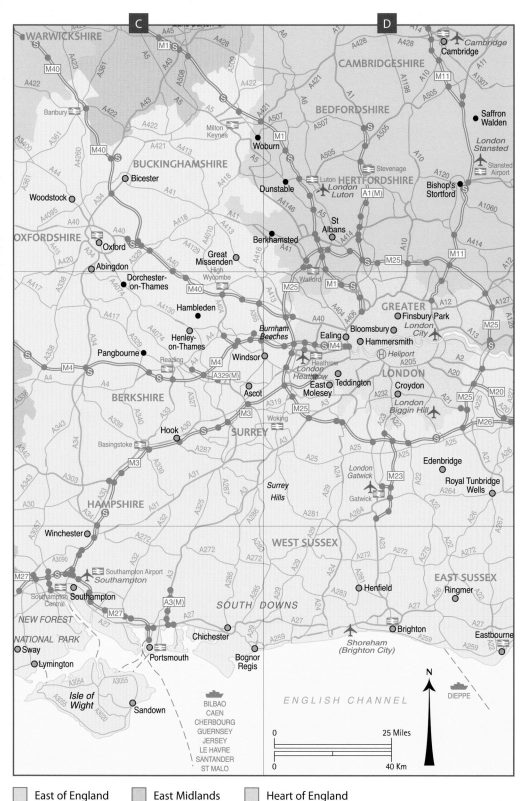

East of England   East Midlands   Heart of England

Orange circles indicate accommodation within the regional sections of this guide

Map 3

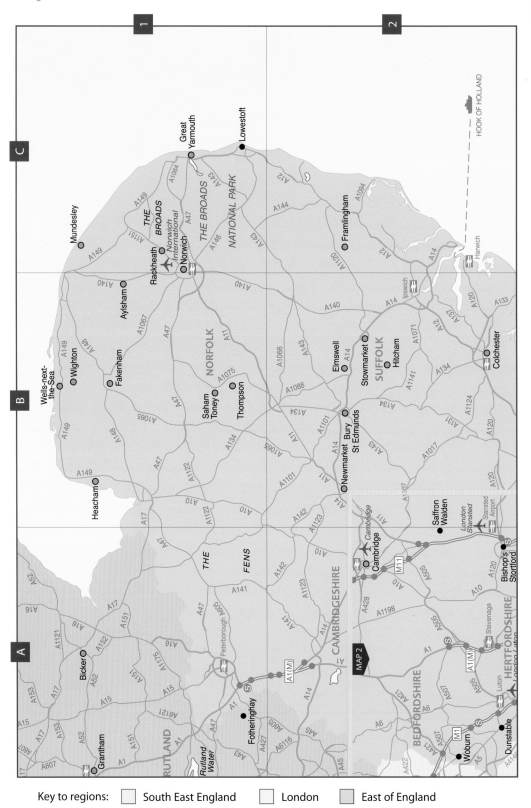

Key to regions: □ South East England □ London ■ East of England

Map 3

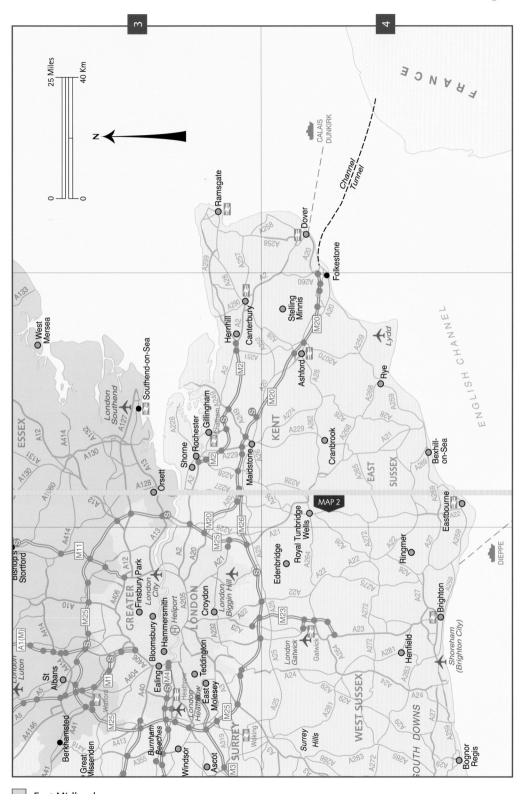

East Midlands

Orange circles indicate accommodation within the regional sections of this guide

Map 4

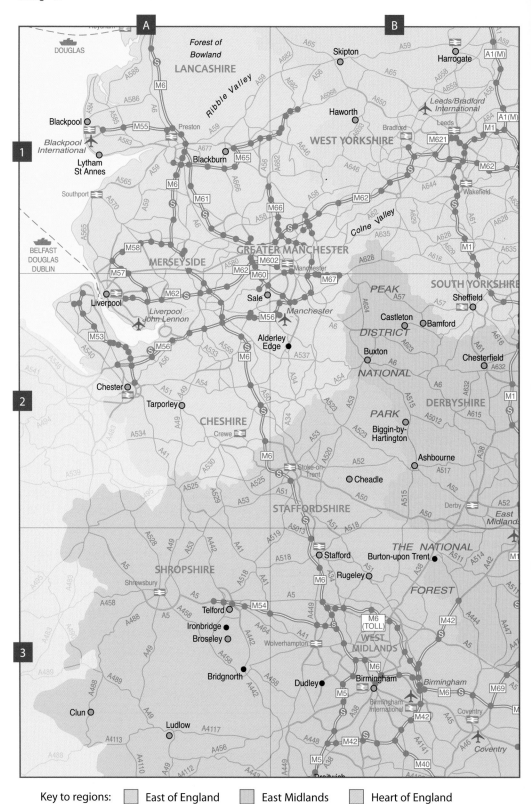

Key to regions: ▢ East of England ▢ East Midlands ▢ Heart of England

Map 4

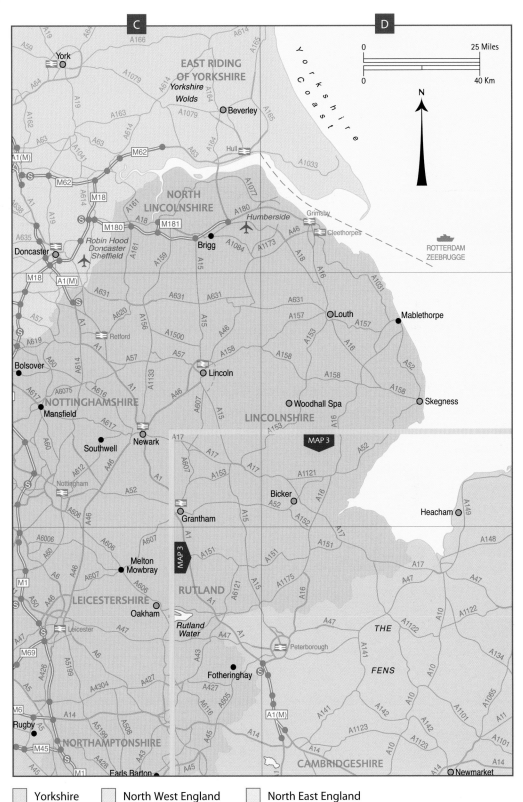

C

D

A59
A19
A64
York
A166
A614
A165
N
0   25 Miles
0   40 Km

EAST RIDING
OF YORKSHIRE
Yorkshire
Wolds

Yorkshire Coast

A64
A19
A1079
A614
A164
A1079
A163
Beverley
A165

A162
A614
A63
A63
M62
A63
A164
Hull
A1033

A1(M)
S
M62
A1041
M18
A161
A1077
NORTH
LINCOLNSHIRE
A180
Humberside
Grimsby

M180
A18
M181
Brigg
A1084
A46
A18
A16
Cleethorpes
ROTTERDAM
ZEEBRUGGE

A638
A1
A19
S
M180
A181
A161
A159
A1173
A15
A1031

M18
A1(M)
Robin Hood
Doncaster
Sheffield
Doncaster

A635
Bolsover
A60
A614
A6075
A617
NOTTINGHAMSHIRE
Mansfield

A631
A620
A156
A631
A631
A631
A157
Louth
A157
Mablethorpe

A57
S
A619
A1
A1500
A15
A46
A153
A16
A52

Retford
A1133
A57
A57
A158
A158
Lincoln
A158
Skegness

A616
A46
A607
A15
Woodhall Spa
A16
A153
A158

Southwell
A612
A46
Newark
A1
A52
LINCOLNSHIRE
MAP 3
A52

Nottingham
A606
A46
A17
A17
A607
A153
A17
A1121
A16
A149

A6006
A60
A46
A607
Bicker
A52
A152
A151
Heacham

Melton
Mowbray
A606
A607
A1
A151
A151
A1175
A16
A17
A148

M1
A6
A46
A607
RUTLAND
A6121
A15
A17
A47
A47
A1122

S
A50
A46
Leicester
Oakham
A47
A1
A43
A1
A47
Peterborough
A1122
A141
A10
A134

LEICESTERSHIRE
Rutland
Water
A43
Fotheringhay
THE
FENS
A47
A10

M69
A6
A5199
A427
A427
A605
A141
A1123
A142
A10
A1101
A11

M6
A5
A426
A4304
A6116
A141
A1065
A1101

Rugby
A14
A5199
A508
A45
A14
A1123
A10
A14

M45
A45
NORTHAMPTONSHIRE
A428
A43
A1(M)
CAMBRIDGESHIRE
Newmarket

M1
S
Earls Barton
A45
A14
A14

Map 5

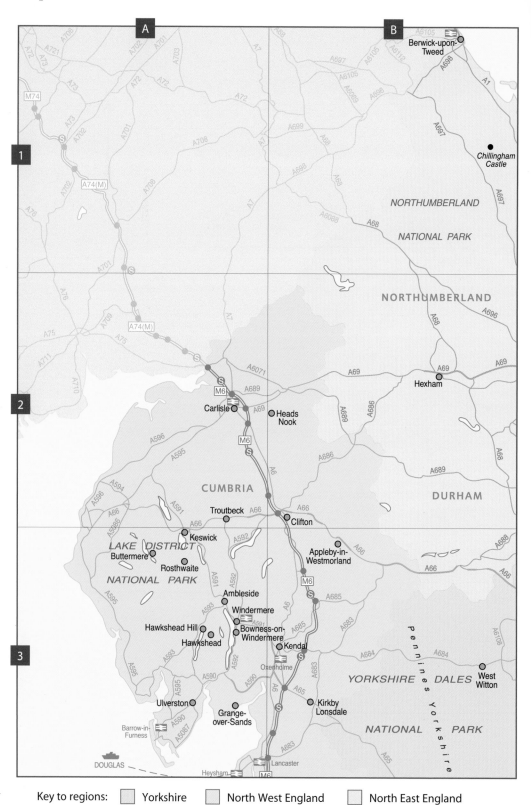

Berwick-upon-Tweed

Chillingham Castle

NORTHUMBERLAND

NATIONAL PARK

NORTHUMBERLAND

Hexham

Carlisle

Heads Nook

CUMBRIA

DURHAM

Troutbeck

Clifton

Keswick

Appleby-in-Westmorland

Buttermere

Rosthwaite

LAKE DISTRICT

NATIONAL PARK

Ambleside

Windermere

Hawkshead Hill

Bowness-on-Windermere

Hawkshead

Kendal

Oxenholme

YORKSHIRE DALES

West Witton

PENNINES YORKSHIRE

Ulverston

Grange-over-Sands

Kirkby Lonsdale

NATIONAL PARK

Barrow-in-Furness

DOUGLAS

Lancaster

Heysham

Key to regions: Yorkshire   North West England   North East England

Map 5

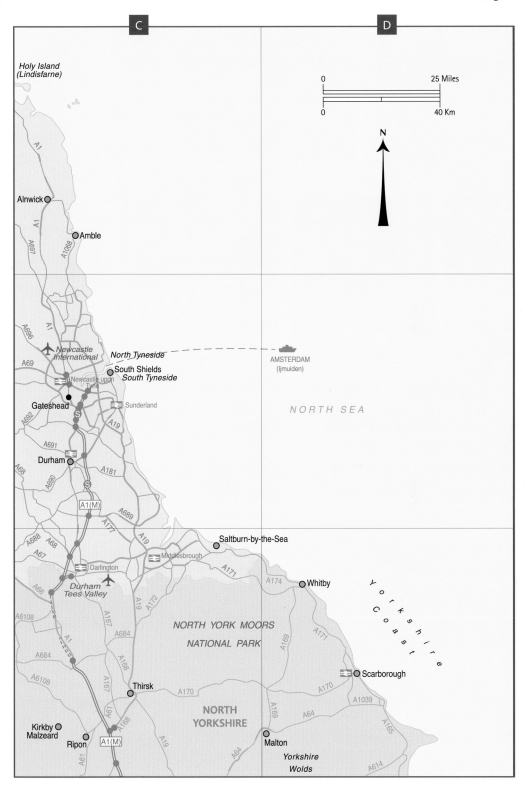

C

D

0   25 Miles

0   40 Km

N

Holy Island
(Lindisfarne)

A1

Alnwick

A1

A1068

Amble

A697

A696

A1

Newcastle
International

A69

North Tyneside

AMSTERDAM
(Ijmuiden)

South Shields
South Tyneside

Newcastle upon
Tyne

Gateshead

Sunderland

NORTH SEA

A692

S

A19

A691

Durham

A68

A680

A181

S

A1(M)

A689

A688

A68

A177

A19

Saltburn-by-the-Sea

A67

Middlesbrough

Darlington

A171

A174

Whitby

A66

Durham
Tees Valley

A19

A172

Yorkshire Coast

A6108

A167

A1

NORTH YORK MOORS

A684

A684

A168

NATIONAL PARK

A169

A171

A6108

A167

A1(M)

Thirsk

A170

Scarborough

Kirkby
Malzeard

A169

A64

A1039

Ripon

A1(M)

A19

Malton

A785

NORTH
YORKSHIRE

A61

A64

A614

Yorkshire
Wolds

Orange circles indicate accommodation within the regional sections of this guide

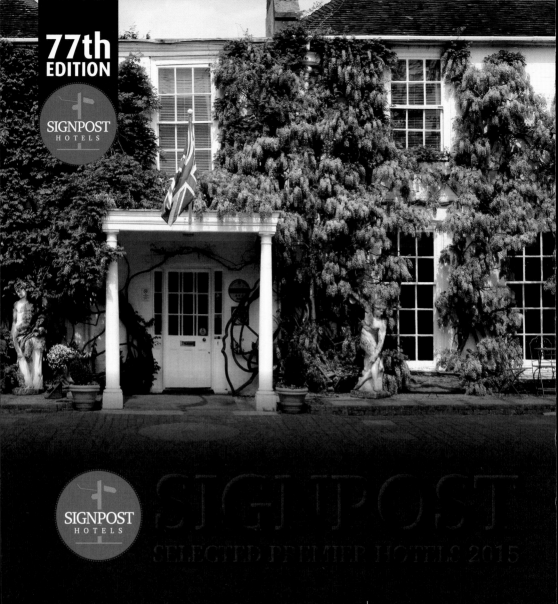

77th EDITION

SIGNPOST
HOTELS

SIGNPOST
HOTELS

SIGNPOST
SELECTED PREMIER HOTELS 2015

Every hotel featured in this guide has that something
special no run-of-the-mill hotels included

•

Available from Signpost hotels and all good book shops

•

Visit our website for up-to-date special offers
and a chance to win a weekend stay at a Signpost hotel

'Gem of a guide...
covers hotels of character'
EXECUTARY NEWS

'For anyone doing any
extensive motoring in
Britain, this guide would
seem invaluable'
NEW YORKER MAGAZINE

'The British Hotel guide for
the discerning traveller'
PERIOD LIVING

Map 6
London

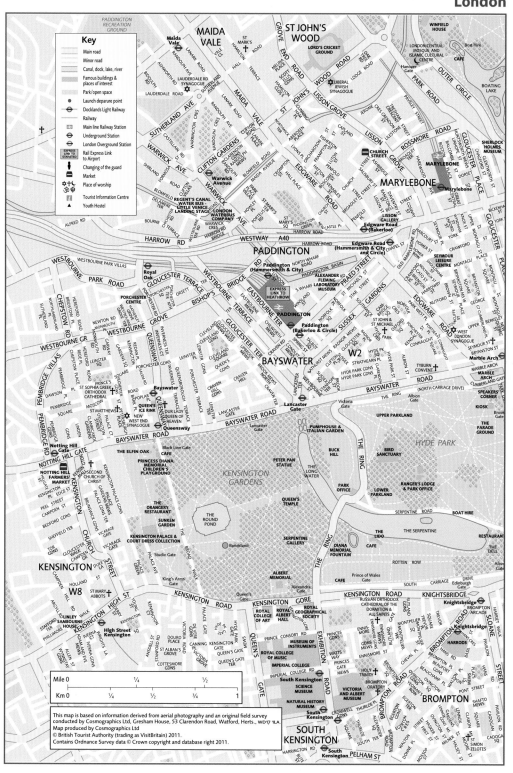

Map 7
London

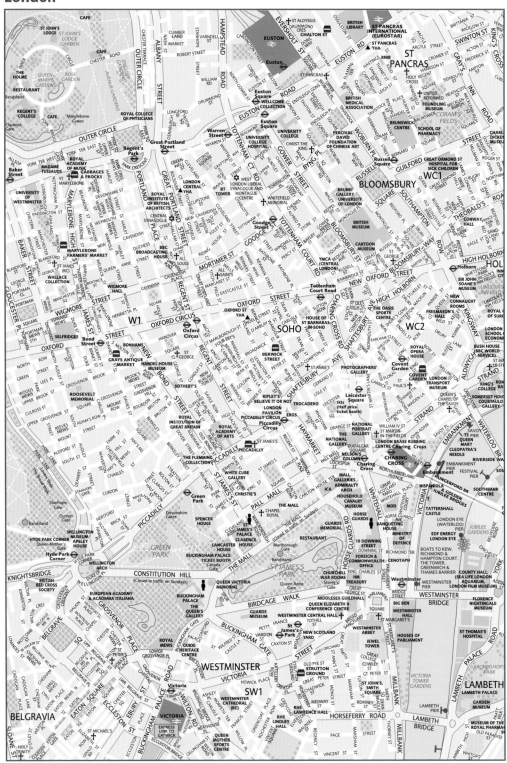

Map 7
London

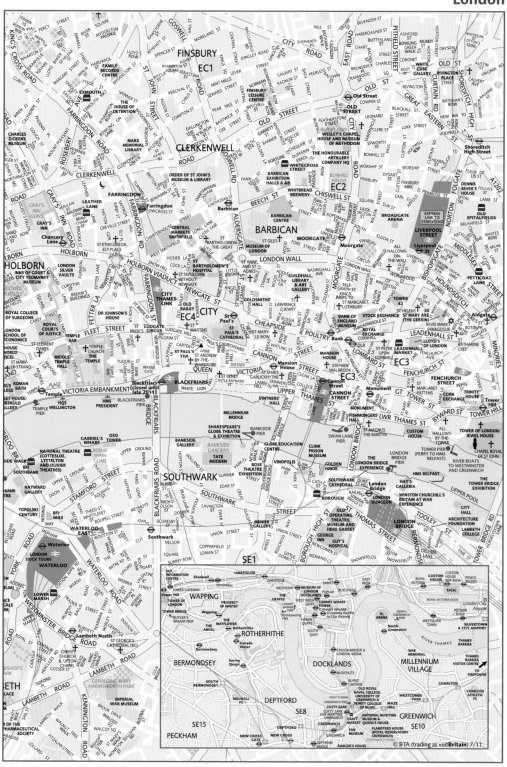

© BTA (trading as visitBritain) 7/11.

Motorway Service Area Assessment Scheme

visitEngland

★★★★★
MOTORWAY SERVICE AREA

Something we all use and take for granted but how good are they?

The star ratings cover over 250 different aspects of each operation, including cleanliness, the quality and range of catering and also the quality of the physical aspects, as well as the service. It does not cover prices or value for money.

OPERATOR: EXTRA

Baldock	★★★★
Beaconsfield	★★★★★
Blackburn	★★★★★
Cambridge	★★★★
Cobham	★★★★★
Cullompton	★★★
Peterborough	★★★★

OPERATOR: MOTO

Birch E	★★★
Birch W	★★★
Bridgwater	★★★
Burton in Kendal	★★★
Cherwell Valley	★★★★
Chieveley	★★★
Doncaster N	★★★★
Donington Park	★★★★
Exeter	★★★
Ferrybridge	★★★★
Frankley N	★★★
Frankley S	★★★★
Heston E	★★★
Heston W	★★★
Hilton Park N	★★★
Hilton Park S	★★★
Knutsford N	★★★★
Knutsford S	★★★★
Lancaster N	★★★★
Lancaster S	★★★★
Leigh Delamere E	★★★★
Leigh Delamere W	★★★★
Medway	★★★
Pease Pottage	★★★
Reading E	★★★★
Reading W	★★★
Severn View	★★★
Southwaite N	★★★
Southwaite S	★★★★

Stafford N	★★★★
Tamworth	★★★
Thurrock	★★★★
Toddington N	★★★★
Toddington S	★★★★
Trowell N	★★★
Trowell S	★★★
Washington N	★★★
Washington S	★★★
Wetherby	★★★★
Winchester N	★★★★
Winchester S	★★★★
Woolley Edge N	★★★★
Woolley Edge S	★★★★

OPERATOR: ROADCHEF

Chester	★★★★
Clacket Lane E	★★★★
Clacket Lane W	★★★★
Durham	★★★
Killington Lake	★★★
Maidstone	★★★★
Northampton N	★★★
Northampton S	★★★
Norton Canes	★★★★
Rownhams N	★★★
Rownhams S	★★★
Sandbach N	★★★
Sandbach S	★★★
Sedgemoor S	★★★
Stafford S	★★★
Strensham N	★★★
Strensham S	★★★
Taunton Deane N	★★★
Taunton Deane S	★★★
Tibshelf N	★★★
Tibshelf S	★★★

Watford Gap N	★★★
Watford Gap S	★★★

OPERATOR: WELCOME BREAK

Birchanger Green	★★★★
Burtonwood	★★★
Charnock Richard N	★★★★★
Charnock Richard S	★★★
Corley E	★★★
Corley W	★★★
Fleet N	★★★★
Fleet S	★★★★
Gordano	★★★★
Hartshead Moor E	★★★
Hartshead Moor W	★★★
Hopwood Park	★★★★
Keele N	★★★
Keele S	★★★★
Leicester Forest East N	★★★
Leicester Forest East S	★★★
London Gateway	★★★★
Membury E	★★★
Membury W	★★★★
Michaelwood N	★★★★
Michaelwood S	★★★★
Newport Pagnell S	★★★
Newport Pagnell N	★★★
Oxford	★★★★
Sedgemoor N	★★★
South Mimms	★★★★
Telford	★★★
Warwick N	★★★
Warwick S	★★★★
Woodall N	★★★
Woodall S	★★★

OPERATOR: WESTMORLAND

Tebay N	★★★★★
Tebay S	★★★★★
Gloucester N	★★★★★

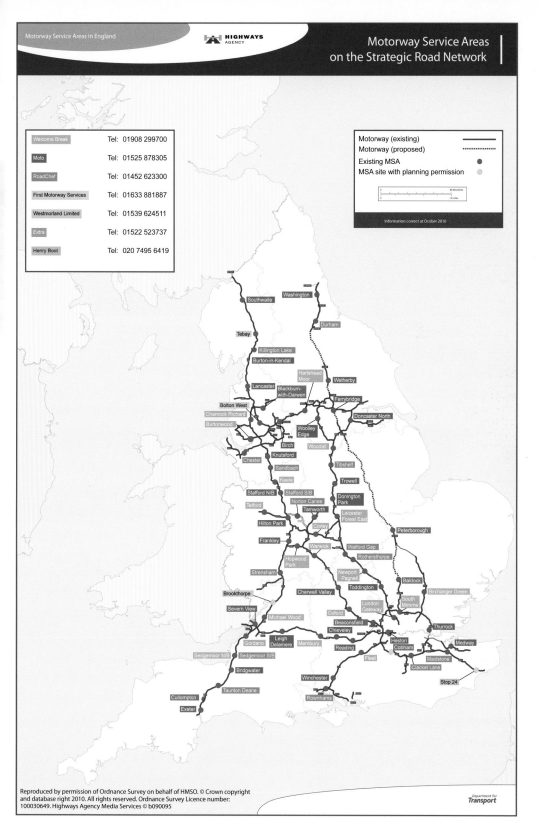

Welcome Break	Tel: 01908 299700
Moto	Tel: 01525 878305
RoadChef	Tel: 01452 623300
First Motorway Services	Tel: 01633 881887
Westmorland Limited	Tel: 01539 624511
Extra	Tel: 01522 523737
Henry Boot	Tel: 020 7495 6419

Motorway (existing)
Motorway (proposed)
Existing MSA
MSA site with planning permission

Information correct at October 2010

Department for
Transport

There are hundreds of "Green" places to stay and visit in England from small bed and breakfasts to large visitor attractions and activity holiday providers. Businesses displaying this logo have undergone a rigorous verification process to ensure that they are sustainable (green) and that a qualified assessor has visited the premises.

We have indicated the accommodation which has achieved a Green award... look out for the symbol in the entry.

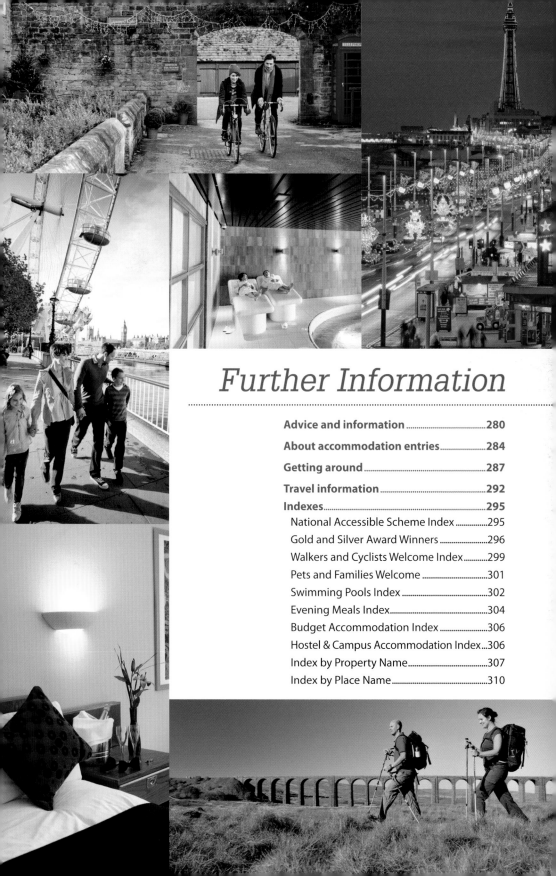

Further Information

Advice and information

Making a booking

When enquiring about accommodation, make sure you check prices, the quality rating and other important details. You will also need to state your requirements clearly and precisely, for example:

- Arrival and departure dates, with acceptable alternatives if appropriate
- The type of accommodation you need – for example, a room with twin beds or an en suite bathroom
- The terms you want – for example, bed and breakfast only; dinner and breakfast (where provided)
- The age of any children with you, whether you want them to share your room or be next door, and any other special requirements, such as a cot
- Any particular requirements you may have, such as a special diet or a ground-floor room.

Confirmation

Misunderstandings can easily happen over the telephone, so do request a written confirmation, together with details of any terms and conditions that apply to your booking.

Deposits

If you make your reservation weeks or months in advance, you will probably be asked for a deposit, which will then be deducted from the final bill when you leave. The amount will vary from establishment to establishment and could be payment in full at peak times.

Payment on arrival

Some establishments ask you to pay for your room on arrival if you have not booked it in advance. This is especially likely to happen if you arrive late and have little or no luggage. If you are asked to pay on arrival, it is a good idea to see your room first, to make sure it meets your requirements.

Cancellations

Legal contract

When you accept accommodation that is offered to you, by telephone or in writing, you enter into a legally binding contract with the proprietor. This means that if you cancel your booking, fail to take up the accommodation or leave early, you will probably forfeit your deposit and may expect to be charged the balance at the end of the period booked if the place cannot be re-let. You should be advised at the time of the booking of what charges would be made in the event of cancelling the accommodation or leaving early, which is usually written into the property's terms and conditions. If this is not mentioned, you should ask the proprietor for any cancellation terms that apply before booking your accommodation to ensure any disputes are avoided. Where you have already paid the full amount before cancelling, the proprietor is likely to retain the money. However if the accommodation is re-let, the proprietor will make a refund to you which normally excludes the amount of the deposit.

Telephone charges

Establishments can set their own charges for telephone calls made through their switchboard or from direct-dial telephones in bedrooms. These charges are often much higher than telephone companies' standard charges (to defray the cost of providing the service).

Comparing costs
It is a condition of the quality assessment schemes that an establishment's unit charges are on display by the telephones or with the room information. It is not always easy to compare these charges with standard rates, so before using a telephone for long-distance calls, you may decide to ask how the charges compare.

Security of valuables

You can deposit your valuables with the proprietor or manager during your stay, and we recommend you do this as a sensible precaution. Make sure you obtain a receipt for them. Some places do not accept articles for safe custody, and in that case it is wisest to keep your valuables with you.

Disclaimer

Some proprietors put up a notice that disclaims liability for property brought on to their premises by a guest. In fact, they can only restrict their liability. By law, a proprietor is liable for the value of the loss or damage to any property (except a car or its contents) of a guest who has engaged overnight accommodation, but if the proprietor has the notice on display, liability is limited to £50 for one article and a total of £100 for any one guest. The notice must be prominently displayed in the reception area or main entrance. These limits do not apply to valuables you have deposited with the proprietor for safekeeping, or to property lost through the default, neglect or wilful act of the proprietor or his staff.

Travelling with pets

Dogs, cats, ferrets and some other pets can be brought into the UK from certain countries without having to undertake six months' quarantine on arrival, provided they meet the requirements of the Pet Travel Scheme (PETS).

For full details, visit the PETS website at
w www.gov.uk/take-pet-abroad
or contact the PETS Helpline
t +44 (0)370 241 1710
e pettravel@ahvla.gsi.gov.uk
Ask for fact sheets which cover dogs and cats, ferrets or domestic rabbits and rodents.

There are no requirements for pets travelling directly between the UK and the Channel Islands. Pets entering Jersey or Guernsey from other countries need to be Pet Travel Scheme compliant and have a valid EU Pet Passport. For more information see
www.jersey.com or www.visitguernsey.com.

Remember, if you book by telephone and are asked for your credit card number, you should check whether the proprietor intends to charge your credit card account, should you later cancel your reservation. A proprietor should not be able to charge your credit card account with a cancellation fee without your consent unless you agreed to this at the time of your booking. However, to avoid later disputes, we suggest you check whether this is the intention before providing your details.

Insurance

There are so many reasons why you might have to cancel your holiday, which is why we strongly advise people to take out a cancellation insurance policy.

Arrival time

If you know you will be arriving late in the evening, it is a good idea to say so when you book. If you are delayed on your way, a telephone call to say that you will be late is often appreciated.

It is particularly important to liaise with the proprietor about key collection as he or she may not be on site.

Service charges and tipping

These days many places levy service charges automatically. If they do, they must clearly say so in their offer of accommodation, at the time of booking. The service charge then becomes part of the legal contract when you accept the offer of accommodation.

If a service charge is levied automatically, there is no need to tip the staff, unless they provide some exceptional service. The usual tip for meals is 10% of the total bill.

What to expect

The proprietor/management is required to undertake the following:

Prior to booking
- To describe accurately in any advertisement, brochure, or other printed or electronic media, the facilities and services provided;
- To make clear to guests in print, electronic media and on the telephone exactly what is included in all prices quoted for accommodation, including taxes and any other surcharges. Details of charges for additional services/facilities should also be made clear, for example breakfast, leisure etc;
- To provide information on the suitability of the premises for guests of various ages, particularly for the elderly and the very young;
- To allow guests to view the accommodation prior to booking if requested.

At the time of booking
- To clearly describe the cancellation policy to guests i.e. by telephone, fax, internet/email as well as in any printed information given to guests;
- To adhere to and not to exceed prices quoted at the time of booking for accommodation and other services;
- To make clear to guests if the accommodation offered is in an unconnected annexe or similar, and to indicate the location of such accommodation and any difference in comfort and/or amenities from accommodation at the property.

On arrival
- To welcome all guests courteously and without discrimination in relation to gender, sexual orientation, disability, race, religion or belief.

During the stay
- To maintain standards of guest care, cleanliness, and service appropriate to the type of establishment;
- To deal promptly and courteously with all enquiries, requests, bookings and correspondence from guests;
- To ensure complaints received are investigated promptly and courteously to an outcome that is communicated to the guest.

On departure
- To give each guest, on request, details of payments due and a receipt, if required/requested.

General
- To give due consideration to the requirements of guests with special needs, and make suitable provision where applicable;
- To ensure the accommodation, when advertised as open, is prepared for the arrival of guests at all times;
- To advise guests, at any time prior to their stay, of any changes made to their booking;
- To have a complaints handling procedure in place to deal promptly and fairly with all guest complaints;
- To hold current public liability insurance and to comply with all relevant statuory obligations including legislation applicable to fire, health and safety, planning and food safety;
- To allow, on request, VisitEngland representatives reasonable access to the establishment, to confirm that the Code of Conduct is being observed or in order to investigate any complaint of a serious nature;

Comments and complaints

Information

Other than rating information, the proprietors themselves supply descriptions of their properties and other information for the entries in this book. They have all signed a declaration to confirm that their information accurately describes their accommodation business. The publishers cannot guarantee the accuracy of information in this guide, and accept no responsibility for any error or misrepresentation. All liability for loss, disappointment, negligence or other damage caused by reliance on the information contained in this guide, or in the event of bankruptcy or liquidation or cessation of trade of any company, individual or firm mentioned, is hereby excluded. We strongly recommend that you carefully check prices and other details before you book your accommodation.

Quality signage

All establishments displaying a quality sign have to hold current membership of VisitEngland's Quality Assessment Scheme.

When an establishment is sold, the new owner has to re-apply and be re-assessed. In certain circumstances the rating may be carried forward before the property is re-assessed.

Problems

Of course, we hope you will not have cause for complaint, but problems do occur from time to time. If you are dissatisfied with anything, make your complaint to the management immediately. Then the management can take action by investigating the matter in attempts to put things right. The longer you leave a complaint, the harder it is to deal with it effectively.

In certain circumstances, the national tourist board may look into your complaint. However, they have no statutory control over establishments or their methods of operating and cannot become involved in legal or contractual matters such as financial compensation.

If you do have problems that have not been resolved by the proprietor and which you would like to bring to their attention, please write to: Quality in Tourism, 1320 Montpellier Court, Pioneer Way, Gloucester Business Park, Gloucester, Gloucestershire GL3 4AH

About the accommodation entries

....

Entries

All accommodation featured in this guide has been assessed or has applied for assessment under a quality assessment scheme.

Start your search for a place to stay by looking in the 'Stay' sections of this guide, where proprietors have paid to have their establishment featured in either a standard entry (includes photograph, description, facilities and prices) or an enhanced entry (photograph(s) and extended details).

Locations

Places to stay are listed by town, city or village. If a property is located in a small village, you may find it listed under a nearby town (providing it is within a seven-mile radius).

Within each region, counties run in alphabetical order. Place names are listed alphabetically within each county, and include interesting county information and a map reference.

Map references

These refer to the colour location maps at the back of the guide. The first figure shown is the map number, the following letter and figure indicate the grid reference on the map. Place names that have a standard or enhanced entry appear on the maps. Some standard or enhanced entries were added at the last minute, therefore they do not appear on the maps.

Telephone numbers

Booking telephone numbers are listed below the contact address for each entry. Area codes are shown in brackets.

Prices

The prices printed are to be used as a guide only; they were supplied to us by proprietors in summer 2015.

Remember, changes may occur after the guide goes to press, therefore we strongly advise you to check prices before booking your accommodation. Prices are shown in pounds sterling, including VAT where applicable. There are many different ways of quoting prices for accommodation. We use a standardised method in the guide to allow you to compare prices. For example, when we show:

Bed and breakfast: the prices shown are per room for overnight accommodation with breakfast. The double room price is for two people. (If a double room is occupied by one person, there is sometimes a reduction in price.) Some places only provide a continental breakfast in the set price, and you may have to pay extra if you want a full English breakfast.

Evening meal: the prices shown are per person per night.

Half board: the prices shown are per person per night for room, evening meal and breakfast. These prices are usually based on two people sharing a room.

Checking prices

There is no specific regulatory requirement for establishments to display prices in the reception, but it is recommended in order to fulfil their obligations under the consumer protection from unfair Trading Regulations 2008.

In your own interests, do make sure you check prices and what they include.

Children's rates

You will find that many places charge a reduced rate for children, especially if they share a room with their parents. Some places charge the full rate, however, when a child occupies a room which might otherwise have been let to an adult. The upper age limit for reductions for children varies from one accommodation to another, so check this when you book.

Seasonal packages and special promotions

Prices often vary through the year and may be significantly lower outside peak holiday weeks. Many places offer special package rates – fully inclusive weekend breaks, for example – in the autumn, winter and spring. A number of establishments taking an enhanced entry have included any special offers, themed breaks, etc. that are available.

You can get details of other bargain packages that may be available from the establishments themselves, regional tourism organisations or your local Tourist Information Centre (TIC). Your local travel agent may also have information and can help you make reservations.

Bathrooms

En suite bathroom means the bath or shower and wc are contained behind the main door of the bedroom. Private bathroom means a bath or shower and wc solely for the occupants of one bedroom, on the same floor, reasonably close and with a key provided. If the availability of a bath, rather than a shower, is important to you, remember to check when you book.

Meals

It is advisable to check the availability of meals and set times when making your reservation. Some smaller places may ask you at breakfast whether you want an evening meal. The prices shown in each entry are for bed and breakfast or half board, but many places also offer lunch.

Open period

If an entry does not indicate an opening period, please check directly with the establishment.

Symbols

The at-a-glance symbols included at the end of each entry show many of the services and facilities available at each establishment. You will find the key to these symbols on page 7.

Smoking

In the UK and the Channel Islands, it is illegal to smoke in enclosed public spaces and places of work. Some establishments may choose to provide designated smoking bedrooms, and may allow smoking in private areas that are not used by any staff. If you wish to smoke, it is advisable to check whether it is allowed when you book.

Alcoholic drinks

Many places listed in the guide are licensed to serve alcohol. The licence may be restricted – to diners only, for example – so you may want to check this when you book. If they have a bar this is shown by the ♟ symbol

Payment accepted

The types of payment accepted by an establishment are listed in the payment accepted section. If you plan to pay by card, check that the establishment will accept the particular type of card you own before booking. Some proprietors will charge you a higher rate if you pay by credit card rather than cash or cheque. The difference is to cover the charges paid by the proprietor to the credit card company. When you book by telephone, you may be asked for your credit card number as confirmation. Remember, the proprietor may then charge your credit card account if you cancel your booking. See details of this under Cancellations on page 280.

Pets

Many places accept guests with dogs, but we advise that you check this with the proprietor before booking, remembering to ask if there are any extra charges or rules about exactly where your pet is allowed. The acceptance of dogs is not always extended to cats and it is strongly advised that cat owners contact the property well in advance of their stay.

Some establishments do not accept pets at all. Pets are welcome by arrangement where you see this symbol ♟. The quarantine laws have changed and now dogs, cats and ferrets are able to come into Britain and the Channel Islands from over 50 countries. For details of the Pet Travel Scheme (PETS) please turn to page 281.

Conferences and groups

Places which cater for conferences and meetings are marked with the symbol ♟. Rates are often negotiable, depending on the time of year, number of people involved and any special requirements you may have.

Awaiting confirmation of rating
At the time of going to press some properties featured in this guide had not yet been assessed therefore their rating for this year could not be included. The term 'Rating Applied For' indicates this throughout your guide.

Getting around

Travelling in London

London transport

Each London Underground line has its own unique colour, so you can easily follow them on the Underground map. Most lines run through central London, and many serve parts of Greater London. Tube services run every day from around 5.30am to around 1am. From Autumn 2015 some services will run all night on Fridays and Saturdays. Buses are a quick, convenient way to travel around London, providing plenty of sightseeing opportunities along the way. There are over 6,500 buses in London operating 700 routes every day. You will need to buy a ticket or Travel Pass before you board the bus.

London's National Rail system stretches all over London. Many lines start at the main London railway stations (Paddington, Victoria, Waterloo, Kings Cross) with links to the tube. Trains mainly serve areas outside central London, and travel overground.

Children usually travel free, or at reduced fare, on all public transport in London.

Oyster cards

The Visitor Oyster Card is a pay-as-you-go smartcard. It's a quick and easy way to pay for journeys on bus, Tube, tram, DLR, London Overground, TfL Rail and most National Rail services in London.

A Visitor Oyster card costs £3 (plus postage) and is pre-loaded with pay as you go credit for you to spend on travel. You can choose how much credit to add to your card: £10, £15, £20, £25, £30, £35, £40, or £50. As a guide a £20 card will usually cover a return journey from Heathrow plus travel around Central London for one 1 or 2 days. If you are visiting for 3-4 days, get a £30 card or if you are here for a week and you will be travelling lots every day, then a £50 card is a good option, The credit on your card never expires - it stays there until you use it. If you run out of credit on your card, it's easy to top it up and use it again. Children under 11 travel free, but children over 11 need their own travel ticket. There is no child version of the Oyster card, but there is a child Travelcard

For further information or to buy cards visit
www.visitbritainshop.com/world/london-visitor-oyster-card or
www.tfl.gov.uk/travel-information/visiting-london/visitor-oyster-card

London congestion charge

The congestion charge is £11.50 daily charge to drive in central London at certain times. Check if the congestion charge is included in the cost of your car before booking. If your car's pick up point is in the congestion-charging zone, the company may pay the charge for the first day of your hire.

Low Emission Zone

The Low Emission Zone is an area covering most of Greater London, within which the most polluting diesel-engine vehicles are required to meet specific emissions standards. If your vehicle does not, you will be required to pay a daily charge.

Vehicles affected by the Low Emission Zone are older diesel-engine lorries, buses, coaches, large vans, minibuses and other heavy vehicles such as motor caravans and motorised horse boxes. This also includes vehicles registered outside of Great Britain. Cars and motorcycles are not affected by this scheme. For more information visit www.tfl.gov.uk

Rail and train travel

Britain's rail network covers all main cities and smaller regional towns. Trains on the network are operated by a few large companies running routes from London to stations all over Britain. Therefore smaller companies that run routes in regional areas. You can find up-to-the-minute information about routes, fares and train times on the National Rail Enquiries website (www.nationalrail.co.uk). For detailed information about routes and services, refer to the train operators' websites (see page 293).

Railway passes
BritRail offer a wide selection of passes and tickets giving you the freedom to travel on all National Rail services. Passes can also include sleeper services, city and attraction passes and boat tours. Passes can usually be purchased from travel agents outside Britain or by visiting the BritRail website www.britrail.net.

Bus and coach travel

Public buses
Every city and town in Britain has a local bus service. These services are privatised and managed by separate companies. The largest bus companies in Britain are First (www.firstgroup.com/ukbus), Stagecoach (www.stagecoachbus.com) and Arriva (www.arrivabus.co.uk), and run buses in most UK towns. Outside London, buses usually travel to and from the town centre or to the busiest part of town. Most towns have a bus station, where you'll be able to find maps and information about routes. Bus route information may also be posted at bus stops.

Tickets and fares
The cost of a bus ticket normally depends on how far you're travelling. Return fares may be available on some buses, but you would usually need to buy a 'single' ticket for each individual journey.

You can also buy your ticket when boarding a bus by telling the driver where you are going. One-day and weekly travel cards are available in some towns, and these can be purchased from either the driver or from an information centre at the bus station. Tickets are valid for each separate journey rather than for a period of time, so if you get off the bus you'll need to buy a new ticket when getting on another.

Domestic flights

Flying is a time-saving alternative to road or rail when it comes to travelling around Britain. Domestic flights are fast and frequent and there are 33 airports across Britain that operate domestic routes. You will find airports marked on the maps at the front of this guide.

Domestic flight advice
Photo ID is required to travel on domestic flights. However it is advisable to bring your passport as not all airlines will accept other forms of photo identification. Please be aware of the high security measures at all airports in Britain which include include restrictions on items that may be carried in hand luggage. It is important that you check the restrictions in place with your airline prior to travel, as these can vary over time and don't forget to allow adequate time for check-in and boarding on arrival.

Cycling

Cycling is a great way to see some of England's iconic scenery and there are many networks of cycling routes available across England. The National Cycle Network offers over 10,000 miles of walking and cycling routes details for connecting towns and villages, countryside and coast across England. For more information and view these routes see page 289 or visit Sustrans at www.sustrans.co.uk.

Think green

If you'd rather leave your car behind and travel by 'green transport' to some of the attractions highlighted in this guide you'll be helping to reduce congestion and pollution as well as supporting conservation charities in their commitment to green travel.

The National Trust encourages visits made by non-car travellers and it offers admission discounts or a voucher for the tea room at a selection of its properties if you arrive on foot, cycle or public transport (you may need to produce a valid bus or train ticket if travelling by public transport.).

More information about The National Trust's work to encourage car-free days out can be found at www.nationaltrust.org.uk.

Here are just some of the most popular long distance routes on the 12,000 mile Sustrans National Cycle Network. To see the Network in it's entirety and to find routes near you, visit **www.sustrans.org.uk**

Sustrans is the UK's leading sustainable transport charity working on practical projects to enable people to choose to travel in ways which benefit their health and the environment.

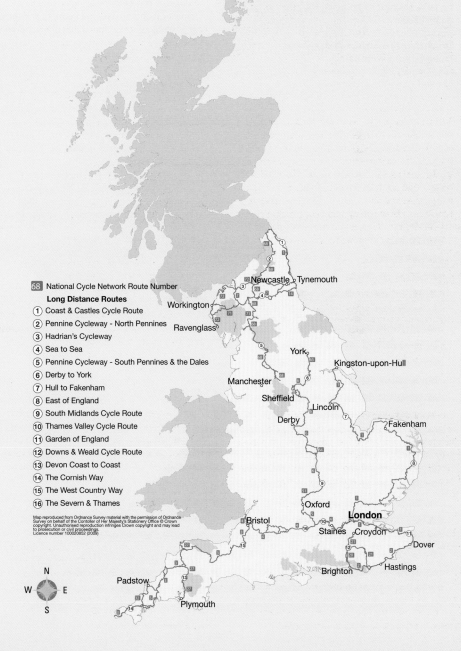

68 National Cycle Network Route Number
Long Distance Routes
① Coast & Castles Cycle Route
② Pennine Cycleway - North Pennines
③ Hadrian's Cycleway
④ Sea to Sea
⑤ Pennine Cycleway - South Pennines & the Dales
⑥ Derby to York
⑦ Hull to Fakenham
⑧ East of England
⑨ South Midlands Cycle Route
⑩ Thames Valley Cycle Route
⑪ Garden of England
⑫ Downs & Weald Cycle Route
⑬ Devon Coast to Coast
⑭ The Cornish Way
⑮ The West Country Way
⑯ The Severn & Thames

Map reproduced from Ordnance Survey material with the permission of Ordnance Survey on behalf of the Controller of Her Majesty's Stationery Office © Crown copyright. Unauthorised reproduction infringes Crown copyright and may lead to prosecution or civil proceedings.
Licence number 100020852 (2009)

By car and by train

Distance chart

The distances between towns on the chart below are given to the nearest mile, and are measured along routes based on the quickest travelling time, making maximum use of motorways or dual-carriageway roads. The chart is based upon information supplied by the Automobile Association.

To calculate the distance in kilometres multiply the mileage by 1.6
For example: Brighton to Dover
82 miles x 1.6 =131.2 kilometres

Diagonal labels (top-left to bottom-right):
Aberdeen, Aberystwyth, Barnstaple, Birmingham, Brighton, Bristol, Cambridge, Cardiff, Carlisle, Carmarthen, Dorchester, Dover, Edinburgh, Exeter, Fort William, Glasgow, Gloucester, Guildford, Hereford, Holyhead, Hull, Inverness, Kendal, Leeds, Lincoln, Liverpool, Maidstone, Manchester, Middlesbrough, Newcastle, Northampton, Norwich, Nottingham, Oxford, Penzance, Perth, Peterborough, Plymouth, Portsmouth, Preston, Salisbury, Sheffield, Shrewsbury, Southampton, Stoke-on-Trent, Stranraer, Taunton, Wick, York, LONDON

```
472
608 214
436 124 180
613 288 210 171
518 130 100 90 169
463 215 267 97 120 170
537 111 128 109 202 44 203
236 236 371 199 376 281 256 300
520 48 190 172 264 107 266 58 284
600 206 94 172 119 62 184 120 364 182
587 325 272 208 82 205 124 233 381 301 200
126 336 471 299 476 381 333 400 100 386 463 458
593 196 44 165 178 64 259 113 356 171 57 248 455
156 435 570 398 576 480 456 499 199 485 562 580 137 554
150 348 467 295 472 377 353 396 96 382 459 477 47 451 102
484 113 126 56 155 36 150 63 248 125 118 192 346 110 445 343
571 224 175 126 44 106 96 139 335 201 97 97 433 150 532 439 97
487 79 144 59 189 54 153 59 250 85 136 225 349 129 448 346 34 133
464 102 339 167 345 249 259 202 238 352 331 368 326 323 425 323 215 302 158
376 227 320 139 258 230 138 250 170 311 312 262 247 304 367 266 196 239 198 218
106 496 631 459 637 541 517 560 260 546 623 641 157 616 66 176 507 595 510 488 430
283 189 324 153 330 234 251 254 47 240 316 354 145 309 245 143 200 288 203 181 164 307
329 173 301 120 262 211 146 230 123 224 293 271 200 265 321 219 177 220 179 165 59 383 110
388 199 275 98 216 185 95 205 182 267 246 220 258 320 379 277 151 173 154 204 44 441 176 74
362 130 272 101 278 182 193 202 126 188 264 302 224 257 224 122 108 128 386 79 74 139
545 284 234 166 50 167 82 200 339 262 161 41 416 209 537 435 153 58 186 327 220 599 313 231 178 261
357 124 261 89 266 171 160 190 112 169 234 253 290 219 245 318 216 236 219 125 97 387 74 44 85 34 248
276 244 357 176 318 267 197 286 95 294 349 322 146 341 283 190 232 276 235 235 89 308 84 64 122 145 280 114
235 215 388 307 349 298 229 317 60 325 380 353 106 312 263 264 153 264 307 266 296 142 267 102 95 154 376 311 145 39
486 174 212 56 133 115 56 162 249 224 159 155 348 196 447 345 79 90 11 217 152 509 203 136 94 131 113 139 189 220
488 277 329 160 168 233 63 266 282 325 241 172 359 313 480 378 210 217 5 147 142 279 174 103 240 130 123 254 218
395 162 232 51 193 142 86 161 189 223 224 210 266 216 387 107 151 101 78 130 161 64 119
510 160 170 68 109 73 82 70 274 146 115 46 373 154 472 370 48 61 81 242 190 534 228 174 132 126 107 164 227 258 44 146 102
702 308 108 274 207 193 368 222 466 264 167 357 564 109 663 562 220 259 238 434 415 726 419 403 370 367 318 356 451 482 326 433 326 265
86 388 523 351 529 433 378 451 152 436 513 467 307 502 60 96 384 460 441 379 291 194 199 245 278 461 275 192 550 400 410 426 617
435 204 263 86 158 173 37 193 229 255 204 162 306 248 427 325 139 115 142 225 110 489 223 121 51 159 120 132 170 201 45 78 58 86 357 351
633 336 82 205 228 218 124 299 192 397 213 98 289 495 44 594 493 151 98 289 495 346 667 350 334 301 296 249 289 243 257 364 275 238 78 544 289
596 244 162 154 53 125 137 153 360 220 73 141 458 112 556 456 118 45 152 328 276 620 314 260 215 262 250 313 344 130 204 188 85 241 508 157 172
326 145 281 110 287 191 209 211 89 207 273 311 188 266 287 338 246 287 456 118 45 152 328 122 243 43 63 134 36 269 30 159 235 121 164 375 237 180 205 272
549 184 118 121 90 52 145 98 313 160 39 160 411 93 509 407 60 62 105 281 203 298 329 173 203 461 165 134 44 223
397 162 272 91 233 182 172 92 161 263 264 241 236 256 359 257 148 191 150 167 66 421 115 38 47 70 205 100 133 104 146 45 92 366 80 93 292 226 73 212
417 75 220 48 226 130 140 111 181 110 212 250 279 205 379 277 96 184 52 105 162 441 135 119 124 65 208 71 190 221 98 203 87 123 314 329 129 245 209 92 161 88
578 229 142 105 66 106 136 147 317 156 52 150 440 111 539 437 90 23 117 312 295 196 246 257 221 480 157 52 23 299 191
392 112 220 48 226 130 140 150 156 211 212 250 245 205 353 251 96 184 99 123 129 415 109 93 91 57 206 46 164 195 98 172 54 123 303 99 245 209 66 161 50 38 191
235 341 477 305 482 387 363 406 106 392 469 487 63 461 181 86 352 446 365 371 237 283 276 263 172 153 229 282 232 445 220 215 361 354 386 295 380 571 149 333 502 466 195 418 267 287 447 261
560 165 50 132 160 51 226 80 323 141 21 125 427 63 525 423 25 44 120 300 225 551 245 209 165 208 201 259 290 130 113 127 80 270 465 81 130 205 270 147 239 60 101 286 148 131 364 285 261
207 577 732 560 738 642 618 662 361 647 724 742 258 716 166 277 608 696 610 588 531 104 408 464 547 648 476 409 704 550 551 625 589 757 721 451 673 925 542 702 516 562 687
323 201 314 133 275 224 154 243 116 221 306 279 193 298 314 212 189 233 192 192 38 376 91 24 79 102 237 71 51 89 146 180 87 184 408 239 125 339 269 96 254 57 146 251 120 223 265 477
550 236 216 121 54 120 59 153 314 215 125 78 413 109 512 410 102 31 126 262 186 574 268 201 143 216 39 254 285 68 218 129 5 310 462 86 241 75 225 85 163 71 161 420 167 167 675 211
```

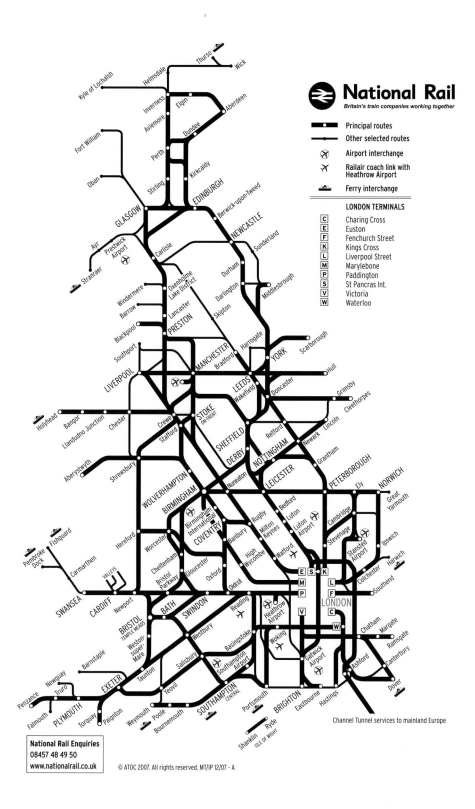

National Rail
Britain's train companies working together

▬▬	Principal routes
●—●	Other selected routes
⊗	Airport interchange
✈	Railair coach link with Heathrow Airport
⛴	Ferry interchange

LONDON TERMINALS

C	Charing Cross
E	Euston
F	Fenchurch Street
K	Kings Cross
L	Liverpool Street
M	Marylebone
P	Paddington
S	St Pancras Int.
V	Victoria
W	Waterloo

Channel Tunnel services to mainland Europe

National Rail Enquiries
08457 48 49 50
www.nationalrail.co.uk

© ATOC 2007. All rights reserved. MT/IP 12/07 - A

Travel information

General travel information

Streetmap	www.streetmap.co.uk	
Transport for London	www.tfl.gov.uk	0843 222 1234
Travel Services	www.departures-arrivals.com	
Traveline	www.traveline.info	0871 200 2233

Bus & coach

Megabus	www.megabus.com	0900 160 0900
National Express	www.nationalexpress.com	08717 818 178
WA Shearings	www.shearings.com	0844 824 6351

Car & car hire

AA	www.theaa.com	0800 085 2721
Green Flag	www.greenflag.com	0845 246 1557
RAC	www.rac.co.uk	0844 308 9177
Alamo	www.alamo.co.uk	0871 384 1086*
Avis	www.avis.co.uk	0844 581 0147*
Budget	www.budget.co.uk	0844 544 3407*
Easycar	www.easycar.com	
Enterprise	www.enterprise.com	0800 800 227*
Hertz	www.hertz.co.uk	0870 844 8844*
Holiday Autos	www.holidayautos.co.uk	0871 472 5229
National	www.nationalcar.co.uk	0871 384 1140
Thrifty	www.thrifty.co.uk	01494 751500

Air

Air Southwest	www.airsouthwest.com	0870 043 4553
Blue Islands (Channel Islands)	www.blueislands.com	08456 20 2122
BMI	www.flybmi.com	0844 848 4888
BMI Baby	www.bmibaby.com	0905 828 2828*
British Airways	www.ba.com	0844 493 0787
British International (Isles of Scilly to Penzance)	www.islesofscillyhelicopter.com	01736 363871*
CityJet	www.cityjet.com	0871 663 3777
Eastern Airways	www.easternairways.com	08703 669100
Easyjet	www.easyjet.com	0843 104 5000
Flybe	www.flybe.com	0871 700 2000*
Jet2.com	www.jet2.com	0871 226 1737*
Manx2	www.manx2.com	0871 200 0440*
Ryanair	www.ryanair.com	0871 246 0000
Skybus (Isles of Scilly)	www.islesofscilly-travel.co.uk	0845 710 5555
Thomsonfly	www.thomsonfly.com	0871 231 4787

Train

National Rail Enquiries	www.nationalrail.co.uk	0845 748 4950
The Trainline	www.trainline.co.uk	0871 244 1545
UK train operating companies	www.rail.co.uk	
Arriva Trains	www.arriva.co.uk	0191 520 4000
c2c	www.c2c-online.co.uk	0845 601 4873
Chiltern Railways	www.chilternrailways.co.uk	0845 600 5165
CrossCountry	www.crosscountrytrains.co.uk	0844 811 0124
East Midlands Trains	www.eastmidlandstrains.co.uk	0845 712 5678
Eurostar	www.eurostar.com	08432 186 186*
First Capital Connect	www.firstcapitalconnect.co.uk	0845 026 4700
First Great Western	www.firstgreatwestern.co.uk	0845 700 0125
Gatwick Express	www.gatwickexpress.com	0845 850 1530
Heathrow Connect	www.heathrowconnect.com	0845 678 6975
Heathrow Express	www.heathrowexpress.com	0845 600 1515
Hull Trains	www.hulltrains.co.uk	0845 071 0222
Island Line	www.islandlinetrains.co.uk	0845 600 0650
London Midlands	www.londonmidland.com	0121 634 2040
Merseyrail	www.merseyrail.org	0151 702 2071
National Express East Anglia	www.nationalexpresseastanglia.com	0845 600 7245
National Express East Coast	www.nationalexpresseastcoast.com	0845 722 5333
Northern Rail	www.northernrail.org	0845 000 0125
ScotRail	www.scotrail.co.uk	0845 601 5929
South Eastern Trains	www.southeasternrailway.co.uk	0845 000 2222
South West Trains	www.southwesttrains.co.uk	0845 600 0650
Southern	www.southernrailway.com	0845 127 2920
Stansted Express	www.stanstedexpress.com	0845 600 7245
Translink	www.translink.co.uk	(028) 9066 6630
Transpennine Express	www.tpexpress.co.uk	0845 600 1671
Virgin Trains	www.virgintrains.co.uk	08450 008 000*

Ferry

Ferry Information	www.discoverferries.com	0207 436 2449
Condor Ferries	www.condorferries.co.uk	0845 609 1024*
Steam Packet Company	www.steam-packet.com	08722 992 992*
Isles of Scilly Travel	www.islesofscilly-travel.co.uk	0845 710 5555
Red Funnel	www.redfunnel.co.uk	0844 844 9988
Wight Link	www.wightlink.co.uk	0871 376 1000

Phone numbers listed are for general enquiries unless otherwise stated.

* Booking line only

If you have
access needs...

Guests with hearing, visual or mobility needs can feel confident about booking accommodation that participates in the National Accessible Scheme (NAS).

Look out for the NAS symbols which are included throughout the accommodation directory. Using the NAS could help make the difference between a good holiday and a perfect one!

For more information on the NAS and tips & ideas on holiday travel in England, go to: www.visitengland.com/accessforall

National Accessible Scheme index

Establishments with a detailed entry in this guide who participate in the National Accessible Scheme are listed below. At the front of the guide you can find information about the scheme. Establishments are listed alphabetically by place name.

Mobility level 1

Abingdon-on-Thames, South East	Abbey Guest House ★★★★ Gold	98
Ashbourne, East Midlands	Peak District Spa ★★★★ Silver	160
Berwick-upon-Tweed, North East	Fenham Farm Coastal Bed & Breakfast ★★★★ Gold	258
Bicker, East Midlands	Supreme Inns ★★★	163
Camelford, South West	Pendragon Country House ★★★★★ Gold	42
Chichester, South East	George Bell House ★★★★ Silver	105
Great Yarmouth, East of England	Decoy Barn ★★★★ Gold	142
Harrogate, Yorkshire	The Station Hotel ★★★★	203
Penzance, South West	Hotel Penzance ★★★★	45
Woodhall Spa, East Midlands	Petwood Hotel ★★★	166
Woodhall Spa, East Midlands	Village Limits Country Pub, Restaurant & Motel ★★★★ Silver	166

Mobility level 2

Abingdon-on-Thames, South East	Abbey Guest House ★★★★ Gold	98
Ashbourne, East Midlands	Peak District Spa ★★★★ Silver	160
Chichester, South East	George Bell House ★★★★ Silver	105
Harrogate, Yorkshire	The Station Hotel ★★★★	203

Mobility level 3

Abingdon-on-Thames, South East	Abbey Guest House ★★★★ Gold	98

Visual impairment level 1

Abingdon-on-Thames, South East	Abbey Guest House ★★★★ Gold	98
Appleby-in-Westmorland, North West	The Hollies ★★★★	227

Hearing impairment level 1

Abingdon-on-Thames, South East	Abbey Guest House ★★★★ Gold	98
Bamford, East Midlands	Yorkshire Bridge Inn ★★★★ Silver	160

Hearing impairment level 2

Appleby-in-Westmorland, North West	The Hollies ★★★★	227

Gold and Silver Award winners

Establishments with a detailed entry in this guide that have achieved recognition of exceptional quality are listed below. Establishments are listed alphabetically by place name.

South West

GOLD AWARD

Barnsley, **Barnsley House** ★★★★	61
Bath, **Marlborough House Guest House** ★★★★	64
Camelford, **Pendragon Country House** ★★★★★	42
Dartmouth, **Cladda House B&B and Self Catering Apartments** ★★★★	48
Sidmouth, **The Barn & Pinn Cottage Guest House** ★★★★	51
Sidmouth, **Hotel Riviera** ★★★★	52
Stroud, **The Close B&B** ★★★★	63
Tetbury, **Calcot Manor Hotel & Spa** ★★★★	63
Torquay, **The Downs, Babbacombe** ★★★★	53
Wareham, **Bradle Farmhouse** ★★★	58
Wells, **Beryl** ★★★★	67

SILVER AWARD

Bath, **Pulteney House** ★★★★	65
Bridgwater, **Gurney Manor Mill** ★★★★	66
Bryher, **Hell Bay Hotel** ★★★★	47
Charlestown, **The Pier House Hotel** ★★★	42
Constantine Bay, **Treglos Hotel** ★★★★	43
Falmouth, **Budock Vean Hotel** ★★★★	43
Lands End, **Bosavern House** ★★★★	44
Moreton-In-Marsh, **Treetops Guest House** ★★★★	63
St. Minver, **Tredower Barton** ★★★	47
Swanage, **Glenlee Guest House** ★★★★	57

Teignmouth, **Ness House** ★★★★	52
Torquay, **The Westgate** ★★★★	54
Trowbridge, **Newhouse Farm** ★★★★	69
Truro, **Spring Cottage B&B** ★★★★	47
Wareham, **Lulworth Cove Inn** ★★★★	59

South East

GOLD AWARD

Abingdon-on-Thames, **Abbey Guest House** ★★★★	98
Ascot, **Coworth Park** ★★★★★	86
Edenbridge, **Hever Castle Luxury B&B** ★★★★★	93
New Milton, **New Forest, Chewton Glen** ★★★★★	89
Rye, **Rye Lodge Hotel** ★★★	107

SILVER AWARD

Bognor Regis, **Willow Tree Cottage B&B** ★★★★	103
Chichester, **George Bell House** ★★★★	105
Cranbrook, **1 Maytham Cottages** ★★★★	92
Eastbourne, **Cavendish Hotel** ★★★★	106
Henley-on-Thames, **The Baskerville** ★★★★	99
Hernhill, **Church Oast** ★★★★	94
Lymington, **Beach House** ★★★★	88
Maidstone, **The Limes** ★★	95
Milton-under-Wychwood, **Hillborough House** ★★★★	99
Ringmer, **Bryn Clai** ★★★★	107
Stelling Minnis, **Great Field Farm B&B** ★★★★	97
Sway, **The Mill At Gordleton** ★★★★★	90

EAST OF ENGLAND

GOLD AWARD

Aylsham, **The Old Pump House** ★★★★★	140
Great Yarmouth, **Decoy Barn** ★★★★	142
Wighton, **Meadow View Guest House** ★★★★★	146

SILVER AWARD

Colchester, **Stoke by Nayland Hotel, Golf & Spa** ★★★★	139
Elmswell, **Kiln Farm Guest House** ★★★★	146
Heacham, **St Anne's Guest House** ★★★★	142
Mundesley, **Overcliff Lodge** ★★★★	143
St. Albans, **St Michael's Manor Hotel** ★★★★	140

EAST MIDLANDS

GOLD AWARD

Grantham, **Glebe House Muston** ★★★★	163

SILVER AWARD

Ashbourne, **Peak District Spa** ★★★★	160
Bamford, **Yorkshire Bridge Inn** ★★★★	160
Castleton, **Causeway House B&B** ★★★	162
Lincoln, **Redhouse Farm Bed & Breakfast** **& Self-Catering** ★★★★	165
Newark, **The Grange Hotel** ★★	167
Oakham, **Barnsdale Lodge Hotel** ★★★	167
Woodhall Spa, **Village Limits Country Pub,** **Restaurant & Motel** ★★★★	166

HEART OF ENGLAND

GOLD AWARD

Rugeley, **Colton House** ★★★★★	185

SILVER AWARD

Broseley, **Broseley House** ★★★★	182
Stratford-upon-Avon, **Adelphi Guest House** ★★★★	185

Yorkshire

SILVER AWARD

Kirkby Malzeard, **Cowscot House** ★★★★	204
Malton, **Old Lodge Malton** ★★★★	204
Scarborough, **Killerby Cottage Farm** ★★★★	206
Skipton, **The Coniston Hotel, Country Estate & Spa** ★★★★	207
Thirsk, **The Gallery Bed & Breakfast** ★★★★	207
York, **Avondale Guest House** ★★★	208

North West

GOLD AWARD

Blackburn, **Stanley House Hotel & Spa** ★★★★	237
Chester, **Mitchell's of Chester Guest House** ★★★★★	226
Grange-over-Sands, **Clare House** ★★	229
Rosthwaite, **Scafell Hotel** ★★★	235
Windermere, **Lindeth Howe Country House Hotel** ★★★★	236

SILVER AWARD

Blackpool, **4 Star Phildene Blackpool** ★★★★	237
Hawkshead Hill, **Yewfield Vegetarian Guest House** ★★★★★	231
Keswick, **Burleigh Mead** ★★★★	233

North East

GOLD AWARD

Berwick-upon-Tweed, **Fenham Farm Coastal Bed & Breakfast** ★★★★	258
Hexham, **Langley Castle Hotel** ★★★★	259

SILVER AWARD

Berwick-upon-Tweed, **Alannah House** ★★★★	258
Durham, **Castle View Guest House** ★★★★	256

OFFICIAL TOURIST BOARD POCKET GUIDE

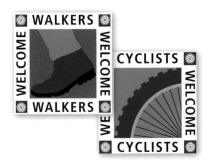

Walkers & Cyclists Welcome

England's star-rated great places to stay and visit

The **OFFICIAL** and most comprehensive guide to England's independently inspected, star-rated guest accommodation specialising in Walkers and Cyclists.

Hotels • Bed & Breakfast • Self-catering • Camping, Touring & Holiday Parks

• Regional round ups, attractions, ideas and other tourist information
• National Accessible Scheme accommodation at a glance
• Web-friendly features for easy booking

www.visitor-guides.co.uk

Walkers Welcome & Cyclists Welcome

Establishments participating in the Walkers Welcome and Cyclists Welcome schemes provide special facilities and actively encourage these recreations. Accommodation with a detailed entry in this guide is listed below. Place names are listed Alphabetically.

▶️⬛ Walkers Welcome & Cyclists Welcome

Abingdon-on-Thames, South East	**Abbey Guest House ★★★★ Gold**	98
Appleby-in-Westmorland, North West	**The Hollies ★★★★**	227
Bamford, East Midlands	**Yorkshire Bridge Inn ★★★★ Silver**	160
Berwick-upon-Tweed, North East	**Alannah House ★★★★ Silver**	258
Berwick-upon-Tweed, North East	**Fenham Farm Coastal Bed & Breakfast ★★★★ Gold**	258
Bicker, East Midlands	**Supreme Inns ★★★**	163
Bognor Regis, South East	**White Horses Bed & Breakfast ★★★★**	103
Camelford, South West	**Pendragon Country House ★★★★★ Gold**	42
Canterbury, South East	**Kipps Independent Hostel ★★★**	91
Carlisle, North West	**University of Cumbria - Carlisle ★★★★**	229
Castleton, East Midlands	**Causeway House B&B ★★★ Silver**	162
Cirencester, South West	**Riverside House ★★★★**	61
Clifton, North West	**George and Dragon ★★★★**	229
Clun, Heart of England	**The White Horse Inn ★★★**	183
Dunster, South West	**Yarn Market Hotel ★★★**	67
Heacham, East of England	**St Anne's Guest House ★★★★ Silver**	142
Hexham, North East	**Langley Castle Hotel ★★★★ Gold**	259
Hitcham, East of England	**Stanstead Hall ★★★★**	147
Keswick, North West	**Lane Head Farm Country Guest House ★★★★**	233
Lincoln, East Midlands	**Welbeck Cottage Bed and Breakfast ★★★★**	165
Maidstone, South East	**Ash Cottage ★★★★★**	94
Mundesley, East of England	**Overcliff Lodge ★★★★ Silver**	143
Norwich, East of England	**Old Rectory Hotel ★★★**	143
Oxford, South East	**Abodes B&B ★★★★**	99
Plymouth, South West	**Caraneal ★★★★**	51
Rackheath, East of England	**Barn Court ★★★★**	143
Rosthwaite, North West	**Scafell Hotel ★★ Gold**	235
Saltburn-by-the-Sea, Yorkshire	**The Arches Country House ★★★★**	205
Stroud, South West	**The Close B&B ★★★★ Gold**	63
Sway, South East	**The Mill At Gordleton 5 Silver**	90
Thirsk, Yorkshire	**The Gallery Bed & Breakfast ★★★★ Silver**	207
Windermere, North West	**Lindeth Howe Country House Hotel ★★★★ Gold**	236

▶️ Walkers Welcome

Ashbourne, East Midlands	**Peak District Spa ★★★★ Silver**	160
Buttermere, North West	**The Fish Inn ★★★★**	228
Buxton, East Midlands	**Old Hall Hotel ★★★**	162
Eype, South West	**Eype's Mouth Country Hotel ★★★**	57
Haworth, Yorkshire	**Leeming Wells ★★★★**	211
Penzance, South West	**Hotel Penzance ★★★★**	45

Welcome Pets!

Want to travel with your faithful companion? Look out for accommodation displaying the **Welcome Pets!** sign. Participants in this scheme go out of their way to meet the needs of guests bringing dogs, cats and/or small birds. In addition to providing water and food bowls, torches or nightlights, spare leads and pet washing facilities, they'll buy in food on request, and offer toys, treats and bedding. They'll also have information on pet-friendly attractions, pubs, restaurants and recreation. Of course, not everyone is able to offer suitable facilities for every pet, so do check if there are any restrictions on type, size and number of animals when you book.

Look out for the following symbol in the entry.

Families and Pets Welcome

Establishments participating in the Families Welcome or Welcome Pets! schemes provide special facilities and actively encourage families or guests with pets. Accommodation with a detailed entry in this guide is listed below. Place names are listed alphabetically.

🏖 🐾 Families and Pets Welcome

Clifton, North West	George and Dragon ★★★★	229
Rackheath, East of England	Barn Court ★★★★	143
Torquay, South West	Best Western Livermead Cliff Hotel ★★★	53

🏖 Families Welcome

Abingdon-on-Thames, South East	Abbey Guest House ★★★★ Gold	98
Bicker, East Midlands	Supreme Inns ★★★	163
Buttermere, North West	The Fish Inn ★★★★	228
Norwich, East of England	Old Rectory Hotel ★★★	143
Sway, South East	The Mill At Gordleton ★★★★★ Silver	90

🐾 Pets Welcome

Dunster, South West	Yarn Market Hotel ★★★	67
Keswick, North West	Lane Head Farm Country Guest House ★★★★	233
Kirkby Lonsdale, North West	Copper Kettle Restaurant & Guest House ★★	234
Oakham, East Midlands	Barnsdale Lodge Hotel ★★ Silver	167
St. Agnes, South West	Little Trevellas Farm ★★★	46
Troutbeck, North West	Troutbeck Inn ★★★★	235

Swimming Pools index

If you're looking for accommodation with swimming facilities use this index to see at a glance detailed accommodation entries that match your requirement. Establishments are listed alphabetically by place name.

Indoor pool		
Ascot, South East	**Coworth Park ★★★★★ Gold**	86
Bicester, South East	**Bicester Hotel Golf and Spa ★★★★**	98
Blackpool, North West	**Doric Hotel ★★**	238
Brixham, South West	**Berry Head Hotel ★★★**	48
Cambridge, East of England	**Cambridge Quy Mill Hotel and Spa ★★★★**	138
Chesterfield, East Midlands	**Abigails Guest House ★★★**	162
Colchester, East of England	**Stoke by Nayland Hotel, Golf & Spa ★★★★ Silver**	139
Constantine Bay, South West	**Treglos Hotel ★★★★ Silver**	43
Dawlish, South West	**Langstone Cliff Hotel ★★★**	49
Falmouth, South West	**Budock Vean Hotel ★★★★ Silver**	43
Great Yarmouth, East of England	**Burlington Palm Hotel ★★★**	141
Haworth, Yorkshire	**Leeming Wells ★★★★**	211
Hexham, North East	**Riverdale Hall Hotel ★★★**	260
Lands End, South West	**Bosavern House ★★★★ Silver**	44
Lincoln, East Midlands	**Branston Hall Hotel**	164
Looe, South West	**Hannafore Point Hotel and Spa ★★★**	44
Lytham St. Annes, North West	**Clifton Park Hotel ★★★**	240

New Milton, New Forest, South East	**Chewton Glen ★★★★★ Gold**	89
Newmarket, East of England	**Bedford Lodge Hotel & Spa**	147
Portsmouth, South East	**Royal Maritime Club ★★**	89
Rye, South East	**Rye Lodge Hotel ★★★ Gold**	107
Saham Toney, East of England	**Broom Hall Country Hotel ★★★**	144
St. Minver, South West	**Tredower Barton ★★★ Silver**	47
Teddington, London	**Lensbury ★★★★**	122
Tetbury, South West	**Calcot Manor Hotel & Spa ★★★★ Gold**	63
Torquay, South West	**The Osborne Hotel ★★★★**	54
Windermere, North West	**Lindeth Howe Country House Hotel ★★★★ Gold**	236
Windermere, North West	**Southview House & Indoor Pool ★★★★**	236

Outdoor pool

Blackpool, North West	**Doric Hotel ★★**	238
Bryher, South West	**Hell Bay Hotel ★★★★ Silver**	47
Dawlish, South West	**Langstone Cliff Hotel ★★★**	49
Manningford Abbots, South West	**Huntly's Farmhouse ★★★★**	68
New Milton, New Forest, South East	**Chewton Glen ★★★★★ Gold**	89
Norwich, East of England	**Old Rectory Hotel ★★★**	143
Penzance, South West	**Hotel Penzance ★★★★**	45
Tetbury, South West	**Calcot Manor Hotel & Spa ★★★★ Gold**	63
Torquay, South West	**Corbyn Head Hotel ★★★**	53
Torquay, South West	**Livermead House Hotel ★★★**	54
Torquay, South West	**The Osborne Hotel ★★★★**	54
Wells, South West	**Beryl ★★★★ Gold**	67

Evening Meal index

The following establishments offer evening meals and all have a
detailed entry in this guide.

Dunster, South West	Yarn Market Hotel ★★★	67
East Molesey, South East	Kings Arms	102
Eastbourne, South East	Cavendish Hotel ★★★★ Silver	106
Eype, South West	Eype's Mouth Country Hotel ★★★	57
Falmouth, South West	Budock Vean Hotel ★★★★ Silver	43
Frogmore, South West	Globe Inn ★★★★	49
Gloucester, South West	English Holiday Cruises ★★★★	62
Grange-over-Sands, North West	Clare House ★★ Gold	229
Grantham, East Midlands	Glebe House Muston ★★★★ Gold	163
Great Yarmouth, East of England	Burlington Palm Hotel ★★★	141
Harrogate, Yorkshire	The Station Hotel ★★★★	203
Hawkshead, North West	Crosslands Farm ★★★★	231
Haworth, Yorkshire	Ashmount Country House ★★★★★	211
Haworth, Yorkshire	Leeming Wells ★★★★	211
Heads Nook, North West	String of Horses Inn ★★★★	232
Henley-on-Thames, South East	The Baskerville ★★★★ Silver	99
Hexham, North East	Langley Castle Hotel ★★★★ Gold	259
Hexham, North East	Riverdale Hall Hotel ★★★	260
Hook, South East	Wellington Arms ★★★★	87
Keswick, North West	Lane Head Farm Country Guest House ★★★★	233
Liverpool, North West	Hope Street Hotel ★★★★	241
Lymington, South East	Beach House ★★★★ Silver	88
Lytham St. Annes, North West	Clifton Park Hotel ★★★	240
Maidstone, South East	The Townhouse Hotel ★★	95
Malton, Yorkshire	Old Lodge Malton ★★★★ Silver	204
Manningford Abbots, South West	Huntly's Farmhouse ★★★★	68
Norwich, East of England	Old Rectory Hotel ★★★	143
Paignton, South West	Redcliffe Lodge Hotel ★★	50
Penzance, South West	Queens Hotel ★★★	45
Rochester, South East	Medway Little Townhouse	96
Rugeley, Heart of England	Colton House ★★★★ Gold	185
Scarborough, Yorkshire	Empire Guesthouse ★★★	205
Sidmouth, South West	Hotel Riviera ★★★★ Gold	52
Skipton, Yorkshire	The Coniston Hotel, Country Estate & Spa ★★★★ Silver	207
Southampton, South East	The Prince Consort ★★★	90
St. Albans, East of England	St Michael's Manor Hotel ★★★★ Silver	140
Stafford, Heart of England	Wyndale Guest House ★★★	185
Swanage, South West	Glenlee Guest House ★★★★ Silver	57
Swanage, South West	The Pines Hotel ★★★	58
Tarporley, North West	Foresters Arms ★★★	226
Teddington, London	Lensbury ★★★★	122
Teignmouth, South West	Ness House ★★★★ Silver	52
Telford, Heart of England	The Old Orleton Inn ★★★★★	184
Torquay, South West	Corbyn Head Hotel ★★★	53
Torquay, South West	The Downs, Babbacombe ★★★★ Gold	53
Wareham, South West	Lulworth Cove Inn ★★★★ Silver	59
West Mersea, East of England	Victory at Mersea ★★★★	139
Weymouth, South West	Smugglers Inn ★★★★	60
Whitby, Yorkshire	Bagdale Hall, No. 4 & Lodge ★★	207
Windermere, North West	Bowfell Cottage ★★★	236
Windermere, North West	Lindeth Howe Country House Hotel ★★★★ Gold	236
Windsor, South East	Stirrups Country House Hotel ★★★	86
Woodhall Spa, East Midlands	Petwood Hotel ★★★	166
Woodhall Spa, East Midlands	Village Limits Country Pub, Restaurant & Motel ★★★★ Silver	166
Woodstock, South East	The Duke of Marlborough ★★★★	102

Budget accommodation

If you are travelling on a budget, the following establishments offer accommodation at £25 per single room per night or less, or £50 per double room per night or less. These prices are only an indication - please check carefully before confirming a reservation. Establishments are listed alphabetically by place name.

South West	
Newquay, **Harrington Guest House** ★★★	45
Paignton, **Redcliffe Lodge Hotel** ★★	50
Salisbury, **Evening Hill**	69
St. Agnes, **Little Trevellas Farm** ★★★	46
St. Agnes, **Penkerris** ★★	46

South East	
Canterbury, **Kipps Independent Hostel** ★★★	91
Ramsgate, **Comfort Inn Ramsgate** ★★★	95

East of England	
Orsett, **Jays Lodge** ★★★★	139

North West	
Blackpool, **Lyndene Hotel** ★★	239
Keswick, **Charnwood Guest House** ★★★★	233
Windermere,	
Southview House & Indoor Pool ★★★★	236

Hostel and campus accommodation

The following establishments all have a detailed entry in this guide.

Hostels		
Bath, South West	**Bath YMCA ★★★ Hostel**	64
Brighton, South East	**Kipps Brighton ★★★ Hostel**	104
Canterbury, South East	**Kipps Independent Hostel ★★★ Hostel**	91
Liverpool, North West	**International Inn ★★★ Hostel**	241

Campus accommodation		
Carlisle, North West	**University of Cumbria - Carlisle ★★★★ Campus**	229

Index by property name

Accommodation with a detailed entry in this guide is listed below.

Index by place name

The following places all have detailed accommodation entries in this guide. If the place where you wish to stay is not shown the location maps (starting on page 312) will help you to find somewhere to stay in the area.

Index to display advertisers

HUDSON'S MEDIA LIMITED

Published by: Hudson's Media Ltd
35 Thorpe Road, Peterborough, PE3 6AG
Tel: 01733 296910 Fax: 01733 209292

On behalf of: VisitBritain, Sanctuary Buildings, 20 Great Smith Street, London SW1P 3BT

Editor: Deborah Coulter
Editorial Contributor: Neil Pope
Production team: Deborah Coulter, Rhiannon McCluskey,
Rebecca Owen-Fisher and Sophie Studd

Creative: Jamieson Eley
Advertising team: Ben Piper, Matthew Pinfold, Seanan McGrory, James O'Rawe
Email: VEguides@hudsons-media.co.uk Tel: 01733 296913
Production System: NVG – leaders in Tourism Technology. www.nvg.net
Printer: Stephens & George, Merthyr Tydfil
Retail Sales: Compass – Tel: 020 8996 5764

Photography credits: © Abbotsbury Subtropical Gardens, Alders Caravan Park, Alnwick Castle, Althorp, Andy Stammers, Anya Campbell, Arley Hall/Val Corbett, Athelhampton House, Beamish Museum, Blenheim Palace, Britain on View, Burghley, Carole Drake, Chatsworth, Commons.Wikimedia.org, Deborah Coulter, Doddington Hall, Edwin Remsberg, English Heritage, Exbury Gardens/Dave Zubraski, Harewood House, Harewood House Trust, Hartland Abbey, Highclere Castle, Historic Royal Palaces, Holker Hall, Kenilworth Castle, Knebworth House, Longleat Safari Park, Oliver Dixon - Imagewise, Pashley Manor Gardens/Helen Sinclair, Renishaw Hall/Chris Dawes, Scampston, Simon Warner, Sudeley Castle, The Alnwick Garden, The Forbidden Corner, VisitEngland, Welcome to Yorkshire, Wilton House, Woburn Safari Park.

© VisitBritain Images: Adam Burton, Alex Nail, Andrew Orchard, Andrew Pickett, Andy Ward, Ben Selway, Choose Suffolk, Chris Renton, County Durham Tourism Partnership, Craig Easton, Craig Easton, Daniel Bosworth, David Clapp, David Sellman, Eric Nathan, Grant Pritchard, Ian Shaw, Ingrid Rasmussen, James McCormick, Jason Hawkes, Joanna Henderson, Joe Cornish, John Millar, John Spaull, Kiyoshi Sakasai, Lancashire & Blackpool Tourist Board, Lee Beel, Liz Gander, Mark Thomasson, Martin Brent, Matt Cant, Melody Thornton, Nadir Khan, Nicolas Chinardet, Olivier Roques-Rogery, Paul Underhill, Pawel Libera, PTomkins/VisitScotland, Richard Allen, Richard Surman, Rod Edwards, Sheradon Dublin, Simon Kreitem, Simon Winnall, Thanet District Council, Tomo Brecj, Tony Pleavin, Visit Chester & Cheshire/NWDA.